Civil Law and Litigation for Paralegals

Second Edition

Aspen College Series

Civil Law and Litigation for Paralegals

Second Edition

NEAL R. BEVANS, J.D.

Western Piedmont Community College

Wolters Kluwer

Published by Wolters Kluwer in New York.

Wolters Kluwer Legal & Regulatory Solutions US serves customers worldwide with CCH, Aspen Publishers, and Kluwer Law International products. (www.WKLegaledu.com)

To contact Customer Service, e-mail customer.service@wolterskluwer.com, call 1-800-234-1660, fax 1-800-901-9075, or mail correspondence to:

Wolters Kluwer
Attn: Order Department
PO Box 990
Frederick, MD 21705

Printed in the United States of America.

1 2 3 4 5 6 7 8 9 0

ISBN 978-1-4548-6904- 7

Library of Congress Cataloging-in-Publication Data

Names: Bevans, Neal R., 1961- author.
Title: Civil law and litigation for paralegals/Neal R. Bevans, J.D., Western Piedmont Community College.
Description: Second edition. | New York : Wolters Kluwer, 2017. | Series: Aspen college series
Identifiers: LCCN 2016020875| ISBN 9781454869047 | ISBN 1454869046
Subjects: LCSH: Civil procedure–United States. | Trial practice–United States. | Legal assistants–United States–Handbooks, manuals, etc.
Classification: LCC KF8841 .B48 2017 | DDC 347.73/5–dc23 LC record available at https://lccn.loc.gov/

2016020875

About Wolters Kluwer Legal & Regulatory US

Wolters Kluwer Legal & Regulatory US delivers expert content and solutions in the areas of law, corporate compliance, health compliance, reimbursement, and legal education. Its practical solutions help customers successfully navigate the demands of a changing environment to drive their daily activities, enhance decision quality, and inspire confident outcomes.

Serving customers worldwide, its legal and regulatory portfolio includes products under the Aspen Publishers, CCH Incorporated, Kluwer Law International, ftwilliam.com and MediRegs names. They are regarded as exceptional and trusted resources for general legal and practice-specific knowledge, compliance and risk management, dynamic workflow solutions, and expert commentary.

For my wife, Nilsa, who has changed my life

Summary of Contents

CONTENTS		xi
PREFACE		xxix
ACKNOWLEDGMENTS		xxxiii
ABOUT THE AUTHOR		xxxv
Chapter 1	Introduction to the Court System	1
Chapter 2	The Participants in the Legal System	31
Chapter 3	Bringing a Legal Action	63
Chapter 4	Civil Complaints	101
Chapter 5	The Defendant's Answer	137
Chapter 6	Evidence	175
Chapter 7	Discovery	209
Chapter 8	Motions Practice	253
Chapter 9	Preparing for and Conducting the Trial	285
Chapter 10	Damages	329
Chapter 11	Arbitration, Mediation, and Settlement	359
Chapter 12	Appeals	387
GLOSSARY		411
INDEX		417

Contents

PREFACE xxix
ACKNOWLEDGMENTS xxxiii
ABOUT THE AUTHOR xxxv

1 INTRODUCTION TO THE COURT SYSTEM 1

Chapter Objectives *1*

I. INTRODUCTION **1**

II. CIVIL LAW **2**
- A. What Is Civil Law? 2
- B. How Does Civil Law Differ from Other Areas of Law? 3
  1. The Parties 3
  2. The Pleadings 4
  3. The Rules 5
  4. The Burden of Proof 5
  5. The Outcome 7

III. SOURCES OF LEGAL AUTHORITY IN THE UNITED STATES **8**
- A. The Constitution 8
- B. Statutes 8
  1. Administrative Rules and Regulations 9
  2. Ordinances 10
- C. Case Law 10
- D. Common Law 11

IV. JURISDICTION **11**
- A. Subject Matter Jurisdiction 12
- B. Personal Jurisdiction 13
  1. Physical Presence in the Forum 13

2. Domicile or Residence in the Forum 13
3. Property Ownership in the Forum 13
4. Consent 14
5. Minimum Contacts 14

V. FEDERAL AND STATE COURT SYSTEMS 14
A. Levels of the Federal Court System 15
1. Trial Courts: U.S. Federal District Court 15
2. Appellate Courts: U.S. Circuit Courts of Appeals 15
3. U.S. Supreme Court 15
B. Levels of the State Court System 16
1. Trial Courts 16
2. Appellate Courts 17
3. State Supreme Courts 17
C. Federal versus State Law 17

Case Excerpt: Peters v. Alpharetta Spa, LLC 19

Chapter Summary 22
Skills You Need in the Real World 22
The Life of a Paralegal 24
Ethical Issues for the Paralegal 25
Websites 25
Forms and Court Documents 26
Key Terms 28
Review Questions 28
Applying What You Have Learned 29
Endnotes 30

2 THE PARTICIPANTS IN THE LEGAL SYSTEM 31

Chapter Objectives 31

I. INTRODUCTION 31

II. JUDGES 31
A. Becoming a Judge 33
1. Judicial Appointment 33
2. Election 33
3. Judicial Selection Committee 33
B. The Role of the Judge 34
1. Judges as Referees 34
2. Judicial Rulings 34
a. Motions 34
b. Evidence 35
3. Judges as Fact Finders 35

III. ATTORNEYS **35**
A. Becoming an Attorney 35
1. Law School Education 36
2. The Bar Examination 36
3. Joining the State Bar 37
4. Specialization 37
a. Plaintiffs' Attorneys 37
b. Defendants' Attorneys 38
c. The Day-to-Day Practice of Law 38

IV. COMPENSATING LEGAL PROFESSIONALS **38**
A. Contingency Fees 38
B. Hourly Rates 40

V. ORGANIZATION OF THE LAW OFFICE **40**
A. Partners 41
B. Associate Attorneys 41
C. Attorney Ethics 42
1. Ethical Codes 42
a. Private Reprimand 42
b. Public Reprimand 42
c. Temporary Suspension of License 43
d. Disbarment 43
e. Criminal Prosecution 43
2. Common Ethical Violations 43
a. Commingling Funds 43
b. Lack of Diligence 44

VI. PARALEGALS **44**
A. Development of the Paralegal Profession 44
B. Daily Activities of Paralegals 45
C. Licensing and Certifying Paralegals 46
D. Paralegal Ethics 48
E. Legal Document Assistants 49

VII. CLIENTS **49**

VIII. COURTHOUSE PERSONNEL **49**
A. Clerk of Court 50
B. Registrar of Deeds 50
C. Probate Court 51
D. Tax Office 51

Case Excerpt: Spoelstra v. Gahn *52*

Chapter Summary *55*
Skills You Need in the Real World *55*

The Life of a Paralegal 56
Ethical Issues for the Paralegal 57
Websites 57
Forms and Court Documents 58
Key Terms 58
Review Questions 59
Applying What You Have Learned 59
Endnotes 61

3 **BRINGING A LEGAL ACTION 63**

Chapter Objectives 63

I. INTRODUCTION 63

II. EVALUATING A CIVIL CASE 64
- A. What Is a Case Evaluation? 64
  - 1. The Nature of the Claim 64
  - 2. The Facts 65
    - a. Factual Analysis 65
    - b. The Legal Requirement to Investigate a Case 66
  - 3. The Defendant's Liability 67
  - 4. The Impact of the Law 68
  - 5. The Likelihood of Recovery 69
  - 6. The Extent of the Plaintiff's Injuries 69
- B. Initial Client Meeting 70
  - 1. Obtaining Authorizations from Clients 72
  - 2. HIPAA Concerns with Medical Records 72
  - 3. Other Information from Client 73
    - a. Details of the Incident 74
    - b. Police Reports 74
    - c. Investigative Reports 74
    - d. Police Accident Reconstructionist Report 74
    - e. Witnesses 75
    - f. Other Critical Information 75
  - 4. Client Intangibles 75
    - a. Client Personality 76
    - b. Will the Client Make a Good Witness? 76
    - c. Cross-Referencing the Client's Version 76
    - d. The Client's Web Presence 76
    - e. Interview Techniques for Clients 76
  - 5. Information the Law Firm Provides to the Client 79

III. INVESTIGATING THE CLAIM **80**
- A. Attorneys and Paralegals as Investigators 80
- B. Paralegal Investigators 81
  - 1. Locating Witnesses 81
    - a. Witness Locator Services 81
    - b. Internet Search 82
  - 2. Interviewing Witnesses 82
    - a. Interviewing Techniques 83
    - b. Purposes of the Interview 84
    - c. Deceitful Witnesses 84
- C. Documenting the Scene of the Accident 84
  - 1. Photographs 85
  - 2. Video 85
  - 3. Diagramming the Scene 86
- D. Gathering Evidence 86
- E. Researching Public Records 87
  - 1. The Clerk of Courts Office 87
  - 2. The Deed Room 87
  - 3. UCC Filings 88
  - 4. Birth, Marriage, and Death Records 88
  - 5. Tax Office 89

Case Excerpt: Oakley v. Nolan *90*

Chapter Summary *94*
Skills You Need in the Real World *94*
The Life of a Paralegal *95*
Ethical Issues for the Paralegal *95*
Websites *96*
Key Terms *96*
Review Questions *96*
Applying What You Have Learned *97*
Endnotes *99*

4 CIVIL COMPLAINTS 101

Chapter Objectives *101*

I. INTRODUCTION **101**

II. PARTIES **102**

III. JURISDICTIONAL ISSUES IN CIVIL SUITS **102**
A. Personal Jurisdiction 102
1. Presence 103
2. Domicile 103
3. Consent 104
4. Minimum Contacts 104
5. Special Appearance 104
B. Subject Matter Jurisdiction 105
1. General Jurisdiction Courts 105
2. Limited Jurisdiction Courts 105
a. Federal Question 106
b. Diversity of Citizenship 106
c. Amount in Controversy 106
d. Pendent and Ancillary Jurisdiction 107
e. Exclusive Jurisdiction 108
f. Removal 108
C. In Rem Jurisdiction 109
D. Concurrent Jurisdiction 109

IV. CAPACITY AND STANDING **109**
A. Capacity 109
B. Standing 111
1. Elements of Standing 111
2. Case or Controversy Requirement 113
a. Ripeness Doctrine 113
b. Mootness Doctrine 113
c. Advisory Opinions 114

V. THE ELEMENTS OF A COMPLAINT **114**
A. Identification of Court 114
B. Style or Caption of a Complaint 115
1. Businesses as Parties 116
2. Plea of Misnomer 116
3. Deceased Parties 116
4. Fugitives 116
C. Title of Action 117
D. Allegation of Jurisdiction 117
E. Factual Contentions 118
1. Liability Allegations 119
2. Sufficiency of the Allegations 119
F. Demand for Judgment/Prayer for Relief 120
1. Request for Damages 120
2. Jury Trial Demand 121

VI. COMPLAINT ATTACHMENTS AND EXHIBITS **121**
A. Verifications 121
B. Exhibits 121
C. Affidavits 122

VII. SUMMONS AND SERVICE OF PROCESS **124**
A. Service by Personal Delivery 126
B. Service by Other Means 126
C. Serving a Corporation or Government Entity 126

Case Excerpt: Emory Univ. v. Metro Atlanta Task Force for the Homeless, Inc. *128*

Chapter Summary *131*
Skills You Need in the Real World *132*
The Life of a Paralegal *133*
Ethical Issues for the Paralegal *134*
Websites *134*
Key Terms *135*
Review Questions *135*
Applying What You Have Learned *136*
Endnotes *136*

5 THE DEFENDANT'S ANSWER 137

Chapter Objectives *137*

I. INTRODUCTION **137**

II. THE ANSWER **138**
A. The Function of the Answer 138
B. The Minimum Requirements of the Answer 138
C. Drafting the Answer 139
1. Denying Claims 141
2. Other Responses in Answers 142
3. Bad Faith 143
D. Serving the Answer on the Plaintiff 144
E. Failure to Respond to the Complaint 145
F. Failure to Respond to Allegations in the Complaint 145

III. DEFENSES **146**
A. Affirmative Defenses 146
B. Counterclaims 148
1. Compulsory and Permissive Counterclaims 148
2. Res Judicata 149
3. Replies to Counterclaims 150

IV. RULE 12(b)(6) MOTIONS 151
A. Purpose of the Rule 12(b)(6) Motion 151
B. When Can a Defendant File a Rule 12(b)(6) Motion? 152
C. Motions to Strike 153

V. CROSS-CLAIMS 153
A. Answers to Cross-Claims 155
B. Time Limits for Cross-Claims 155

VI. THIRD-PARTY CLAIMS 155
A. Impleader 156
B. Interpleader 158
C. Intervention 158

VII. CLASS ACTIONS 161

Case Excerpt: Flores v. Skaro 163

Chapter Summary 166
Skills You Need in the Real World 167
The Life of a Paralegal 167
Ethical Issues for the Paralegal 168
Websites 168
Forms and Court Documents 168
Key Terms 172
Review Questions 172
Applying What You Have Learned 173
Endnotes 173

6 EVIDENCE 175

Chapter Objectives 175

I. INTRODUCTION 175

II. WHAT IS EVIDENCE? 176
A. Relevance 177
B. Competence 178
C. Admissibility 178

III. THE ROLE OF EVIDENCE 179
A. Laying the Foundation 180
B. Tendering Evidence 182

C. Objecting to Evidence 183
1. Improper Conclusion 183
2. Relevance 184
3. Prejudice 184
4. Other Issues 184

IV. TYPES OF EVIDENCE 184
A. Direct Evidence 185
1. What Qualifies as Direct Evidence 185
2. Eyewitness Testimony 185
B. Circumstantial Evidence 186
C. Documentary Evidence 187
D. Other Categories of Evidence 187
1. Testimonial Evidence 188
2. Demonstrative Evidence 188
3. Scientific Evidence 190

V. SPECIFIC EVIDENTIARY RULES 190
A. The Best Evidence Rule 190
B. Hearsay 190
1. Hearsay in Documents 191
2. Exceptions to the Hearsay Rule 192
a. Excited Utterance 192
b. Business Records 193
c. Statements for Purpose of Medical Diagnosis 193
C. Authentication 194
1. Judicial Notice 195
2. Self-Authenticating Document 196
D. Privileges 197
1. The Marital Privilege 198
2. The Attorney–Client Privilege 198

Case Excerpt: Jenkins v. CACH, LLC *199*

Chapter Summary *203*
Skills You Need in the Real World *203*
The Life of a Paralegal *204*
Ethical Issues for the Paralegal *205*
Websites *205*
Key Terms *206*
Review Questions *206*
Applying What You Have Learned *206*

7 DISCOVERY 209

Chapter Objectives *209*

I. INTRODUCTION **209**

II. PURPOSE OF DISCOVERY **210**
A. Clarification of the Facts 210
B. Preservation of Testimony for Later Use 211
C. Avoiding Surprise at Trial 211
D. Narrowing the Issues 211

III. SHORT HISTORY OF DISCOVERY **211**

IV. DISCOVERY IN MODERN CIVIL PRACTICE **212**
A. Rules of Civil Procedure 213
B. Sequence of Discovery 213
C. Supplementing Discovery Responses 214
D. Expert Witnesses in Modern Discovery 215
E. Electronic "E-Discovery" 215

V. DISCOVERY METHODS **217**
A. Interrogatories 218
1. Limitations on Interrogatories 219
a. Unreasonably Cumulative or Burdensome 219
b. Objections to Specific Questions 219
2. Drafting Interrogatories 220
3. Answering Interrogatories 222
4. Time Limits on Interrogatories 222
B. Requests for Production of Documents 223
C. Depositions 224
1. Preparing for a Deposition 225
2. Setting a Deposition 226
3. Conducting the Deposition 228
a. Opening Stipulations 228
b. Reserving Objections 229
c. Permissible Questions 229
d. Cross-Examining a Witness During the Deposition 230
e. Use of Exhibits 230
4. Persons Present at the Deposition 231
a. The Witness 231
b. The Attorneys 231
c. The Court Reporter 231
d. The Parties 232

5. Duration of the Deposition 232
6. After the Deposition 232
D. Requests for Physical and/or Mental Examination 235
E. Requests to Admit 236

VI. OBJECTIONS TO DISCOVERY REQUESTS 236
A. Work Product 237
B. Unduly Burdensome, Cumulative, and/or Expensive 237
C. Constitutional Rights 237
D. Trade Secrets 238
E. Protective Orders 238

VII. FAILURE TO RESPOND TO DISCOVERY REQUESTS 240

VIII. COMPELLING DISCOVERY 240

IX. SOFTWARE THAT ASSISTS IN DISCOVERY 241

Case Excerpt: Maynard v. Nygren 242

Chapter Summary 248
Skills You Need in the Real World 248
The Life of a Paralegal 248
Ethical Issues for the Paralegal 249
Websites 250
Key Terms 250
Review Questions 250
Applying What You Have Learned 251

8 MOTIONS PRACTICE 253

Chapter Objectives 253

I. INTRODUCTION 253

II. BRINGING A MOTION 254
A. Construing the Language in a Motion 254
B. Drafting a Motion 254
C. Serving a Motion 255
1. Certificate of Service 256
2. Attaching Affidavits to the Motion 256
D. Filing a Motion 258
E. Arguing a Motion 259
F. Ruling on a Motion 261
G. Written Motions 261
H. Oral Motions 261

III. ISSUES THAT CAN BE ADDRESSED IN A MOTION 261
A. Motion for Summary Judgment 262
B. Motion for Partial Summary Judgment 264
C. Judgment on the Pleadings 264
D. Affirmative Defenses 264
1. Lack of Jurisdiction Over the Subject Matter 265
2. Lack of Jurisdiction Over the Person 265
3. Improper Venue 265
4. Insufficiency of Process and Service of Process 265
5. Failure to Join a Necessary Party Under Rule 19 265
E. 12(b)(6) Motion 266
F. Motion for More Definite Statement 266
G. Motion for Default Judgment 268

IV. THE JUDGE'S ROLE IN CONSIDERING MOTIONS: MOTIONS FOR SUMMARY JUDGMENT 268

V. USING MOTIONS TO CLARIFY ISSUES IN LITIGATION 270

VI. PRETRIAL, TRIAL, AND POST-TRIAL MOTIONS 270
A. JNOV Motions 271
B. Motion for Directed Verdict 271
C. Motion for New Trial 271

Case Excerpt: Niepsuj v. Doe 273

Chapter Summary 277
Skills You Need in the Real World 278
The Life of a Paralegal 278
Ethical Issues for the Paralegal 279
Websites 279
Forms and Court Documents 280
Key Terms 281
Review Questions 281
Applying What You Have Learned 282
Endnotes 283

9 PREPARING FOR AND CONDUCTING THE TRIAL 285

Chapter Objectives 285

I. INTRODUCTION 285

II. PREPARING TOOLS FOR THE TRIAL **286**
A. The Attorney's Role 287
B. The Paralegal's Role 287
1. Chronology of Events 288
2. Master Index 290
3. Issue Table 291
4. Witness Cross-Reference 291
5. Witness Summaries 293
6. Trial Timetable 293
7. Organized Client File 294
8. Trial Notebook 294
9. Paralegal Trial Notebook 295
10. Preparing Exhibits 296

III. PREPARING WITNESSES FOR THE TRIAL **297**
A. Review Deposition Testimony 297
B. Double- and Triple-Check Documentation 298
C. What to Tell Witnesses about Testifying 298
1. Do: Review the File 299
2. Do: Dress Professionally 299
3. Do: Make Eye Contact 299
4. Do: Be Polite 299
5. Do: Tell the Truth 299
6. Don't: Guess 300
7. Don't: Get Angry or Use Sarcasm 300
8. Don't: Take Notes to the Witness Stand 300

IV. PREPARING FOR THE TRIAL: ROLE OF THE PARALEGAL **300**
A. Reconnoiter the Courtroom 301
B. Rehearse Your Equipment 301
C. Learn the Layout of the Courthouse 301
D. Master the Trial Notebook or the Case Files 302
E. Get Ready for Stress 302
F. Anticipate Problems 302

V. MOCK TRIALS **303**

VI. PHASES OF THE TRIAL **303**
A. Pretrial Conference 303
B. Calendar Call 306
C. Jury Selection 307
1. Trial Paralegals and Jury Selection 307
2. Peremptory Jury Strikes 307
3. Challenges for Cause 307
D. Opening Statements 308

E. Presentation of the Plaintiff's Case 308
1. Witnesses 308
a. Direct Examination 309
b. Cross-Examination 310
c. Paralegal Assistance during the Testimony Phase of the Trial 310
2. Resting the Case 311
3. Motion for Directed Verdict 311
F. Presenting the Defense 312
1. Defense Witnesses 312
2. Resting the Defense Case 312
G. Charge Conference 312
H. Closing Argument 314
I. Jury Instructions 314
J. Jury Deliberation 315
K. Verdict 315
L. Judgment 316
M. Enforcing the Judgment 316

Case Excerpt: In re Lowell *317*

Chapter Summary *323*
Skills You Need in the Real World *323*
The Life of a Paralegal *324*
Ethical Issues for the Paralegal *325*
Websites *325*
Key Terms *326*
Review Questions *326*
Applying What You Have Learned *326*

10 **DAMAGES 329**

Chapter Objectives *329*

I. INTRODUCTION 329

II. TYPES OF DAMAGES 330
A. Compensatory Damages 330
1. General Damages 331
a. Calculating Damages 331
b. Pain and Suffering 332
2. Special Damages 332
a. Lost Wages 332
b. Medical Bills 333
c. Future Losses 333
d. Emotional Distress 334

e. Loss of Consortium 334
f. Bad Faith Damages 334
B. Punitive Damages 335
C. Nominal Damages 336

III. PROVING DAMAGES 336
A. Distinguishing between General and Special Damages 336
B. Presenting Proof at Trial 337
C. Proving Property Losses 338
D. The Collateral Source Rule 338
E. Mitigation of Damages 339
F. Prior Injuries 340

IV. EQUITABLE REMEDIES 340

V. EVALUATING POTENTIAL DAMAGES 341
A. Reviewing the Facts of a Case 341
B. Asset Searches 342
C. The Jury's Role 342
1. Jury Instructions 342
2. JNOV 343

Case Excerpt: Zak v. Riffel 344

Chapter Summary 354
Skills You Need in the Real World 355
The Life of a Paralegal 355
Ethical Issues for the Paralegal 356
Websites 356
Key Terms 356
Review Questions 357
Applying What You Have Learned 357
Endnotes 358

11 ARBITRATION, MEDIATION, AND SETTLEMENT 359

Chapter Objectives 359

I. INTRODUCTION 359

II. ARBITRATION 360
A. The History of Arbitration 360
B. The Federal Arbitration Act 361

C. Comparing Arbitration to Appraisal 361
D. Types of Arbitration 362
E. Issues That Can Be Submitted to Arbitration 362
F. Limitations on Arbitration Cases 363
G. Arbitrators 363
H. The Arbitration Agreement 364

III. MEDIATION 364
A. State Mediation Programs 365
B. Certified Mediators 365
C. The Mediation Conference 366
D. Persons Required to Be Present at Mediation 366
E. The Mediator's Authority 367
F. Impasse 367

IV. SETTLEMENT 368
A. Reasons to Settle 368
B. Settlements Are Contracts 369
1. Mutual Assent 369
2. Capacity 370
3. Consideration 370
4. Legality 370
C. Procedures in Bringing About a Settlement 370
1. Settlement Brochure 370
a. Factual Basis of Plaintiff's Claim 371
b. Summary of Plaintiff's Damages 371
c. Overview of the Law 371
d. Summary of Recent Jury Awards 372
e. Offer to Settle 372
2. Demand Letter 372
3. Offers of Judgment 375
D. Releases 377

Case Excerpt: Joyner's Mech., Inc. v. Miller *377*

Chapter Summary *381*
Skills You Need in the Real World *381*
The Life of a Paralegal *381*
Ethical Issues for the Paralegal *382*
Websites *383*
Key Terms *383*
Review Questions *383*
Applying What You Have Learned *384*
Endnotes *385*

12 APPEALS 387

Chapter Objectives 387

I. INTRODUCTION **387**

II. STARTING AN APPEAL **388**

III. CHANGING COURTS **388**
A. Notice of Appeal 389
B. Terminology on Appeal 390
C. The Record 390
D. Appellate Docket Number 391

IV. BRIEFS **391**
A. Appellant's Brief 391
1. Contents of an Appellate Brief 392
a. Title Page 392
b. Statement of Facts 392
c. Enumerations of Error 393
d. Argument 394
e. Conclusion 394
2. Filing Deadlines 394
3. Serving Copy on Appellee 395
B. Appellee's Brief 395
C. Oral Argument 396

V. THE POWERS OF THE APPELLATE COURTS **396**
A. Affirming 396
B. Reversing 397
C. Modifying 397
D. Remanding 397

VI. THE STATE SUPREME COURT **397**
A. Petition for Cert 398
B. Granting Cert 398
C. Denying Cert 399

VII. THE U.S. SUPREME COURT **399**

Case Excerpt: City of Riverside v. Horspool 400

Chapter Summary 406
Skills You Need in the Real World 406
The Life of a Paralegal 407

Ethical Issues for the Paralegal 408
Websites 408
Key Terms 409
Review Questions 409
Applying What You Have Learned 409
Endnotes 410

GLOSSARY 411
INDEX 417

Preface

Civil litigation is the lifeblood of private legal practice, as well as an important part of government practice. Paralegal students are far more likely to be involved in civil lawsuits than criminal cases, business disputes, and intellectual property suits combined. Civil litigation courses are part of the core curriculum in every paralegal program in the country. In this second edition, the author has incorporated many of the electronic developments that have changed the day-to-day practice of civil law, especially in regard to e-discovery. In addition to discussing theoretical constructs, the text also offers extensive ancillary materials and supplemental material.

In *Civil Law and Litigation for Paralegals*, the author provides the student with an in-depth analysis of the wide variety of civil cases, laying out the basic foundation of the American legal system, proceeding through the investigation and implementation of a civil case, and following the case through to appeal. The premise of the book is to teach the basics of civil litigation and to give students the chance to build a skill set and create material that could go into a portfolio that they can then show to prospective employers.

The text also addresses the specific duties of paralegals in civil practice. Each chapter provides examples of the important role that paralegals play in every stage of civil litigation, from client intake to bringing an appeal. The text balances the theoretical underpinnings of the law with the practical examples and hands-on experience that all students need to completely understand the topic.

KEY CHARACTERISTICS OF *CIVIL LAW AND LITIGATION FOR PARALEGALS*:

THE WRITING STYLE

The author's clear and coherent writing is one of the best features of the text. The author clearly communicates his enthusiasm for the topic throughout the text.

CHAPTER FEATURES

Each chapter has a standard format, including:

- **Clearly stated chapter objectives**
  Each chapter sets out 10 objectives for the student-reader.

- **Introductory paragraph**
  The major topics in the chapter will be set out in this introductory chapter.

- **Material presented in a logical way**
  The topics discussed in the chapter flow in a logical, commonsense manner.

- **Material supplemented by numerous sidebars, charts, diagrams, etc.**
  The text contains numerous charts, diagrams and illustrations, and sidebars designed to illuminate specific topics throughout the chapter.

- **Learning styles are taken into consideration**
  The topics in the chapters are discussed in a variety of ways to take advantage of different student-reader learning styles.

- **Significant cases**
  The text will also place strong emphasis on seminal or otherwise important cases in specific areas of practice to help demonstrate the importance of case law to civil litigation.

- **Terms and legal vocabulary**
  All terms and legal vocabulary are defined immediately for the student—the first time a key word or legal term is mentioned in the text, a definition of it appears in the margin. This helps students grasp the meaning without breaking into the flow of the reading by having to turn to the glossary.

- **Extensive use of hypotheticals**
  The author uses hypothetical questions and other scenarios to illustrate the points under discussion in each chapter. These scenarios also provide an excellent foundation for classroom discussion.

- **Case excerpts**
  Each chapter contains a significant case designed to expand on the topics discussed in the chapter. There are also questions for students based on the case to further assist their understanding of the case and its relevance to the chapter concepts.

- **"Real world" flavor**
  The text also places heavy emphasis on the practical aspects of civil litigation practice. Each chapter presents interview excerpts from paralegals who actually work in the field, presenting an overview of what brought them into the law, as well as their daily activities. This is outlined in the "Life of the Paralegal" section that appears at the conclusion of each chapter.

- **Ethical issues**
  Ethics is crucial for any legal professional. Each chapter explores an important ethical question and explains the relevance of ethical systems for the day-to-day practice of civil law.

- **Examples of court documents**
  The text will also present numerous court documents for the student-reader, including contracts of representation, complaints, answers, discovery requests, motions, and many others. Each of these court documents will be annotated with explanations of the various component parts.

PEDAGOGY

The text has numerous features that take advantage of the varying learning styles that students apply to learning. Because students who apply their newly acquired knowledge often retain it much better than those who do not, this text requires students to apply the knowledge that they have gained. Each chapter has practical examples of court documents, pleadings, motions, and other real-life exercises that emphasize the material discussed in each chapter.

The text is written in clearly presented language that engages the student, keeps the reader's interest, and presents information in a variety of styles to take advantage of different learning styles. Each new concept is presented in a multilayer fashion, first with the basic concepts and then adding greater complexity once the intellectual foundation is laid. Charts and diagrams are provided to illustrate concepts as they are discussed and to provide the instructor with additional material for class discussion. Sidebars, tables, and interviews are also presented to supplement the chapter information in a different format for students who may not fully grasp the concepts on initial presentation. Finally, practical hands-on assignments and discussion questions are presented to reiterate and emphasize the concepts. This allows for greater comprehension and retention by the student. The author fills the text with a balance of theoretical discussions and practical examples, all presented in a well-written, enjoyable style.

INSTRUCTOR'S MANUAL

The author has developed an impressive instructor's manual to accompany the text. Recognizing the needs of instructors for multiple resources, the author has provided the following features:

- **Suggested syllabi and lesson plans**
- **Annotated outlines for each chapter**
- **Answers to all end-of-chapter questions**

- **Test bank**
  The test bank includes a variety of test questions, including:
  - Essay questions (5 per chapter)
  - Short answer (10 per chapter)
  - Multiple choice (25 per chapter)
  - True-false (10 per chapter)
- **PowerPoint slides for each chapter**

Acknowledgments

The author would like to thank Betsy Kenny, David Herzig, Christine Becker, and Sarah Dawson for their assistance in creating this book.

About the Author

Neal Bevans is a former assistant district attorney and private attorney. A veteran of over 150 trials, Bevans has tried every major felony from rape, murder, and narcotics to armed robbery. One of his cases was televised nationally on Court TV. He also worked in a private firm handling primarily medical malpractice and personal injury defense. He has a Juris Doctor degree from the University of Georgia (Order of the Barrister) and has been a college instructor for over 20 years. A multiple-year honoree in *Who's Who Among America's Teachers,* Bevans is the author of numerous textbooks and magazine articles.

1

Introduction to the Court System

Chapter Objectives

- **Explain the differences between civil law and other types of law**
- **Describe the burden of proof in civil cases**
- **Explain the role of pleadings in civil cases**
- **Explain the difference between a finding of liability and a finding of guilt**
- **Describe the function of damages in civil cases**
- **Define the role of the U.S. Constitution in the American legal system**
- **Explain the difference between statutes and case law**

I INTRODUCTION

Before we can discuss the many fascinating aspects of civil litigation, we must begin with an examination of the American judicial system. The purpose of this chapter is to introduce you to the important distinctions between civil law and other types of law, as well as the sources of judicial authority. Finally, we will examine the major features of both the federal and state court systems. As you will see, there any many different sources of legal authority, and each plays an important role in the overall pattern of civil litigation.

CIVIL LAW

Civil law is a broad category encompassing an enormous variety of cases. Divorce actions, medical malpractice, child custody, and personal injury cases are all types of civil law. Because this is a book about civil litigation and procedure, we will touch on many of these disparate areas of law as we discuss the course of a civil case. Before we examine the details of civil litigation, however, we must address a more fundamental question: What is civil law?

A. WHAT IS CIVIL LAW?

Civil law refers to the large body of cases that are brought by individuals against other individuals. When a person sues someone for defamation or a corporation seeks to enforce an employment contract against an employee, these are both civil cases. What makes civil litigation so interesting is that there is an almost infinite variety of cases that falls under the general heading of civil law. Unlike criminal law or other specialized areas, legal professionals who work in civil litigation must be prepared for a wide assortment of cases. Fortunately, the rules that govern civil cases are uniform and relatively straightforward, even if they do apply to a myriad of case types.

Tech Topic
THE TECHNOLOGY GAP

Individuals who are new to the practice of law are often surprised to learn of the technology gap between this profession and nearly every other. Law is a conservative profession and has been traditionally very slow to adopt new technology. Devices that have found immediate acceptance in accounting and medicine have been slow to find their way into the legal field. Given the vast adoption of personal computers, it is surprising to learn that there is still a significant percentage of attorneys who have not used a laptop or desktop computer. Many still dictate memoranda and other items to secretaries, who transcribe them in much the same way that they did 30 years ago.

However, that predisposition against technology has finally begun to change. Younger lawyers who have used computers and other devices since childhood are in the forefront of this movement, but there are other reasons for law as a profession to adopt computer software and other labor-saving devices. Throughout this book, we will examine the expanding role of technology in the practice of law and show how you, as a paralegal, can increase your marketability to a firm by demonstrating your understanding of and ability to use various technological innovations.

B. HOW DOES CIVIL LAW DIFFER FROM OTHER AREAS OF LAW?

There are dozens of branches of law. Administrative law deals with the rules and regulations that manage government agencies. Admiralty law governs the rules of the sea. Bankruptcy law is concerned with discharging debts through a court proceeding. Criminal law focuses on punishing lawbreakers. Domestic law involves divorce, alimony, and child custody issues.

Civil law is different from these and other areas of law in several important respects. A civil action is usually based on a private wrong suffered by an individual, corporation, or other entity. The plaintiff brings suit when he or she has suffered a financial, emotional, or physical loss. The right to bring a civil suit is not limited to people. Corporations and businesses may also sue in their own right. There are even provisions that allow government agencies to bring civil suits. Civil actions encompass these and many other types of actions. We will address the many ramifications of these actions throughout this text.

In particular, civil cases differ from other types of cases in all of the following ways:

- Parties
- Pleadings
- Rules
- Burden of proof
- Outcome

1. THE PARTIES

In civil suits, private parties sue other private parties. Unlike criminal cases, which are brought by the government against an individual, a civil case involves private issues and grievances. Although government agencies can bring civil suits against individuals, the point of the litigation is to enforce a right or to sue for damages.

There are some important terms regarding civil suits that all legal professionals should know. The person who brings a civil suit is referred to as the **plaintiff**. The person who is being sued is the **defendant**. These terms are almost exclusively reserved for civil cases; other names are used to refer to the parties in noncivil cases. The person or business filing a bankruptcy, for instance, is referred to as a *petitioner*. In criminal cases, the government brings an action against an individual or corporation to enforce statutes and is simply termed *the state*, *the people*, or *United States* (among others).

Plaintiff
The individual, company, or institution that initiates a lawsuit

Defendant
The individual, company, or institution against whom a lawsuit is brought

As you read pleadings in civil cases, you will see that the **caption** or **style** of the case always lists the names of the plaintiffs and defendants. Civil cases are captioned *Plaintiff A v. Defendant B*. By contrast, criminal cases are captioned *Government (or State) v. Defendant*, and bankruptcy cases are captioned *In re John Doe* (in the matter of John Doe). By examining the caption or style of the case, you can easily decipher if it is a civil or other type of action.

Caption (Style)
The heading or title used in all legal pleadings

The caption of any pleading reflects the identities and status of all parties to the suit. The plaintiff is identified by full legal name when he or she is a person and by full title when it is a business or government entity. Similarly, the caption must correctly identify the defendant. A caption that lists the incorrect name of the defendant may be subject to dismissal for failing to correctly identify exactly who is the subject of the action. Beyond identifying the parties, the caption also identifies the court where the action is pending and provides information about the case file number, sometimes called the *civil action number*. This number is important because it is the docketing number assigned by the court system to that action. Case file numbers are unique to each case and must be included on all documents subsequently filed in the case. Many courts also require that in addition to identifying the parties, the court, and the case file number, the caption must also identify the document filed.

Complaint
Also known as a *petition*, it is the pleading filed by the plaintiff and served on the defendant that sets out the plaintiff's factual allegations that show the defendant is responsible for the plaintiff's injuries.

2. THE PLEADINGS

Petition
A request made to a government entity; often used synonymously with *complaint*, although *petition* is a more general term

Answer
The document filed by the defendant in a civil action that responds to each of the allegations raised in the plaintiff's complaint, denies or admits to the factual allegations, and denies or admits to responsibility for the plaintiff's injuries

Civil actions are also unique in the type of pleadings that are used to initiate lawsuits. In a civil case, the plaintiff files a **complaint**, also known as a **petition**. This complaint sets out the plaintiff's factual allegations against the defendant and asks a court to award monetary damages to the plaintiff as a result of the defendant's actions. The defendant, on the other hand, responds with an **answer**, also known as a *reply*. In the answer, the defendant denies the plaintiff's factual allegations and any responsibility for the plaintiff's injuries. See Figure 1-1 for an example of the caption of a civil case complaint.

It is important to note that the term *pleadings* has different meanings in different jurisdictions. For instance, in some areas, *pleadings* refers exclusively to the complaint and answer, while in others it broadly refers to all documents filed in the civil action.

FIGURE 1-1

Civil Case Caption

STATE OF EDWARDS
COUNTY OF PLACID
SUPERIOR COURT OF PLACID COUNTY

		CIVIL ACTION FILE NO.: ________
Elizabeth Louise,	)	
	)	
Plaintiff,	)	
	)	
v.	)	**COMPLAINT**
	)	
Wilson Johnson,	)	
	)	
Defendant.	)	
	)	
____________________	)	

LEGAL LEGWORK ■ FINDING SOURCES

You will find a section in each chapter where you will be asked to research specific legal topics raised in the chapter. The purpose of this feature is to emphasize specific material from the chapter and to assist you in learning about additional and important legal topics. For the purposes of this first assignment, research the available sources online as well as any print media you may have in your local law library. There are more and more online sites available every day, and these can be a tremendous help in researching, organizing, and preparing for civil cases. Try an online search through Google, Yahoo!, or another search engine, using the search string "online legal research."

3. THE RULES

As we will see throughout this book, civil actions follow their own set of rules in regard to the filing of pleadings, the various stages of a civil action, and even the enforcement of the ultimate verdict. All states have enacted their own versions of the Federal Rules of Civil Procedure, which we will discuss throughout this book. See Figure 1-2 for an example of the Rules of Civil Procedure.

(a) Claim for Relief. A pleading that states a claim for relief must contain:
- (1) a short and plain statement of the grounds for the court's jurisdiction, unless the court already has jurisdiction and the claim needs no new jurisdictional support;
- (2) a short and plain statement of the claim showing that the pleader is entitled to relief; and
- (3) a demand for the relief sought, which may include relief in the alternative or different types of relief.

FIGURE 1-2

Federal Rules of Civil Procedure — Rule 8. General Rules of Pleading

4. THE BURDEN OF PROOF

Whenever a party brings an allegation in any type of case, that party must prove the allegation. The **burden of proof** varies depending on the type of case involved. In civil cases, for example, the burden of proof is usually a **preponderance of the evidence**. This is a standard that requires the plaintiff to prove that the allegations in the complaint are more likely true than not. Many commentators have described it as the plaintiff's burden to tip the scales of proof in the plaintiff's direction. Others have attempted to quantify it by saying that if the plaintiff can establish the facts to 51 percent, then the plaintiff has satisfied preponderance of the evidence.

There are different burdens of proof in different types of actions. Prosecutors in a criminal trial, for instance, must prove that the defendant is guilty **beyond a reasonable doubt**. Although legal commentators and authorities have wrestled for centuries over the exact meaning of this term, most define it as substantial or overwhelming evidence that the defendant committed the crime charged. Proof beyond a reasonable doubt means that the

Burden of proof
The amount of proof that the plaintiff must present in order to substantiate his or her claims as made in the complaint

Preponderance of the evidence
The level of proof required in a civil case: "more likely than not to be true"

Beyond a reasonable doubt
Proof of the elements of a crime against the defendant to a point where a juror has no substantive uncertainty about the defendant's guilt

individual jurors in the case are convinced of the evidence against the defendant and have no major objections to the case presented. If preponderance of the evidence is considered to be a slight tipping of the scale in the plaintiff's favor, proof beyond a reasonable doubt would require the plaintiff to swing the scale entirely to its side. This higher standard is required in criminal cases for the very simple reason that it should be more difficult to imprison a person than it is to assess monetary damages against him or her.

Although preponderance of the evidence is the most commonly seen burden of proof in civil law, there are situations where a civil litigant might have to prove his or her case by **clear and convincing evidence**. The standard of "clear and convincing evidence" is higher than preponderance of the evidence and less than proof beyond a reasonable doubt, falling somewhere between the two. Clear and convincing evidence requires the fact finder to determine to a substantial certainty that the party's allegations are true.

Clear and convincing evidence
Having a high probability of truthfulness; a higher standard than preponderance of the evidence

The question often arises, why would civil cases usually require preponderance of the evidence and then, in rare instances, require a higher degree of proof? Clear and convincing evidence is reserved for instances where the result for the parties will have a substantial impact on their lives. A court might require clear and convincing evidence in any of the following actions:

- Committing an individual to a mental institution
- Deciding to withdraw life support from a patient in a persistent vegetative state
- Determining parental rights
- Disbarring an attorney
- Committing fraud
- Alleging improper actions in an election

In each of the examples provided here, the issues involved have such a potential impact on the parties that courts routinely require a higher standard of proof before allowing the action. These actions will have such drastic consequences that many states require the standard of clear and convincing evidence before a judge is authorized to make a ruling on them.

PRACTICE POINTER ▶ RESOURCE FOLDER

One important aspect of working in the legal field is organizing all of the information that you will need on a daily basis. One way of doing this is to create your own paralegal resource folder. This can be an actual file folder or a computer folder on your computer. You need this folder for one simple reason: time. When you work in the legal field, time is money. The more time you can save on a particular job, the sooner you can move on to the next. Creating a paralegal resource folder is one of the best ways to save time and effort. The couple of hours that you spend creating one will save you hundreds of hours over your career. Besides that, having a resource that contains virtually everything you need, from telephone numbers to notes about how certain judges like their orders submitted, will make you look even better to your firm. In fact, having all of this information at your fingertips will make you seem almost superhuman.

Whether you create your resource in physical file folders, notebooks, or on a computer, a good resource should have all of the following information:

- Telephone numbers, addresses, and e-mail contact information
- Calendar
- Where to find certain courthouse records
- Attorney and judge "peculiarities"
- Forms, forms, and more forms
- Brief and memo bank
- Frequently asked questions
- Computer passwords and login information
- Vendor/supplier information

If putting together your own paralegal resource folder sounds unusual, it isn't. Legal professionals have been creating their own handy references for decades. Many attorneys keep important data in manila file folders or word processing files or stored on digital devices. In the modern world, many paralegals keep all of this information in databases. Whatever method you currently use to hang on to important information, you will need to pull it all together and put it in one place. It might be a large file folder on your desk. It might just as easily be on your laptop, stored in a network folder, or backed up on CD. However you decide to store it, you should organize your important information, put it in one place, and start using it to make your job easier.

5. THE OUTCOME

In a civil trial, jurors are asked to determine which side has presented a more believable version of the facts. Unlike criminal cases, where jurors are called upon to determine guilt or innocence, the juries in civil cases face a determination of **liability**. Civil juries determine whether one party is liable to the other party. A civil jury never determines, for instance, that a party is **guilty**. Instead, if the jury believes the plaintiff, it finds the defendant liable to the plaintiff. On the other hand, if the jury determines that the defendant has the more likely version of the truth, the jury might easily find that the plaintiff is liable to the defendant or that the defendant is not liable to anyone.

Liability
A jury's determination that one party is responsible for injuries to another party; the basis for an award of damages

Guilty
A verdict only available in criminal cases where the jury determines that the defendant is responsible for committing a crime

Once a determination of liability has been made, the next step in a civil case is the determination of **damages**. *Damages* refer to monetary payments made by one party to another that attempt to compensate the party for his or her losses. In situations where the jury believes that the defendant is not liable, the jury will order that no damages be awarded. On the other hand, if the jury sides with the plaintiff, the jury must make a determination about damages — specifically, how much money the defendant should pay to the plaintiff.

Damages
Monetary payments assessed against a party who has been deemed liable to another party in a civil case

SOURCES OF LEGAL AUTHORITY IN THE UNITED STATES

One of the first questions that any legal professional must answer is, "What is the law?" Is the law simply a body of statutes, or is it something more? As we will see throughout this book, there is no easy answer. For instance, one could easily argue that the source of all legal authority in the United States derives from the U.S. Constitution.

A. THE CONSTITUTION

The U.S. Constitution took effect in 1789. It is one of the most influential documents in world history. The Constitution sets out the basic framework for the federal and state governments, creates three separate branches of government, and details the rights allotted to citizens (Fig. 1-3). Constitutional law is a complex subject and not one that we will address in any depth here, except to say that all governmental authority flows from the provisions of the Constitution. In addition to the federal Constitution, each state also has its own constitution, setting out the rights, duties, and obligations of state governments.

FIGURE 1-3

U.S. Constitution

Article I:	Legislative Branch
Article II:	Executive Branch
Article III:	Judicial Branch

Although the Constitution provides the framework for the government, it does not provide much guidance on issues such as bringing civil actions, prosecuting crimes, or enforcing judgments. For answers to those questions, we must turn to other sources of the law, including statutes, case law, and common law.

B. STATUTES

Statute
A law that is voted on by the legislative branch and enacted by the executive branch

Statutes consist of legislative bills that are voted on by the legislative branch of government and enacted by the executive branch. On the federal level, the U.S. Congress is the legislative branch, and it votes on bills before sending them to the president (the executive branch) for signature. If the president signs the legislation, it becomes a binding law. On the state level, the legislature votes on bills and submits them to the governor for signature. In both instances, the laws that are created are referred to as *statutes*. But that is only one small part of the large body of what American legal scholars consider to be the *law*.

1. ADMINISTRATIVE RULES AND REGULATIONS

Once a statute has been created, a government agency may create an administrative rule or regulation to put the statute into effect. For instance, the 16th Amendment gives the federal government the power to levy income taxes but provides no details about the process of actually carrying out tax collection (Fig. 1-4). Instead, the Treasury Department, acting through its Internal Revenue Service, creates administrative rules and regulations that govern how, when, and who should pay income taxes. These rules and regulations carry the same force as a statute.

FIGURE 1-4

Amendment XVI

The Congress shall have power to lay and collect taxes on incomes, from whatever source derived, without apportionment among the several states, and without regard to any census or enumeration.

PRACTICE POINTER ▶ WRITTEN COMMUNICATION

If there is one skill that all legal professionals should have in abundance, it is the ability to communicate clearly and succinctly in writing. Written communication is still the cornerstone of the legal profession, even in this era of e-mail, faxes, and the Internet. We will examine written and other forms of communication throughout this text, but in this chapter, we will focus on written communication.

Why are written communication skills so important? For most people, clear writing indicates clear thinking. The ability to effectively communicate an idea or a position in writing is the core of what an attorney does. We all tend to think of attorneys as individuals who communicate through the spoken word, either in closing arguments to juries, motions before a judge, or simply discussing legal implications with clients. But the reality of legal practice is just the opposite of the popular impression. Attorneys spend large portions of every day reading and writing. They read case decisions, statutes, law reviews, and a wealth of other material, and they write letters to clients, briefs to appellate courts, complaints, answers, motions, and a myriad of other materials. If they cannot present themselves well in writing, their legal practice will suffer.

Attorneys expect the same high level of writing skills on the part of their staff. Paralegals and others who work closely with attorneys must have mastered the basics of written communication. That is one reason why we devote a section to it in every chapter of this book. In future chapters, you can anticipate assignments ranging from questions surrounding basic grammar to the development of motions that would be submitted to a judge.

2. ORDINANCES

Ordinance
A law passed by a local government, such as a town council or city government

As we have seen, statutes are laws passed by a state or federal government. However, there is an entire class of laws passed by local governments, such as municipalities and towns, that regulate behavior at a local level. These are not referred to as statutes. Instead, they are called **ordinances**. An ordinance has limited application. Ordinances have strict geographic limits, such as the town limits or the county boundary. Ordinances cannot conflict with statutes. If they do, the ordinances are ruled unconstitutional and the statutes take precedence.

C. CASE LAW

Case law
The decisions written by appellate courts explaining the outcome of a case on appeal

In addition to statutory law, there is another, and equally important, source of law: **case law**. Case law is the huge body of decisions published by appellate courts. Laypersons do not realize the significance of case law. When an appellate court reaches a decision in a case on appeal, the reasons for the decision are encapsulated in a written opinion. In many instances, case law is synonymous with common law, discussed later.

An opinion discusses not only the facts of the particular case on appeal, but also the law that applies to those facts. For legal professionals, case law can be one of the most important sources of legal authority in the United States. The importance of case law can be demonstrated by reviewing a decision by the U.S. Supreme Court.

Suppose that the U.S. Congress passes a bill stating that the punitive damages available to civil litigants are limited to a specific formula. The formula set out by the federal legislation is that punitive damages (those monetary payments made above and beyond the monetary damages intended to compensate the plaintiff for his or her injuries) must be limited to twice the amount of proven actual damages. The statute is clear and unambiguous. The most that an injured plaintiff could receive in any case, no matter how egregiously the defendant acted, is a sum that is twice the plaintiff's actual damages. This means that if the plaintiff's proven damages are $1,000, the most that the plaintiff could receive in punitive damages is $2,000. However, if a litigant who falls under this statute appeals to the U.S. Supreme Court, that court is free to rule that Congress overstepped its bounds by limiting awards in this way. The court's written opinion in that case would be vitally important case law for anyone else with a pending case involving punitive damages. That case law would be as important as any statute.

The significance of case law is that it both explains and expands on statutes and other sources of law. The true power of appellate courts is their ability to review the decisions of lower courts. All courts have the responsibility of interpreting the Constitution, statutes, ordinances, and even other case law, but the appellate courts can review the decisions of lower courts and modify those interpretations in accordance with their own views. The appellate court's interpretation of these issues is binding on the parties in a particular appeal and on all others who have similar issues. Once an appellate court, such as the U.S. Supreme Court, adopts a new interpretation of a law or rules that a particular statute is unconstitutional, that interpretation becomes the law of the land and is just as binding as any statute.

There are quite literally hundreds of examples of the impact that appellate decisions have had on civil litigation. A court's ruling on evidence may affect whether or not a plaintiff is permitted to introduce evidence of the defendant's previous driving record in a personal injury case. Another court's ruling on collateral source payments might well allow the defendant to present evidence to the jury that the plaintiff has already been compensated for some of his or her injuries through insurance.

One might be tempted to think that the only important source of case law in the United States is the U.S. Supreme Court. However, case law comes from every level of the court system. As we will see later in this chapter, both state and federal courts generate case law, and they do so at different levels, from trial courts, to appellate courts, to the U.S. Supreme Court.

D. COMMON LAW

The final category of sources of legal authority is **common law**. This is an ancient source of legal authority. Stretching back to our legal roots in England, common law was literally the law of the common people. In an age when most people were illiterate, judges were one of the few professionals who could read and write. As a result, there were very few statutes created by the government. Instead of using statutory law, judges were forced to create their own rules.

Common law
The large body of decisions and principles created by judges as they decide individual cases

For instance, the "year and a day" law stated that if a man was attacked and it took longer than a year for him to die of his injuries, then the person who attacked him could not be tried for murder. This rule was a common law rule that governed English (and American) jurisdictions for years. The theory behind the law was simple: Given the standards of the medical profession in the Middle Ages, if a victim lingered for at least 12 months, then it was quite likely that he died from something other than the injuries he sustained in his attack. Similarly, as judges continued to reach decisions in cases, they amassed a huge body of legal principles and standards that came to be called *common law*.

The reason that we continue to focus on common law, even after many states have abolished it, is that it remains binding law in a small number of states and it also functions as a reservoir of legal knowledge that can be relied upon by courts. Common law exists alongside statutory law in states like North Carolina and Virginia. That alone would justify studying it. However, even in states where common law has long since been abolished, courts may still turn to the ideas and principles found in common law when they are wrestling with a new issue on appeal. It may be true that there is nothing new under the sun, and over the centuries, common law had addressed virtually every legal topic. This makes common law a great resource when other legal authorities come up short.

Sidebar

The year and a day rule has been abolished in all jurisdictions in the United States, but only recently in some states.

IV JURISDICTION

No discussion of judicial authority could be complete without an examination of the topic of jurisdiction. **Jurisdiction** refers to the power of a court to decide issues in the

Jurisdiction
The power of a court to make rulings

case and to impose those decisions on the parties. There are many different types of jurisdiction, including the two major types:

- Subject matter jurisdiction
- Personal jurisdiction

A. SUBJECT MATTER JURISDICTION

Subject matter jurisdiction
The power of a court to consider specific types of cases

When a court has **subject matter jurisdiction**, it means that the court is permitted to entertain the issues raised in the suit and to make binding rulings on those issues. There are many examples of courts that lack subject matter jurisdiction to consider specific types of cases. Small-claims court, for instance, is often listed as a court of limited jurisdiction precisely because it is barred from considering criminal cases and may only consider litigation concerning civil cases for which a specific amount of money is contested. Besides small-claims courts, many other courts have strict rules about subject matter jurisdiction. If a person or business wishes to file bankruptcy, that filing must occur in the federal bankruptcy courts, simply because those are the only courts authorized to hear such actions.

On the local level, there are some courts that have broad subject matter jurisdiction. In states where the most powerful local court is referred to as *superior court* (also known as *district court* or *county court* in some states), this court may have the power to hear a broad range of actions, from felony crimes to divorce cases (Fig. 1-5). In fact, in many states, superior court was the original court and other local courts were created out of its vast powers.

FIGURE 1-5

Subject Matter Jurisdiction of Superior Court (Georgia)

The superior courts shall have jurisdiction in all cases, except as otherwise provided in this Constitution. They shall have exclusive jurisdiction over trials in felony cases, except in the case of juvenile offenders as provided by law; in cases respecting title to land; in divorce cases; and in equity cases. The superior courts shall have such appellate jurisdiction, either alone or by circuit or district, as may be provided by law.[1]

General jurisdiction
The power of a court to hear a broad range of case types, including civil and criminal issues

Limited jurisdiction
The expressly confined powers of a court to hear specific types of cases only

In addition to issues surrounding subject matter jurisdiction, there are other issues that litigants must address; these include the basic powers of the court. Courts of **general jurisdiction** are empowered to hear a broad range of cases, including civil, criminal, probate, divorce, and child custody issues, among many others. A court of general jurisdiction may consider any of these issues and make binding rulings. However, there are also many courts in the United States that are classified as courts of **limited jurisdiction**. A limited jurisdiction court may only hear specific types of cases. Small-claims court is one such example. This court is authorized to consider civil cases where the parties contest a monetary amount below a specific level. If the amount in controversy is higher than the threshold amount, or if the case involves additional issues outside of the court's authority, the court must transfer the case to another court. On the federal level, bankruptcy court is an example of a court with limited jurisdiction. It may entertain all issues associated with personal or business bankruptcies, but it is not empowered to consider other issues, such as criminal charges or wrongful death claims.

B. PERSONAL JURISDICTION

In addition to subject matter jurisdiction, courts must also have power over the parties, called **personal jurisdiction**. Personal jurisdiction is often described as the court's power to adjudicate the issues in the case and to reach a decision that affects the parties' legal rights. These jurisdictional issues are concomitant: They must exist together. A court may have subject matter jurisdiction, but if it lacks personal jurisdiction, it is barred from considering the case. The opposite scenario is also true. When both types of jurisdiction exist in a case, then the court may proceed to consider the issues. Both subject matter jurisdiction and personal jurisdiction must combine to provide the **forum** with the authority to consider the issues in the case. Here, the "forum" refers to the actual location where the case must be brought. A court with sufficient personal and subject matter jurisdiction becomes the forum where the action is brought and decided.

Personal jurisdiction
The power of a court to enter rulings that are binding on the parties to the action

Forum
The location of the court; a court that possesses both personal and subject matter jurisdiction over the case

A court may acquire personal jurisdiction over a party by a number of methods, including:

- physical presence in the forum;
- domicile or residence in the forum;
- property ownership in the forum;
- consent; or
- minimum contacts.

1. PHYSICAL PRESENCE IN THE FORUM

When a party is present within the geographic limits of the court's power, the party may be served with service of process, and by the party's mere presence the court will acquire personal jurisdiction in the case. Although there are many extrapolations of this rule, including a prohibition against the use of trickery or deceit to get the party into the forum, we will limit our discussion to the fact that presence alone can equate to personal jurisdiction.

2. DOMICILE OR RESIDENCE IN THE FORUM

A court may also acquire personal jurisdiction over a party by the simple fact of the party maintaining a domicile in the county. In many cases, a **domicile** refers to a permanent residence in a particular area. For instance, when a person maintains several different homes in different areas, it may become necessary for the party urging the court to exercise personal jurisdiction to prove that the opposing party's main residence is in the forum.

Domicile
A party's permanent residence, where the party has lived and where the party intends to return

3. PROPERTY OWNERSHIP IN THE FORUM

There are provisions that allow certain types of cases to proceed simply because a party owns property in a particular forum. This is referred to as **in rem jurisdiction**.

In rem jurisdiction
The power of a court to exercise jurisdiction based on the location of real property within the forum

Although actions based on in rem jurisdiction are generally limited to litigation concerning real estate, such as boundary disputes, tax evaluations, and similar actions, the mere fact that real property is located within the forum may be enough to give the court personal jurisdiction over a party.

4. CONSENT

A party may always consent to the court's jurisdiction. In its pleadings, for example, a party may decide to forgo a challenge to the court's jurisdiction, consent to personal jurisdiction, and then proceed to a defense of the allegations.

5. MINIMUM CONTACTS

All states have provisions that allow a forum to acquire jurisdiction, especially in business cases when a party has had sufficient minimum contacts with the forum state to justify a finding that the party has submitted to the court's personal jurisdiction. This rule was first announced in the case of *International Shoe Co. v. Washington*, 326 U.S. 310 (1945), where the U.S. Supreme Court announced a complex test to determine if a specific party has availed itself of sufficient contacts with the forum to have essentially submitted itself to the court's authority. The bane of law students since it was decided, *International Shoe* remains a difficult case to decipher.

SEARCH SUGGESTION • NOT ALL SOURCES ARE CREATED EQUAL

Throughout this text, you will be given specific tips and maxims to assist you in researching issues raised in the chapter. For instance, in this first chapter, you should be aware that not all online research services are created equal. Some online sources cover only a few years' worth of case decisions. For legal researchers, depth of coverage is always important, and you should always seek out sites that provide decades of case analysis, not simply the most recent cases from a state or federal court. For example, this chapter mentions the famous *International Shoe* case. If you are doing online legal research on a site that provides coverage for only the last 10 years or so, your research would never reveal this case. You would be hard-pressed to call your research complete if you were unable to locate one of the most important cases on jurisdiction.

V FEDERAL AND STATE COURT SYSTEMS

Now that we have discussed the important role played by case law in providing a source of legal authority, we will address the issue of how the court systems in the United States are organized. We will begin our discussion with the federal court system and then proceed to the various state systems.

A. LEVELS OF THE FEDERAL COURT SYSTEM

The federal court system is authorized under Article III of the U.S. Constitution. That article provides the structure for the federal court system and clearly establishes the judiciary as a separate and equal branch, moderating the power of the executive and legislative branches. Federal judges are appointed by the president and confirmed by the Senate. Once appointed, federal judges serve for life. They cannot be removed from their positions unless they commit a crime or violate some other law. Federal judges are thus insulated from the day-to-day world of politics and are free to make unpopular decisions. Over the centuries, federal judges have made many controversial decisions, from forced desegregation to a woman's right to receive an abortion.

1. TRIAL COURTS: U.S. FEDERAL DISTRICT COURT

If we think of the federal court system diagrammed as a pyramid, then the U.S. District Courts would be at the bottom of the pyramid. These are the trial courts for the federal system, and they are empowered to hear both civil and criminal cases. There are 94 federal judicial districts scattered across the United States and Puerto Rico.

Federal district courts empanel juries, consider evidence, hear witness testimony, and reach verdicts. As we will see in Chapter 5, federal courts have limited jurisdiction; they are only able to hear certain types of cases. When a final verdict is reached in a federal district court, the losing party usually has the right to appeal to the U.S. Circuit Court of Appeals.

2. APPELLATE COURTS: U.S. CIRCUIT COURTS OF APPEALS

Because federal courts cover the entire nation, cases from federal district courts are appealed to specific appellate courts. There are 13 separate judicial circuits. As you can see in Figure 1-6, some judicial circuits cover large swaths of the United States, while some, like the Second Judicial District, cover a relatively small geographic area. Population determines the boundaries of judicial circuits. The eastern seaboard of the United States has a denser population, and this accounts for the smaller size of its judicial circuits.

3. U.S. SUPREME COURT

The U.S. Supreme Court is one of the most famous courts in the world. In terms of authority and prestige, it is easily one of the most important. Decisions of the U.S. Supreme Court can affect everyone in the United States and can even have ramifications for other countries. The U.S. Supreme Court is the nation's highest appellate court. Its decisions on federal appellate issues are final. Composed of nine justices, the U.S. Supreme Court begins its term on the first Monday of each October and continues

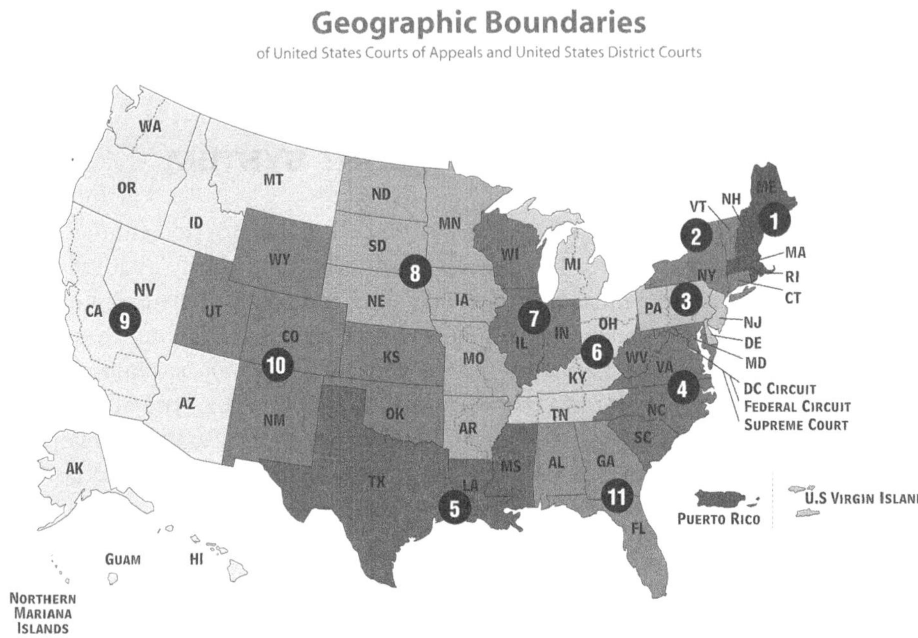

FIGURE 1-6

Geographic Boundaries of United States Courts of Appeal

through June or July of the next year. Authorized by Article III of the U.S. Constitution, the U.S. Supreme Court is the final authority on issues related to the interpretation of the Constitution. The court also has the power to rule federal statutes unconstitutional and therefore unenforceable. Although many cases are submitted to the Supreme Court, the vast majority never make it past the hurdle of certiorari.

Certiorari
The power of an appellate court to decide which cases it will hear

The federal Supreme Court, like many state supreme courts, is vested with the authority to decide which cases it will hear. If the court believes that a specific case lacks merit or does not present any significant issue for the justices to review, the court will deny **certiorari** or *cert.* A denial of cert means that the court refuses to hear the appeal. On the other hand, if the court decides that the case should be heard, it will grant cert. The decision to grant cert does not mean that a party has won on appeal; instead, it simply means that the court has agreed to consider the appeal.

B. LEVELS OF THE STATE COURT SYSTEM

In many ways, the state court systems are a mirror of the federal system. However, state courts are limited to the geographic limits of the state, and therefore they have far less bureaucracy than the federal system. Just as we did with the federal system, we will start our discussion at the bottom of the court pyramid with trial courts.

1. TRIAL COURTS

Trial courts on the state level fulfill many of the same roles as federal district courts. These are the courts where witnesses testify, juries consider verdicts, and judges make rulings on evidence. Because there is a great deal of variation among the states, there is no clear consensus when it comes to the names applied to trial courts. Some states might refer to their trial courts as *superior court*, while others refer to them as *district court* or *state court*. Many states have different levels of trial courts, with one level empowered to hear only specific types of cases, while another is empowered to hear others. In any event, just as we saw with federal district courts, losing parties in trial courts on the state level have the right to appeal to an appellate court.

2. APPELLATE COURTS

All states have appellate courts. In many states, the layers are virtually identical to those found on the federal level, with a trial court, an intermediate court of appeals, and a state supreme court. However, it is important to note that not all states follow this arrangement. Some have only a single layer of appellate courts. In the states with two layers of appellate courts, most refer to the first layer as the state court of appeals. This is the court where losing parties from the trial court level appeal their cases. These courts have appellate justices who are empowered to review the issues on appeal and produce written opinions about the merits of the case. In most states, the losing party in the state court of appeals has the option of appealing to the state's highest court: the state supreme court.

3. STATE SUPREME COURTS

Just like the U.S. Supreme Court, all states have a court of final authority on appellate issues. Although this court is usually referred to as the *state supreme court*, this court may go by a different name in some states. In New York, for example, the state's highest court is referred to as superior court. State supreme courts share many similarities with the U.S. Supreme Court. For instance, these courts also have cert authority in most of their cases. This gives them the right to decide which cases they will hear and which they will not. See Figure 1-7 for a diagram of the typical state court system.

C. FEDERAL VERSUS STATE LAW

The final point we must consider in this chapter regarding the legal system in the United States is the different layers of law that may affect the proceedings in any civil case. For instance, the United States is composed of states that have their own statutory and case law binding on cases brought in state courts, but each state is also a member of the union and is therefore bound by federal law. This often leads to a conflict, especially when an action may be filed as either a state or a federal action. Which court has precedence? Where should the plaintiff file a complaint?

Sidebar

There are some cases that are an exception to cert. Death penalty cases, for example, may be appealed directly to the state and U.S. Supreme Courts without first applying for cert.

The general rules, first promulgated in Article VI of the U.S. Constitution, establish that when there is a conflict between state and federal laws, federal laws will predominate. This "supremacy clause" controls the outcome in situations where there is a conflict between federal and state laws, giving preference to federal actions. Throughout the United States, the interplay of federal and state laws can be represented as two systems overlaid, with the federal on top and the state system below.

FIGURE 1-7

Diagram of Typical State Court System

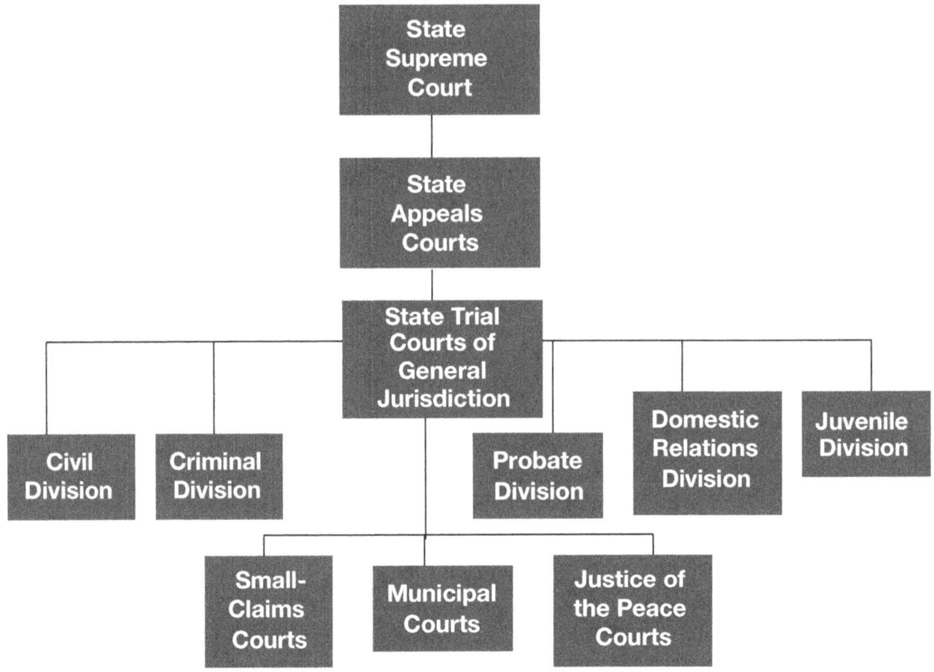

Tech Topic

PORTABLE, HIGH-CAPACITY DIGITAL STORAGE

Like any other business, law offices have realized that storage is a major issue. In the old days, it was file cabinets, sometimes hundreds of them, that would house the paper files of pending and past cases. But over the last 20 years, physical storage has given way to digital storage. These days, digital backup is common; in fact, it may be a violation of ethics and good practice to fail to keep current files on a backup. For small firms that can't afford off-site cloud storage of client files, one method is to purchase high-density, quick-transfer, portable hard drives. These can be programmed to back up once a day or even several times a day. The idea of backup storage has been around for a long time, with old tape backup systems connected to the firm's computer network, but the tapes often presented real issues. For one thing, they were not that convenient to use and often difficult to restore after a major network failure. These days, there are backup drives that store terabytes of data at rates of 400 MB per second; these can be accessed quickly and used to restore missing files in a matter of minutes. These drives are compatible with both Mac and Windows platforms and have a footprint that is as small as a iPad. The only real downside to such a system is that unless they are stored in a secure area, someone can unplug them and take them away quite easily.

Case Excerpt

What is personal jurisdiction and how does the court address it when a defendant is a nonresident? What constitutes "minimum contact" to make it sufficient for a court to exercise jurisdiction over a person or a corporation?

PETERS V. ALPHARETTA SPA, LLC
915 So. 2d 908, (La. App. 1 Cir. 2005)

CARTER, C. J.

In this appeal, we review whether the trial court correctly found insufficient minimum contacts to support personal jurisdiction in Louisiana courts over the nonresident defendant. For the following reasons, we affirm.

Facts

Mark H. Peters, M.D. (Dr. Peters) filed a lawsuit in Terrebonne Parish, Louisiana, seeking protection from "collection activity" on the part of defendant, Alpharetta Spa, L.L.C. (Alpharetta), a Georgia limited liability company in which Dr. Peters was a member prior to relocating to Terrebonne Parish. The lawsuit was filed in response to a demand letter that had been mailed by Alpharetta directed to Dr. Peters for an alleged deficiency/penalty pursuant to the terms of an Operating Agreement (the Agreement) between Dr. Peters and Alpharetta. Dr. Peters alleged that the Agreement was "not freely negotiated" and that he had grounds to dissolve the Agreement, thereby voiding any alleged deficiency/penalty amount that Alpharetta was seeking to collect from him.

Alpharetta maintains and operates a medical business used to enhance its members' plastic surgery practice. Alpharetta operates exclusively in the state of Georgia. The Agreement between the parties was negotiated and executed in the state of Georgia. During the entire time that the Agreement was in effect between the parties, Dr. Peters was a resident of the state of Georgia. He later relocated to the state of Louisiana after the Agreement was terminated. Dr. Peters currently resides and practices medicine in Terrebonne Parish.

In response to Dr. Peters' lawsuit, Alpharetta filed a declinatory exception raising the objections of lack of personal jurisdiction and improper venue. Alpharetta maintained that it had absolutely no contact with the state of Louisiana, and that therefore, no Louisiana court could exercise jurisdiction over it. Additionally, Alpharetta argued that the Agreement between the parties contained a valid and enforceable forum selection clause, designating the courts in the state of Georgia as the exclusive forum for "any dispute or matter arising under" the Agreement.

After a hearing, the trial court sustained Alpharetta's exception and dismissed Dr. Peters' petition. Dr. Peters appeals, assigning one error: "the trial court erred in interpreting too narrowly the scope of Louisiana courts' specific personal jurisdiction over a party that has committed a wrongful act against a Louisiana citizen in this State." Essentially, Dr. Peters argues that the demand letter mailed by Alpharetta and received by him in the state of Louisiana constituted a "wrongful collection" activity, because it was an "improper and oppressive attempt to harass and collect" pursuant to an invalid contract, causing him an injury in this state.

Law and Analysis

We must decide whether a nonresident defendant's mailing of a demand letter to a Louisiana domiciliary is sufficient contact with the state of Louisiana so as to exercise personal jurisdiction over the nonresident defendant. An appellate court conducts a de novo review of the legal issue of personal jurisdiction over a nonresident by a Louisiana court. However, the trial court's factual findings underlying the decision are reviewed under the manifest error standard of review.

In determining whether there is personal jurisdiction, we must look to the long-arm statute of Louisiana, which provides that "a court of this state may exercise personal jurisdiction over a nonresident on any basis consistent with the constitution of this state and of the Constitution of the United States." LSA-R.S. 13:3201B. The limits of the Louisiana long-arm statute and of constitutional due process are coextensive; the sole inquiry into jurisdiction over a nonresident is whether it comports with constitutional due process requirements.

For the exercise of personal jurisdiction over a nonresident defendant to comport with constitutional due process requirements, the defendant must have purposefully established certain "minimum contacts" with the forum state such that he could reasonably anticipate being haled into court there, and the exercise of personal jurisdiction must be such that it "does not offend traditional notions of fair play and substantial justice." *International Shoe Co. v. Washington*, 326 U.S. 310, 316, 66 S.Ct. 154, 90 L.Ed. 95 (1945). Minimum contacts are established when the nonresident defendant "purposely avails itself of the privilege of conducting activities within the forum state."

A court's exercise of personal jurisdiction may be "specific" or "general." A court may exercise specific jurisdiction over a defendant when the alleged cause of action arises out of, or is related to the defendant's purposeful contacts with the forum state. A court may exercise general jurisdiction over a defendant when the defendant has engaged in "continuous and systematic contacts" with the forum, but the contacts are not necessarily related to the lawsuit.

The "purposeful availment" requirement ensures that the nonresident defendant will not be haled into a jurisdiction solely as a result of a random, fortuitous, or attenuated contact, or by the unilateral activity of another party or a third person. There has developed a two-part test in personal jurisdiction analysis. First, it must be shown that the defendant has established minimum contacts with the forum state — i.e., it has purposefully directed its activities at the residents of the forum state. Once that is shown, "a presumption arises that jurisdiction is reasonable and the burden of proof and persuasion shifts to the defendant opposing jurisdiction to present 'a compelling case that the presence of some other considerations would render jurisdiction unreasonable.'"

In this case, Dr. Peters does not argue that the trial court has general jurisdiction over Alpharetta. He does not allege any contacts by Alpharetta other than the demand letter sent to him in Louisiana. He does not allege that Alpharetta owns property in Louisiana, that any of its members reside in Louisiana, that any of its members ever traveled to Louisiana, or that it conducts any type of business in Louisiana. Alpharetta is a limited liability company with its principal place of business near Atlanta, Georgia. From the facts alleged, we do not find the level of "continuous and systematic contacts" necessary to justify the exercise of general jurisdiction. Thus, in order to justify the exercise of specific personal jurisdiction, we must consider only whether Alpharetta's purposeful contact of sending a demand letter to Dr. Peters, who was domiciled in Louisiana, gave rise to or relates to Dr. Peters' cause of action.

After a thorough review of the record, we find that Dr. Peters' cause of action against Alpharetta did not arise out of any transaction of business conducted by Alpharetta in the state of Louisiana. Alpharetta is not in the collection business. Alpharetta's medical business is, and always was, conducted solely in the state of Georgia. The demand letter was the result of Alpharetta's attempt to enforce the terms of the Agreement between it and Dr. Peters. Accordingly, the demand letter did not give rise to Dr. Peters' lawsuit. Rather, the basis of this cause of action was to determine the legal effect of the Agreement. Dr. Peters' allegations revolve around the negotiations between the parties prior to the execution of the Agreement, as well as the actual terms and provisions of the Agreement. The Agreement was negotiated and executed in the state of Georgia. Dr. Peters relocated to Louisiana after the Agreement and the relationship he had with Alpharetta were terminated. Alpharetta sent the demand letter to Dr. Peters in Louisiana simply because that is where Dr. Peters resided at the time that Alpharetta sought to enforce a provision in the Agreement. It was merely fortuitous that Dr. Peters relocated to Louisiana. By mailing the letter to Dr. Peters in Louisiana, Alpharetta never anticipated being haled into a Louisiana court to resolve a dispute arising out of the Agreement. To the contrary, both parties specifically anticipated that any dispute or matter involving the Agreement would be litigated in the state of Georgia.

We conclude that Dr. Peters' cause of action did not arise out of the mailing or receiving of the demand letter. It follows that Alpharetta cannot be said to have purposefully availed itself of the privilege of conducting activities within the state of Louisiana, such that it should have reasonably anticipated Louisiana litigation. Therefore, we find that the trial court correctly sustained Alpharetta's declinatory exception raising the objection of lack of personal jurisdiction and properly dismissed Dr. Peters' petition.

Conclusion

For the reasons assigned, the trial court judgment dismissing Dr. Peters' petition for lack of personal jurisdiction over the nonresident defendant/appellee, Alpharetta Spas, L.L.C., is affirmed. Costs of this appeal are assessed against plaintiff/appellant, Mark H. Peters, M.D.

Affirmed.

QUESTIONS ABOUT THE CASE

1 According to the ruling in this case, how was Dr. Peters involved with Alpharetta Spa, LLC?
2 What business does Alpharetta Spa, LLC, conduct?
3 Where is Alpharetta Spa, LLC, located?

4 What is the "forum selection clause" contained in the agreement between the parties?
5 According to the court, does the demand letter create a sufficient basis for personal jurisdiction? Why or why not?
6 Did Alpharetta Spa, LLC, have sufficient minimum contacts with the state of Louisiana? Explain your answer.
7 What effect does the court ruling have on Dr. Peters's action against Alpharetta Spa, LLC?

Chapter Summary

Civil law is a distinct specialty within a much broader field of legal areas. Unlike criminal law, civil law is concerned with a finding of liability and assessing damages against a party. Civil litigants must prove their cases to a preponderance of the evidence.

The authority for the American legal system derives from the U.S. Constitution. This document creates the framework of the federal and state systems and also provides basic rights for citizens. However, the legal system is also built on other forms of legal authority, such as statutes. Statutes are created by legislatures and enacted by the executive branch. Case law, on the other hand, consists of the large body of written judicial opinions in cases on appeal. Common law is another form of legal authority. Common law stretches back for centuries and was originally an embodiment of judicial principles that would be applied in routine cases.

The federal court system is organized into three levels. At the bottom are the trial courts, called U.S. District Courts. Appeals from these courts go to the U.S. Circuit Courts of Appeal. A litigant may appeal from the circuit court of appeals to the U.S. Supreme Court, which is the final authority on appeal. Many state court systems mirror the federal system, with trial courts and two levels of appeal courts.

SKILLS YOU NEED IN THE REAL WORLD

Visiting the Courthouse

One of the most important skills you can acquire as a paralegal is the ability to navigate successfully among the various courts in your area. As you embark on your career as a paralegal, you should take time to visit the local courthouse.

The problem with going to the courthouse is that it is an intimidating place. That's why you should read through these 10 tips to help you feel more assured when you visit the courthouse for the first time:

1 Realize that everybody had to walk through that door for the first time. Everyone once felt anxious when they walked in. Every one of them was intimidated by the courthouse, no matter how blasé they act now. This is as true for attorneys as it is for paralegals. Sometimes it's even worse for attorneys, because everyone expects them to know their way around.

2 Don't give in to nervousness. Part of the problem with the courthouse is that it was designed to be an intimidating place. As you pass through the front door, keep that in mind. The architecture was created with the goal of making the average citizen feel respectful and maybe even a little bit afraid. When you walk in, look like you've been there a hundred times before. Get a self-confident, slightly bored look on your face. Sometimes looking like you know what you're doing is half the battle.

3 When in doubt, ask questions. Having said that, however, there are some tricks to asking questions.

   Many people think that the first rule in asking questions is knowing what to ask, but actually it is knowing the right to person to ask. Look around the courthouse. Find someone who looks sympathetic. Skip the obviously busy people; they don't have the time or the inclination to answer questions. Next, smile. Always smile before you ask a person a question. They will almost always smile back. Finally, get to the point. Don't beat around the bush; fire away. Don't be afraid that it is a stupid question.

4 Get the lay of the land. If you're nervous about where to go or what to do, get there early and see what other people do. Find a place to sit where you can pretend to read the newspaper and see what other people are doing. Then do it yourself.

5 Project confidence. You are a legal professional there to do a job. You may not know exactly where everything is, but you can find it. By the same token, you shouldn't be cocky or arrogant. That won't get you anywhere.

6 Be polite. Say "please" and "thank you." You'd be surprised how rarely people in the courthouse hear those magic words. It doesn't help to go marching in there and demanding things. Being nice pays off. You really do catch more flies with honey than vinegar.

7 Look the part. You should dress professionally if you want to be treated like a professional. It also gives you just a little bit more confidence.

8 Don't think you can learn it all in an hour. You can't. If you could pick up everything that you needed to know about the courthouse in one trip, it wouldn't be such an intimidating place. Think of your trips to the courthouse as learning sessions. Each time you go, you learn more. There are lawyers who've practiced for 20 years who still learn something new about the courthouse that they didn't know before.

9 Clean up after yourself. Put the books, microfilm, and other things back where you got them. If you can't remember where you got something, then ask someone. You'll score

big points with court personnel if you just put things back where they belong. Also, if the courthouse has rules preventing you from pulling your own files, follow them.

10 Let the Internet work for you. Many courthouse offices now have official Web pages. You can find out a lot of information without having to leave your office. There is plenty of information on the Web these days, and the nice thing is that you can find it 24 hours a day, 7 days a week.

If you follow these tips, you should find that the courthouse isn't as intimidating as you first thought. You might even discover that after a few trips there, you'll start feeling like a veteran. Then you can take pity on someone who has just walked through the metal detector and seems anxious and lost.

THE LIFE OF A PARALEGAL

A Typical Day in the Life

Lisa Mazzonetto has worked for a small firm for several years. Although the firm handles a large percentage of divorce and child custody cases, it also takes on other cases, including contract disputes and other claims.

"The thing I like about [our practice] is that I get to go to court a lot," she says. "There is a lot of client contact in being a paralegal at a family law practice. You manage a lot of cases, and you get a lot of phone calls from upset clients. There is also a lot of paperwork. The pleadings are extensive, and then you have equitable distribution of the marital estate. That involves a lot of affidavits. Then you've got discovery. I do my best to stay on top of it all.

"I also spend a lot of time making sure that my attorney stays organized. I check the file to make sure that the most recent correspondence is there, and any other communications. I also often summarize the opposing side's stand on particular issues, to help [my attorney] stay on top of any new developments.

"Clients are always nervous about going to trial. I help prepare them for trial. Based on the initial meeting, I'll set up an outline of questions that we may ask. I like to go through the questions before they testify. It helps them get a little more comfortable with testifying. People get very nervous about taking the stand. I'll take them to an empty courtroom a few days before the trial so that they can see what it's like. The hardest part for clients when they testify is staying focused on the issues in the hearing. Some of them want to go off on tangents. I find that it helps them focus to have them work on the files with us."

For Lisa, a typical day involves a lot of client contact:

"I'll have them go through their inventory lists and organize their files with me. I want them to be involved and not obsess about issues. Sometimes you get late-night phone calls from clients who have questions about their case or sometimes just want to vent.

"Unfortunately, we're always dealing with domestic violence issues. A lot of our clients take out domestic violence orders to keep their husbands from hurting them. That also means that I'm pulling a lot of criminal files and digging up convictions on opposing parties. I hire a lot of private investigators. They not only investigate the other party, but they sometimes act as civil process servers.

"Sometimes, I'll talk directly with opposing attorneys. They'll want to know about specific issues or want to talk over some points. It's not like the old days; there are a good amount of attorneys who will talk with a paralegal. Of course, there are some who won't have anything to do with you."

ETHICAL ISSUES FOR THE PARALEGAL

Introduction

Throughout this text, we will address important ethical issues for paralegals. Although attorneys have a code of ethics that paralegals must be familiar with, paralegals have their own code of ethics as well. As we go through the material in this book, we will tackle many ethical issues, from confidentiality to fee splitting. Does your state have a paralegal code of ethics? Locate a copy of it and print it off. You will find that ethics is one of the most important aspects of day-to-day legal practice.

Websites

- **Federal Courts**
  http://www.uscourts.gov/
- **National Center for State Courts**
  http://www.ncsc.org/
- **U.S. Supreme Court**
  http://www.supremecourt.gov/
- **Michigan Trial Courts**
  http://courts.mi.gov/Pages/default.aspx
- **Supreme Court of Ohio**
  http://www.sconet.state.oh.us
- **Florida State Courts**
  http://www.flcourts.org/

Forms and Court Documents

Complaint in a Car Wreck Case

STATE OF EDWARDS
COUNTY OF PLACID
SUPERIOR COURT OF PLACID COUNTY

CIVIL ACTION FILE NO.: ________

Elizabeth Louise,	)	
Plaintiff,	)	
v.	)	**COMPLAINT**
Wilson Johnson,	)	
Defendant.	)	
____________________	)	

Complaint

COMES NOW, the plaintiff, Elizabeth Louise, and complaining of the defendant alleges the following:

1.

The Plaintiff is a citizen and resident of Placid County, State of Edwards.

2.

The Defendant is, upon information and belief, a citizen and resident of Springfield County, Edwards.

3.

On or about April 6, 2015, at approximately 12:45 a.m., the Plaintiff, Elizabeth Louise, was operating a 2004 Buick LeSabre automobile, owned by the Plaintiff and Plaintiff's husband, Von Louise, in an easterly direction on Home Street, within the City Limits of the Town of Harrisburg, County of Placid, State of Edwards.

4.

At the time and location averred in paragraph number three, the Defendant was operating a 2001 Honda Civic automobile in an easterly direction on the same street as the plaintiff.

5.

It is further alleged upon information and belief that at all times relevant hereto, the Defendant owned the 2001 Honda Civic automobile being driven by the Defendant.

6.

At the time and place stated above, the Plaintiff, Elizabeth Louise, had slowed and stopped her 2004 Buick LeSabre automobile in respect and in obedience to a traffic light emitting a signal compelling her to stop.

7.

At the time and place stated above, the automobile operated by the Defendant did, without justification, and without warning, drive into and collide with the rear of the vehicle operated by the Plaintiff, while the Plaintiff's automobile was at a complete stop in obedience and in conformity with the traffic signal.

8.

The Defendant was negligent in that he:

a. Failed to keep reasonable and proper control of his vehicle;
b. Failed to keep a proper lookout in his direction of travel and to operate his automobile in a safe manner; and
c. Drove his vehicle carelessly and in willful and wanton disregard of the rights and safety of others including the Plaintiff, Elizabeth Louise.

9.

That as a proximate cause of the Defendant's negligence, the Plaintiff, Elizabeth Louise, suffered severe and permanent injuries in excess of $10,000.00

WHEREFORE, the Plaintiff prays that the Court as follows:

1. That the Plaintiff, Elizabeth Louise, have and recover a judgment against the Defendant in an amount in excess of $10,000.00 for personal injuries.
2. That the Plaintiff have and recover of the Defendant a sum to be determined at trial, but in any event, no less than $10,000.00 for damage to personal property.
3. That prejudgment interest be awarded as provided by law.
4. That the costs of this action be taxed against the Defendant.
5. That all issues raised be tried before a jury.
6. For such other and further relief as the Court may deem just and proper.

This the ___________ day of October, 2015.

Debra Blum

Attorney for Plaintiff

State Bar No. 00-0000

Key Terms

Answer
Beyond a reasonable doubt
Burden of proof
Caption (style)
Case law
Certiorari
Clear and convincing evidence
Common law
Complaint
Damages
Defendant
Domicile
Forum
General jurisdiction
Guilty
In rem jurisdiction
Jurisdiction
Liability
Limited jurisdiction
Ordinance
Personal jurisdiction
Petition
Plaintiff
Preponderance of the evidence
Statute
Subject matter jurisdiction

Review Questions

1. Compare and contrast the different burdens of proof in civil and criminal cases.
2. What is the relationship of the U.S. Constitution to statutes and case law?
3. What is common law?
4. What is case law?
5. How do statutes compared to ordinances?
6. What is the top court in the U.S. federal court system?
7. What responsibilities does the top court in the federal system have?
8. Name the trial courts in the federal court system.
9. What duties do federal trial courts have?
10. How many circuit courts of appeal are there in the United States?
11. Create a diagram showing the organization of your state-level court systems. How are these courts organized? How do appellate courts factor into your diagram?
12. Describe how civil litigation is different from criminal law.
13. What is jurisdiction?
14. Compare and contrast personal and subject matter jurisdiction.
15. What is certiorari?

16 Why are ethical issues so important for paralegals?

17 Create a chart showing the differences between civil and criminal cases.

18 How are the monetary damages paid to a party in a civil case different than the fine that a criminal defendant must pay as part of his or her sentence? How are they alike?

19 Explain why it is important to understand the organization and function of a courthouse.

20 What is the significance of the *Peters v. Alpharetta Spa, LLC* case in regard to a discussion of personal jurisdiction?

21 We have seen that there are several layers of courts on both the state and federal level. When the country was originally created, there were very few courts. What does the number and complexity of the American court system say about our nation? Are we a nation of laws or a nation of lawyers?

Applying What You Have Learned

1 Contact a local law firm and interview a paralegal who works there. Ask some basic questions, such as why this person decided to become a paralegal. Then, proceed to other issues, such as the most common misconceptions about the practice of law and what things a new paralegal should know before going to work for a firm. Ask this person what he or she finds appealing about the legal practice. What are some of the things about law that the paralegal likes least, and why? What are some important skills that a paralegal can bring to a practice specializing in civil actions?

2 Prepare a complete list of all of the courts in your area, including federal, state, traffic, small-claims, and any other courts that you might come into contact with. List the judges who work in those courts, the names of support personnel, and addresses, including websites, if any. Put this information into a file in your portfolio labeled, "Important Contacts."

3 Locate your state's statutes that govern the jurisdiction of the various courts. Pinpoint the jurisdictional requirements of each. Which courts have subject matter to hear cases such as divorce, child custody, felony charges, adoption, name change, cases involving $1,000 or less in controverted amount, and actions involving claims for $20,000 or more?

4 In a double-spaced, three-page paper, describe the organization of federal and state courts in your state. This will require you to research the structure and function of both state and federal courts in your state and to provide an explanation of the function of the courts. You should also discuss how these various courts interact with one another.

5 Review the following factual scenario and then determine, based on the material in this chapter, whether this is a civil case or a criminal case: Juan is driving home one day, and while he is proceeding through a green light, a driver from the intersecting lane of traffic runs the red light and plows into Juan's car. Juan is severely injured. When police and emergency workers arrive on the scene, the other driver appears to be driving under the influence of alcohol. Is this potentially a civil case or a criminal case?

6 Review the following factual scenario and then discuss the legal implications of the material presented. You should work through the factual presentation and attempt to summarize as many different significant legal issues as possible. This is an excellent way to train yourself as a legal professional in civil practice.

> Marie has recently opened a craft store and has ordered a large amount of merchandise from a single supplier, Crafts 'R Us. When she negotiated the order, which is for more than $10,000, the supplier agreed to provide terms. Marie was authorized to receive the material after paying 10 percent of the total price with the balance due within 90 days of the receipt of the material. Marie submitted a check to Crafts 'R Us for $1,000, and the check was cashed. The supplier shipped only half of the total order and is now refusing to ship the rest until Marie pays the balance of $9,000. Marie was counting on being able to sell some of the merchandise as a way of paying for the outstanding balance. Without the merchandise, she will be unable to generate enough income to pay for the rest of the order, and she has very little savings, certainly not enough to pay the balance of the order.

Marie has come to our firm. What legal issues are presented by her situation?

Endnotes

[1] O.C.G.A.§15-1-2

2

The Participants in the Legal System

Chapter Objectives

- Explain the function of judges in civil litigation
- Describe the day-to-day functions of paralegals who specialize in civil practice
- Explain how a person becomes an attorney
- Demonstrate understanding of how various legal professionals work together
- Describe the various courthouse personnel and their duties

I INTRODUCTION

In this chapter, we will examine the various participants involved in civil litigation, including judges, lawyers, clients, and paralegals. It is important to understand not only the role played by each of these participants, but also how they all work together.

II JUDGES

Judge
A person either appointed or elected to serve as the final arbiter for legal questions in a court of law

We have all seen **judges** portrayed on television and in movies. Although fictional judges often break the rules, real-life judges have vast authority and exercise it in vital ways in our legal system. Judges preside in both civil and criminal cases, but we will focus on the role played by judges in civil cases. At the most basic level, judges are responsible for the orderly administration of justice in our legal system. They are given powers to compel parties and witnesses to act in a reasonable way. Judges also ensure that cases do not get bogged down and move steadily toward resolution.

Judges are required by court rules and their own ethical codes to be neutral and objective in all suits. They are not permitted to influence the jury to vote in a particular way or to control the events in a trial in such a way that one side is guaranteed to win. A judge who engages in such behavior would receive a reprimand from the judicial ethics board and would also face the prospect of having a ruling overturned by a higher court.

Judges are bound by a strict code of ethical conduct that prohibits them from engaging in many outside activities. They cannot, for instance, own stock in companies that have cases pending before them. They cannot be members of any group that knowingly discriminates against members of society. The judicial code for judges prohibits actions that may be illegal or any activity that has even the appearance of impropriety. Under that strict code, a judge must avoid any conduct that could cause a potential ethical concern. As a result, most judges are vigilant in their personal and financial relationships in order to uphold the ethical standards of their profession (Fig. 2-1).

FIGURE 2-1

Summary of the Rules Governing Judges

- Judges are required by their ethical codes to avoid even the appearance of impropriety in their actions. As such, they cannot allow friendships or other relationships to influence their conduct either in the courtroom or outside it.
- Judges cannot use their prestige to advance someone's business interests or otherwise endorse some product.
- Judges are not even permitted to testify as character witnesses unless they are subpoenaed.
- Judges are barred from holding memberships in any organization that has discriminatory practices.

A judge is a civil servant. Judges work for and are paid by local, state, or federal governments. In most situations, judges are attorneys. In fact, many work as attorneys for several years before being appointed to a judicial position. However, there are some judicial positions that do not require any legal training and very little higher education. There are magistrate and other low-level judicial positions that are held by individuals who have a bachelor's degree or less. These individuals are responsible for issuing warrants and hearing small claims. Higher-level judicial positions, such as Superior Court judges, are filled by individuals with law degrees.

As you can see in Figure 2-2, judges are usually paid well but not as well as successful attorneys. Given the earnings discrepancy between judges and attorneys, a person would be tempted to ask why an attorney would give up a lucrative practice in order to become a judge. There are several reasons: First, judges often feel a strong commitment to the community and want to contribute. Second, some attorneys grow tired of the grind of a legal practice and seek the relative security and predictable work schedule that most judges enjoy. Finally, the position of judge is still widely respected.

The respect and service to the community often offset the financial losses in taking the position.

Federal district court judges earned on average $201,100 in 2015.[1]

FIGURE 2-2
Judicial Pay

A. BECOMING A JUDGE

In most situations, judges are attorneys before they ever put on a black robe. Most states require that their judicial positions be filled by attorneys licensed to practice in that state. In addition to membership in the state bar, most attorneys who become judges have significant experience practicing law and bring that practical knowledge to bear in their role as judge. States use many different methods to select their judges. The methods outlined here are not exclusive of one another; some states use multiple methods, depending on the judicial position to be filled. For instance, a state may use any or all of the following methods to choose an individual to fill a vacant judicial position:

- Judicial appointment
- Election
- Judicial selection committee

1. JUDICIAL APPOINTMENT

When a new judicial position is created or a current position is vacated, some states allow the state governor to appoint an individual to fill it. The governor may use a committee to assist in judicial selection or may make the selection entirely himself. In either case, the governor may choose a qualified individual to fill the judicial position.

2. ELECTION

Many states elect judges in the same way that they elect other officials. A person who meets the minimum requirements would file to run for the post of judge, and voters would have the opportunity to choose between several contestants. Some states not only elect local judges, but also justices for the court of appeals and State Supreme Court. In many states, these judicial elections are as partisan — and sometimes as bitterly contested — as any political election.

3. JUDICIAL SELECTION COMMITTEE

Another method used by some states to choose a new judge is by a judicial selection committee. This committee, working directly for either the governor or the State Supreme Court, recommends candidates to fill specific judicial openings.

LEGAL LEGWORK ■ JUDGE SELECTION

Does your state elect or appoint judges? How does the process work? Research your state statutes and determine exactly how judges are selected to serve in various courts. Locate recent cases from your state's highest appellate courts that clearly define the practice of law and that delineate the roles of paralegals and attorneys. Are these rules clear? Do they make clear distinctions between the two roles?

B. THE ROLE OF THE JUDGE

Judges are responsible for the orderly administration of justice. To that end, they control the various phases of a civil lawsuit and can force the parties to abide by the rules of civil procedure.

1. JUDGES AS REFEREES

One of the primary duties of a judge is to essentially act as referee between the litigating parties. A judge can enforce rulings, control the behavior of the parties, and even dismiss claims, all to maintain the dignity of the proceedings. A judge's determination about issues in the case remains in effect until the case is finished. A party is usually not permitted to appeal a judge's ruling in the middle of the proceedings, only when the case has been resolved. We will discuss appellate issues in general, and the exceptions to this rule in particular, in Chapter 12.

2. JUDICIAL RULINGS

A judge not only controls the proceedings, but also makes rulings on the law, motions, and evidence during the lawsuit. A judge interprets the law, and her decision on legal points remains in effect until a higher court changes that decision. In addition to ruling on points of law, the judge is also responsible for ruling on motions and evidence.

a. Motions

Motion
A request by a party to a judge

A **motion** is a request by a party for a court to take some action (Fig. 2-3). Motions come in a variety of forms. When a judge grants a motion, he agrees to the request. When a judge denies a motion, he disagrees with the request. We devote all of Chapter 8 to a discussion of motions.

FIGURE 2-3

Motions

(1) An application to the court for an order shall be by motion, which, unless made during a hearing or trial, shall be made in writing, shall state with particularity the grounds therefor, and shall set forth the relief or order sought. The requirement of writing is fulfilled if the motion is stated in a written notice of the hearing of the motion.[2]

b. Evidence

A judge not only rules on motions, but also on evidentiary matters. We will discuss evidence in greater detail in Chapter 6. If a judge rules that evidence is admissible, it means that the jury will be allowed to see and hear it. A ruling of inadmissibility means that the jury will not be allowed to consider it. Judges must determine if evidence is relevant to the proceedings and if the evidence will cause prejudice to one side.

3. JUDGES AS FACT FINDERS

There are times when the judge has additional duties. For instance, when the parties request a bench trial, the judge considers the legal issues and acts as the jury. In a bench trial, there is no jury present and the judge must act as fact finder. In such a situation, the judge will enter a verdict at the conclusion of the evidence that serves the same function that a jury's verdict would. The verdict is the fact finder's determination about which side has presented the more believable version of the case.

III ATTORNEYS

Attorneys are essential to the American legal system. They are responsible for representing clients and safeguarding their interests. Attorneys not only act as advocates, but also as counselors, delegates, and guardians. The process of becoming an attorney is demanding, and the profession offers immense challenges and rewards. We will begin our discussion of the important role that attorneys play by first addressing the question of how a person becomes an attorney.

A. BECOMING AN ATTORNEY

Prior to the 20th century, becoming an attorney was a relatively straightforward proposition. A person, almost always a man, would work as an apprentice for an established attorney. After working with the attorney for several years, the apprentice would then qualify for admission into the state bar. In some cases, the members of the bar would question the applicant. In other situations, the fact that a senior attorney vouched for the applicant would be enough to admit the person into the profession. Once admitted, the new attorney would remain a member of the bar for the rest of his life, unless stripped of his license for committing an offense. Stripping a lawyer of his or her license is still referred as **disbarment**.

Disbarment
Temporary suspension or permanent revocation of an individual's license to practice law

In the early 20th century, many state bars began changing their admittance policies. Law schools, which have existed in the United States for over two centuries, solidified their hold on the profession by requiring any applicant for the state bar to have graduated from an approved school. In addition to graduation from an approved law school, an applicant must also have earned a bachelor's degree, had his background investigated, and have successfully passed a written examination.

Tech Topic
INFORMATION ABOUT ATTORNEYS

In previous years, one of the few ways to locate information about attorneys was through the Martindate-Hubbell legal directory. This multivolume publication included short biographies of all attorneys who had contributed, listed their office information, and provided details about their specializations. Although Martindale-Hubbell still exists, there are many more sources for learning information about attorneys, including:

Attorney locate	**www.attorneylocate.com**
Attorney pages	**www.attorneypages.com**
Lawyers.com	**www.lawyers.com**
Martindale-Hubbell	**www.martindale.com**

In addition to these sites, many state bars now also list members on their main Web pages. These listings include some biographical information as well as the areas of practice for the attorneys. This information is important not only for individuals who are seeking legal advice, but also for those who are looking for potential employers.

Sidebar

Most law schools have the following minimum requirements:

- *Applicant must have a bachelor's degree.*
- *Applicant must have achieved a specific minimum score on the LSAT (Law School Admission Test).*
- *Applicant must have a minimum GPA in his undergraduate courses.*
- *In some cases, applicant must submit a writing sample and be recommended by a selection committee.*

Bar examination
A test administered to graduates from approved law schools that determines the applicant's knowledge of the law and suitability to practice in the state

1. LAW SCHOOL EDUCATION

These days, all attorneys must graduate from a law school before they will be admitted into the state bar. When a person graduates from law school, she receives a *juris doctor* degree. This degree, somewhere between a bachelor's degree and a PhD, entitles a person to sit for the state bar examination and to practice law. Although there are night law schools around the country, and at least one online program, most law schools follow a format that has remained virtually unchanged for centuries. Law school lasts for three years, on a full-time basis, and is extremely rigorous. Even when the student graduates, the work isn't over. Simply graduating is no longer enough to qualify a person for the practice of law. Now, a graduate must also take and receive a passing score on the state bar examination.

2. THE BAR EXAMINATION

After the hard work that it takes to enter and complete law school, one might think that a **bar examination** would be redundant. However, all states require graduates to take such an examination before they will be admitted into the profession. The bar examination consists of multiple choice and essay questions and can last as long as three days. Studying for and taking the bar examination can be an enormously stressful event. After all, if the applicant fails the bar exam, she cannot practice law, although she is free to retake the exam in the future. Some very prominent attorneys did not pass the bar examination on their first attempt, yet went on to have very successful careers after passing it on the second or even third attempt.

3. JOINING THE STATE BAR

Once the law student has taken and passed the examination, he is admitted into the **state bar**. This is a joyous day for individuals who have literally spent years and tens of thousands of dollars to achieve the goal of becoming an attorney. New members are sworn in and receive a printed license to practice law. From that point on, the person is an attorney, qualified to give legal advice, represent clients in trials, and collect fees for services provided.

State bar
The organization that licenses and oversees the practice of law and the conduct of attorneys in the state. An attorney must be a member of the state bar before she will be allowed to practice in that state.

4. SPECIALIZATION

In an age where every profession seems to have specialized, it might seem odd to realize that attorneys do not graduate with specialties in particular areas of law. A new member of the bar is free to practice any type of law that appeals to him. Unlike medical doctors, they do not receive any specialized education in civil or criminal law. Instead, they learn their trade as they go. However, once they are licensed, all attorneys have the obligation of continuing their education by attending mandatory continuing legal education courses, which cover topics as varied as ethics, litigation, trial practice, law office management, and the proper handling and disposition of client funds.

Many state bars also offer attorneys the chance to receive certification as specialists in certain areas of the law. States such as Ohio and Georgia, for example, offer specialist certificates to attorneys in the areas of personal injury or medical malpractice. An attorney receives such recognition by successfully completing courses in these areas and by handling a minimum number of these types of cases. Once certified, an attorney is permitted to add this information to business cards and advertisements.

Even though law school students do not specialize in particular areas of law as they proceed through law school, most graduates have a firm idea of the area of law that appeals to them most. For some, it will be probate or tax law. For others, trial work will be a strong pull. Others may be drawn to education or writing. A law degree opens up many opportunities in both private and government work. Many new attorneys go to work for private law firms and specialize in civil cases.

A civil attorney is an attorney who routinely represents one side or another in a lawsuit. There are an amazing variety of civil suits, from personal injury cases to divorce actions, and an attorney could easily spend her entire career handling just one type of case. Personal injury cases, such as suits arising from car wrecks, are some of the most common types of civil cases in the Untied States and offer plenty of business for law firms. Most attorneys involved in personal injury cases specialize as plaintiffs' or as defendants' attorneys.

a. Plaintiffs' Attorneys

Attorneys who routinely represent individuals who have been injured in personal injury cases are usually referred to as *plaintiffs' attorneys*, because *plaintiff* is the name for the party who initiates a suit. As we will see in the next chapter, classification as a plaintiffs' attorney brings special concerns. These attorneys are compensated in specific ways and have particular concerns about how they will prove their cases against defendants.

b. Defendants' Attorneys

On the other side of a civil suit are the defendants' attorneys. These lawyers routinely represent people who have been named in civil actions. They are compensated differently than plaintiffs' attorneys, and their focus in a civil case is also different. Because they represent people who have been sued, they work hard to prove that the plaintiff has failed to prove all allegations against their clients.

c. The Day-to-Day Practice of Law

The day-to-day practice of law can bring many challenges and also many rewards. Although an attorney's work can be very stressful, it does offer financial rewards. Not all attorneys are rich, but most make comfortable salaries. Some earn millions of dollars each year and represent high-profile clients in publicized cases. However, the vast majority of attorneys report to work just like any other professional. Their daily activities might include meeting with new clients, appearing in court, drafting pleadings, writing letters, and conducting depositions. We will examine the day-to-day role of attorneys in civil cases throughout this book.

IV COMPENSATING LEGAL PROFESSIONALS

We have already stated that the practice of law is a business, and as such, an attorney expects to be paid by her clients. This is true whether she represents plaintiffs or defendants. There are, however, some important differences in the way that attorneys who primarily represent plaintiffs are compensated compared to the common method for compensating attorneys who routinely represent defendants. The two primary methods are:

- contingency fees and
- hourly rates.

A. CONTINGENCY FEES

Although attorneys can represent plaintiffs or defendants in different cases, most attorneys specialize in one type or the other. An attorney who regularly represents individuals injured in automobile collisions (the most common type of litigation) is commonly referred to as a *plaintiffs' attorney*. These lawyers enter into an agreement with their clients called a **contingency fee** arrangement.

Contingency fee
The attorney's fee calculated as a percentage of the final award in a civil case

In the most common type of contingency fee agreement, the client signs a contract agreeing to pay the attorney one-third of the total recovery from the case (Fig. 2-4). If the client eventually receives $10,000, for example, then the attorney who represents him will receive $3,333. A contingency fee arrangement is often the only way that some individuals can afford legal representation. Of course, there is an element of risk in the arrangement. One-third of the total recovery sounds like excellent compensation, as long as the final settlement amount is large. But one-third of nothing is nothing. If the client loses the case, the attorney will receive nothing.

FIGURE 2-4

Contingency Fee Agreement

THIS AGREEMENT, made this 7th day of April, 2015, between the foregoing named person(s) being herein called "Client," and Allison Attorney, herein called "Attorney(s)." It is understood that litigation can be expensive, and that the Attorneys are prohibited by law from becoming liable for its costs, expenses, disbursements, and deposits. Attorneys may advance them, but they cannot become ultimately liable for them. The Client and the Attorney(s) have agreed as follows:

1. The Client this day retains, employs, and authorized the Attorney(s):

(a) To prosecute, administratively and judicially, if necessary in his judgment, each of the Client's following claims; and

(b) To prosecute or defend any and all appeals that may be taken in connection with the Client's claims; and

(c) To receive and collect any final recovery that may be realized on the Client's claims and to satisfy the same upon the records of the appropriate agency or court. The words "final recovery" when used anywhere in this Agreement means the total gross amount of any and all monies, property, and compensation of any and every kind whatsoever realized or received by any Client for any claim, whether realized as the result of settlement or litigation or otherwise, and shall include, but not be limited to, any and all monies, funds, awards, verdicts, judgments, determinations, damages, principal, interest of every kind and nature, penalties, allowances, costs, and any and all compensation of every kind, nature, and description; and

(d) To deduct and retain their Attorney(s)' fees out of the proceeds of the final recovery, and to remit the balance, less their costs, expenses, disbursements, and deposits, to the Client.

2. The Client agrees to pay the Attorney(s), and the Attorney(s) agree to accept for all of the legal services rendered in accordance with this Agreement, the following fee:

(a) A contingent fee, paid within thirty (30) days of a final recovery or any portion thereof, computed as follows: thirty three percent (33%) of any final recovery obtained if the claim is settled without suit.

IN WITNESS WHEREOF, the parties have executed this Agreement the day and year first above written.

____________________ ____________________

CLIENT ATTORNEY(S)

Sworn to and subscribed before me

this _____day of ___, 201___

____

Notary Public

In most situations, the contingency fee arrangement does not apply to routine costs, such as filing or copying fees, but will apply to the attorney's time and all costs incurred by the attorney's support staff. There are also certain types of cases where contingency is either inappropriate or not permitted by state bar rules. In California, as in many other states, an attorney cannot enter into a contingency fee arrangement in a family law case, such as divorce or child custody. The contingency fee agreement can cause the attorney a great deal of stress, especially if the attorney is risk-averse. On the other hand, some attorneys thrive on the prospect of a one-third recovery. For those who find the prospect daunting, there is the flip side of the coin: hourly billing.

B. HOURLY RATES

The attorneys who represent defendants in a civil case generally charge by the hour. Contingency fees are rare for defendants' attorneys for the simple reason that most civil cases settle, and the settlement amount comes from the defendant's personal assets or the defendant's insurance policy. As a result, basing the defendant's fee on the final amount would not be a fair reflection of the attorney's work. Instead, the attorney may charge a flat fee or an hourly rate. Some attorneys charge extremely high hourly rates, such as $500 per hour. This does not mean that the attorney actually pockets $1,000 for two hours' work. The attorney's fee pays a large portion of the firm's expenses, from the electric bill to the employee payroll. However, $500 per hour is still an excellent pay rate.

If we again return to the example of automobile collision (commonly called *personal injury*) cases, there is another reason for the defendant's attorney to bill by the hour. The defendant-driver is required to have an insurance policy covering collisions, and this policy provides for attorney expenses related to litigation following an accident. The attorney will bill the defendant's insurance company instead of the defendant, and insurance companies insist on accurate and itemized billing.

Sidebar

Attorneys who work with insurance companies to represent policyholders are commonly referred to as "insurance defense" attorneys.

In addition to addressing the topic of how attorneys are compensated, it is just as important to note that paralegals also bill for their time. Whether the ultimate fee comes from a contingency fee agreement, flat fee, or hourly rate, paralegals must pay particular attention to itemized billing. Paralegals should track their time spent on every activity related to a case. These itemized statements will help support the firm's claim for services to a client who is reluctant to pay and may also become an issue in litigation should the court find that the losing party must pay the winner's attorney's fees. Courts allow the imposition of fees to cover the activities of both attorneys and paralegals.

V ORGANIZATION OF THE LAW OFFICE

We will assume for purposes of the discussion that the firm we describe in this section exclusively handles civil litigation matters. There are many firms that limit themselves to civil matters, ranging from divorce to contract disputes. However, it is also true that many law firms are generalists, taking on additional matters, including criminal matters, probate, and real estate issues. We will ignore the specialized issues raised by these other matters and concentrate exclusively on civil cases. Civil litigation is broad enough to encompass a huge variety of lawsuits and will also serve as a method to introduce various members of a typical law office and the actions they carry out on a daily basis.

In general, it should come as no surprise that an average law firm consists of lawyers and other support staff. There is only so much that a single attorney can do on a daily basis, and having support staff is essential if a lawyer wishes to expand his practice to a size where it will generate substantial income. Within this general parameter of attorneys and support staff there are numerous subcategories of specialized professions, including associate attorneys, legal secretaries, paralegals, clerks, private investigators, legal nurse consultants, and others.

A. PARTNERS

Because the practice of law is both a noble profession and a business, the internal organization of a law office reflects both the hierarchy imposed on the legal field and the practical considerations of running a business for profit. The traditional organization model for a law office is a **partnership**. The general definition of a partnership is a business run for the benefit of two or more individuals. A partnership brings several distinct advantages to a business that outweigh the advantages of a sole proprietorship. Business **partners** can pool their resources and share profits and losses. In its simplest form, a law partnership consists of two or more attorneys who share profits and losses.

Partnership
A business model wherein two or more individuals pool assets, run a business for profit, and share in the profits and losses of the business

Partner
A person or corporation who is a co-owner of a business and shares in profits and losses

B. ASSOCIATE ATTORNEYS

An **associate attorney** is an employee of the firm, not a partner. As a result, the associate attorney has no say in the business dealings of the firm, has no authority to negotiate on behalf of the firm, and does not share in the firm's profits. On the other hand, an associate attorney is also not obligated to pay any of the firm's debts. Associate attorneys are paid a salary, although many firms have provisions that provide for a base salary plus a percentage of profits from new clients whom the associate brings to the firm. The associate attorney is usually someone who has recently graduated from law school and learns her trade on the job. An associate's salary is not in the same realm as that of a partner. In a successful firm, the associate's salary may be a fraction of the partner's income. Associates also work long hours and are expected to bill a minimum number of hours each year or to bring in a minimum number of new clients each quarter.

Associate attorney
An attorney who is an employee of an attorney partnership

One might wonder why an attorney would accept a position as an associate, given the workload and the fact that the associate does not share in the firm's profits. The answer is simple: Most associates hope to become a partner. A successful associate will, one day, be invited to join the firm as a partner and then enjoy the fruits of all of his labors on behalf of the firm. Of course, an associate might just as easily be fired and replaced by another associate. This element of uncertainty contributes to a general sense of stress for associates.

C. ATTORNEY ETHICS

1. ETHICAL CODES

Each state bar maintains a strict ethical code for attorneys licensed in the state. These ethical codes are often closely modeled on the American Bar Association's (ABA) Model Rules of Professional Conduct. Although the ABA promulgates rules and makes many suggestions about ethical practices, the enforcement of ethical rules falls to the individual state's bar association or state courts. The American Bar Association does not have the power or the responsibility of policing individual attorneys. Instead, the ABA is a national organization that lobbies for attorney rights, promotes greater respect for the law, and has a role in accrediting legal educational programs.

Attorneys' ethical rules are usually found in state statutes and the bylaws for the individual state bar associations. The ethics rules govern all aspects of an attorney's professional life, from admittance to the bar to actions that will result in an attorney being suspended or disbarred. Although state bars maintain records about admitted members, most bars do not actually sanction attorneys. They create rules and investigate claims, but the authority to sanction attorneys normally falls to the state's highest court (usually called the *State Supreme Court*). When an attorney violates an ethical rule, there are several possible sanctions that can be imposed against him. The sanctions run from the lowest form (private reprimand) to the ultimate bar sanction (disbarment) and include:

- private reprimand;
- public reprimand;
- temporary suspension of license;
- disbarment; and
- criminal prosecution.

a. Private Reprimand

Private reprimand
A private letter to an attorney advising of possible ethics violations

Attorneys who commit minor ethical violations are subject to a **private reprimand**. This sanction, the lowest form of punishment for an ethics violation, is usually imposed when an attorney has neglected some aspect of a case, but not to the extent of seriously injuring a client's legal rights. A private reprimand often comes in the form of a letter from the state bar to the offending attorney discussing the violation and strongly urging the attorney to refrain from such activity in the future. Private reprimands are not published, and the only people with knowledge of the reprimand are the offending attorney and the investigating arm of the state bar.

b. Public Reprimand

Public reprimand
A published notice concerning an attorney's ethical violation

A **public reprimand** is a more serious ethical sanction than a private reprimand, and details of the attorney's misdeeds are usually published in the state's appellate reporter. Public reprimands are considered to be a midpoint between a private reprimand and the much more serious sanction of temporary suspension. They are imposed after an attorney has received a private reprimand and continues to engage in questionable conduct.

c. Temporary Suspension of License

Temporary suspension
A sanction that prevents an attorney from practicing law for a specified period, usually because of a serious ethics violation

An attorney who receives a temporary suspension is barred from the practice of law for a specified period. This period could be as short as a few days to as long as several years, depending on the seriousness of the offense. A temporary suspension is authorized where the attorney has committed a serious breach in handling a case for a client, has neglected to pursue a legal claim, or has not been diligent in handling client affairs.

d. Disbarment

An attorney who has committed a serious ethical violation or been convicted of a major crime can be disbarred. Disbarment strips the attorney of her license to practice law. An attorney who is disbarred in one jurisdiction is usually disbarred in all other jurisdictions as well. When an attorney is disbarred, she cannot practice law in any form; it is essentially a professional death sentence. A disbarred attorney can sometimes petition to have her license reinstated, but many disbarments are permanent. An attorney who has been convicted of a felony, stolen client funds, or abandoned a client in the midst of a legal action is eligible for disbarment.

e. Criminal prosecution

An ethical violation can also rise to the level of criminal activity. When an attorney embezzles client funds, for example, it is both an ethical violation and a crime. In such a situation, the offending attorney faces state bar sanctions as well as a fine and prison sentence if convicted of the crime.

2. COMMON ETHICAL VIOLATIONS

Although there are many different types of ethical violations, attorneys who commit ethical violations can be classified into one of three very broad categories:

1. The attorney has financial trouble.
2. The attorney has a drug or alcohol problem.
3. The attorney is suffering from a personal or mental health problem.

In such a situation, an attorney might easily be tempted to commit one of the most common forms of ethical violation: commingling funds.

a. Commingling Funds

Commingle
Combining funds from different sources into one, such as using a client's money as personal funds

When an attorney **commingles** funds, he takes money from a client's trust account and uses it as personal funds. An attorney who transfers proceeds from a client's settlement or trust account into the attorney's personal account, even with the intention of paying the money back, has committed the offense of commingling funds and is liable for disbarment and criminal prosecution. Commingling is a form of embezzlement and is one of the most serious ethical violations. The end result of commingling is loss of the attorney's license to practice law and criminal prosecution for embezzlement.

b. Lack of Diligence

Some attorneys are sanctioned for their failure to follow through on important client matters. An attorney who agrees to represent a client has the duty of diligence toward her clients. The requirement of diligence means that she must follow through on the client's problems and take all legal actions to bring the case to a successful resolution. An attorney is required by state ethics rules to zealously represent the interests of the client, and when the attorney fails to do so, she can be cited by the bar for lack of diligence.

VI PARALEGALS

Paralegal
A legal professional who handles many aspects of legal practice but is not authorized to give legal advice; also know as a *legal assistant*

Paralegals play an absolutely vital role in the American legal system. This entire book is devoted to setting out the day-to-day activities of paralegals in civil practice, so we will only touch on the fundamentals here. Paralegals may be present at the very first interview with a new client and may take notes on the client's potential legal problems. The paralegal may also work with that new client to ferret out additional information and documents to assist with those claims. In addition to client intake, paralegals play a central role in drafting motions, issuing subpoenas, reviewing correspondence, conducting legal research, filing documents at the courthouse, arranging depositions, preparing settlement brochures, and billing clients, to name just a few tasks. We will discuss all of these topics and many others throughout this text. Although their status may not be as clearly defined as that of attorneys, even that shortcoming is gradually being rectified. Many states have begun certifying individuals as paralegals or legal assistants, and this certification process is helping to further define a profession without which the legal system would come to a crashing halt. Paralegals act as assistants to attorneys at every level of the legal system, from one-person local firms to huge multinational corporations. What is even more surprising than the broad diversity of the roles played by paralegals is that they are actually finally receiving the recognition that they deserve. This certainly was not always the case.

A. DEVELOPMENT OF THE PARALEGAL PROFESSION

Attorneys have always had assistants. Whether referring to them as clerks, legal secretaries, or some other name, attorneys have always needed individuals to help them in their practice. An attorney with no support staff can actually accomplish very little. However, attorneys have always jealously guarded their roles as legal professionals and have been traditionally unwilling to recognize the validity of any other class of legal workers as fellow professionals. That mind-set has been very slow to change.

In the mid-1970s, the group that had always worked as legal assistants, and sometimes as the attorneys' right arms, finally began to organize themselves. Local paralegal associations gave rise to national movements and the formation of groups such as the National Association of Legal Assistants and the National Federation of Paralegal Associations. These groups promoted professional standards and better pay for what had always been a high-stress, intensively trained profession. See Figure 2-5 for paralegal employment statistics.

2014 median pay	$48,350 per year $23.24 per hour
Typical entry-level education	Associate's degree
Work experience in a related occupation	None
On-the-job training	None
Number of jobs, 2014	279,500
Job outlook, 2014–24	8% (as fast as average)
Employment change, 2014–24	21,200

FIGURE 2-5

Bureau of Labor Statistics: Paralegals

There has been a split about what to call the legal professionals who help attorneys almost from the time that the first assistant was hired. Is the person who works hand in glove with the attorney, helping to draft pleadings, dealing with clients, and performing an essential service, a "paralegal" or a "legal assistant"? Actually, there is no clear answer. Some groups are attracted to the term *legal asistant* because they feel the name is a more accurate description of what this profession actually does. Others cling to the term *paralegal* because of its historical antecedents. Some states, such as California, have actually quantified the difference between a paralegal and a legal assistant, but most have not. Throughout this text, we will refer to the profession as *paralegals*, for the sake of clarity and for the simple reason that the term has existed longer but not ignoring the strong argument that can be used to label these professionals as *legal assistants*.

B. DAILY ACTIVITIES OF PARALEGALS

It is not an overstatement to say that paralegals are involved in every level of legal practice. They are the bedrock of the profession, and their day-to-day activities make the practice of law possible. Depending on the type of firm for which they work, they might interview witnesses, draft legal documents, or meet with clients. Paralegals may also work as trial specialists, helping an attorney to try a case. Their daily activities can present constant challenges. They can find themselves interviewing clients, obtaining police reports, drafting motions, and preparing discovery materials, while also fielding telephone calls and making sure that files are properly documented. In fact, paralegal duties are so extensive that we will discuss them at length in every chapter of this text.

Paralegals not only play an important role at private firms, but also in government agencies. Prosecution offices across the country now use paralegals to draft indictments, work with witnesses, and track criminal convictions. Government agencies have begun to see the advantages of having someone who is trained in the law to assist attorneys with cases.

SEARCH SUGGESTION • CITATIONS

Whenever you conduct any type of legal research, it is absolutely essential to learn the proper method to cite the cases and statutes that you locate. Any good book on legal research will tell you how to do this, but two of the most influential works on legal citation are *The Bluebook* and the *ALWD Citation Manual.* Both works provide substantial information on the correct ways to cite cases and statutes on both the state and federal level.

A citation is a shorthand method to tell others where to locate the case or statute to which you are referring. In a basic example, suppose that you wish to direct another person to the *Smith v. Jones* case. Because there may be more than one *Smith v. Jones* case, you must direct your reader to the correct one. Legal citation is the way to do that. For instance, your citation to the particular *Smith* case could look like this:

Smith v. Jones, 123 Pl. App. 456 (2005).

This citation tells the reader that the *Smith* case can be found in volume 123 of the Placid State Court of Appeals Reporter, page 456. Of course, there is no state of Placid. Instead, a citation from your state would insert the appropriate abbreviation for your state's appellate courts.

C. LICENSING AND CERTIFYING PARALEGALS

In recent years, many states have either passed or considered passing legislation that regulates the paralegal profession in the same way that other professionals are licensed. In the states that have passed these bills, paralegal licensing boards have been created. These boards are responsible for licensing paralegals, creating minimum standards for admission, and setting up educational requirements for new paralegals. Eventually, all states will regulate paralegals in the same way that nurses, dentists, and lawyers are currently monitored.

Paralegals and legal assistants have existed for decades, but it was only in the 1970s that they formally organized themselves under the title of paralegals. National paralegal organizations trace their origins to this period. Of the many national paralegal organizations, two stand out: the National Federation of Paralegal Associations (NFPA) and the National Association of Legal Assistants (NALA). Each group has created its own model rules of ethical conduct for paralegals. The NFPA has even maintained an ethics board since 1995, which posts ethical opinions on its website so that other paralegals can obtain guidance on specific issues.

National paralegal associations resemble the ABA in that they have created model ethical rules but cannot actually impose on them on a state level. Many states have codified paralegal ethical codes in the same way that they have codified attorney ethical standards. However, there are some important differences between the professional standing of paralegals and that of attorneys. One of these important differences revolves around the issue of certification versus licensure.

Licensure is the process of requiring governmental approval of an individual before he is allowed to practice a profession. Doctors, lawyers, and many other professionals are required to possess a license issued by the state before they are allowed to practice there. As we have already seen, the process for an attorney to become licensed involves graduation from a law school, a background investigation, and successful completion of the state bar examination. It might seem odd, then, to consider that a process so much a part of an attorney's professional life is virtually nonexistent when it comes to paralegals. As of this writing, no state requires licensure of a paralegal before that person can work with an attorney. In fact, the vast majority of states have no regulatory control over paralegals at all. In these states, the paralegal works under the direct supervision of the attorney, who still bears the full brunt of all legal responsibility for that work. However, that situation has begun to change. For instance, there are several states that have enacted or have pending legislation that creates a voluntary certification program for paralegals.

Licensure
The requirement of governmental approval before a person can practice a specific profession

The biggest difference between **certification** and licensure, at least as these issues are defined for paralegals, concerns the mandatory nature of the proceeding. In states such as North Carolina, Delaware, Texas, and Louisiana, a person may register with a state agency and receive the designation of *certified paralegal.* Usually, this designation comes at the end of a registration process that requires graduation from an approved paralegal program and a minimum number of hours on the job, as well as continuing legal education requirements. Given the fact that certification in these states is voluntary, why would a paralegal even bother to go through the process? Even more startling, why do statistics show that in states where voluntary certification procedures have been set in place, applications have skyrocketed?

Certification
The recognition of the attainment of a degree of academic and practical knowledge by a professional

There are several possible answers. For one, paralegals have been organizing for several decades and are now beginning to exert some pressure on the legal field to receive the recognition that they have long deserved. Certification is one way to address that issue. Paralegals may also wish to receive the personal recognition and satisfaction that state certification brings. Of course, there are also monetary issues to consider. A certified paralegal would be justified in demanding a higher salary than a noncertified paralegal. Finally, some paralegals may see certification as the first step down a long road toward licensure and believe that obtaining certification may give them a head start or even a possible waiver when the licensure process is finally instituted. Regardless of the reasons, there is a slow but steady pressure building across the United States to recognize the critical role played by paralegals in the day-to-day practice of law.

Although several states are actively considering the issue of licensing paralegals, most do not. Paralegals in these states operate in a gray area: They are not attorneys, but they work closely with them. They engage in legal activities on a daily basis, but they have no state license that clearly states their qualifications. Faced with this dilemma, many paralegals opt for certification from one of the national paralegal associations. The NALA offers a certification program that entitles paralegals to use the credential "certified legal assistant" when they successfully complete the intensive testing.

PRACTICE POINTER ▶ WRITING WELL

One of the most common complaints made by attorneys is that their support staff cannot write well. Although it may be true that the American education system has not emphasized written communication skills as much now as they have in the past, it is also true that attorneys expect a high standard of literacy. For an attorney, reading and writing is a daily practice, and the ability to communicate effectively and correctly is an absolutely essential skill. Because of that, anyone contemplating a career in the legal profession must be aware of and use proper grammar and spelling. Some practices that will help you maintain good written communication skills include:

- always using your grammar and spell check feature on your word-processing software;
- always double-checking your writing before submitting it to anyone;
- never using a word unless you can define it; and
- always using a guide for tricky questions.

On the last point, many writers keep a copy of Strunk & White's *The Elements of Style* close at hand. This small book has had a huge impact on American writing since its publication in the early 1900s.

D. Paralegal Ethics

An important component of any licensure or certification scheme is the implementation of continuing education programs that focus on ethics. Even in states without any programs to recognize paralegals, ethics remains an extremely important topic. Ethical concerns point out the interdependence of attorneys and paralegals. Attorneys need paralegals in order to assist them with the practice of law, but the attorney is ultimately responsible for any legal malfeasance. Paralegals in nearly all states have no regulatory body that can revoke their license to practice as a legal professional when they violate ethical rules, but their unethical actions can have dire consequences for the attorneys with whom they work. Not only can an ethical violation result in a legal malpractice action against an attorney, but also a paralegal who engages in such activities as giving legal advice can find herself the subject of a criminal prosecution. **Unauthorized practice of law** (UPL) is considered a misdemeanor offense in states such as California[3] and a felony in states such as Texas.[4]

Unauthorized practice of law
When a person who is not an attorney gives legal advice or counsel to a client

Other than criminal prosecution, paralegals in most states are regulated indirectly. The attorneys with whom they work are closely regulated by their state bar, and any unethical activities carried out by their staff, including paralegals, are imputed to them. In states that have a certification regime, unethical paralegals may have their certifications stripped away in much the same way that an attorney may be disbarred. Unlike attorneys, however, a paralegal who has lost his certification is not prohibited from working, though he may have great difficulty securing employment when attorneys learn why he lost certification.

E. Legal Document Assistants

Some states, such as California, recognize another class of legal professionals: independent paralegals or **legal document assistants**. These individuals are authorized to assist members of the public who choose to represent themselves in litigation or who wish to file documents with the state (Fig. 2-6).

Legal document assistant
A specialized type of paralegal, legally able to provide assistance to clients in preparing forms

Definition:

(1) Any person who is not exempted under Section 6401 and who provides, or assists in providing, or offers to provide, or offers to assist in providing, for compensation, any self-help service to a member of the public who is representing himself or herself in a legal matter, or who holds himself or herself out as someone who offers that service or has that authority. This paragraph does not apply to any individual whose assistance consists merely of secretarial or receptionist services.[5]

FIGURE 2-6

Legal Document Assistant (California)

VII CLIENTS

Although attorneys and paralegals are absolutely essential to the justice system, without clients there would be no need for either. When someone hires an attorney, it is often because that person has been unsuccessful in resolving the problem herself. Most people are reluctant to speak with attorneys and would much prefer to avoid conflict and controversy. However, there are times when hiring an attorney is inevitable. When a client first appears at an attorney's office, she is often confused and anxious. Clients often turn to paralegals not only for information, but also for reassurance. Throughout this text, we will draw a distinction between the unauthorized practice of law, such as giving legal advice, and the very real need to help and reassure clients about their cases. Clients need good legal representation. When a case is resolved, the client will be satisfied with the result and will be able to move on with her life.

VIII COURTHOUSE PERSONNEL

So far, our discussions about the legal field have been tied to the participants. However, there is an entire group of professionals who are indirectly involved in lawsuits, without whom the legal system could not function. These are the agencies and departments responsible for maintaining public records and administering the day-to-day functions of legal professionals. We will group all of these professionals together under the slightly misleading name of *courthouse personnel*. However, you should keep in mind that not all of these people actually work in the courthouse; many work at other locations. It is absolutely essential for anyone considering a career as a legal professional to understand what courthouse personnel actually do.

It is important to understand that there is a great deal of variation from state to state in the names that are used to describe various public offices. There is no standard system in place across the United States to describe the office that houses records of civil and criminal actions, hears probate matters, or keeps records concerning real estate transactions. Because of this variation in names, you must familiarize yourself with your own local system, learning what the various departments are called and what each contains.

A. CLERK OF COURT

Clerk
A government official responsible for maintaining public records

Clerks are responsible for storing and maintaining all records of court proceedings. Clerks' offices are open to the public. Clerks and deputy clerks keep track of every case filed in the courthouse and store documents relating to all cases. Their role is central to the orderly administration of justice, because it is the clerks who keep track of the payment of fines, the assessment of sentences, and the organization of the mountain of paperwork generated by even the most routine cases. Deputy clerks are often found in the courtroom during calendar calls and hearings because they are charged with the duty of keeping a record of the disposition of every case.

The clerk's office maintains records about all civil and criminal cases in the county. Most clerks' offices are computerized, and simply by entering a person's last name, you can find out whether he has been sued, divorced, or convicted of a crime. The clerk's office is a good place to start if you are investigating anyone or trying to locate information about other pending or closed cases.

B. REGISTRAR OF DEEDS

Also called the *registrar's office* or the *land office*, the deed room is where all records of real estate transactions are stored. Here, you can find out how much a person paid for her house and get a complete picture of what real estate this person owns. However, the deed room has a wealth of other information. Uniform Commercial Code (UCC) filings can tell you whether a person has financed her car and for how much. Does a defendant claim that she has no assets and therefore cannot pay a judgment? UCC filings can show you that she recently purchased a boat or a recreational vehicle. Many deed rooms also maintain a record called *vital statistics*, or birth and death records. These records will show the names of a person's children and whether they were born in that county. They will also show whether a person was the beneficiary of a will. Attorneys often check these records — called *asset searches* — before bringing a lawsuit to make sure that they can recover something from the other side. A defendant who has no assets cannot pay a judgment and may not be worth the trouble of suing.

C. PROBATE COURT

The **probate court** is responsible for administering the estates of people who have died in the county. If a person has had his estate probated in that county, you can locate a record of the will, the names of any beneficiaries, and a list of what each received in the probate court. In many states, the probate court also keeps records of marriages.

Probate court
The court empowered to settle estates for those individuals who have died with or without a will

D. TAX OFFICE

The tax office is required to keep extensive records about real estate, and all of this information is open to the public. Many people never think about going to the tax office for information, but it has more raw data than any other office. Of course, the tax office keeps records about whether or not a person has paid her property taxes, but there is also a great deal of other data there. If you want to find a person's address, and her name doesn't appear in the telephone book, it's a simple matter to enter the name in the tax office database and find out where she lives. Tax offices even keep information about the basic floor plan of a house and list how many bedrooms and bathrooms the house has. In some areas, the tax office has a digital photograph of every structure in the county, and you can see these photos simply by clicking on them. The tax office also maintains information about sales, acreage, and assessed value of real estate parcels.

TECHNOLOGY AND THE LAW ♦ IS YOUR STATE READY FOR LIMITED LICENSE LEGAL TECHNICIANS?

As you will see throughout this book, technology has made huge inroads in the practice of law. Along with the technical innovations, the very role of the paralegal is being reviewed. In the past, paralegals were seen as little more than glorified legal secretaries, but that has changed significantly in the last 10 years. Many states now license or certify paralegals, while others have expanded the role that paralegals can play in the day to day practice of law. Legal document assistants are one example, but another is limited license legal technicians (LLLT). The LLLT is seen as a way of expanding legal services in high-demand areas, such as family law. An LLLT must graduate from an ABA-approved paralegal program and must pass a state-based test. The test focuses on one area of law. Because of the widespread need for legal services in family law issues, the states that are considering enacting LLLT programs have focused on that area almost exclusively. Washington State began its LLLT program in 2015. A licensed LLLT can advise clients on basic family law issues and in some cases to appear in court with clients. While some attorneys see this trend as a direct threat to their livelihoods, others acknowledge that there is an ever-growing need for direct and inexpensive legal assistance. Other states are considering legislation that will authorize the designation of limited license legal technicians.

Case Excerpt

When does a paralegal cross the line between assisting a client and actually practicing law without a license? Does preparing a quit claim deed for someone qualify as the practice of law?

SPOELSTRA V. GAHN
2013 Wash. App. LEXIS 1041, 2013 WL 1897159 (Wash. Ct. App. May 6, 2013)

Opinion

Lau, J. — Daniel Gahn appeals the trial court's verdict and order on John and Sharla Spoelstra's claim that he engaged in the unauthorized practice of law. Because Gahn fails to establish reversible error, we affirm.

Facts

In 2004, the Spoelstras filed suit against Gahn in Snohomish County Superior Court. In an amended complaint filed in May 2008, the Spoelstras alleged that Gahn, who is not an attorney, prepared a quit claim deed for a portion of their property worth $700,000 to secure payment of legal fees to an attorney, Royce Ferguson. When the Spoelstras discovered that Ferguson had not required the quit claim deed and asked Gahn to return it, Gahn refused, claiming that he had performed legal services for them in the amount of $40,000. The Spoelstras claimed that Gahn obtained the quit claim deed without the necessary disclosures, thereby engaging in the unauthorized practice of law. The Spoelstras sought an order quieting title to the property as well as damages.

After a four-day trial in which Spoelstra and Gahn appeared pro se, a jury answered "yes" to the following special interrogatory: "Did Mr. Gahn engage in the practice of law in his dealings with Mr. Spoelstra from 2002 until the signing of the Quit Claim Deed, Exhibit 1?" The trial court made the following additional findings:

1. Mr. Gahn advised Mr. Spoelstra that in order for Mr. Gahn to continue working on his legal matters, Mr. Spoelstra would have to secure payment of his fees, in the approximate amount of $40,000.
2. That in order to secure said fees, Mr. Gahn would accept a Quit Claim Deed on a piece of property selected by Mr. Spoelstra and that the property selected should be one involved in the Kaufman litigation.
3. That Mr. Ghan [sic] represented to Mr. Spoelstra that the Quit Claim Deed would serve two purposes: One, it would secure his fees and two, it would allow Mr. Gahn to intervene in the Kaufman litigation as a party in interest and allow him to argue in court. Both Mr. Gahn and Mr. Spoelstra testified to this dual purpose.
4. In fact, Mr. Gahn did intervene and did appear in court as a party in interest in the Kaufman litigation pursuant to the rights conferred on him by the Quit Claim Deed.
5. Mr. Gahn or his wife, drafted the Quit Claim Deed using a form obtained by them at a store, and entered the legal description given to them by Mr. Spoelstra.
6. The fees to be secured for work done on behalf of Mr. Spoelstra from 2002 to 2004 totaled approximately $40,000. However, there has never been a written accounting of the fees incurred that has been produced to Mr. Spoelstra.

7. The value of the property quit claimed, while generally in dispute, clearly exceeded $100,000.
8. Mr. Gahn testified that he would return the property to Mr. Spoelstra upon payment of his fees and that he held the Quit Claim for security purposes.

Based on these findings, the trial court concluded that Gahn "was engaging in the unauthorized practice of law in his dealings with Mr. Spoelstra," ordered Gahn to disgorge his fees, and quieted title to the property in favor of the Spoelstras.

Analysis

We review the trial court's findings of fact and conclusions of law to determine whether the findings are supported by substantial evidence and, if so, whether the findings support the trial court's conclusions. *Sunnyside Valley Irrigation Dist. v. Dickie*, 111 Wn. App. 209, 214, 43 P.3d 1277 (2002), aff'd, 149 Wn.2d 873, 73 P.3d 369 (2003). "Substantial evidence is evidence in sufficient quantum to persuade a fair-minded person of the truth of the declared premise." This court defers to the trier of fact for purposes of resolving conflicting testimony and evaluating the persuasiveness of the evidence and credibility of the witnesses. In determining the sufficiency of the evidence, this court need only consider evidence favorable to the prevailing party. There is a presumption in favor of the trial court's findings, and the party claiming error has the burden of showing that a finding of fact is not supported by substantial evidence. If the standard is satisfied, an appellate court will not substitute its judgment for that of the trial court even though it may have resolved a factual dispute differently.

Gahn challenges findings of fact 1 through 4, 6, and 8, claiming that the trial court mischaracterized his testimony. Gahn claims that he was the only witness who testified about certain matters and then assigns error to the trial court findings that do not directly adopt his theory of the case and explanation of the evidence. He complains that the trial court used words that he did not use in his testimony. Gahn also repeatedly argues that Spoelstra deeded the property to him for "consideration given" and not as security for his fees. Brief of Appellant at 12.

Gahn's challenges to the findings fail. First, Gahn has provided only excerpts of the trial transcript, including his cross-examination of Spoelstra and his own direct testimony. It is the appellant's burden to provide a record sufficient to review the issues raised on appeal. To the extent the findings reflect the trial court's resolution of factual disputes based on other testimony and evidence not included in Gahn's trial record excerpts, we cannot review them.

Also, Gahn's claims are, in essence, a challenge to the trial court's credibility determinations and resolution of conflicting evidence. For example, despite Gahn's repeated claim to the contrary, Spoelstra testified on cross-examination that he agreed to sign the quit claim deed in order to use the property for security. As the trier of fact, the trial court was entitled to resolve such disputes based on its assessment of the credibility of the witnesses, and we do not review such determinations.

And Gahn testified that in February 2004, he "informed Spoelstra that I would no longer perform any work for him until he paid me for the work that I did" and that his total fees for the work he had performed "at that time was roughly in the neighborhood of about $40,000." Verbatim Report of Proceedings (VRP) (Feb. 4, 2011) at 116. Gahn also testified that he "agreed" to Spoelstra's request to "hold" the deed without recording it, and "not to sell" the property, until Spoelstra wanted to "buy it back . . . for the $40,000." VRP (Feb. 4, 2011) at 118. The trial court was not bound by Gahn's use of particular words or his own interpretation of his actions. Under these circumstances, Gahn fails to demonstrate any error in the trial court's findings of fact.

In several of his assignments of error, Gahn argues that the trial court failed to sufficiently describe the basis of liability, consider his asserted defenses, and properly enforce the quit claim deed as written. Each of these arguments constitutes a claim that the trial court's findings do not support its conclusions of law. We disagree.

A layperson may appear and act in court as his own attorney, and a party to a legal document may draft that document without fear of liability for the unauthorized practice of law. *Wash. State Bar Ass'n v. Great W. Union Fed. Sav. & Loan Ass'n*, 91 Wn.2d 48, 56-57, 586 P.2d 870 (1978). However, these "pro se" exceptions are limited and do not apply to a layperson who receives compensation for such legal services. Wash. State Bar, 91 Wn.2d at 56-57. "The receipt of compensation is conclusive evidence that the layperson is not merely acting for himself but has assumed the additional burden of acting for another." Wash. State Bar, 91 Wn.2d at 57.

Nonattorneys who practice law are liable for negligence for the breach of the duties of an attorney practicing law. *Bowers v. Transamerica Title Ins. Co.*, 100 Wn.2d 581, 586-87, 675 P.2d 193 (1983). A lawyer entering a business transaction with a client or acquiring an ownership or security interest adverse to a client has the burden to prove fair and reasonable terms, full disclosure, opportunity to consult outside counsel, and consent.

Here, the jury found that Gahn engaged in the practice of law in his dealings with Spoelstra from 2002 until the time of the preparation of the quit claim deed. The trial court found that Gahn prepared and accepted the quit claim deed for the Spoelstras' property with a value clearly exceeding $100,000 to secure payment of his undocumented claim of $40,000 in fees for past legal work and to continue working on the Spoelstras' legal matters. Given Gahn's failure to prove at trial that he strictly complied with the duties of an attorney acquiring an ownership or security interest adverse to a client, the trial court properly concluded that Gahn's actions constituted the unauthorized practice of law.

Gahn also claims that the trial court committed various procedural errors justifying reversal. In particular, he claims that the trial court (1) failed to give him sufficient notice of its "proposed" order reciting its findings of fact and conclusions of law in violation of court rules, (2) violated his right to a jury trial, and (3) denied his right to a fair trial by refusing to instruct the jury as he requested. However, Gahn has not provided a record sufficient to review these issues. Gahn has not provided transcripts of any hearings at which the trial court considered argument or made rulings on any procedural matter before, during, or after trial. Because we cannot determine what arguments the trial court considered or what objections, if any, Gahn made, we will not review these claims.

We affirm.

Cox and Verellen, JJ., concur.

QUESTIONS ABOUT THE CASE

1. What did the Spoelstras allege against Gahn?
2. What was the trial court's determination of whether or not Gahn was engaged in unauthorized practice of law?
3. What was the basis of Gahn's defense at trial and on appeal?
4. What does the appellate court have to say about reviewing the facts as determined by the trial judge and the trial judge's credibility?
5. How were Gahn's actions any different than a person who is allowed to appear in court to represent himself as pro se?

Chapter Summary

There are many participants in the American legal system. Judges are responsible for administering justice, maintaining order, and making rulings on legal issues that arise in a court action. Judges act as impartial and neutral third parties in trials. They are employed by the government, and although they generally receive salaries that are less than prominent attorneys, a judgeship offers security and a lighter workload as well as prestige in the community. Attorneys are also an important part of the American legal system. These days, a person becomes an attorney by attending law school and successfully completing the state bar examination. Once a person has been admitted to the state bar, she is entitled to practice any type of law. Most attorneys specialize in particular areas of law, such as civil litigation practice.

Paralegals are legal professionals who work closely with attorneys. They carry out many of the daily activities in a legal practice, from drafting pleadings to conducting telephone conference calls and interacting with clients, to name just a few. Several states have recently passed laws to certify or license paralegals, in the same way that nurses and other professions are also regulated. Other important participants in the American legal system can be called *courthouse personnel*, including the clerk's office, which is responsible for maintaining public records of all pending cases; the deed room, which stores records pertaining to real estate transactions; the probate court, which is responsible for administering wills and estates; and the tax office, which keeps extensive records on both personal and real property.

SKILLS YOU NEED IN THE REAL WORLD

Keeping Track of Your Time

Whether you are working for a plaintiff's firm or a defense firm, it is important for you to keep track of your billable hours. As we will see in Chapter 4, plaintiffs' firms are generally only paid when the case settles. Because the amount of payment does not depend on the hours billed, why would it be important to keep track of the hours you spend working on a particular case? The simple answer is that by keeping track of your hours, you can have a better idea of where you are spending a majority of your time and whether or not your activities ultimately benefit the firm. You may find, for example, that most of your time is spent dealing with clients on the telephone. Keeping track of your activities and the amount of time you spend on those activities will give you a better idea of how to streamline your workday and eliminate some of the nonproductive periods. This will help you be a better paralegal and consequently even more indispensable to the firm.

Billable Hours at Defense Firms

When a paralegal works for a defense firm, keeping track of billable hours is often the only way to ensure that the firm is paid for its services. Defense firms are not paid based on the ultimate settlement amount. Instead, most defense firms bill their clients with an hourly charge. In such a situation, the attorneys working at the firm will want to make sure that they bill for every possible activity. Some firms do this by requiring you to keep track of your activities and assigning how much time you spend on those particular activities and for whom the activities were carried out. For instance, you may have spent 30 minutes writing a letter on the *Joe Doe v. Sue Doe* case. Most firms bill their clients on the basis of one-tenth of an hour, which equates to 6 minutes. Therefore, if you spend half an hour working on a letter, your time would appear as 0.5 hours. Defense firms spend a great deal of time and energy making sure that all activities at the firm are billed to the appropriate client.

THE LIFE OF A PARALEGAL

Locating Information

Darlene Burgess has worked as a paralegal since she was 16 years old. She began her legal career by working with her mother, also a paralegal. "The attorney we worked for was blind," she explains, "and he often had me read the law to him." In addition to her reading duties, Darlene slowly worked up from answering the phones to handling increasingly more difficult and detailed activities at the firm.

These days, she works for the tax office, collecting delinquent real property taxes. In addition to working for the tax office, Darlene is also a certified legal assistant. Following the receipt of her bachelor's degree from a local college, she started teaching part-time in a paralegal program. She uses her legal education every day, not only in locating delinquent taxpayers, but also in training future paralegals.

In Darlene's average day, she may visit several different parts of the courthouse. Although there is a wealth of information available in the tax office where she works, she may also visit the clerk's office, the deed room, and other departments. Here is a summary of the information that she can locate about an individual:

- Full legal name
- Whether the person has a criminal record

- Whether the person has ever been sued or brought a suit
- The basic floor plan of the person's home
- Maps of all of the person's real estate holdings
- Whether the person has ever received property through probate
- Information on the person's cars, boats, trailers, or other financed items

This information is helpful to individuals who work for the tax office and to any legal professional who wishes to gather information about witnesses or simply wishes to find out if a potential party to a civil suit has enough property or assets to pay a judgment.

ETHICAL ISSUES FOR THE PARALEGAL

Freelance Paralegals

The role of the paralegal in the United States has been slowly changing. The traditional arrangement, wherein a paralegal works full-time for an attorney, is slowly giving way to independent contractors: freelance paralegals who hire themselves out to attorneys on a case-by-case basis. Freelance paralegals are part of a new movement of paralegals taking greater control of their own destinies.

Although becoming a freelance paralegal has many attractions, there are some downsides. For one thing, there is the issue of unauthorized practice of law. Freelance paralegals, especially those in the more conservative parts of the country, have felt the pressure from attorneys who do not like competition.

In some states, such as California, where paralegals are regulated and distinctions are made between document preparers and legal assistants, the rule about unauthorized practice of law remains the same: When it comes to giving legal advice, you can't.

Legal document assistants are not permitted to practice law. They can help people complete legal forms, but they cannot give legal advice.

Websites

- **Concord Law School**
  www.info.concordlawschool.edu

- **U.S. Department of Labor — overview of process of becoming a judge**
  www.dol.gov/

- **Overview of Paralegal Certification — National Association of Legal Assistants**
  www.nala.org/

- **National Association of Legal Professionals**
  www.nals.org/

Forms and Court Documents

Contract of Representation

STATE OF EDWARDS
COUNTY OF PLACID
EMPLOYMENT CONTRACT

THIS AGREEMENT, made and entered into this the ___________ day of ___________, 2015, by and between ___________, hereinafter referred to as "Client"; and ALLISON ATTORNEY, P.A., hereinafter referred to as "Attorneys";

IN WITNESS OF THE FOLLOWING:

WHEREAS, Client has a claim against ___________
___________ arising out of an incident which occurred on or about the ___________ day of ___________, ___________, and desires to employ the Attorneys on a contingent fee basis;

NOW, THEREFORE, the Attorneys agree to represent, through trial court, as attorney for the Client and the Client agrees to pay the Attorneys thirty-three and one-third (33 1/3%) percent of the amount recovered or which may be recovered in this matter, whether by compromise or settlement at any time before suit is instituted or by compromise, settlement or judgment after suit is instituted, plus expenses incurred in the preparation of the case. Both parties agree that neither party will compromise or settle this action without consent of the other party.

This the ___________ day of ___________, 2015.

____
Attorney
ALLISON ATTORNEY, P.A.

Key Terms

- Associate attorney
- Bar examination
- Certification
- Clerk
- Commingle
- Contingency fee
- Disbarment
- Judge
- Legal document assistants
- Licensure
- Motion
- Paralegal
- Partner
- Partnership
- Private reprimand
- Probate court
- Public reprimand
- State bar
- Temporary suspension
- Unauthorized practice of law

Review Questions

1 What are some of the activities the judges perform in civil cases?
2 What are some of the selection processes used in various states to select individuals to serve as judges?
3 What are some of the ethical guidelines that judges must follow?
4 What is a motion?
5 What are some considerations that judges must take into account when ruling on evidence?
6 How does a person become an attorney?
7 What is disbarment?
8 What is the bar examination?
9 What is the difference between plaintiffs' attorneys and defendants' attorneys?
10 Why is it important for a paralegal to know and understand an attorney's code of ethics?
11 When did paralegals first begin to organize themselves on a national level?
12 What are some of the daily activities of paralegals?
13 Explain the paralegal licensing and certification initiatives that have been passed in several states.
14 What is the function of the clerk of court?
15 What is the function of the deed room?
16 What kind of information can you learn at the tax office?
17 Explain the holding in this chapter's case excerpt as it applies to paralegals.
18 What are some of the arguments for and against state licensure of paralegals?
19 Based on the case provided in this chapter, what are some ways that you could avoid an allegation that you are practicing law without a license?
20 Are the restrictions governing paralegals a way to protect society from individuals who do not understand the legal implications of their actions or a way for attorneys to maintain a monopoly on the practice of law?
21 What are the ethical guidelines for paralegals and attorneys?
22 What is the attorney licensing and disciplinary process for your state?

Applying What You Have Learned

1 Visit your local courthouse and locate the various departments. Prepare a list showing the following:
- The name of the department, such as tax office, deed room, etc.
- The name of the person who heads the department
- The phone number for the department
- A contact person within the department
- A summary of the public records stored there

This list will come in handy later, when you begin your practice, to help you quickly and accurately locate pertinent information.

2 Most firms that bill clients do so in one-tenths of an hour. The basic premise behind billing is that you list, down to tenths of an hour, exactly how much time you spent doing any particular task. Here is an example from a billing statement:

File No.	*Activity*	*Amount*	*Entry*
101-1231	Telephone call	0.1	Confirmed witness for case

Breaking this entry down, we see that the first item is the file number assigned for this particular case and the entity that will be billed for this activity. The activity is a telephone call. The length of time for the telephone call is 0.1 hours. Because an hour is 60 minutes and computers like everything to be in decimals, law firms break an hour down into tenths, with one-tenth equal to 6 minutes. Most firms bill 6 minutes as the absolute minimum that it takes to do anything. When you create an itemized billing, your end product may look something like this:

File No. 101-1231

Activity: Researched legal issues in contributory negligence, especially concerning possible federal claim.

2.7 hours

Activity: Researched medical literature on possibility of recurrent amnesia for client injured in car wreck.

3.4 hours

Activity: Prepared brief to trial court on evidentiary issue of subsequent remedial measures for repairs to stairs completed after the client was injured.

1.4 hours

File No. 101-1231 Total billed: 7.5 hours

Using the above examples, create a few sample billing statements to get some practice calculating time in tenths of an hour.

3 In a three-page paper, research and discuss the development of the paralegal profession from the 1970s to the certification and licensure movements of the early 2000s.

4 Review the case excerpt provided in this chapter and then research the question of unauthorized practice of law. Prepare a checklist showing what actions by paralegals are and are not permissible in your state. For instance, may a paralegal prepare legal pleadings, child custody materials, settlement brochures, and so forth?

5 Consider the following: Carl works as a freelance paralegal in a state that has a statute providing that the unauthorized (or unlicensed) practice of law is a misdemeanor. One day, an individual approaches Carl and asks his advice on how best to proceed on filing for a divorce. Carl informs the man that he is a paralegal, not an attorney, and then proceeds to prepare the complaint for divorce, arranges to have the complaint served on the man's wife, prepares a motion to accompany the complaint, interrogatories to the man's wife, and tells the man about the possible dispositions of his marital property. However, Carl refuses to sign any of the paperwork. Is Carl practicing law without a license?

Endnotes

[1]U.S. Courts.gov, cite visited on October 22, 2015.
[2]O.C.G.A. §9-11-7 (Georgia).
[3]Business and Professions Code, California.
[4]Code of Judicial Conduct, Texas.
[5]CA. Bus & Prof, Section 6400 (c)(1).

Bringing a Legal Action

3

Chapter Objectives

- Explain the importance of determining a cause of action prior to filing a lawsuit
- Describe the process of evaluating a potential civil case
- Explain the legal requirement to an independent factual investigation prior to filing a claim
- Document the significance of Rule 11 of the Rules of Civil Procedure
- Explain cause of action
- Describe the initial client meeting and important documentation that must occur there
- Prepare a basic client questionnaire
- Detail the importance of client authorizations for release of records
- Explain how witnesses should be interviewed about the potential case
- Describe how a paralegal can conduct basic factual investigations

I INTRODUCTION

The steps preliminary to initiating a civil action are some of the most important that a paralegal can learn. There are many requirements that must be satisfied before a civil lawsuit can be brought against a defendant. We will discuss those numerous preliminary steps in this chapter, concentrating not only on the rules of civil procedure, but also on the practical steps of research, investigation, and preparation that must be carried out.

EVALUATING A CIVIL CASE

In any civil practice, both paralegals and attorneys must develop the skills to evaluate a case. Evaluation takes into account the merits of the case and the applicable law and statutes, as well as an in-depth analysis of the witnesses and the client. Like any skill, the ability to accurately analyze the basic facts leading to a civil action takes time to develop. Why should anyone take this time? The simple answer is that the better paralegals are at evaluating cases, the better they are at their jobs. **Case evaluation** skills also make paralegals even more indispensable to their firms, help them understand the legal elements of claims, and build important skills that can also apply in other legal settings.

Case evaluation
The process of investigating the facts, issues, and legal implications of a proposed lawsuit before it is ever filed

A. WHAT IS A CASE EVALUATION?

Evaluating the facts of a case is necessary because the firm must decide whether to represent a client in a particular action based on the merits of the case. In many instances, such an evaluation is also a legal requirement. We will discuss these reasons throughout this chapter, but first we must address a more fundamental question: What is a case evaluation? Case evaluations take into account the following issues:

- The nature of the claim
- The facts
- The defendant's liability
- The impact of the law
- The likelihood of recovery
- The extent of the plaintiff's injuries

1. THE NATURE OF THE CLAIM

The nature of the claim is perhaps the single most important item in a case evaluation. In this section, we will assume that you are building your case evaluation skills by working for a firm that represents plaintiffs. The most typical way for a case to begin is when a person schedules an appointment with the firm to review a specific situation.

Consider the following example: Martha is a single mother. On a rainy evening last month, around eight o'clock, Martha and her daughter, Rachel, were heading home. Martha was driving a route that she had traveled many times before. She had just picked up Rachel from a late basketball practice, and the two were talking as Martha came into a wide arc in the road that leads to their home. As Martha came to the midpoint of the curve, she noticed a large tractor-trailer rig in the oncoming lane. According to Martha, the truck had come into her lane as it negotiated the curve. Martha was unable to avoid a collision. The back end of the tractor-trailer sideswiped Martha's car, and the impact caused her car to go into a spin. Fortunately, the front air bags deployed, cushioning the impact as Martha's car ran off the road and struck a tree. Martha suffered several broken ribs, a broken wrist, and neck trauma. Her daughter suffered numerous scrapes and bruises but no major injuries. Martha and her daughter were taken to the hospital after the collision. Rachel was released within a few hours, but Martha remained in the hospital for three days. She lost time from work, had no medical insurance, and is still in constant pain. Today, she came to your firm with a very basic question: Is the defendant liable?

Before answering Martha's question, the firm must evaluate the case. The first question that must be answered about this case is what type of case is contemplated? As we have already seen, there are many different subspecialties in the law. Martha's claim appears to center on negligent driving by the truck driver. This would place it squarely in the field of personal injury or negligence law. However, there may be other theories that would allow Martha the right to recover. In future chapters, we will address concepts such as product liability, strict liability, and other actions that might be authorized under these facts. For the purpose of this chapter, however, we will limit our discussion to a civil action based on negligence.

Once the initial determination of case type is made, the next question that must be answered in the case evaluation concerns the facts.

2. THE FACTS

Injuries do not always equate to financial recovery. There are many injuries, from minor scrapes to accidental deaths, that do not provide a means for seeking compensation from anyone. A person who is struck by lightning does not have the legal right to recover for an act of God. This is why the process of evaluating the facts is so important. Without the right set of facts, there is no case.

a. Factual Analysis

Factual analysis of any civil case must clearly demonstrate that someone other than the plaintiff is at fault. Without such a showing, there can be no lawsuit. Although an initial review of the facts in Martha's case seems to indicate a strong case against the truck driver, case evaluation contemplates a thorough check of all facts. Are there facts in this case that would have a dramatic effect on the outcome? If it were proven that Martha was operating her car under the influence of alcohol or another drug, that she was in fact across the centerline, or that she had lied about critical facts in this case, her case would be significantly different. Factual investigation will answer the question of the defendant's liability. Was the defendant clearly at fault? What evidence supports this contention? Are there witnesses to the incident? These and many other — questions must be answered as part of the factual analysis.

b. The Legal Requirement to Investigate a Case

Although it would seem obvious that a firm should investigate the basic facts of an incident before filing suit, in recent decades there has been a steady expansion of the number of civil lawsuits filed. Some of these suits have involved frivolous or unfounded claims. Because such claims subject individuals to significant costs, even when the case is resolved in their favor, all states have created a rule that requires attorneys to investigate claims prior to filing suit. The most common version of this requirement is seen in **Rule 11** of the Federal Rules of Civil Procedure, which is closely followed by a similar rule on the state level.

Rule 11
One of the major rules under the Rules of Civil Procedure; it requires an attorney to investigate an action before bringing it

The Federal Rules of Civil Procedure govern the conduct of all phases of a lawsuit, and Rule 11 specifically addresses the topic of how a civil case is begun. Rule 11 provides the following:

> (a) Signature.
>
> Every pleading, written motion, and other paper shall be signed by at least one attorney of record in the attorney's individual name, or, if the party is not represented by an attorney, shall be signed by the party. Each paper shall state the signer's address and telephone number, if any. Except when otherwise specifically provided by rule or statute, pleadings need not be verified or accompanied by affidavit. An unsigned paper shall be stricken unless omission of the signature is corrected promptly after being called to the attention of attorney or party.
>
> (b) Representations to Court.
>
> By presenting to the court (whether by signing, filing, submitting, or later advocating) a pleading, written motion, or other paper, an attorney or unrepresented party is certifying that to the best of the person's knowledge, information, and belief, formed after an inquiry reasonable under the circumstances —
>
> > (1) it is not being presented for any improper purpose, such as to harass or to cause unnecessary delay or needless increase in the cost of litigation;
> >
> > (2) the claims, defenses, and other legal contentions therein are warranted by existing law or by a nonfrivolous argument for the extension, modification, or reversal of existing law or the establishment of new law;
> >
> > (3) the allegations and other factual contentions have evidentiary support or, if specifically so identified, are likely to have evidentiary support after a reasonable opportunity for further investigation or discovery; and
> >
> > (4) the denials of factual contentions are warranted on the evidence or, if specifically so identified, are reasonably based on a lack of information or belief.
>
> (c) Sanctions.
>
> If, after notice and a reasonable opportunity to respond, the court determines that subdivision (b) has been violated, the court may, subject to the conditions stated below, impose an appropriate sanction upon the attorneys, law firms, or parties that have violated subdivision (b) or are responsible for the violation.

Rule 11 has served as the model for various state sanctions for frivolous lawsuits. Consider Figure 3-1.

FIGURE 3-1

Rule 11, Idaho Rules of Civil Procedure

Rule 11(a)(1). Signing of pleadings, motions, and other papers; sanctions.

Every pleading, motion, and other paper of a party represented by an attorney shall be signed by at least one (1) licensed attorney of record of the state of Idaho, in the attorney's individual name, whose address shall be stated before the same may be filed. A party who is not represented by an attorney shall sign the pleading, motion or other paper and state the party's address. Except when otherwise specifically provided by rule or statute, pleadings need not be verified or accompanied by affidavit. The signature of an attorney or party constitutes a certificate that the attorney or party has read the pleading, motion or other paper; that to the best of the signer's knowledge, information, and belief after reasonable inquiry it is well grounded in fact and is warranted by existing law or a good faith argument for the extension, modification, or reversal of existing law, and that it is not interposed for any improper purpose, such as to harass or to cause unnecessary delay or needless increase in the cost of litigation.

If a pleading, motion or other paper is not signed, it shall be stricken unless it is signed promptly after the omission is called to the attention of the pleader or movant. If a pleading, motion or other paper is signed in violation of this rule, the court, upon motion or upon its own initiative, shall impose upon the person who signed it, a represented party, or both, an appropriate sanction, which may include an order to pay to the other party or parties the amount of the reasonable expenses incurred because of the filing of the pleading, motion, or other paper, including a reasonable attorney's fee.[1]

The provisions for Rule 11, whether based on state or federal regulations, require that any attorney filing an action on behalf of another person must have thoroughly investigated the claim, and by affixing his signature to the pleadings attests to this prefiling investigation. As you can see in Figure 3-1, Rule 11 also provides sanctions for attorneys and others who file frivolous, harassing, or groundless lawsuits. These sanctions include paying the other party's legal fees and expenses.

LEGAL LEGWORK ■ RULE 11

Does your state have a corollary to Rule 11? If so, what does the rule say? Locate a copy of it. Then research any cases under this rule. Locate a case where Rule 11 (or its equivalent in your state) played a major role in the case outcome.

3. THE DEFENDANT'S LIABILITY

One of the questions that should be answered early on in the case evaluation process is, How liable is the defendant? If the case against the defendant is shaky, then the rest of the evaluation will be affected. On the other hand, if the case against the defendant establishes clear **liability**, then that part of the legal evaluation will indicate a strong case against the defendant. One important point is to ensure that this portion of the evaluation is both realistic and objective. This is a situation where sympathy for the client can actually cause problems. Legal professionals must be able to take a cold, hard look at the facts presented and make a declarative statement about the extent of the defendant's liability. If the case against the defendant is weak, the final case evaluation must reflect it.

Liability
A party's legal responsibility for injuries to another

4. THE IMPACT OF THE LAW

A proper case evaluation must consider the facts of the possible case, as well as the applicable law. The first question that must be answered as part of the legal analysis is, Does the law provide a remedy for the plaintiff's injuries? If, as we have already seen, the plaintiff has suffered an act of God or cannot point to anyone else as the responsible agent for her injuries, she will have no legal option, no matter how severe the injuries. Legal research will focus on the basic facts of the case and whether the law grants a cause of action to the plaintiff.

Cause of action
A personal, financial, or other injury for which the law gives a person the right to receive compensation

A **cause of action** is the right of the plaintiff to maintain an action against another for specific injuries. Researching a cause of action involves comparing the facts of the current case with prior cases and reviewing case law and statutes. Legal research into the cause of action not only answers the question of whether a civil action is authorized, but also where the case should be filed. For instance, case law might demand that the case be brought in federal court instead of state court. This would be required if the defendant is a citizen of another state or some other federal question is involved.

There are many different types of causes of action. Individuals involved in business relationships might bring a breach of contract action when one party alleges that the other failed to meet the obligations created by their contract. A person injured in an automobile accident might bring a personal injury or negligence suit against the person responsible for causing his injuries. A short list of causes of action includes:

- invasion of privacy;
- defamation;
- tort;
- medical malpractice;
- wrongful death; and
- intentional infliction of emotional distress.

In each case, a plaintiff's cause of action is not only the basis for her claim for financial, emotional, or physical injuries, but also the plaintiff's legal theory about why she should prevail against the defendant. Seen in this context, a cause of action is the basis of the lawsuit and the theory setting out why the plaintiff is entitled to damages or equitable relief against the defendant. We will discuss cause of action further in the next chapter and address damages and equitable relief in Chapter 10.

As you can see, applicable law can have a drastic effect on the case. For instance, in the minority of states that follow a contributory negligence model, the plaintiff's fault might bar all possibility of recovery. This rule would bar Martha's recovery if the defense can show that she was also at fault during the collision, such as driving too fast for conditions. Other jurisdictions follow a comparative negligence rule, where the plaintiff's recovery will be reduced by the amount of her own negligence. Obviously, the legal research portion of case analysis must determine the applicable law and the possible impact on the case of various statutes, evidentiary standards, and prior cases.

SEARCH SUGGESTION • INVESTIGATING LAW

Remember that adequate investigation of a case involves not only the facts, but also the law. Does your state require specific affidavits or expert reports in certain types of cases? For instance, does your state require expert affidavits in medical malpractice cases prior to filing? Locate the applicable rules and summarize them.

5. THE LIKELIHOOD OF RECOVERY

Although it might seem mercenary to include the extent of the defendant's assets as part of the decision to accept or reject a possible case, the likelihood of financial recovery is as critical a factor in case analysis as any other. Law firms are businesses and must generate income. For plaintiffs' firms, this income comes in the form of contingency fees, or a percentage of the plaintiff's recovery from the case. As we saw in Chapter 2, contingency fees are usually one-third of the total recovery. If the defendant is unable to pay a judgment after successful completion of the action, then the firm will recover nothing for all of its efforts. Any plaintiff's firm that engaged in such practices would quickly go bankrupt. The investigation that goes into evaluating a potential case must take into account the defendant's financial resources. This portion of the evaluation centers around the defendant's personal finances and whether the defendant is insured.

For example, automobile insurance is required for motorists. In the preceding example, it is more than likely that the truck driver defendant has the statutorily required insurance. This fact can be established by reviewing the police and accident reports, as discussed later. When the defendant has insurance, this can increase the likelihood of recovery and be a positive factor in evaluating the case overall. We will examine issues related to insurance in greater detail in Chapter 7.

6. THE EXTENT OF THE PLAINTIFF'S INJURIES

The last part of a case evaluation concerns the extent of the plaintiff's injuries. Once the facts have been investigated and confirmed, the applicable law researched and found to be favorable, the defendant's liability clearly established, and the possibility of recovery verified, the question then turns to the plaintiff's injuries. Many people might be tempted to begin with this question, rather than saving it for last. However, the other elements of a case evaluation must be established. If the other elements are either unclear or negative, the plaintiff's injuries, no matter how severe, will dictate that the firm should refuse to take the case.

The plaintiff's physical injuries should be listed in detail. All medical procedures, treatments, and issues related to the plaintiff's injuries must be documented, including any prior injury that might have a bearing on the case. The best way to gather this information is through extended meetings with the client, followed by cross-references with all available records.

B. INITIAL CLIENT MEETING

Initial client meeting
The first meeting with a prospective client, where information will be gathered, additional information requested, and the attorney–client relationship formed

In the earlier example, the situation concluded with Martha appearing at the firm to inquire about suing the truck driver who collided with her car. The **initial client meeting** is a vital tool to establish the working relationship with the client, create the attorney–client relationship, and gather essential information about the case. When a person meets with a law firm, he is often anxious and in trouble. People who have had no previous experience with lawyers and paralegals base their expectations on the wildly inaccurate view provided in the media. Given the range of mind-sets found in clients at the initial client meeting, one method that many legal professionals employ in order to ensure that all relevant information has been gathered is to use a client questionnaire.

Please review the client questionnaire in Figure 3-2. As you can see in that questionnaire, there is a great deal of information that can and must be gathered from the client. At a minimum, this information should include the client's full name, address, and home, work, and cell phone numbers. It is also important to note the client's e-mail addresses, both at work and at home. When you need to contact the client on short notice, this information will come in handy.

FIGURE 3-2

Client Questionnaire

CLIENT'S NAME:

ADDRESS:

PHONE # WORK:

PHONE # HOME:

E-MAIL ADDRESS:

HOW LONG AT PRESENT ADDRESS?

WITH WHOM DOES CLIENT LIVE?

SPOUSE:

CHILDREN: ____________ AGE: ____________
____________ AGE: ____________
____________ AGE: ____________

OTHER PRIOR RESIDENCES:

PERSONS CLIENT SUPPORTS: ____________ AGE: ____________
____________ AGE: ____________

CLIENT'S AGE:

CLIENT'S DATE OF BIRTH:

CLIENT'S SOCIAL SECURITY NUMBER:

CLIENT'S PLACE OF BIRTH:

CLIENT'S EDUCATIONAL BACKGROUND:

CLIENT HAVE A FACEBOOK PAGE? ______________ WILL ACCEPT FRIEND REQUEST? ______________ CLIENT HAVE ANY OTHER SOCIAL MEDIA POSTS?

CLIENT GOOGLED? RESULTS: ______________________________

CLIENT'S EMPLOYMENT HISTORY:

CLIENT'S CURRENT EMPLOYMENT:

EMPLOYER:

ADDRESS:

SUPERVISOR:

TYPE OF WORK:

LENGTH OF EMPLOYMENT:

PRESENT JOB STILL AVAILABLE?

PAY:

MILITARY HISTORY:

CLIENT EVER TREATED BY PSYCHIATRIST OR BEEN IN MENTAL INSTITUTION?

PHYSICAL AILMENTS?

PHYSICAL AILMENTS OF FAMILY MEMBERS?

OTHER NAMES BY WHICH CLIENT HAS BEEN KNOWN?

BRIEF EXPLANATION OF WHAT HAPPENED:

PRIOR ACCIDENTS/LAWSUITS?

YEAR	COURT	DISPOSITION	PARTY

PRACTICE POINTER ▶ MEETING RECORDS

It is always important to create a written record of all meetings with clients. This is important because there may be an allegation of legal malpractice. Such a claim could come years after the initial meeting with the client, and the paralegals and attorneys may be hard-pressed to remember the specific details of that meeting, especially in the context of similar meetings with hundreds of other clients. The best practice is to write a follow-up letter to the client as soon as possible after the meeting, detailing what was discussed, problems presented, potential issues, and any additional information that may be needed from the client. Such a letter is even more important when the firm decides not to accept representation of a client. The letter must be specific about why the firm has decided against taking on the case and set out any issues about impending statute of limitations concerns.

1. OBTAINING AUTHORIZATIONS FROM CLIENTS

Medical authorization
A form, signed by the client, that allows the legal team to review and obtain copies of the client's medical records

In addition to signing a contract of representation and gathering information about the client and the incident, the firm will usually obtain a series of signed medical authorizations from the client as well. A **medical authorization** is a legal document that gives a legal representative the right to obtain copies of the client's medical records. This information is confidential, and the only way that medical providers will release it to anyone other than the patient is through an authorization. These medical authorizations must comply with the requirements of state law and must also conform to the requirements imposed by HIPAA.

2. HIPAA CONCERNS WITH MEDICAL RECORDS

The Health Insurance Portability and Accountability Act (HIPAA) of 1996 imposes requirements on health providers that limit the information that they may release about a patient's condition or course of treatment. Any authorization obtained by the firm must take into account these stringent requirements. See Figure 3-3 for a sample authorization form. Many firms have the client sign several copies of these authorizations so that they can serve originals on medical providers (many will not accept copies). In many situations, a HIPAA authorization form only remains valid for one year. In addition, the medical provider may require that the client sign an attorney designation statement, identifying the attorney and the law firm representing the client in a pending action.

FIGURE 3-3

Authorization Form for Medical Records (HIPAA Compliant)

To: Anywhere Medical Services, LLC

Re: Jane Doe

Address: 21 Maple Drive, Anywhere, AP 00030

I, Jane M. Doe, do hereby authorize the release of all medical documentation, including, but not limited to, medical treatment, diagnosis, medical reports, medical billing, and all other health and medical information to which I am legally entitled, currently in the possession of:

Anywhere Medical Services, LLC

Anywhere, AP 00030

I further authorize the release of said information in full knowledge of and in compliance with the Health Insurance Portability and Accountability Act of 1996 ("HIPAA") to: Smith and Jones, PC, my attorneys. Under the provisions of HIPAA, I grant and authorize my attorneys full and immediate access to my medical records.

Upon presentation of this medical authorization, you are hereby authorized to release any and all medical records of any kind to my attorneys.

____
Jane M. Doe

____
Date

3. OTHER INFORMATION FROM CLIENT

When questioning the client about the incident, do not neglect obvious points. Does the client know of any witnesses to the collision? Has anyone taken photos of the car the client was driving? Does the client know if the local press did a story about the wreck? The only way to find out this information is by asking.

When a new client meets with a law firm, she can usually provide only the most basic facts of the incident. In the example above, for instance, Martha can provide an overview of what happened but will probably not be able to provide the kind of detail that the firm must have before it can initiate a lawsuit. Sometimes clients bring documentation with them, but most clients do not. What kind of information does the firm need in order to begin an investigation of a claim? At a minimum, the legal team needs the following:

- Details of the incident
- The police report
- Any investigative report
- Any police accident reconstructionist report
- Witness names and contact information

a. Details of the Incident

The client should be questioned in detail about the incident. This is the time to pin down as many facts as possible. It is important to record all relevant data, not only because it is necessary to assist in further investigation, but also as a way of confirming the client's version of the incident. If the client's narrative differs in significant ways from the details provided by others, this is a strong indicator that the client is either misinformed or actively deceiving the legal team.

The most critical piece of information is the date and time of the incident. In Martha's collision, it is absolutely essential to confirm the date of the accident. This date determines the statute of limitations period.

Statute of limitation
A statute that imposes a time limit on the initiation of a civil action

A **statute of limitation** is a statutory time limit on legal actions (Fig. 3-4). Different causes of action have different statutes of limitations. In negligence cases, the statute of limitations may be as short as one or two years. In such a situation, the client must file an action before the statutory period expires. If no action is filed within this time period, then the action is barred and the client will have no recourse.

FIGURE 3-4

Statute of Limitation for Personal Injury Cases (Illinois)

§13-202. Personal injury — Penalty. Actions for damages for an injury to the person, or for false imprisonment, or malicious prosecution . . . shall be commenced within 2 years next after the cause of action accrued.[2]

b. Police Reports

If the police were called to the scene of the accident or were in any other way involved, they will create a police report. The police report is an excellent resource because it is created by a neutral third party with no vested interest in the outcome of a possible civil case. It also lists important details, including the date, time, weather conditions, and other relevant data.

c. Investigative Reports

In some cases, a police officer or detective may generate a second report, referred to as an *investigative report*. This report differs from a traditional police report by showing follow-up investigations by the police department. Although investigative reports are common in criminal investigations, they are rare in situations involving routine traffic accidents. However, if such a report exists, it behooves the legal team to locate a copy of it and to review it closely. An investigative report will provide additional detail not found in the police report, including additional witness statements, forensic investigation, and evidence not mentioned in the original police report.

d. Police Accident Reconstructionist Report

In the hypothetical case that begins this chapter, we outlined a fairly routine traffic accident. These cases are all too common in the United States and are one of the most frequently brought actions in lawsuits in the American court system. Because of the prevalence of automobile accidents, many police officers have received training in accident reconstruction. An accident reconstructionist can gather details from the scene of a car collision and prepare a report showing the most probable sequence of events that led to the injuries. Police officers trained in accident reconstruction will measure skid marks, the pattern of glass shards from broken headlights and windshields, and the relative position of the automobiles and can reach conclusions about which driver was at fault based on those measurements. These conclusions can be invaluable to the legal team considering bringing a lawsuit. If the conclusions of the accident reconstructionist run against the client, then the legal team should reconsider bringing the case.

e. Witnesses

The police report will often contain the names and contact information of any witnesses to the incident, but any good prefiling investigation will attempt to locate additional witnesses. The police may not have located all witnesses to the incident; the client may know of others who have information about the case. All of these individuals should be noted and marked for later interview. Important witness information includes:

- name;
- address;
- telephone numbers, including work, residence, and cell, if known;
- place of work; and
- general description (particularly if name is incomplete or not known).

f. Other Critical Information

In addition to gathering all of the information outlined above, there may be a need to gather specific information unique to each case. In Martha's case, for instance, it will be important to know if the truck driver was employed for a company at the time, whether he was on duty at the time of the incident, whether he was under the influence of alcohol, whether either driver was cited by the police, whether trucks were permitted on that particular section of road, and a host of other details. As you can see, other critical information depends on the nature of the claim and the specifics surrounding the actual incident.

4. CLIENT INTANGIBLES

It is important to understand that the initial and subsequent meetings with the client are not simply limited to gathering information about the case. There is another important evaluation that the legal team must take into account: the client. Under the heading of "Client Intangibles" are such things as the client's personality, background, previous medical history, and other factors.

a. Client Personality

Why is the client's personality an important part of any case evaluation? The answer is simple: If the case goes to a jury, the client's personality will have a profound impact on the case. We would all like to believe that cases are decided solely on their factual and legal basis, but in truth, the personalities of the main players in the case are also critical. If the client has a pleasant disposition and will make a positive impact on the jury, the case will have a better chance of positive resolution than a situation where the client is rude, obnoxious, and annoying. One of the most important parts of the preliminary evaluation of the client involves the answer to a very basic question: Will the client make a good witness?

b. Will the Client Make a Good Witness?

If the case goes to trial, the client will take the stand. The client is a witness to the events in the case and must testify about important aspects of the case, including the incident and subsequent events. If the client is someone who will make a positive impression on the jury, this fact should be noted prominently in the materials used to record important details of the case. If, on the other hand, the client is someone who will obviously make a terrible impression on the jury, this fact should be noted just as prominently.

c. Cross-Referencing the Client's Version

One of the final elements involved with evaluating the client is the confirmation of the client's version of the facts with other sources. Does the client's version of the events correspond to the record? Are there significant discrepancies? If so, is there a good reason for these discrepancies? A client might, for instance, have been so traumatized by the incident that his memory has been affected. On the other hand, significant discrepancies might indicate a client who is either exaggerating injuries or actively trying to deceive the court. In any event, these discrepancies must be cleared up before the case is filed.

d. The Client's Web Presence

Another key element to take into account whether representing a plaintiff or a defendant is the client's Web presence. Broadly speaking, this refers to any posting, blog, Facebook entry, or any other information the opposition can access about the client. The client should be closely questioned about any websites that she maintains or any information that is available about the client on the Internet, even if she believes that the information is positive. You can rest assured that the opposition is investigating the Web presence of each party and every important witness.

e. Interview Techniques for Clients

Although we would all like to believe that our clients tell the absolute truth about every issue in their case, experience has shown that that is not the case. Even the best of us tend to shade the truth a bit when an event shows a person in a negative light. With that in mind, there are some interviewing techniques that paralegals should follow when interviewing clients. Bear in mind that clients may also exclude information simply because they are not aware of what is and what is not important. There are several different approaches to interviewing clients, and legal professionals may use some or all of them when assessing whether to take a case. There are many steps that a person may follow to develop a successful interview:

- Doing research before the meeting
- Being tactful, sympathetic, and professional during the meeting
- Reviewing and expanding on the information already provided
- Building a rapport
- Reminding the client that all information given is confidential
- Asking open-ended questions and getting the client to talk
- Studying body language
- Ending the meeting with specific directions

Research Before the Meeting

Almost everyone has some kind of Web presence, and it is vitally important to investigate your potential client's social media presence before meeting with him. An amazing amount of details can be learned about a person before ever meeting with him. With Facebook, LinkedIn, and other websites, a paralegal can build a strong picture of the person before the client walks through the door for the first time. It is also important to note what kind of social media postings the client has that may be reviewed by the opposition should the firm accept the case. But researching the client goes beyond simply viewing whatever Web presence he may have. It is also possible to check a person's litigation and criminal record, often without ever leaving your desk.

Being Tactful, Sympathetic, and Professional during the Meeting

Before a client decides to come to an attorney for possible representation, this person may have gone through a long history of pain, second-guessing, and general anxiety. She may be receiving request calls from debt collectors or insurance adjusters. A potential client may not be in her best state when the interview begins. This is where tact and sympathy pay off. Be aware that people who are under stress react in very different ways. Some may be belligerent while others are docile. Some may think that no one will believe them. Along with tact and sympathy, however, it is also important to maintain professionalism. You may feel sorry for this person and may believe that she has suffered a massive injustice. However, it is also possible that this injustice is not something the firm will be able to assist the client to overcome. A firm that takes all cases, especially without investigating them, is soon a firm that is out of business. For an example of the kind of investigation that is required before an action is filed, see this chapter's Case Excerpt.

Reviewing and Expanding on the Information Already Provided

When the interview starts, it is important to make the client feel comfortable. This can be accomplished in a variety of ways, but often just following up on the details that the client has already provided is a good way to get started. Go over the client information sheet and fill in any missing data. Make sure that you have alternate phone numbers and e-mail addresses in case it is necessary to get in touch with the client in a short time frame.

Building a Rapport

Establishing a rapport with a client is more art than science. For some legal professionals, developing a positive relationship with a potential client is easy. For others, it may not be. A good way to start is to review the already provided by the client and to engage in a bit of small talk. Get the client used to talking. Ask about the client's job or children or any topic that is not a potential hot button. Do not ask about their religion, ethnic origin, or their accent — if they have one. These questions are almost always irrelevant and tend to put clients on the defensive, which is the exact opposite of what you are hoping to achieve.

Reminding the Client That All Information Given Is Confidential

Clients and potential clients should be reminded several times that what they say to the legal team will be held in strict confidence. In fact, some would argue that an attorney's guarantee of confidentiality, like that of a medical doctor, is the cornerstone of the profession. When a client actually believes that the conversation will be confidential, she is far more likely to be candid and to bring up not only the good points of the case, but also the potential pitfalls. No case is perfect and no client is totally good (or totally bad). A case will have good and bad points, and finding out about these before bringing suit is not just a good idea — it is actually required by Rule 11 or its state corollary.

Asking Open-Ended Questions and Getting the Client to Talk

One of the best ways to get information from someone is to simply listen. Ask open-ended questions and listen to what the person says. Take some notes, but spend more of your time making eye contact. Use your body language to convey that you are interested. An interested person leans forward and takes an attentive pose. An interested person smiles and reacts in nonverbal ways to what he is hearing. The benefit of asking open-ended questions, such as, "What happened after that?" is that it gets the client talking and tends to relax him. It may also reveal some inconsistencies that may need to be investigated later on.

Studying Body Language

Just as you are aware of your own body language and the nonverbal cues you are giving the client, observe the client's body language. While a person who never looks you in the eye might not always be lying, body language can tell you some important things about the client. When the client becomes especially nervous or closed off when discussing a particular point, this may suggest a potential problem. The client may simply be uncomfortable discussing this issue or there may be another reason why the client's body language is signaling discomfort.

Ending the Meeting with Specific Directions

When the meeting concludes, give the client your card and assure her that you will make contact within a specific time period. One of the biggest complaints that the general public has about legal professionals is that their phone calls are not returned. Get ahead of that potential issue by telling the client that it will be 24 to 48 hours before she hears from the firm, but that she will definitely hear something. Even if the firm hasn't made a decision about taking the case, contact the client within that agreed-upon time period anyway. No one likes to feel abandoned or ignored, so if you promise to call, then honor your promise, even if there isn't anything in particular to report. If you promise to send a document, then send it. Stay in contact with the client until a decision is made. If the firm takes the case, then make routine contact with the client two or three times a month or perhaps more often. Your clients will appreciate the extra effort. If you request information from clients, then follow up with them and make sure that they produce it.

5. INFORMATION THE LAW FIRM PROVIDES TO THE CLIENT

So far, we have limited our discussion to the information that the client provides to the legal team. But there is another important information exchange that must be addressed: the information that the firm provides to the client.

The original reason that the client sought out legal advice was to inquire about his rights and the possibility of bringing a lawsuit against another. The client may not have any experience with the court system and so may not understand many of the procedures. For instance, clients are often confused and frustrated by the length of time it takes from filing the complaint to actually trying the case. They do not understand why this process can take a year or more. Explaining it to them at this stage will often prevent a lot of the client's frustration later on. The legal team must explain the various stages involved in bringing a suit and also frame the process in such a way that the client understands that the court system has many other cases currently pending and that it may take months or years to resolve his case. The initial meetings with the client are the time to explain all of these aspects of bringing or defending a civil suit. Paralegals should keep in mind that many times a client will not ask basic questions out of fear that he will appear stupid or misinformed. Take the time to explain the entire procedure of a civil case to the client, and give the client numerous opportunities to ask questions.

Many law firms provide the client with a printed handout or brochure that explains the legal process in detail. The client can take the printed material home and review it later. If you are called upon to create such a brochure, it should spell out in uncomplicated terms exactly what happens at each stage of the lawsuit. When they are well written, these brochures can also serve as a marketing tool for the firm. When the case concludes, the satisfied client may give the brochure to a friend who has just been injured in a car wreck, generating additional income for the firm.

As another option, there are also currently several different professionally produced online videos and DVDs that discuss all phases of civil litigation. Companies market this media to law firms, who in turn provide them to clients at no charge. They answer most of the common questions raised by new clients, and clients can watch them several times in order to better understand the legal process.

INVESTIGATING THE CLAIM

Now that we have established the need for a proper investigation of an incident before a lawsuit is ever filed, the next question becomes, How is such an investigation carried out? Although you might be tempted to think that attorneys hand the responsibility of the factual investigation off to a private detective, there are several reasons why this is not the case. For one thing, private detectives are expensive, and there are numerous cases where this investment is simply not cost-effective. A case that might potentially only earn a few thousand dollars would quickly turn into a losing proposition if a large chunk of that ultimate recovery went to pay a private detective's wages. Another consideration concerns the time line of the case.

As a general rule, both sides in a civil case tend to wait too long before involving a private investigator. Normally, the parties only justify the additional expense when the case is likely to go to trial, but that can be months or even years after the complaint was filed. By that time, critical information may already be lost. Thus, time and money are both reasons why attorneys conduct their own investigations or insist that their paralegals do so.

PRACTICE POINTER ▶ CONFLICTS CHECK

Whenever the firm considers representing a new client, one of the most important practical applications that should be followed is a conflicts check. This is a review of the current and past client list to make sure that the action brought by the new client will not affect a previous client. An attorney is barred from representing the plaintiff in one action and the defendant in another. This raises the specter of a conflict of interest, where the interests of one client are in direct conflict with the interests of another. This places the attorney and the firm in an untenable position: They have access to privileged and sensitive information about a client who is now about to be sued by the firm. In such a situation, the attorney and the firm should disqualify themselves from representing the new client when there is even a possibility that the new client's action will impinge on the interests of a previous client.

Sidebar

Deborah Reusher is a paralegal investigator for the Missouri Public Defender in Kansas City, Missouri. "We work on a case from the beginning, doing the pre-work for the trial, and then help out through the trial. We touch on all phases of a case." Her work involves going to the scenes of crimes, taking photos, shooting video, and interviewing witnesses. According to Deborah, investigation is all about people. "To be a good investigator, bottom line, you need good people skills. You really have to know how to read people. You have to know what kind of situations to walk into, [and] when to take a buddy with you."

A. ATTORNEYS AND PARALEGALS AS INVESTIGATORS

Having an attorney or paralegal conduct the preliminary investigation solves many of the problems that are created by using private detectives. For one thing, the legal professional is already on the payroll. For another, a paralegal can go to the accident scene within days of the initial client meeting. The photographs, videos, and witness contacts made at this early juncture can mean the difference between winning and losing a case at trial.

B. PARALEGAL INVESTIGATORS

Although many attorneys conduct the prefiling investigation, it is becoming increasingly common for attorneys to entrust this duty to paralegals. The reason is simple economics: While the attorney is generating additional income by meeting with new clients, conducting depositions, or participating in a trial, the paralegal can do the basic investigative work and then present a complete picture to the attorney at a later time. Of course, the final decision to take the case will rest with the attorney, but it may be your responsibility, as paralegal, to gather all of the information to help the attorney make an informed decision. The attorney may not have the time to visit the scene right away, and there are other reasons why the attorney should not be the person to create certain forms of documentation.

For example, if the attorney does go to the scene and learns something about the case, he cannot testify about it. Attorneys are legally barred from being both witnesses and advocates in the same case. That is one reason why an attorney should not interview witnesses with no one else present: If a witness gives a statement and then later contradicts it, the attorney cannot take the stand and dispute it. But if a paralegal took that statement, the paralegal is perfectly capable of being sworn in and questioned about it. Because of this, paralegals must know the basics of investigating a case, including how to locate and interview witnesses, document testimony, and gather evidence.

1. LOCATING WITNESSES

We have already seen that there are several potential resources for locating witnesses in civil cases. The client, for example, can provide names of witnesses. The names will also be provided in police and accident reports. Once located, individual witnesses may be able to provide information about other witnesses. It is important to note, though, that simply obtaining a person's name does not always mean that you will be able to actually find that person. Some witnesses are difficult to locate and may challenge your ability to track them down.

a. Witness Locator Services

A **witness locator service** is a company that locates individuals for a fee. They can be private investigators, **skip tracing agencies**, or other types of businesses that specialize in locating people who do not wish to be found. However, in most civil cases, a well-trained paralegal can find a witness without having to use such companies.

Witness locator service
A company that provides information about a witness's former addresses, telephone numbers, employment, and current location

Skip tracing agency
A company or individual who charges a fee for locating a witness or potential civil litigant

How do you locate witnesses? Go to the witness's last reported address and talk to her neighbors. If you can locate family members, ask them. There is one person who can often provide a gold mine of information about a person: her ex-spouse. You can request a person's new address from the U.S. post office, although a written request, on office letterhead, signed by an attorney, is usually required. The Internet offers several free services to locate people by last name, region, or other identifying information. Most public libraries have telephone books for cities across the nation. Look up the witness's name there; you might actually find it. If you have reason to believe that

Tech Topic
EVALUATING ONLINE SOURCES

The widespread availability of the Internet has made it much easier to locate information, but that availability does not always guarantee the quality of the sources. The biggest problem with the Internet is that there is no method for ensuring the pedigree of a particular site. Websites may offer substantial resources or may simply be platforms for individuals to express radical views. As a general rule, legal professionals can trust websites established by government agencies or higher education institutes, but even these may not always have the most up-to-date information. Your own critical thinking skills are still your best guide: You must be able to locate information online and have the ability to sort through the sites for the best and most accurate data.

the person is actively avoiding being found, however, then it may be necessary to resort to a professional service.

b. Internet Search

In addition to hiring a witness locator service, it is also possible to glean a great deal of information about a person through a simple Internet search. Using Google or Yahoo! or any number of other online services, you can gather a lot of information about a person, including any references to a person mentioned in a newspaper article, address and telephone numbers, age, whether they have created their own website, and even a satellite image of their home (e.g., using Google Earth).

2. INTERVIEWING WITNESSES

When it comes to talking to witnesses, keep your pen and paper handy. Although you might think that tape-recording the person's statement would make better use of time, many individuals become nervous and noncommunicative when a tape recorder comes out. Of course, you should never record a person's statement without his permission, so if the person does not wish to be recorded, the next best thing is to write out what he tells you. It is important to record the data that the person provides, as well as the phrases and vocabulary that the witness uses to describe the incident. Later, you may need to type up your notes, or even prepare an affidavit, and a witness is more likely to sign such a document when the writing actually sounds like the person.

Even if your recorder is working perfectly, you should still take notes. Good note-taking is an important skill that pays off in many different contexts. When interviewing a witness, for example, keeping notes helps you stay focused on the important issues in the case while also giving you the opportunity to follow up on interesting points that the witness has raised during the interview. Having a prepared list of questions is a good starting point, but when it comes to interviewing, your best assets are your ability to take good notes and actually listen to what the witness has to say. You may find that the witness brings up issues that you had not considered when you originally created your list of questions. Sometimes, witnesses surprise you with information you never expected them to possess. Being able to track these issues with careful note-taking can save a great deal of additional follow-up work.

Interviewing witnesses is a skill that only comes with practice. Establishing a rapport with a person before getting her to provide details of the incident is often the best way to approach an interview. If you like to talk to people, then you will probably make a good interviewer. Find a way to create common ground with a witness before asking the pertinent questions. People are reluctant to talk with lawyers or other legal professionals. A good paralegal investigator must overcome that hurdle and get the person to relax. An uncomfortable, nervous person will never provide as much information as a comfortable, relaxed person will. Hopefully you will already have a copy of the police and accident reports with you that you can use to cross-reference what the witness tells you. You should also compare the information provided by the witness with what you have previously received from the client. Is there a disparity between the two? It is not unusual for witnesses to disagree about minor points in a story, but the main points should remain the same from witness to witness. For instance, they might disagree about the color of the cars, but there shouldn't be any disagreement about the fact that there was a collision.

PRACTICE POINTER ▶ POLICE OFFICERS

You can always get better ideas about how to research from speaking with police officers. Call up a local detective and ask for pointers about how to do some basic investigative work in civil cases. Also make sure that you know what you can and can't do under the law.

a. Interviewing Techniques

Interviewing others is both a skill and an art. It takes practice to master the ability to get people to speak to you, especially when they learn that you are a legal professional. The first reaction most people give is that they do not want to become involved in any legal action, even as a witness. You can explain that you are gathering information, but you should not promise that the person will never be called to testify. At this early point in the investigation, it is far too soon to rule anyone out as a potential witness at the trial. However, there is no reason to be overly aggressive. Most paralegals who interview witnesses try to be approachable and courteous. After all, you are simply doing a job that has been assigned to you, and this person may have information that is critical to your client's case.

When questioning witnesses, it is extremely important to let the witness tell her story. Allow the witness to tell the story in a narrative, and then follow up with questions after the main facts have been filled in. From the plaintiff's perspective, the important facts to be learned from a witness are those facts that either help the case or hurt it. Witnesses who corroborate the client's version of what happened are just as important as witnesses who disagree with the client's version of the facts. Witnesses often know of other people with more information, and asking them about other witnesses is always an excellent idea. It also helps to go to the scene. Whether the scene is the site of a car wreck or the office space in a sexual harassment case, knowing the lay of the land prior to talking with key witnesses helps the paralegal understand the facts being related. Such knowledge also helps when a witness begins to exaggerate or on the few occasions when a witness actually lies. Beyond this, the basic facts of the lawsuit — who, what, when, where, and why — should always be asked and recorded for later review. Any discrepancies between the versions of the witnesses should be prominently noted.

Of course, it is equally important for the paralegal to make sure that the witness is under no illusions about the role of the paralegal. Any paralegal conducting an investigation should always properly identify himself as a paralegal, not as an attorney, private investigator, detective, or police officer. Such identification is an ethical requirement, and misidentifying yourself as a police officer or attorney is against the law.

b. Purposes of the Interview

The purpose behind any witness interview is to learn as much information about the case as possible and to plan how the witness's testimony may be used. Will it be necessary to depose this witness? Is the witness likely to testify at trial? Although it isn't possible to answer these questions conclusively in a preliminary investigation, there are times when the answers are plain. An eyewitness will almost certainly testify. During the interview, the paralegal should also make notations about the witness's attitude. The witness should be classified as friendly, neutral, or hostile. The witness's attitude will often determine to what extent the legal team will rely on the person's testimony in later hearings or at trial.

c. Deceitful Witnesses

It is an unfortunate fact of life that some witnesses shade, exaggerate, or deliberately lie about critical facts in a case. How can you tell when someone is lying to you? Even trained investigators sometimes have trouble spotting a lie. Usually, no single factor will demonstrate a person's credibility. For instance, if a witness fails to make eye contact with you, that could indicate deceit, or it might just indicate a person who is anxious or nervous. Instead of looking for one telltale sign, weigh the person's entire story. Do the facts add up? Could the person have seen what he claims to have seen? Does this person have a vested interest in the outcome of the case? Do you, as the interviewer, have some reservations about the person's testimony? These are just some of the factors that go into evaluating the veracity of a person's statement.

C. DOCUMENTING THE SCENE OF THE ACCIDENT

Another important aspect of a preliminary investigation concerns documenting the scene where the accident occurred. This is important no matter what the issues are in the case. Obviously, the scene of an automobile accident will prove to be a critical element of a case, but the scene is just as important in other types of cases. As people move through their lives, they are constantly negotiating their way around other people and inanimate objects that affect their actions. In a sexual harassment case, for example, where does the plaintiff allege that the harassment occurred? Is this area secluded? Could others have witnessed the incident? In almost all civil and criminal cases, the location where the incident occurred is critical.

Accident scenes can change their appearance quickly. If you wait even a few weeks before going out to record the site, the scene may have changed dramatically. For instance, road crews may have come through and put up barriers where none existed before. A change in seasons can mean that the foliage and underbrush have changed in appearance. Skid marks and other evidence of the crash fade and disappear over time. All of these are excellent reasons to go to the scene as soon as possible. When the client informs the legal team about the location, the paralegal should go to that scene armed with a still camera, a video camera, and some blank paper for drawing a diagram.

1. PHOTOGRAPHS

Photographs of the scene of the accident are absolutely essential and should be taken as soon as possible. We have all heard the old maxim that a picture is worth a thousand words. In litigation, it can be worth thousands of dollars. The jury may not understand what happened from two hours of testimony, but a single snapshot can bring the case home for them. Photographs should take in all of the available angles of the scene. When you are taking photographs, try to duplicate the conditions of the accident as close as possible. If the collision occurred in the morning, make sure that you go to the scene in the morning. Shadows, the angle of the sun, the position of trees, and more can have a huge impact on the case.

When in doubt, take your photographs with an eye toward what the jurors will ultimately see in the case. Remember that most jurors will be unfamiliar with the scene and may not have a frame of reference. You should take camera shots from as many different angles as possible, but don't neglect the obvious. Still shots are great for pinpointing exact details, but video can sometimes make or break a case.

2. VIDEO

If a paralegal has taken still shots of the scene, why would it be necessary to also take video? Moving video is more interesting to watch, and jurors can get a better idea of what happened in the case by watching a moving picture. This is particularly true for automobile accidents, but video is commonly used in other types of cases, too. For instance, plaintiffs' attorneys routinely present "day in the life" videos to support damage claims. A day in the life video follows the plaintiff through a normal day, showing how the plaintiff's injuries impact everyday activities from getting out of bed, to taking out the trash, to going to work. Videos can have a huge impact on jurors.

Although it is always best to have a professional shoot your video footage, that isn't always feasible. There may not be sufficient funds to hire a professional, and early on in the case, while the firm is still evaluating the facts, the only person available to take video is the paralegal. If you are called upon to shoot video of any scene, here are some guidelines:

- Move the camera slowly. Some people find this to be a lot more difficult than it sounds. We all have a natural tendency to aim the video camera at one thing and then at another. The problem with that is that when you view the tape later, your eyes get whiplash because the scene is changing so quickly.
- Hold the camera with a steady hand. Shaky video can be a terrible distraction and take away effectiveness.
- Keep perspectives in mind. Start your video from a known landmark and follow a commonsense route, either right to left or left to right.
- Avoid comments. If your video camera has a way to mute the audio part of the recording, use it. Do not talk while the video is running. You should certainly avoid inserting comments such as, "Wow! Our guy must have really been speeding to go this far off the road!" For videos, the best course is no audio at all.
- Do not use dramatic effects. These days, many video cameras come with a host of special effects. Do not use them for your video. It might make the video more dramatic to put a warning sign in the shot that wasn't actually there when the accident occurred, but you are there to record, not to improvise. In the same vein, you shouldn't rearrange the site to make it more picturesque or dramatic. Record the scene as it appears, not as you would like it to appear.

3. DIAGRAMMING THE SCENE

If you have taken the time to capture the scene in still photos and video, why do you need a diagram of the scene? A diagram gives you a different perspective on the scene, and you want as many different perspectives as possible. The time to draw your diagram is while you are still at the scene. You should not concern yourself with making the diagram to scale, but you should make sure that you capture important features, especially landmarks that are already on film or videotape. Later, you can compare the photos and video to the diagram. It should give you and your witnesses a better understanding of what the scene is like.

D. GATHERING EVIDENCE

When you do get photographs, videotape, and witness statements, you must save it for future use. Put in a clearly marked box in the firm's basement or in a storage unit that belongs to the office. Never store it in a box in your office. Somehow, when you need it, the box will mysteriously disappear. Worse, the cleaning crew might think that it's trash and throw it out for you. Of course, you should store all of this information in the case file, but you might also want to consider making backup copies of everything.

When you want to preserve evidence, take a cue from *CSI* or other law shows. The reason that they store evidence in plastic bags is to keep people from handling or tampering with it. Plastic bags are see-through, so you don't have to keep taking your evidence out of the bag to see what it is. *CSI* also has a couple of other good tips, such as labeling the bag with information like:

- who collected it;
- when it was collected; and
- where it was found.

For example, a few years ago, a woman was getting ready to feed her cat. When she picked up a can of cat food, it exploded. She had severe injuries, and after numerous trips to the doctor, she sought out a lawyer to sue the cat food company. The attorney was eager to take on the case, seeing the possibility of a huge settlement against a multinational corporation. "So," he said, "where's the can?"

The woman looked at him blankly. "The can? Oh, I threw that away a long time ago."

You be the judge: What result? Can they bring their case? Why or why not?

E. RESEARCHING PUBLIC RECORDS

When it comes to evaluating a case, it is also important to review the public records. These can provide valuable information about the defendant, the witnesses, and even your client. One of the best places to start a review of the public records is the clerk of court's office. Besides actually visiting the courthouse, there are many websites available that can help a legal professional learn a great deal about clients, opposing clients, judges, and many others. These sites include LexisNexis's CourtLink Strategic Profiles or Westlaw's PeopleMap, but there are many others.

1. THE CLERK OF COURTS OFFICE

The local clerk's office maintains records about all civil and criminal cases in the county. Most clerks' offices are now computerized, and this speeds up information gathering tremendously. Using the computer databases, a paralegal can learn whether someone has been sued, divorced, or convicted of a crime. Some of these terminals can provide you with statewide information on both civil and criminal cases. If you'd like to know if one of your witnesses has a criminal record, this is the best place to start. Private detectives use these resources all the time, but you don't have to be a licensed private investigator to get access.

Just around the corner is another information treasure trove: the deed room.

2. THE DEED ROOM

Sometimes called the registrar's office or the land office, the deed room is where the records of all real estate transactions are stored. Although it doesn't sound very promising, this is one of the best places to gather information about a person. In this office, for instance, a paralegal can find out what real estate a person owns (useful in evaluating the likelihood of enforcing a judgment). You can also find out how much this person paid for her property. Although in most cases the purchase amount is not stated directly on the deed, the tax assessed on the purchase can help you figure out the sale price. You can also find out if someone has recently transferred property out of her name into someone else's — a close family member, for instance. This is a common act in domestic cases where someone is trying to shield assets. Most deed rooms also have plats or maps of the properties owned to help you locate exactly where the property is. Information is available about first and second mortgages. How much does this person owe? Has she recently obtained a second or even a third mortgage on the property? This might indicate financial trouble.

3. UCC FILINGS

There are also other sources of information that can help you build a picture of a witness or a potential defendant. For instance, there are the Uniform Commercial Code (UCC) filings. These filings are required for financed items like cars and boats, and the information is free and open to the public. Has your witness purchased a boat lately, had a garage door installed, or bought a new car? The UCC filings will tell you all of this. You might think that this information isn't very helpful, but imagine that you are about to interview someone, and this person has critical information. Wouldn't it be a great icebreaker to mention in passing that you like to waterski, knowing full well that this witness just purchased a powerboat? Establishing a rapport with a person is essential if you are going to get any information out of him. Obviously, this information also helps you build a better picture of the defendant's finances and his ability to pay a substantial civil judgment.

4. BIRTH, MARRIAGE, AND DEATH RECORDS

It is always helpful to know who someone's family members are. You can get this information from birth and death records. In some states, this information is stored in the deed room; in others, you'll find it in the probate court. Wherever it is stored, these records are worth a look. In the past, when people didn't relocate as often as they do these days, you could glean a person's entire history from these records alone. However, these records may only be of limited use today. People relocate so often these days that it is rare to find someone who has lived in the same area her entire life. The birth records will show the names of the person's parents and children, but only if they were born in that county. In some states, this information is linked with probate records, which show if the person was the beneficiary of a will. Along with birth and death records, marriage licenses can also tell you a lot about family relationships. These records, along with the others mentioned above, are important for asset searches, too. Knowing what someone owns is always helpful in determining if they should be sued in the first place.

Tech Topic
LITIGATION SOFTWARE SUPPORT

It is quite common for even an average civil case to balloon in file size from a few papers to reams of documents. The ability to scan all of this material, organize it, and review it from a desktop and from mobile devices like tablets and phones has become a reality in the legal system. Attorneys and paralegals who find themselves with downtime can use that time more efficiently by reviewing digitized documents that have been provided through discovery, police reports, accident reconstruction reports, and even photographs, all from their own mobile device. Litigation software has come a long way in the last two or three decades. Now it is possible to allow everyone assigned to the case to review documents and to include notes, emphasize certain portions of documents, and even correlate them in different ways. For instance, medical files can be organized chronologically and by provider, giving the legal professional a new way to look at the material on hand.

As has been true with all technological innovations, however, a paralegal must keep in mind that the old rules about confidentiality still apply. Just because files are easily available on a tablet does not mean that others should have access to that tablet and the information contained should not be discussed with others outside the firm or, worse, leave the mobile device in some location, with no password protection that could allow others access to highly sensitive information.

5. TAX OFFICE

The tax office is required to keep extensive records about real estate, and all of this information is open to the public. Many people never think about going to the tax office for information, but it has more raw data than any other office. The tax office is the perfect place to start if the only information you have about someone is his name. Most people don't realize just how extensive the tax office information is. The tax office can give the basic floor plan of the person's house, including the number of bedrooms and bathrooms; total square footage, including heated and unheated spaces; amenities like decks or pools; and even information about recent renovations. In some tax offices, you can see a digital photo of the house. In larger counties, such as metropolitan Atlanta, this information is available at public access terminals. A picture of the house and all of the details are just a mouse click away. See Figure 3-5 for a list of all the information available from these sources.

FIGURE 3-5
Witness Information

The information that you can develop about witnesses includes:

- full name, address, and telephone number (clerk's office, deed room, tax office);
- where the house is located, what it looks like, and so on (tax office);
- a rough picture of his finances (clerk's office, UCC filings, deed room);
- his criminal record, if any (clerk's office; Internet);

- prior contact with the legal system, such as if he has ever been a plaintiff or a defendant in a civil suit (clerk's office);
- any pending litigation, either civil or criminal (clerk's office);
- whether he has a relationship with anyone else in the suit (birth/death records; marriage records; probate court);
- what kind of assets this person owns (deed room; tax office);
- what he does for a living (neighbors; deed room);
- anything he has in common with you (all of the above);
- whether the client appears in a Google search. Is information positive or negative? Should you preserve this information for discovery? Advise client not to change information? (Internet); and
- advising client not to post anything about the case at any stage of the process (Internet).

Case Excerpt

When is a party subject to sanctions for failing to sufficiently investigate a case as required by Rule 11?

OAKLEY V. NOLAN
2007-Ohio-4794, 2007 Ohio App. LEXIS 4288 (Ohio Ct. App., Athens County Sept. 11, 2007)

Opinion

DECISION AND JUDGMENT ENTRY

McFarland, P.J.:

Jack Oakley and James Nobile ("Appellants") appeal from a sanctions judgment in favor of Appellees Michael Nolan and First National Bank of Nelsonville, Ohio ("FNB"). On appeal, the Appellants contend the trial court erred when it granted the Appellees' request for expenses and attorney fees. Because we find that the trial court did not abuse its discretion when it found frivolous conduct under R.C. 2323.51(A)(2)(a)(ii)-(iv), we affirm its judgment.

On January 30, 2006, Mr. Oakley, by and through his counsel, Mr. Nobile, filed a complaint against Mr. Nolan and FNB, asserting two causes of action: defamation and invasion of privacy. The claims arose out of Mr. Oakley's bankruptcy case. Prior to the time at which Mr. Oakley filed for bankruptcy, he and FNB were involved in litigation over several banking transactions. By and through its counsel, Mr. Nolan, FNB answered Mr. Oakley's complaint and filed a motion for summary judgment. Mr. Oakley also requested additional time to conduct discovery, which the trial court denied.

Both parties submitted evidence to the trial court pursuant to Civ.R. 56. Included was evidence detailing that the bankruptcy court scheduled a hearing regarding the settlement of one of Mr. Oakley's claims against another bank. Mr. Nobile, who also represented Mr. Oakley in the bankruptcy, sent a letter about the hearing to Mr. Nolan. Mr. Nobile related in the letter that Mr. Oakley was in the process of finalizing a deal to sell certain real property. Mr. Nolan then contacted the bankruptcy trustee to alert her to the sale of the real property. Mr. Nolan also faxed the trustee a copy of a newspaper article stating that Mr. Oakley had "closed" on the real property in question.

The bankruptcy trustee was interested in the real property at issue because of Mr. Oakley's alleged interest in it. Title to the real property was not in Mr. Oakley's name, but he owned fifty-four percent of the stock in the company that held title. The trustee wanted Mr. Oakley's interest in the sales proceeds from the real property to be deposited into the bankruptcy estate. She stated that Mr. Nolan informed her of the newspaper article on the property and about Mr. Oakley's attempts to sell "star bricks."

Mr. Oakley did not deny trying to sell the property at issue or the star bricks for his personal benefit. He also failed to contest or dispute the information set forth in the newspaper article that Mr. Nolan faxed to the bankruptcy trustee. Mr. Oakley claimed, however, that Mr. Nolan's communication to the bankruptcy trustee was intentionally false and defamatory. He also contended that his bankruptcy proceedings did not go favorably for him because of Mr. Nolan's actions.

After considering the aforementioned evidence, the trial court granted Mr. Nolan's and FNB's motion for summary judgment. Mr. Nolan and FNB then filed a motion for expenses and attorney's fees against Mr. Oakley and Mr. Nobile, alleging that Mr. Nobile's filing of the complaint at Mr. Oakley's request was frivolous. The trial court subsequently held a hearing on the matter wherein the parties stipulated to the evidence submitted on the motion for summary judgment. The trial court also heard testimony from several witnesses, summarized infra.

At the time Mr. Oakley filed the defamation suit, he knew Mr. Nolan had a conversation with the bankruptcy trustee about Mr. Oakley's company selling the aforementioned property. After this conversation, he felt that the trustee's behavior shifted. Mr. Oakley was not apprised of the bankruptcy trustee's thoughts until after he filed the defamation suit, when Mr. Nolan and FNB secured her affidavit for use in summary judgment proceedings; however, it appeared to Mr. Oakley and Mr. Nobile prior to the filing that Mr. Nolan's communications with the trustee were extensive and had negative consequences for Mr. Oakley.

Subsequent to filing the defamation suit, Mr. Oakley did not deny the truth of what Mr. Nolan claimed to have told the trustee, but Mr. Oakley believed that Mr. Nolan had related other things to the trustee that were not true. Mr. Oakley alleged he did not think that the real property in question and the star bricks were the property of the bankruptcy estate because they were not titled in his name. He also alleged he knew an attorney other than Mr. Nolan represented FNB in his bankruptcy case, and that Mr. Nolan never made an appearance in the bankruptcy case as counsel for FNB.

At the conclusion of the hearing, the trial court granted Mr. Nolan and FNB's request for expenses and attorney's fees against Mr. Oakley and Mr. Nobile, as it found frivolous conduct on their part in violation of R.C. 2323.51(A)(2)(a)(ii)-(iv). Mr. Oakley and Mr. Nobile now appeal this decision, asserting the following assignments of error:

1. THE TRIAL COURT COMMITTED AN ABUSE OF DISCRETION AND/OR ERROR AS A MATTER OF LAW WHEN IT GRANTED DEFENDANTS' MOTION FOR SANCTIONS.

2. THE TRIAL COURT COMMITTED ERROR AS A MATTER OF LAW WHEN IT DETERMINED THAT AN ATTORNEY AND THE PARTY BEING REPRESENTED, ALSO AN ATTORNEY, WERE BOTH ENTITLED TO LEGAL FEES PURSUANT TO §2323.51.

In their first assignment of error, Mr. Oakley and Mr. Nobile allege that the trial court abused its discretion when it granted Mr. Nolan and FNB's motion for sanctions. In their second assignment of error, they argue that the trial court erred when it determined that Mr. Nolan and FNB were entitled to attorney's fees. For ease of analysis, we will address these assignments of error jointly.

Sanctions are addressed in Civ.R. 11, which states, "every pleading, motion, or other document of a party represented by an attorney shall be signed by at least one attorney of record in the attorney's individual name." The attorney's signature constitutes certification by the attorney of the following: (1) that he or she has read the pleading, motion, or document; (2) that to the best of the attorney's knowledge, information, or belief, the pleading, motion, or document is supported by good grounds; and (3) that the pleading, motion, or document is not interposed for delay. See Civ.R. 11. If the rule is willfully violated, or if a scandalous or indecent matter has been inserted, the attorney can be subject to sanctions, including attorney fees. Id. Any violation must be willful; negligence is insufficient to invoke Civ.R. 11 sanctions. Id. Civ.R. 11 employs a subjective bad faith standard.

R.C. 2323.51 addresses sanctions and attorney's fees where frivolous conduct is at issue. HN3 Under R.C. 2323.51(A)(2)(a)(ii)-(iv), "frivolous conduct" is defined in the following manner:

> (a) Conduct of an inmate or other party to a civil action, of an inmate who has filed an appeal of the type described in division (A)(1)(b) of this section, or of the inmate's or other party's counsel of record that satisfies any of the following:
>
> (ii) It is not warranted under existing law, cannot be supported by a good faith argument for an extension, modification, or reversal of existing law, or cannot be supported by a good faith argument for the establishment of new law.
>
> (iii) The conduct consists of allegations or other factual contentions that have no evidentiary support or, if specifically so identified, are not likely to have evidentiary support after a reasonable opportunity for further investigation or discovery.
>
> (iv) The conduct consists of denials or factual contentions that are not warranted by the evidence or, if specifically so identified, are not reasonably based on a lack of information or belief.

The trial court's decision to impose sanctions pursuant to R.C. 2323.51 rests within its sound discretion and cannot be reversed absent an abuse of that discretion. An abuse of discretion connotes more than a mere error of law or judgment; rather, it implies an unreasonable, arbitrary, or unconscionable attitude on the part of the trial court.

The law concerning R.C. 2323.51 was advanced by the Second Appellate District in *Hickman v. Murray* (1996), Montgomery App. No. CA 15030, 1996 WL 125916, 1996 Ohio App. LEXIS 1028:

> "The statute is to be applied carefully so that legitimate claims are not chilled. *Beaver Excavating Co. v. Perry Twp.* (1992), 79 Ohio App.3d 148, 606 N.E.2d 1067. A party is not frivolous merely because a claim is not well-grounded in fact. Furthermore, the statute was not intended to punish mere misjudgment or tactical error. Instead, the statute was designed to chill egregious, overzealous, unjustifiable, and frivolous action.
> "Whether a claim is warranted under existing law is an objective consideration. The test, we find, is whether no reasonable lawyer would have brought the action in light of the existing law. In other words, a claim is frivolous if it is absolutely clear under the existing law that no reasonable lawyer could argue the claim."

1996 Ohio App. LEXIS 1028, at 13-14, 1996 WL 125916, at 5. Additionally, "when . . . reasonable inquiry by a party's counsel of record should reveal the inadequacy of a claim, a finding that the counsel of record has engaged in frivolous conduct is justified, as is an award, made within the statutory guidelines, to any party adversely affected by the frivolous conduct." *Ron Scheiderer & Assocs. v. City of London* (1998), 81 Ohio St.3d 94, 97, 689 N.E.2d 552, 1998 Ohio 453.

In the case sub judice, there was no evidentiary support for Mr. Oakley's defamation suit. Mr. Oakley never denied the truth of Mr. Nolan's communications to the bankruptcy trustee. He merely asserts that Mr. Nolan made additional defamatory remarks about him to the trustee. There is no support for this allegation in either Mr. Nolan's or the trustee's affidavit or elsewhere in the record. Reasonable inquiry by Mr. Nobile, as Mr. Oakley's counsel of record, would have revealed the inadequacy of the defamation claim, and thus, its frivolity. Therefore, the trial court's levy of sanctions was not an abuse of its discretion.

Likewise, the trial court's imposition of attorney's fees pursuant to R.C. 2323.51 was not an abuse of its discretion. As noted supra, awards made within statutory guidelines to a party affected by the frivolous conduct of another party are justified. Id. at 98. Additionally, Mr. Nolan and FNB called attorney William Walker to testify regarding the legal fees and expenses they incurred in defense of the suits filed by Mr. Oakley and Mr. Nobile. Mr. Walker testified that the legal fees and other expenses were reasonable. Mr. Oakley, by and through Mr. Nobile, did not object to Mr. Walker's testimony or the trial court's admission of Mr. Nolan's invoices. In fact, Mr. Nobile stipulated to the reasonableness of the time spent and the amount of the legal fees incurred. Because Mr. Oakley and Mr. Nobile did not object to the trial court's admission of these items into evidence, they have waived all but plain error. We find no error in the trial court's award, let alone plain error. As such, we overrule both of Mr. Oakley and Mr. Nobile's assigned errors.

In our view, the trial court did not abuse its discretion when it granted Mr. Nolan and FNB's motion for sanctions and awarded those parties reasonable attorney's fees. Accordingly, we affirm its judgment.
JUDGMENT AFFIRMED.

QUESTIONS ABOUT THE CASE:

1 Although the heart of this case involved a bankruptcy, how did a claim of defamation come up?

2 At the conclusion of the trial, why did the trial court award expenses and attorney's fees to Nolan?
3 How does Rule 11 (virtually identical to Federal Rule of Civil Procedure Rule 11) impact this case?
4 How do the rules define "frivolous conduct"?
5 According to the court, was there any evidentiary support for Oakley's claim of defamation against Nolan?

Chapter Summary

The process of evaluating a potential civil case involves many different elements. A case evaluation must take into account various factors, including the nature of the possible claim, the facts setting out the defendant's liability, the law, the likelihood of recovery, and the extent of the plaintiff's injuries. Rule 11 of the Federal Rules of Civil Procedure — or its analog found in most state court rules — requires that an attorney must investigate a claim before bringing it. This investigation must focus on the facts of the case and on a review of the applicable laws. Before a plaintiff can bring an action against a defendant, the plaintiff must have a cause of action. A cause of action is a legally recognized wrong committed against the plaintiff that entitles the plaintiff to recovery in a court of law.

In order to adequately investigate a claim, the law firm must first meet with the client and consult with him to gather as much information as possible. The initial client consultation will involve obtaining extensive information from the client, including the details of the plaintiff's injury, background on the plaintiff, and additional details. At the initial client consultation, the law firm will often obtain authorization forms that allow the law firm to collect copies of the client's medical and other personal files. This material is essential to an adequate review of the case. Additional investigation will be required before the lawsuit can be filed. This additional information will come in the form of review of accident or police reports and medical records and interviews with witnesses, among others. A paralegal must know some basic investigative techniques in the event that she is called upon to go to the scene and record important details.

SKILLS YOU NEED IN THE REAL WORLD

Investigating Accident Scenes

Go to the courthouse or your local paper and find a recent automobile accident. Investigate this case as though you were the paralegal assigned to it from your firm. What facts can you develop about the main players in the case? Is there a viable case? Would you recommend that your firm take this case? Provide specific examples and facts to justify your recommendation.

THE LIFE OF A PARALEGAL

Interviewing

For Jane Huffman, a litigation paralegal, preparing a case begins with a review of the police or accident reports. She reviews these extensively before speaking with any witnesses. "These reports can give you a lot of information about the case, and you can use it to test your witness's knowledge of the case. Before I speak with regular witnesses," says Jane, "I try to speak with the police officers involved."

Interviewing the police officers offers several advantages. "For one thing," she says, "police officers are trained to remember and record details. They can give you a lot information about the case in a short period of time." Jane follows a normal procedure when speaking with police officers. "First, I introduce myself and tell them right up front that I'm a paralegal and we're thinking about bringing a suit for client X." After that, "I ask the police officer if he has any drawings or photographs that will help me understand what happened." She is surprised how often they do. Then she tries to find out what they think about the case. A police officer may have developed a feel for the case by watching all of the people involved and can often tell a paralegal early on about a particular problem in the case.

Jane finds that most police officers are easy to talk to. "The attorney I work for has a good reputation in the community, and that helps." But there are some guidelines that she follows when she speaks with police officers. "For one thing," she says, "don't be too aggressive. Police officers, like everybody else, are turned off if you're too aggressive in your questions."

When Jane interviews witnesses in civil cases, she keeps in mind some basic rules. "First of all, always be honest and straightforward. I'll call the witness and tell them that the attorney asked me to call. I say we need some information about the case. Sometimes they talk to me, and sometimes they don't. Sometimes I call just to find out if they're willing to speak with us at all."

There are some questions that a paralegal can always expect to get from a witness. One of them involves whether they will have to testify. "I always tell them that I don't know if the case is going to go to court or not." Jane never promises that the witness will not have to testify. "At this stage, I don't know what is going to happen, and I tell them that. I try to get as much information as possible without pressing too hard. Some people just are not going to tell you anything." Later, the legal team may use subpoenas and scheduled deposition to get at what these people know, but it's always helpful to get as much information as early as possible in the process.

ETHICAL ISSUES FOR THE PARALEGAL

The Initial Meeting

One area that is filled with potential problems concerns the initial meeting with the client. We have already mentioned the dangers involved in unauthorized practice of law. This meeting is the most common place for a client to ask you a legal question, such as, "Does my case look good?" There is almost no way to answer this question without getting into some form of legal advice. When this question comes up, the safest course is to simply say that you can't give legal advice and leave it at that. However, not all clients will let the issue go so easily. They will ask what you think when they really want some assurance that things are going to work out all right. If you understand that the real reason behind this question is to seek assurance, you can speak to the client's real concerns and still avoid giving legal advice.

Websites

- **Reverse Phone Directory**
  www.reversephonedirectory.com
- **Locating Individuals — Yahoo!**
  www.people.yahoo.com
- **Whowhere People Search Engine**
  www.whowhere.com
- **InfoSpace**
  www.infospace.com

Key Terms

Case evaluation
Cause of action
Initial client meeting
Liability
Medical authorization
Rule 11
Skip tracing agency
Statute of limitation
Witness locator service

Review Questions

1. What are the preliminary steps to bringing a lawsuit?
2. Why is it important to evaluate a civil case before bringing it?
3. Explain the steps involved in evaluating a case.
4. Why should the nature of the claim have an impact on the decision about whether the law firm should accept the case?
5. Explain the steps involved in a factual analysis of a potential lawsuit.
6. What legal requirements are imposed on attorneys to conduct a thorough evaluation of the case prior to filing?
7. What is Rule 11, and what impact does it have on filing a lawsuit?
8. Explain the sanctions that can be imposed for violations of Rule 11.

9 How does an investigation into the defendant's liability affect the decision about whether to file the case?
10 What is a cause of action?
11 Explain how having very little likelihood of recovery can damage case evaluation.
12 Discuss how the existence or nonexistence of insurance can impact a case evaluation.
13 How do the plaintiff's injuries impact the case evaluation?
14 What is an initial client meeting?
15 What kind of information should the legal team obtain from a client during the initial client meeting?
16 What are medical authorizations?
17 What is HIPAA, and what impact does it have on obtaining medical authorizations?
18 Explain the statutes of limitations concerns in evaluating a case.
19 What kind of information can be gleaned from accident and police reports?
20 What information should be obtained from witnesses to the incident?
21 Why would state and federal courts impose such stringent requirements on attorneys to conduct such thorough investigations of cases before they are filed? Wouldn't it make more sense for the facts to come out as the case proceeds?
22 Why would a paralegal be called upon to conduct some basic investigation into a civil case? What type of investigation is detailed in this chapter? Would you feel confident conducting such investigations?

Applying What You Have Learned

1 Before you can carry out some basic investigative work, you need the right tools. Here are some things to pull together to form your own investigative tool kit:
- Tape recorder
- Still camera
- Video camera
- Hammer and nails
- Pen and paper
- 100′ tape measure
- 12″ ruler
- Extra tapes and batteries for all your machines
- Latex or rubber gloves

You should always have a tape recorder with you, even when you don't plan on talking to any witnesses. You'd be surprised to learn how many times a little trip to the accident scene for a couple of photos will turn up additional witnesses whom no one has spoken to.

Not all witnesses like to be recorded, and you shouldn't record anyone without permission. But tape recorders aren't just for witness interviews. When you go to the scene, you may not always have the time to sit down and write out your impressions. Instead, you may have to dictate what you see and transcribe it later.

We have already discussed the important need to visually document any scene that will have importance in a lawsuit. Although we tend to think of the importance of photos and video in automobile accidents, visual documentation is important in almost all cases. In contract cases, the issues often center on performance, or the lack thereof. A photo showing the level of completion can answer that question better than several live witnesses. In divorce cases, evidence of physical trauma from violence can offer dramatic testimony. Visual documentation should be an element of the prefiling research in all cases.

As far as photographs go, paralegals should take lots of them. When you do, you'll find that you can never shoot enough. Too much is better. Some paralegals deliberately fill an entire roll or two of film, just to make sure that every possible angle and element of the claim is documented.

Why should a hammer and nails be an important part of your investigative tool kit? Ask any private investigator. They routinely hammer a nail at the beginning of a skid mark and put another at the end of the skid mark. That way, even if the road is later paved over, they can use a metal detector to find skid marks. A hammer is also a useful tool for brushing away debris and other items that you don't necessarily want to put your hands in.

Rounding out your investigative toolbox, we have some of the more obvious items. You should never go anywhere without pen and paper. A 100-foot tape measure comes in handy for measuring. But if you have a measuring tape, why do you need a ruler? The ruler is important in order to give you some measuring technique for close-up photographs. Suppose you want to show the size and indentation of a gouge in the roadway or the size of blood stains on the front of the car. The problem with close-up pictures is that it is hard to get any perspective. By placing a ruler in the picture, you give the viewer a frame of reference.

Finally, you always need extra film, tapes, batteries, and chargers. Remember Murphy's law of recording equipment: If something can go wrong, it will, right when you are about to get something that will win the case. Finally, always have several pairs of surgical or rubber gloves handy. You never know when you may need to handle something that is either dirty or potentially harmful. Having several pairs of gloves handy will help keep your hands clean.

2 We have reviewed the case recently brought to us by Jane Doe. Our firm has reviewed the applicable law and does not feel that her claim of psychic distress, created by an overbearing boss and his obvious mental powers, is a sufficient cause of action. We must inform our client of this fact in such a way that she understands that we will not be representing her in this case, but also inform her that the statute of limitations for such an action, at least as she has described it, will run in three weeks. Create your own firm letterhead and draft a letter that explains these concerns as well as the decision not to accept the case.

3 Locate a fellow student who has been involved in a car accident. Interview this person, using the detail provided in this chapter as a guide to the comprehensive nature of your interview. Pretend that this student is a new client. Prepare a complete client questionnaire and include as much detail as possible about the incident.

4 Your firm has scheduled a meeting with a potential new client. When you and the attorney meet with the client, he describes the following facts:

> He works at a local factory, and his boss, who is female, has on several occasions touched him in what he describes as inappropriate ways. She often tells him that his skin is beautiful and that his eyes are the bluest that she has ever seen. She has recently promoted him to become her office assistant, even though he has very little office training. She schedules late evening meetings and tries to give him back rubs. The entire situation has made him uncomfortable. When he complained to the department supervisor, the supervisor told him that he was crazy and that a man can't bring a sexual harassment suit against a woman.
>
> Is this a case for sexual harassment, based on your own state's decision on the topic? Do we advise this client that, based on our review of the applicable law, this is a case we will take or one that we will turn down?

Endnotes

[1]Idaho R.Civ.Pro. Rule 11.
[2]IL ST CH 735 §5/13-202.

4 Civil Complaints

Chapter Objectives

- Identify the basic components of a complaint
- Describe the important procedural rules that affect how complaints are drafted
- Explain subject matter jurisdiction
- Define the term *limited jurisdiction* and how it applies to federal courts
- Explain the requirements of capacity and standing in civil suits
- Define the "case or controversy" requirement
- Identify the importance of the concepts of mootness and ripeness
- Describe the caption or style of a complaint
- Explain the importance of notice pleading
- Define the role of factual allegations in a complaint

I INTRODUCTION

In this chapter, we will examine the issues that surround commencing a civil action, including jurisdictional questions, standing, and other legal elements of complaints. We will also examine the elements of a complaint, explaining the significance of each feature and showing how a complaint raises a legal claim against the defendant.

PARTIES

Plaintiff
The party who has a cause of action; the person who initiates a suit against another

Defendant
The party who is named in the complaint and against whom the plaintiff has a cause of action

Before we can discuss the issues pertinent to filing a complaint, we must answer a basic question: Who are the parties to a lawsuit? The easiest answer is that the **plaintiff** is the party who files suit, and the **defendant** is the party who is served with the complaint. But that answer does not provide sufficient detail. We also need to know how someone becomes a plaintiff and what rules govern how and when a person can be sued. We will begin by defining the term *party* and then proceed to the issues that give a party the right to claim a legally recognized injury so that he can be called *plaintiff.*

Under the federal rules, the definition of a *party* is relatively simple. A party is one who seeks relief or against whom relief is sought. Under this definition, a party can be a person, a business, a government entity, or even a corporation. Any of these can sue or be sued. This definition also does not limit itself to the named plaintiffs and defendants. Anyone who has an interest in the proceedings can be a party in a federal civil action. As we will see in later chapters, simply because a plaintiff brings suit against a specific defendant does not mean that other parties are barred from entering the action. Under the theories of cross-claims, interpleader, and impleader, additional parties may join the action. However, in order to become officially designated as a defendant, some procedural issues must be satisfied, including service of process. We will discuss service of process later in this chapter.

In any lawsuit, there must be two adverse parties. If the court dismisses the case against the defendant, the suit is dismissed. This is true in situations where there is more than one defendant and each is eliminated from the case. Without adverse parties, there can be no suit.

JURISDICTIONAL ISSUES IN CIVIL SUITS

One of the first points that a plaintiff must establish is that a court has the power to hear the action contemplated. At its simplest, *jurisdiction* refers to a court's power to make rulings that are binding on the parties involved. Jurisdiction comes in many forms. Before a court can make binding decisions, it must have two basic forms of jurisdiction: personal and subject matter.

A. PERSONAL JURISDICTION

Personal jurisdiction
A court's power over the individuals involved in the case; when a court has personal jurisdiction, it can compel attendance at court hearings and enter judgments against the parties.

Before a court can consider the issues involved in any suit, the judge must make a determination that she has **personal jurisdiction** over the parties. Personal jurisdiction is the power of the court to create binding decrees on the parties and to enforce those court orders on all parties. A court does not acquire personal jurisdiction simply because the court exists. Instead, the plaintiff must investigate the issues in the case, carry out legal research, and then name the basis of personal jurisdiction in the complaint to establish that the court has personal jurisdiction over all of the parties.

Personal jurisdiction can be established by any number of methods. The important basis of any allegation of personal jurisdiction is that, at some time, the defendant had contact with the geographic area where the court is located. That geographic component gives the court the power to fashion orders that require the defendant to appear in court, answer pleadings, and, ultimately, to pay any judgment assessed against him. This means that personal jurisdiction has both a geographic and a legal basis. The geographic basis, referred to as the *forum*, requires that the defendant must have either lived, worked, or done business within the geographic boundaries of the court. Let's suppose that a particular court's forum is contained within a single county. In order for the court to exercise personal jurisdiction over the defendant, the plaintiff must show that the defendant had a presence within that county. That establishes the forum where the court's authority can be expressed.

The legal basis of personal jurisdiction is the consideration of how the court can determine that the defendant had sufficient contacts within the county to make it fair to sue the defendant there and also to require the defendant to appear before that court. There are several different legal tests that courts can use to justify personal jurisdiction over the defendant. They include the defendant's:

- presence;
- domicile;
- consent; and
- minimum contacts.

1. PRESENCE

The simplest and most obvious way to establish that the court has personal jurisdiction over the defendant is for the defendant to be physically located within the court's forum. Physical presence automatically gives the court personal jurisdiction over the parties. This is true even if the defendant is within the jurisdiction for a limited period of time. If the plaintiff can show that the defendant was served with a copy of the summons and complaint while the defendant was in the forum, then the court has personal jurisdiction over that defendant. The court can then require that the defendant appear for future court hearings and can sanction the defendant if she fails to appear.

2. DOMICILE

Another way that a plaintiff can establish the court's personal jurisdiction over the defendant is to prove that the defendant is domiciled in the forum. **Domicile** is the legal term for a residence. If the defendant has a residence in the area, that can be sufficient to establish personal jurisdiction. A domicile is something more than mere presence in a state. In order to qualify under domicile, a person must reside in a specific location and have the intent to remain there indefinitely.

Domicile
A person's residence

3. CONSENT

Another method to establish the court's personal jurisdiction over the defendant is by the defendant's consent. If the defendant agrees to appear in court and submits himself to the court's authority, then the defendant has consented to personal jurisdiction and waived any objection.

4. MINIMUM CONTACTS

The last category used to establish personal jurisdiction over the defendant is based on a legal test created in the case that has been the bane of law students' existence for decades: *International Shoe Co. v. Washington*, 326 U.S. 310, 66 S.Ct. 154, 90 L.Ed. 95 (1945). In a long and complicated opinion, the U.S. Supreme Court established that a court can acquire personal jurisdiction over a commercial enterprise when it has had sufficient minimum contacts with the forum to make it reasonable for the defendant to answer lawsuits there. The premise here is that the defendant has had business contacts within the forum, has had the advantage of profits, and has even paid taxes in the forum; therefore, it is not unreasonable to require said defendant to answer a complaint in the same forum.

Special appearance
A temporary appearance authorized by the Rules of Civil Procedure that allows a defendant to contest a court's personal jurisdiction without submitting to it through the challenge

5. SPECIAL APPEARANCE

A defendant who wishes to challenge a court's personal jurisdiction may do so through a **special appearance**. When the defendant comes before the court through the vehicle of a special appearance, she contests the court's power to enter any order in the matter,

Tech Topic
FORMS

There are numerous sources to obtain forms for nearly every type of civil filing it is possible to bring. You can search through various online sources and find a plethora of forms. Some of these forms are in PDF format, provided by the local or state court system. Others are completed or sample legal filings. There are even companies that advertise sample civil forms that are "legal in all 50 states." With the exception of blank forms provided by the court system, you should view all sample pleadings and forms with skepticism. The same holds true for the more traditional method of disseminating forms: form books. A form or sample pleading is only as good as the person who put it together. Although you can certainly review sample pleadings in other cases as a guide in your own case, never rely on them exclusively. This is especially true for any company producing forms that claim to be valid through the country. There is such a wide variation in legal practice from state to state that it is virtually impossible to create any form that is valid in every state court, from Alaska to Florida. In the end, you must rely on your own state or federal Rules of Civil Procedure, statutes, and case law. There is no perfect sample pleading that will work in every case.

without simultaneously triggering personal jurisdiction through the appearance. Consider the implications for a defendant who, in contesting personal jurisdiction, unwittingly submits to it. By making a special appearance before the court, defendants insulate themselves from a claim that they have opened themselves up to the court's personal jurisdiction simply by appearing before the court to contest its authority. Without this ability, a defendant would be faced with two grim possibilities: (1) fail to appear in court, have judgment entered against her, then attempt to attack the judgment when the plaintiff seeks to enforce it, or (2) appear in court to contest the action and by so doing submit to the court's personal jurisdiction. A special appearance avoids both of these unpleasant alternatives. If a court should rule that it has no personal jurisdiction over the defendant, the defendant may have the case dismissed, and the plaintiff will be forced to refile in a jurisdiction that does have authority over the defendant.

B. SUBJECT MATTER JURISDICTION

In addition to establishing personal jurisdiction over the defendant, the plaintiff must also prove that the court has **subject matter jurisdiction** over the issues in the case. Subject matter jurisdiction is the power of the court to hear certain types of cases. Federal courts, and many state courts, are circumscribed by limited jurisdiction. They are permitted to hear only specific types of cases, and if the plaintiff cannot prove that the court is empowered to hear the issues in his case, the court will dismiss the suit.

Subject matter jurisdiction The power of a court to entertain specific legal actions and to make rulings on those issues

1. GENERAL JURISDICTION COURTS

All states have at least one court that is empowered to hear a broad range of lawsuits, from divorces to personal injuries to contested wills. These are referred to as *general jurisdiction courts*. They have subject matter jurisdiction over a wide variety of cases. In many states, this court is referred to as *superior court*. The state legislature has granted superior court this wide general jurisdiction in order to provide a mechanism for litigants. In some situations, superior court may have transferred the authority to hear certain types of cases to other courts. For instance, when a superior court authorizes the creation of a small-claims court, it transfers its jurisdictional power to that court. In situations involving claims below a specific amount, such as $1,000, small-claims court would then be authorized to hear those cases. If we were to diagram the subject matter jurisdiction of superior court, we would see that it was originally vested with general jurisdiction, then transferred a portion of its jurisdictional power to another court, creating a court of limited jurisdiction.

2. LIMITED JURISDICTION COURTS

A court of limited jurisdiction is empowered to hear only certain types of cases. On the state level, small-claims court is an excellent example. When a person wishes to sue another for a small amount of money, it must take the case to small-claims court because that is the court that is specifically empowered to hear such cases. If the litigants have a case involving other issues, then they would be required to file their suit in a court of general jurisdiction.

Limited jurisdiction courts are significant in that they can consider only specific issues. Although all states have at least one court of general jurisdiction, limited jurisdiction courts are the rule, not the exception, in federal court.

Article III of the U.S. Constitution authorizes the creation of the federal court system, but it also imposes restrictions on that court system. For one thing, all federal courts are courts of limited jurisdiction. Federal courts are only empowered to hear cases that fall within certain specified classifications, including:

- federal question;
- diversity of citizenship; and
- amount in controversy.

a. Federal Question

Federal courts are specifically authorized to consider questions involving the application of the U.S. Constitution or the U.S. Code. In order to bring a case within the confines of federal court, the plaintiff must prove that the federal court has subject matter jurisdiction. The practical result of this rule is that the plaintiff's preliminary allegations in a federal complaint are more detailed than those typically found in a state court complaint. After all, the state court will often be a court of general jurisdiction, giving it broad discretion to hear a wide variety of issues. Federal courts, on the other hand, have always been courts of limited jurisdiction, and given a general interpretation against granting federal jurisdiction, the plaintiff must specifically prove federal jurisdiction at the outset of the lawsuit.

b. Diversity of Citizenship

Diversity cases involve lawsuits between citizens of different states or territories. Because of the potential for abuse and the wide disparity between state-based laws, requiring the suit to be brought in federal court only makes sense. All federal courts follow the same procedures and are at least arguably free of local prejudices in favor of one litigant or the other.

The rules about establishing citizenship resemble and are actually based on the rules we previously discussed concerning domicile. If a plaintiff is domiciled in one state and the defendant is domiciled in another, then that will satisfy the diversity of citizenship rule to invoke federal court jurisdiction.

c. Amount in Controversy

However, diversity of citizenship does not always guarantee that a federal court will accept a particular case. There are additional requirements. For instance, the plaintiff must also establish a minimum monetary threshold before the federal courts will become involved. In order to bring a case in federal court, the plaintiff must prove that the amount in controversy between the parties exceeds $75,000, not counting court costs and interest. The plaintiff must make an allegation in the complaint that his damages exceed this amount and that the parties are domiciled in different states before the federal court would be authorized to hear the case.

When considering the complexities of federal cases, the question often arises about the interplay between subject matter jurisdiction and personal jurisdiction. Proof of one does not negate the requirement of proof of the other. The plaintiff must prove both subject matter and personal jurisdiction before federal court jurisdiction is triggered (Fig. 4-1). If a plaintiff can establish one but not the other, a federal judge would be forced to dismiss the plaintiff's complaint.

FIGURE 4-1

Federal Court Jurisdiction

(a) The district courts shall have original jurisdiction of all civil actions where the matter in controversy exceeds the sum or value of $75,000, exclusive of interest and costs, and is between —

(1) citizens of different states;

(2) citizens of a state and citizens or subjects of a foreign state . . . ;

(3) citizens of different states and in which citizens or subjects of a foreign state are additional parties; and

(4) a foreign state, defined in section 1603(a) of this title, as plaintiff and citizens of a state or of different states.[1]

Consider the following example: Anna has a claim against Stewart. They are both citizens of different states and have clearly established domiciles in different states. Anna wishes to bring her claim in federal court because she has heard that these courts are generally more favorable to plaintiffs. Can Anna establish subject matter jurisdiction in federal court?

Answer: No. Anna must establish diversity of citizenship and that her claim involves an amount of at least $75,000. Without such proof, a federal court will not consider the case.

d. Pendent and Ancillary Jurisdiction

What happens in cases where there are multiple issues, some of which clearly fall within a federal court's jurisdiction and some that do not? Put another way, does the fact that some of the claims do not satisfy federal jurisdiction mean that none of the claims can be heard in federal court?

If a party can establish that some of her claims fall under federal subject matter, then that party can take advantage of the concepts of pendent and ancillary jurisdiction in order to have all claims heard in one court. This negates the only other option: that the parties would litigate some of their claims in federal court and some in state court. That would be an unnecessary duplication of effort and result in an unnecessary waste of time and effort, especially when the claims are all related to one another.

Ancillary jurisdiction is the power of a federal court to consider issues that do not technically fall within the court's subject matter jurisdiction but are part of other claims that do. In such a case, the court would be authorized to make rulings on closely related issues. Ancillary jurisdiction involves parties. As we have already seen, one of the basic requirements of a federal action is that there is diversity of citizenship between the parties. If a defendant wishes to bring a claim against a third party but that third party is a resident of the same state, ancillary jurisdiction allows cross-claims against individuals who would ordinarily not meet the minimum federal requirements. In such a case, the plaintiff would be from State A, the defendant from State B, and the third-party defendant also from State B. We will discuss third-party complaints and related issues in the next chapter.

Where ancillary jurisdiction focuses on the parties, *pendent jurisdiction* focuses on the nature of the claims. Once the plaintiff has established subject matter jurisdiction on some of the claims, he can rely on pendent jurisdiction to request that the court rule on other, closely linked issues, even when they do not technically meet the requirements of federal jurisdiction. Because the claims are closely linked to one another, the court can rely on pendent jurisdiction to make final determinations on all. Both ancillary and pendent jurisdiction require that the claims be closely interlinked with one another. If they are not, then the federal court will refuse to consider them and insist that the parties bring a separate state action to resolve them.

e. Exclusive Jurisdiction

Exclusive jurisdiction
The authorization of a specific court to hear particular actions

When we say that a court has **exclusive jurisdiction**, it means that a particular action must be brought in a specific court. When a business or person wishes to file bankruptcy, for example, the court with exclusive jurisdiction is the U.S. bankruptcy court. Similarly, on the state level, cases involving particular disputes, from child support to cases where the amount in controversy are above a specific amount, must be brought in the court that possesses the appropriate exclusive jurisdiction.

f. Removal

Removal
The transfer of a case from a state court to a federal court

In situations where a state action has commenced but the state judge determines that the issues actually qualify under federal jurisdiction, the judge is authorized to transfer the case to federal court. This is called **removal**. A defendant has the right to file for removal by bringing a motion requesting it. This motion must allege that although the case was filed in state court, it properly requires federal court jurisdiction. A defendant might file a motion to remove a case where she is domiciled in another state and the claim involves $75,000 or more. In that case, the minimum federal threshold would be met and the case would then qualify for federal court (Fig. 4-2).

(a) Except as otherwise expressly provided by Act of Congress, any civil action brought in a State court of which the district courts of the United States have original jurisdiction, may be removed by the defendant or the defendants, to the district court of the United States for the district and division embracing the place where such action is pending. For purposes of removal under this chapter, the citizenship of defendants sued under fictitious names shall be disregarded.[2]

FIGURE 4-2

Actions Removable Generally

C. IN REM JURISDICTION

Although our discussion has centered on personal and subject matter jurisdiction, it is important to note that although these are the most common types of jurisdiction, they are not the only forms. For instance, in some situations the fact that the defendant owns property in a particular venue may be enough to submit him to the jurisdiction of the court, at least for some matters. Basing jurisdiction on the location of real property is referred to as **in rem jurisdiction**.

In rem jurisdiction
Jurisdiction based on the property located within the forum

D. CONCURRENT JURISDICTION

There are times when a party may have the right to bring an action in one of several possible courts. Suppose that a plaintiff located in one state wishes to bring a civil action against a defendant located in another state. The plaintiff may bring this as a federal action, based on diversity of citizenship, or may travel to the defendant's home state and bring the action there. **Concurrent jurisdiction** is a term that encompasses a situation where more than one court has the power to hear a particular matter. In such a case, the plaintiff may decide to choose one court over another because the rules or applicable laws weigh more in the plaintiff's favor. As we have already seen, however, when a plaintiff brings a case in state court where federal courts have concurrent jurisdiction, the defendant may have the case transferred to federal court.

Concurrent jurisdiction
When two or more courts have contemporaneous jurisdiction over a civil action

IV CAPACITY AND STANDING

Once the jurisdictional issues have been resolved, a plaintiff must also establish other legal prerequisites, including the parties' capacity and the plaintiff's standing, to bring the suit.

A. CAPACITY

In all civil suits, the parties must have the capacity to know and understand the legal effect of the claim. *Capacity* is a word that is used in different ways throughout the law.

Capacity to enter into a contract is not the same as the capacity necessary to make a will. In civil cases, capacity takes on yet another meaning. In order to initiate a complaint, the plaintiff must establish that she is free of a legal disability, such as insanity, incompetence, or infancy. In any of these situations, the plaintiff would be unable to prove the ability to know and understand the consequences of bringing suit. In fact, in situations where the plaintiff has been declared mentally incompetent or is under the age of 18, the courts will presume that the plaintiff lacks capacity and dismiss the case.

Unlike most other aspects of a civil suit, there is no requirement to list a party's capacity in the complaint. Instead, if capacity becomes an issue, the other party can raise it once the suit has commenced (Fig. 4-3).

FIGURE 4-3

Federal Rules of Civil Procedure, Rule 9(a) Capacity

(a) Capacity or Authority to Sue; Legal Existence.

(1) In General. Except when required to show that the court has jurisdiction, a pleading need not allege:

(A) a party's capacity to sue or be sued;
(B) a party's authority to sue or be sued in a representative capacity; or
(C) the legal existence of an organized association of persons that is made a party.

(2) Raising Those Issues. To raise any of those issues, a party must do so by a specific denial, which must state any supporting facts that are peculiarly within the party's knowledge.

Capacity is listed as a separate element because courts consider it independently of other questions such as cause of action or other action. As is often seen in other situations, when a person lacks the ability to understand the legal action, the courts are short-circuited from taking any further action. Before any developments in the case, the court must be satisfied that the parties understand what is occurring.[3]

Is capacity an issue when dealing with businesses? Certainly. A corporation that has been dissolved lacks the capacity to be sued in the same way that a natural person who has been declared mentally incompetent lacks capacity to be sued.[4] Because corporations are artificial persons, the fact that they no longer legally exist is an issue of capacity. Other business models, especially ones that do not enjoy the recognition of "artificial person" under statutory laws, have different capacity issues. In those situations, the plaintiff normally sues the natural persons who make up the business, not the business itself.

SEARCH SUGGESTION • RULES OF CIVIL PROCEDURE

Before you ever begin developing a case for possible litigation, it is important to have a solid grasp of the Rules of Civil Procedure. These rules exist on both the state and federal levels, and you—like the attorney—must know every rule that has any bearing on your case. Failure to adhere strictly to the rules can have disastrous consequences, such as dismissal of pleadings in the case and court sanctions. The Rules of Civil Procedure are available in print form, as part of your state code, and online. Many paralegals find it convenient to purchase a copy of the Rules of Civil Procedure as a separate printing. That makes it easier to locate specific rules and to include your own notations beside the rules.

When a plaintiff or defendant lacks capacity, it does not mean that he is unable to be a party in a suit; it simply means that he must have a representative appointed to represent his interests. That representative must be appointed by a court and must act with the party's best interests in mind.

PRACTICE POINTER ▶ BEGIN WITH THE END IN MIND

When the firm decides to take on a new case, you should always begin the case with the end in mind. For litigation purposes, the end is the trial. Your preparation should anticipate potential trial issues. Although most civil cases settle, you should act as though each case you handle will definitely go to trial. With that in mind, you will find yourself focusing on visual aids, such as photographs and diagrams that will show the jury important information. You will also need to record as much detail as possible. If you receive evidence from a client, keep it in a safe place. It may be used during the trial, and there could be a question concerning tampering with the evidence. Prepare the client for the real prospect that the case will take a long time to resolve, especially if it goes to trial.

B. STANDING

Standing is a separate issue from capacity to sue. When a person has standing, she can establish that a particular court has the constitutional power to hear the case and that one or more of the plaintiff's guaranteed rights have been infringed upon or that the plaintiff has a property interest that will suffer as the result of another's actions. Standing ensures that the persons who bring actions have some stake in the outcome. It is not enough for a party to claim that a court's decision might eventually impact her potential rights; the party must show that the certain, specific actions are having an adverse effect on the party.

Standing
The requirement that a party to a suit have a legally recognized interest in the proceedings or that a party's rights will be infringed upon by the rulings in the litigation

In federal court, establishing standing has two parts: The plaintiff must show (1) that the federal court has the authority to resolve the dispute and (2) that the party's constitutional, financial, or property rights are involved.[5] The reason that standing is a requirement has mostly to do with the underlying theories of the separation of powers among the three branches of government. Requiring a party to establish standing places the court outside the realm of actively seeking out potential government problems and hypothetical issues. Instead, the court concerns itself with concrete controversies between real parties and leaves it to the other branches to anticipate problems and create solutions for them.[6] Under these rules, a plaintiff must prove to the court three different elements. The first is that he has suffered an "injury in fact."

1. ELEMENTS OF STANDING

Courts have defined the concept of injury in fact as an invasion of a legally protected interest that is "concrete and particularized." This excludes hypothetical questions, advisory opinions, and other issues that have not yet been brought before the court by litigants.[7] Other courts have defined standing by a requirement that the plaintiff must have suffered a distinct and palpable injury. Without such a showing, the plaintiff lacks standing and the case will be dismissed. But simply showing an injury in fact is only the first step in establishing standing.

Once the plaintiff has established an injury in fact, the courts will next look to the causal connection between the injury that the plaintiff is complaining about and the conduct of the defendant. We all know of situations where individuals receive terrible injuries, but there is no one for them to sue. Natural disasters are an excellent example. A hurricane or earthquake can cause widespread and terrible damages, but at the end of the day, an injured person will be hard-pressed to establish standing for a suit against a particular individual for these injuries.

The third and final element of standing involves the prospect that a court decision will likely resolve the issue. This does not mean that the plaintiff must prove his case before it has even begun, but the plaintiff must establish that a court decision will have an impact on the case (Fig. 4-4). This third element explains why third parties cannot sue in the names of friends or relatives: The court's decision, whatever it might be, will have no direct effect on the third party. In such a case, the friend or family member must sue in his own name or through a personal representative appointed for that purpose.

FIGURE 4-4

Standing — Rule 17, Federal Rules of Civil Procedure

(a) Real Party in Interest.

(1) Designation in General. An action must be prosecuted in the name of the real party in interest. The following may sue in their own names without joining the person for whose benefit the action is brought:

(A) an executor;
(B) an administrator;
(C) a guardian;
(D) a bailee;
(E) a trustee of an express trust;
(F) a party with whom or in whose name a contract has been made for another's benefit; and
(G) a party authorized by statute.

Sidebar

In order to establish standing, a party must have "alleged such a personal stake in the outcome of the controversy as to assure that concrete adverseness which sharpens the presentation of issues upon which the court so largely depends for illumination of difficult constitutional questions."[8]

Consider the following example: Debbie and Dawn were married two years under the provisions of New Hampshire's civil union statute. Last month, they were granted a final divorce by a local judge. A citizens' group filed suit against the judge, challenging the judicial decree on the basis that homosexual unions offend contemporary community standards. They based their standing on the fact that they are "concerned citizens." The judge has sought dismissal on the grounds that the group lacks standing. How is the court likely to rule?

Answer: The court will dismiss the suit because the citizens' group has failed to establish standing.[9]

2. CASE OR CONTROVERSY REQUIREMENT

Closely intertwined with the requirement of standing is the case or controversy requirement, one of the few guidelines provided to the federal court system in Article III of the U.S. Constitution. Under that article, which has been adopted in whole or in part by every state constitution, a court only has the power to hear "cases" or "controversies." These words have been interpreted to mean situations where the parties have standing and where the issue between the parties has reached a stage where court intervention is proper (Fig. 4-5).

The judicial power shall extend to all cases, in law and equity, arising under this Constitution, the laws of the United States, and treaties made, or which shall be made, under their authority; — to all cases affecting ambassadors, other public ministers and consuls; — to all cases of admiralty and maritime jurisdiction; — to controversies to which the United States shall be a party; — to controversies between two or more states; — between a state and citizens of another state; — between citizens of different states; — between citizens of the same state claiming lands under grants of different states, and between a state, or the citizens thereof, and foreign states, citizens or subjects.

FIGURE 4-5

Article III, Section 2, U.S. Constitution

As you can see, courts labor under specific limitations that prevent them from taking all cases filed. In addition to the requirement that the plaintiff must prove standing, there are also the issues of ripeness and mootness.

a. Ripeness Doctrine

The ripeness doctrine requires that the issues in the case have reached a point where court intervention is proper. Federal courts, and many state courts, will refuse to hear hypothetical cases. They require that there be actual litigants with specific, concrete complaints against one another. Under the ripeness doctrine, if the issues have not progressed to the point where a court order is warranted, the judge is authorized to dismiss the case and order the parties to refile in the future when the issues have progressed to that stage.

Consider the following example: Mary and Andy are married but considering divorce. Andy files a petition seeking a court order establishing his rights to the vacation home that the couple owns. He would like to have his title established so that he'll know for sure whether he owns half of the property. How does the court rule?

Answer: The court will refuse to rule because the issues in this case are not ripe. There is no divorce action pending, and until there is, the court will not rule on speculations. When the parties actually file a divorce action, then the issues will be ripe and the court can rule about the disposition of the marital property.

b. Mootness Doctrine

In many ways, mootness is the opposite of ripeness. Under the ripeness doctrine, a court will not consider issues until they are actually being litigated. Under the mootness doctrine, the court will refuse to hear a case because the issues have already been resolved. The court will base a decision to dismiss a case on mootness when there is no longer a valid, pending controversy between the parties.

Consider the following hypothetical situation: Terry has suffered irreparable brain damage, and her husband wishes to take her off life support. Her parents sue to have the life support system left on, but while the case is pending, Terry dies. Terry's parents would still like the court to rule because it would set a precedent for parental rights in other cases. What action does the court take?

Answer: The court dismisses the case because of mootness. Because Terry is no longer alive, the only issue pending in this case is now moot. The court will not continue to consider the matter, even if the case has broad national importance. Instead, the court will wait to tackle the issue in a future case where the patient is still alive.

c. Advisory Opinions

Federal and most state courts also refuse to give advisory opinions, under the same principles that underlie the doctrines of ripeness and mootness. The courts have no desire to anticipate problems or to commit themselves to rulings before the litigants have actually brought them. Although there are some state appellate courts that will give advisory opinions under limited circumstances, the vast majority delay any ruling until the full facts and pleadings are presented to the court for review.

V THE ELEMENTS OF A COMPLAINT

Our discussions so far have centered on the prerequisites to initiating a civil action. In the last chapter, we examined the legal research and factual investigation that must be carried out to support a complaint. In the early part of this chapter, we saw that there are many different legal issues that must be established before the complaint can be brought. In this section, we will examine the specific elements of a complaint. We will analyze each aspect of a complaint, from beginning to end, explaining the significance of each and how these elements come together to initiate a civil suit.

The basis of our discussion centers on the complaint that might appear in any civil case. We use the example of a personal injury because such actions are among the most common types of lawsuits brought in the United States today and because these complaints do not raise too many complex issues. In future chapters, we will discuss more detailed pleadings, including answers, cross-claims, counterclaims, interpleader, and impleader.

A. IDENTIFICATION OF COURT

The first element of a complaint is the correct heading identifying the court where the action is brought. This entry must list the court by its correct name.

B. STYLE OR CAPTION OF A COMPLAINT

One of the first issues for the legal team is to determine the appropriate caption of the civil suit. In this regard, both the plaintiff and the defendant must be identified in the correct, legal capacity. For persons, this means their full legal name, whether as defendant or plaintiff. Where there are multiple parties, all must be listed (Fig. 4-6).

FIGURE 4-6

Caption with Multiple Parties

IN THE SUPERIOR COURT OF BURKE COUNTY
STATE OF GRACE

CHARLES DICKENS,	)	
	)	
Plaintiff,	)	CIVIL ACTION NUMBER: ___________
	)	
vs.	)	COMPLAINT
	)	JURY TRIAL DEMANDED
	)	
SCROOGE & MARLOWE, INC.	)	
ROBERT CRATCHIT,	)	
TIMOTHY CRATCHIT.	)	
	)	
Defendants.	)	
	)	
______________________________	)	

Complaint

The caption of a complaint must set out and correctly identify all parties; however, the rules change slightly when there are multiple parties to be identified in other pleadings. In those situations, the legal team can simply list the full names of the plaintiff and the defendant (Fig. 4-7).

FIGURE 4-7

Names of Parties in Complaint; Names in Other Pleadings (California)

In the complaint, the title of the action shall include the names of all the parties; but, except as otherwise provided by statute or rule of the Judicial Council, in other pleadings it is sufficient to state the name of the first party on each side with an appropriate indication of other parties.[10]

The purpose of the caption (or style) is to identify all parties to the action, both plaintiffs and defendants. As such, the caption must correctly spell and designate each party. As you will notice in Figure 4-8, each party is designated by full legal name and with the suffix "plaintiff" or "defendant." This eliminates any possibility of confusion over the precise parties in the case.

FIGURE 4-8

§422.30. Caption; Contents (California)

(a) Every pleading shall contain a caption setting forth:

(1) The name of the court and county in which the action is brought.

(2) The title of the action.

(b) In a limited civil case, the caption shall state that the case is a limited civil case, and the clerk shall classify the case accordingly.[11]

1. BUSINESSES AS PARTIES

Businesses can be parties in civil actions; however, the rules about naming business are more complicated than those that apply to persons. For instance, a business might be formed under one name but doing business under another. In such a situation, the legal team must ensure that the proper name is used in the pleadings.

2. PLEA OF MISNOMER

Later, we will address the issues that arise when a defendant is incorrectly named in the suit. A defendant has the right to file a motion with the court requesting dismissal or other appropriate remedy when she has been incorrectly identified. We will discuss pleas of misnomer and other motions in Chapter 8.

3. DECEASED PARTIES

Individuals cannot sue on behalf of deceased persons, nor can an action be brought against a person who has died.[12] In either situation, the right to sue or be sued dies with the person — although states often have survivors' statutes that do allow an heir or guardian to continue a case originally brought by a party who has since died. There are also situations where family members and others can maintain an action based on the death of a person, such as a wrongful death claim. In such a situation, the person is suing based on the impact the other person's death had on him, not because a dead person can maintain a suit.

4. FUGITIVES

In a similar vein, a fugitive from justice is also not permitted to bring suit against another. To allow a contrary ruling would put the court in an unusual situation: On the one hand, there is an outstanding warrant for a person that must be served. On the other hand, the court would have to allow a person who has flaunted justice in one context to employ it in another. In order to avoid this dilemma, courts simply bar fugitives from bringing suit.[13]

C. TITLE OF ACTION

Federal and state courts have adopted rules concerning "notice" pleading. Under these rules, a party must correctly entitle her action and must provide sufficient detail to put the other party on notice as to the exact nature of the claim and the facts that support it. The first time that notice pleading rears its head in a complaint is with the title of the action.

The civil suit must be correctly identified. Although we have used the term *complaint* to describe the pleading that sets out the plaintiff's wrong against the defendant, not all jurisdictions follow this rule. For instance, in some states, the document filed by the plaintiff is referred to as a *petition*. By whatever name, the purpose of the pleading remains the same: to set out the claims against the defendant and the facts that the plaintiff claims support his demands against the defendant. For the sake of clarity, we will use the term *complaint* to describe such a document.

D. ALLEGATION OF JURISDICTION

The actual wording of the pleadings is governed by Rule 8, or its state equivalent. Under that rule, pleadings must be short, concise, and put the other party on notice of all the claims. As you can see in Figure 4-9, Rule 8 requires a "short and plain statement" setting out the court's jurisdiction and an equally short and plain statement regarding the claims and relief sought.

FIGURE 4-9

Federal Rules of Civil Procedure, Rule 8. General Rules of Pleading

(a) Claim for Relief. A pleading that states a claim for relief must contain:

(1) a short and plain statement of the grounds for the court's jurisdiction, unless the court already has jurisdiction and the claim needs no new jurisdictional support;
(2) a short and plain statement of the claim showing that the pleader is entitled to relief; and
(3) a demand for the relief sought, which may include relief in the alternative or different types of relief.

The basis of Rule 8 of the federal rules, and the various state rules that closely follow it, is that a party should receive as much information as possible from the pleadings. Rather than waiting for trial to reveal the facts of the case, modern civil practice is based on a theory of learning as much as possible about the case prior to trial. This theory underlies not only notice pleading but also the mechanics of discovery that we will examine in Chapter 7. This principle is amplified in other provisions of Rule 8, including (e), as seen in Figure 4-10.

FIGURE 4-10

Rule 8, Pleading to be Concise and Direct; Consistency

Each allegation must be simple, concise, and direct. No technical form is required.

Following the guidelines created in Rule 8, the first paragraph of a complaint sets out the plaintiff's contention that the court identified at the top of the document is the appropriate forum to consider the issues raised in the complaint. Because federal courts have limited jurisdiction, the plaintiff must set out specific allegations to satisfy the court that it does have such jurisdiction. In cases involving state courts, the plaintiff's jurisdictional allegation may contain only an allegation that the defendant is subject to the jurisdiction of the court because of domicile, as in Figure 4-11.

FIGURE 4-11

Jurisdictional Allegations in Complaint

Complaint

Plaintiff, by and through his attorneys, complains of the defendant as follows:

1 Plaintiff is, and all times hereafter was, a citizen and resident of the Town of New Haven, County of Berry, State of Anystate.

2 Plaintiff alleges upon information and belief that the defendant Rideway Transport Truck Company (Truck Company) is, and at all times hereafter was, a corporation organized and existing under the laws of the State of Anystate, licensed to do business, and in fact doing business, in the State of Anystate and having a registered agent for the service of process by the name of Darryl P. Putnam, located at 230 N. Tree Street, Suite 2000, New Haven, Anystate, 27401.

3 Plaintiff alleges upon information and belief that the defendant Martin W. Jerry is a citizen and resident of the County of Berry, State of Anystate.

E. FACTUAL CONTENTIONS

In the next paragraphs, which can vary in number considerably from complaint to complaint, the plaintiff slowly builds his case against the defendant by establishing the basic facts that the plaintiff contends resulted in his injury and that determine the defendant's legal responsibility for the action. The best practice in this regard is to separate different factual allegations into different paragraphs. For instance, consider Figure 4-12, where the plaintiff's attorney sets out each disparate set of facts as a separate paragraph. This has the benefit of satisfying the requirements of Rule 8, while also narrowing down the elements of the plaintiff's claim.

FIGURE 4-12

Specific Factual Allegations from Plaintiff's Complaint

4 That at all times relevant to this Complaint the defendant Martin W. Jerry was an agent, servant, and employee of the defendant Rideway Transport Truck Company (Truck Company) and was acting within the course and scope of his employment with it.
5 Truck Company, at the time of the accident, owned, maintained and used, a fourteen (14') foot tractor-trailer rig, license plate number PMH 3032, VIN JXR123456989.
6 Katie Street is a public street in the Town which runs in a north-south direction through the town of New Haven.
7 On May 23, of last year, at approximately 1:55 p.m., plaintiff was driving his automobile south on Katie Street. Defendant Martin Jerry was operating his tractor-trailer rig in the oncoming lane of traffic, in a northerly direction.
8 At approximately the point where Katie Street intersects with Ben Avenue, the tractor-trailer rig operated by Defendant Martin Jerry crossed over the double yellow lines and into the oncoming flow of traffic.
9 Truck Company's truck struck plaintiff's automobile with great force, causing substantial damage to the automobile.

A plaintiff's factual allegations must establish her cause of action and also provide sufficient notice of the relevant dates, times, and actions that the plaintiff states were committed by the defendant. Following the factual allegations, the plaintiff then proceeds to her theory of liability, again setting it out by specific, numbered allegations.

1. LIABILITY ALLEGATIONS

The plaintiff must set out the specific facts of the claim and must make a clear case why the defendant is the person who is liable to the plaintiff for the injuries sustained. In the sample complaint that we are using in this chapter, those allegations are found in paragraphs 10 through 13, with subparts.

2. SUFFICIENCY OF THE ALLEGATIONS

How do the courts evaluate the sufficiency of the complaint? That is, how much information must the plaintiff provide to support his claims so that the plaintiff meets the threshold of Rule 8 (or its state equivalent)? The complaint must provide enough information on its own to withstand the court's scrutiny. The plaintiff must establish a **prima facie** case for jurisdiction, standing, and other issues, without reliance on other pleadings. Case decisions have placed the burden squarely on the plaintiff to meet all of the material elements to place the defendant on notice of the claims against him as well as the facts that support this claim. A complaint that fails to meet that standard is subject to dismissal. We will discuss how the defendant seeks to dismiss an insufficient complaint in the next chapter.

Prima facie
Latin for "At first sight"; the presentation of a minimum of evidence to establish the party's case

F. DEMAND FOR JUDGMENT/PRAYER FOR RELIEF

Sidebar

A complaint that fails to meet the minimum requirements of notice pleading is subject to a dismissal for failure to state a claim.[14]

Once the plaintiff has made out her case against the defendant, the plaintiff must then make a specific request to the court. Here, the plaintiff requests that the court take some action based on the contentions in the case. This is referred to as the *demand for judgment* or the *prayer for relief.* By whatever name, the purpose is the same: The plaintiff requests that the court carry out an action to award the plaintiff compensation for the injuries alleged in the complaint, as in Figure 4-13.

FIGURE 4-13

Prayer for Relief

WHEREFORE, the plaintiff prays the Court as follows:

1. That the plaintiff have and recover from the defendants, jointly and severally, a sum in excess of Ten Thousand Dollars ($10,000.00) for compensatory and punitive damages as alleged above.
2. That the plaintiff have and recover the costs of this action.
3. For a trial by jury.
4. For such other and further relief as the Court may deem just and proper.

As you can see in Figure 4-13, the plaintiff requests a nonspecific sum, but one in excess of $10,000. The plaintiff also requests other relief, including a jury trial, that the defendant pay all costs associated with bringing the suit, and a final, catchall phrase, "for such other and further relief as the Court may deem just and proper." This phrase is inserted for the express purpose of allowing the plaintiff to receive any other compensation the court may deem proper. After all, if the plaintiff doesn't ask for all possible remedies, he may not receive them.

1. REQUEST FOR DAMAGES

In addition to the other requirements listed above, a complaint must also contain a specific allegation about the damages that the plaintiff suffered and is demanding from the defendant. On the federal level, the rule is that plaintiffs must state their damages in "definite and certain" terms. For instance, a plaintiff might state that she has suffered damages in "excess of $1 million." The plaintiff can simply allege a total or lump sum of the requested damages.

The rule about specifying damages is different when the plaintiff claims *special damages.* A "special damage" is a request for compensation for a specific out-of-pocket expense, such as medical bills, damage to personal property, or lost wages, among others. Where a claim involves a request for damages for these items, they must be pled with specificity (Fig. 4-14). We will discuss possible damages in Chapter 10.

FIGURE 4-14

Federal Rules of Civil Procedure, Rule 9(g), Special Damages

(g) Special Damages. If an item of special damage is claimed, it must be specifically stated.

2. JURY TRIAL DEMAND

Among the demands raised by the plaintiff, there is usually a request that the case be heard before a jury. The rule in most states and on the federal level is simple in regard to jury trials: If a party does not request a jury, then she will not receive one. In order to avoid any potential waivers on this point, attorneys usually place their request for trial by jury prominently and in several different parts of the complaint. You will notice, for example, that the plaintiff's request for a jury trial in our sample complaint is mentioned twice: once at the beginning and again in the prayer for relief.

VI COMPLAINT ATTACHMENTS AND EXHIBITS

Now that we have addressed the common aspects of the body of a civil complaint, there are additional issues to consider. For instance, how common is it for a complaint to contain additional documents that seek to prove the plaintiff's allegations? This brings us to the issues surrounding verifications, exhibits, and affidavits.

A. VERIFICATIONS

As we saw in the last chapter, the attorney's signature on the complaint acts as his representation that the basic facts alleged in the complaint are true and that they were investigated. But are there additional requirements? In years past, many states required not only the attorney's signature, but also a signed **verification** from the client. A verification is a sworn statement that the facts set out in the complaint are true. Verifications often follow along the lines of the statement set out in Figure 4-15.

Verification
A sworn statement by a party attesting to the truth and accuracy of the statements made in a complaint

"I hereby declare, under penalty of perjury, that the foregoing facts and statements contained in this complaint are true and known to me of my own knowledge."

FIGURE 4-15
Verification

Rule 11 abolished the need for verifications in the vast majority of suits, although verifications remain a feature of specific types of pleadings, such as zoning ordinance actions, defamation, tortious interference with contract, and actions against the government, among others.

B. EXHIBITS

Exhibit
A document attached to a pleading that is incorporated by reference into the body of the pleading

An **exhibit** is a document attached to a pleading that is referred to in or incorporated into the main body of the pleading. Attaching exhibits to all types of pleadings, including complaints and answers, is common practice. Again, Rule 8 requires that the wording of the complaint seek to establish the basic allegations made by the plaintiff, and exhibits help to facilitate such notice pleading.

C. AFFIDAVITS

Affidavit
A written statement, made under oath, that details specific facts

Just as it is rare to attach exhibits to a complaint (Fig. 4-16), so it is unusual to attach an **affidavit** to a complaint. An affidavit is a written, sworn statement that declares certain facts to be true.

FIGURE 4-16

Complaint in a Car Wreck Case

STATE OF PLACID

DISTRICT COURT

LONDON COUNTY

Sherlock Holmes
(Plaintiff)
v.
Professor James Moriarty, individually and as owner, operator of Moriarty Transport Trucking Co.
(Defendant)

CIVIL ACTION: 15-100

COMPLAINT
(Jury Trial Requested)

JURISDICTIONAL ALLEGATIONS

1 The plaintiff, Sherlock Holmes, age 57, is a citizen and resident of London County, PLACID.
2 The defendant, Moriarty Transport Trucking Co., is a corporation organized under PLACID laws and headquartered in Lestrade, N.C. and doing business in PLACID in London County.
3 The cause of action happened in Baskerville, PL. in London County.

GENERAL ALLEGATIONS

4 On August 23, 2013, at approximately 3:30 p.m., the plaintiff was driving his car on Watson Street, in Baskerville, PL. with his wife, Irene Adler Holmes, in the passenger seat.
5 As he passed through the intersection of Watson Street and Roylott Avenue, a truck belonging to, owned, and operated by the defendant failed to stop at a red light and caused a collision with the automobile driven by the plaintiff.
6 Irene Adler Holmes died at the scene of the accident from injuries she sustained in the crash.
7 Mr. Holmes was seriously injured by the collision with defendant's truck. He suffered head wounds, broken bones, and internal injuries.
8 At the time of the accident, Mr. Holmes was self-employed as a private consulting detective with a large client list. Since the collision, he has been unable to return to work.

9 Mr. Holmes has been severely disabled by the accident.
10 Mr. Holmes's quality of life has been severely diminished as a result of the accident injuries and the loss of his wife.
11 Mr. Holmes's life expectancy has been dramatically shortened as a result of the collision.
12 The injuries suffered by the plaintiff from the accident were caused by the defendant's negligence.
13 Defendant driver Moriarty failed to maintain a proper lookout.
14 Defendant driver Moriarty failed to abide by the rules of the road.
15 Defendant driver Moriarty was driving too fast for conditions prior to the collision.

PRAYER FOR RELIEF

The plaintiff incorporates by reference Paragraphs 1 through 21 in support of this claim for relief.

The plaintiff prays to the court for the following relief:

1 Judgment be made against the defendant for negligence described in Paragraphs 13–15.
2 Compensatory damages be awarded to the plaintiff in excess of $10,000.
3 The defendant be required to pay the costs of this action, including the attorney fees of the plaintiff.
4 For such other and further relief as the court may deem necessary and in the interests of justice.
5 The plaintiff requests that a jury trial be held.

November 18, 2014

Respectfully Submitted,

By: ______________

____

(PL. Bar No.)

Neal Bevans

Attorney for the plaintiff

Bevans & Bevans, P.A.

1001 Burkemont Avenue

Bohemia, PL. 28655

828-555-1212 (phone)

828-555-1213 (fax)

AFFIDAVIT OF VERIFICATION BY THE PLAINTIFF

I, Sherlock Holmes, do hereby swear that I have read and understand the attached complaint against the Moriarty Transport Trucking Co. and that the facts and allegations contained within this complaint are true except those matters stated to be upon information and belief, and as to those matters, I believe they are true.

____________ Date: November 18, 2014

Sherlock Holmes

STATE OF PLACID

COUNTY OF LONDON

On this day, November 18, 2014, Sherlock Holmes personally appeared before me and signed this affidavit.

____

Notary Public

Notary Seal

My Commission expires ____________.

LEGAL LEGWORK ■ MEDICAL MALPRACTICE

As you will see in this chapter's "The Life of a Paralegal" section, many states now impose requirements on medical malpractice cases before they can be filed. For instance, a state might require an affidavit from a licensed doctor setting out a claim that the defendant–doctor in the complaint breached the standard of care. This affidavit is required to be filed with the complaint. Does your state have similar requirements? Research the issue and determine what limitations or requirements your state imposes on the filing of medical malpractice cases.

VII SUMMONS AND SERVICE OF PROCESS

Preparing the complaint is only the first step in beginning a lawsuit. Just as important are the summons and service of process. All states require that when a complaint is drafted, it be served on the defendant. In this situation, "service" means that the defendant must receive a copy of the complaint and a summons directing the defendant to appear in court on a specific date and time. In this section, we will discuss the issues that arise under the requirement of service of process.

Once the complaint has been drafted, the next issue for consideration by the legal team is the manner in which the defendant will be served with a copy. Only when the defendant has been physically served with the complaint will the lawsuit have actually commenced. Service often raises a host of issues. For instance, how is service actually accomplished? State and federal rules provide for several different mechanisms for serving defendants. Local rules also state who is responsible for actually contacting the defendant.

In some states, private process servers are paid to locate defendants and to physically hand them a copy of the complaint. There is a long history of case law regarding what is considered to be proper service. For instance, the defendant must receive a copy of the complaint, but there is no requirement that she must actually read it before valid service is perfected. Defendants cannot avoid valid service by claiming that they refused to read the complaint. The certification by the process server, often referred to as *proof of service*, establishes that the defendant received a copy of the complaint on a particular date and time. Proof of service is essential because it determines when the lawsuit begins.

While some states use private process servers, many, including federal courts, rely on law enforcement officers to carry out service (Fig. 4-17). Using police officers, marshals, and deputies tends to mitigate the violent reaction that a defendant often has to being presented with a lawsuit.

(a) In General. Process — other than a summons under Rule 4 or a subpoena under Rule 45 — must be served by a United States marshal or deputy marshal or by a person specially appointed for that purpose. It may be served anywhere within the territorial limits of the state where the district court is located and, if authorized by a federal statute, beyond those limits. Proof of service must be made under Rule 4(l).

FIGURE 4-17

Federal Rules of Civil Procedure, Rule 4.1. Service of Other Process

PRACTICE POINTER ▶ MEMORANDA TO FILE

Whenever you speak with someone important to a case or discuss an issue that can have any significance to a client, always write up a memorandum about it. You might think that you will remember any significant conversation or discovery in a case, but the human memory is a great deal more fragile than most of us are willing to believe. Whenever you discuss anything of significance with a client, witness, judge's secretary, or anyone else having a bearing on the case, immediately create a memo and put it into the file. Save the digital version of the memo to the client's file on the computer or network, and make a backup hard copy. If this sounds like overkill, keep in mind that a short telephone conversation could become the major focus of a legal malpractice action several years from now. See Figure 4-18. Being able to produce a contemporaneously written memo may short-circuit a potential claim and also assure others that you took the action that you claimed you took. In the era of ubiquitous computers, there is no reason not to create a quick memorandum to file about any conversation. Consider this example:

To: File
From: Paula Paralegal
RE: TC with John Smith
Date: May 24, 2015

I spoke with client John Smith this morning, and he said that he definitely does not want his aunt, Myra Smith, called to testify in this case. I explained to him that Ms. Smith has critical information in this case and that by not calling her we put the entire case in jeopardy, but he was adamant. I discussed this decision with Allison Attorney, and she agreed that we would not call the client's aunt to the stand in this case. Ms. Attorney suggested that I send a letter to the client confirming this decision, and I followed up this conversation with a letter to Mr. Smith, setting out his decision.

A. SERVICE BY PERSONAL DELIVERY

Whether service of process is carried out by private individuals or law enforcement officers, the requirements are that the defendant must receive a copy of the complaint, along with any exhibits, verifications, and other attachments. *Personal service* means handing the complaint and related material directly to the defendant. It is not sufficient service to leave a copy with a friend or at the defendant's place of business. There are provisions that allow service of process by posting at the defendant's residence or by leaving it with the defendant's spouse, but the best means is by hand-delivering it to the defendant. However, that is not always possible.

B. SERVICE BY OTHER MEANS

In situations where the defendant cannot be located or where the defendant is avoiding service of process, there are other provisions for service. For instance, a plaintiff might rely on a provision that allows proof of service by posting notice and summons in the local newspaper for successive weeks or by posting the service on the front door of the defendant's residence. However, the preference is always for physical delivery to the actual defendant.

C. SERVING A CORPORATION OR GOVERNMENT ENTITY

Service of process on corporations or other entities raises interesting questions. Because there is no human defendant, who must be served in order for the plaintiff to establish adequate service of process under the law? In these situations, service is accomplished by hand-delivering a copy of the complaint and summons to a registered agent. As part of a corporation's registration with the state, it must designate a specific individual who will act as an agent for the corporation. This person's name and address remain on file with the state, and when a plaintiff wishes to sue a corporation or other entity, this person must be served with the appropriate paperwork. Once served, the registered agent forwards this information on to the corporate directors and officers, but when proof of service is established on the registered agent, the lawsuit has commenced, regardless of how much or how little the actual corporate officers and directors know about the case.

FIGURE 4-18

Letters to Clients Declining Representation

After meeting with a client, the legal team must carry out some basic investigations into the factual allegations raised by the client. What if the firm decides that there is not a sufficient basis to bring a suit? The firm must contact the client and inform him that the firm will not be handling the matter and also advising the client of potential consequences. Consider the following example:

Allison Attorney & Associates
1001 Maple Street
Lake Placid, PL 22202
904-555-1212

May 24, 2015

Ms. Jane Marple
1001 Mary's Lane
St. Mary Mead, PL 22202

Dear Ms. Marple:

Thank you for meeting with me on February 12, 2015. At that time, you requested that I review the materials you provided me and to reach a conclusion about the possibility of bringing an action against Detective John Slack. The materials you provided included the following:

- Newspaper clippings detailing your involvement in various criminal cases
- Letters from local law enforcement praising you for your efforts
- Character references from local community residents, detailing your high character and reputation for honesty
- Your own scrapbook of cases in which you have been involved
- An excerpt from the "St. Mary Mead Gazette," dated December 14, 2014, which includes statements by Det. Slack about you and your involvement in the recent investigation of the murder of Belle Girdler.

Based on our review of this case, we do not believe that there is sufficient evidence to support a claim of libel against Detective Slack. We do not believe that the statements rise to the level required by Placid law to bring such an action. The fact that you have become a celebrity in your own right substantially raises the bar for any slander or libel cases and that requires a showing of actual malice on the part of Det. Slack that is not reflected in this newspaper clipping.

Please do not construe our decision as a reflection on the merits of your claim; our firm simply does not believe it can prevail in an action against Det. Slack. Feel free to consult with other attorneys. Keep in mind that the statute of limitations for a libel action is 12 months from the date of publication. In this case, that means that any action you intend to file against Det. Slack for his statement in the newspaper must be filed on or before December 14, 2016, or it will be barred forever.

I'm sorry that we cannot assist you with this case.

Sincerely,

Allison Attorney, Esq

Encl: Newspaper clippings, letters, scrapbook

Tech Topic
CASE MANAGEMENT SOFTWARE

There is a wide variety of case management software suites available for small, midsized and large, multinational law firms. What all of these programs have in common is the ability to track clients and provide easy access to information about a pending case, from pleadings to matters on appeal. One example of such software is Clio. It helps a law office do such things as creating a thorough intake file, complete with mailing addresses, telephone numbers, and e-mail addresses as well as documents directly related to the pending case. But this software does more than generate a database of client information. Case management software also allows law firms to track billable hours on cases; set appointments, depositions, and court appearances; and generate bills for clients and other vendors. Some of these software packages essentially create a turnkey operation: a single software platform that can establish a law firm from the ground up. In addition to creating and storing valuable information about a case, many of these software packages also allow legal professionals to access important information from the cloud or with mobile devices.

Case Excerpt

When a case requires a verification, when must the verification be filed? Can it be filed after the complaint has been served or must it be made part of the record before such action is taken?

EMORY UNIV. V. METRO ATLANTA TASK FORCE FOR THE HOMELESS, INC.
320 Ga. App. 442, 740 S.E.2d 219, 2013 Ga. App. LEXIS 209, 2013 Fulton County D. Rep. 804, 2013 WL 1092848 (Ga. Ct. App. 2013)

Opinion

Ray, Judge.

These cross-appeals stem from a complaint filed by Metro Atlanta Task Force for the Homeless, Inc. ("Metro") which asserted claims against Emory University and Emory Healthcare, Inc. ("Emory") for tortious interference with business and contractual relations, violation of the Georgia Racketeer Influenced and Corrupt Organizations (RICO) Act, and defamation. Emory moved to dismiss or to strike the complaint based on Metro's failure to comply with the verification requirements of OCGA §9-11-11.1, Georgia's anti-SLAPP (Strategic Lawsuits Against Public Participation) statute. Metro then filed verifications "out of an abundance of caution." After a non-evidentiary hearing, the trial court denied the motion to dismiss or to strike the complaint, finding that the claims did not come within the scope of the anti-SLAPP statute. The trial court further found that, had the anti-SLAPP statute applied, Metro had been placed on notice of such defense at the time of Emory's answer and that Metro's subsequent filing of the verifications was untimely. Emory filed a request for a certificate of immediate review, but Metro voluntarily dismissed its complaint without prejudice before the trial court could address the request. Emory then filed a motion to strike the voluntary dismissal, which the trial court denied.

On appeal, we conduct a de novo review of the denial of a motion to dismiss. In reviewing the trial court's order, "we construe the pleadings in the light most favorable to the plaintiff with any doubts resolved in the plaintiff's favor."

The complaint indicates that Metro is a nonprofit enterprise that relies on government grants and private donations to provide shelter and other services to the homeless population in Atlanta. In 1997, Metro obtained a 95,000 square-foot facility in which to base its operations on the corner of Peachtree and Pine streets in midtown Atlanta ("Peachtree Pine building"). Thereafter, Metro received $900,000 in loans from private entities to renovate the facility. These loans were secured by security deeds on the property.

In its complaint, Metro alleged that Emory initiated efforts to interfere with its business operations and oust it from the Peachtree Pine building. Metro generally alleged that Emory, acting alone or through unidentified co-conspirators, engaged in "deceptive, covert, and malicious actions designed to drive Metro from the Peachtree Pine building." The alleged actions included Emory's efforts to undercut public and private funding using a "defamatory propaganda campaign," as well as efforts to "deceptively purchase the notes on the Peachtree Pine building and oust Metro from the property through a foreclosure process." Metro further alleged that, as a consequence of these actions, it sustained a loss of public and private funding which resulted in its loss of title to the Peachtree Pine building. It is this alleged conduct that forms the general basis of each of the claims in the complaint.

Case No. A12A1841

1. Emory argues that the trial court erred in denying its motion to dismiss or strike Metro's complaint because of the alleged untimely verifications. Specifically, Emory argues that the trial court erred in finding that the anti-SLAPP statute does not apply to the claims asserted in Metro's complaint and that Metro was not required to file verifications in accordance with OCGA §9-11-11.1 (b). Finding no error, we affirm.

"If the anti-SLAPP statute applies to a claim asserted in a complaint, and the plaintiff fails to timely file the required subsection (b) verifications, the defendant is entitled to have the claim stricken and the complaint dismissed." However, where a complaint asserts multiple claims and allegations, only those claims that are based on an act that falls under the scope of the anti-SLAPP statute are afforded the procedural protections of the statute and are subject to its verification requirements.

The purposes of Georgia's anti-SLAPP statute are to encourage citizens to participate in matters of public significance by exercising their constitutional rights to free speech and to petition the government for redress of grievances, and to prevent the chilling of those rights through abuse of the judicial process. To those ends, the statute requires the timely filing of a written verification when the complaint asserts a claim "against a person or entity arising from an act by that person or entity which could reasonably be construed as an act in furtherance of the right of free speech or the right to petition government for a redress of grievances . . . in connection with an issue of public interest or concern." The statute defines such an act as

> any written or oral statement, writing, or petition made before or to a legislative, executive, or judicial proceeding, or any other official proceeding authorized by law, or any written or oral statement, writing, or petition made in connection with an issue under consideration or review by a legislative, executive, or judicial body, or any other official proceeding authorized by law.

In denying Emory's anti-SLAPP motion to dismiss, the trial court found that the claims did not fall within the scope of the anti-SLAPP statute because "the statements at issue in the complaint were made neither to any official proceeding authorized by law nor in connection with an issue under consideration by any official proceeding."

On appeal, Emory contends that the trial court's denial is in error and argues that two types of official proceedings were implicated by Metro's claims: (1) any legislative proceedings involving Metro's public funding, and (2) the foreclosure proceeding regarding the Peachtree Pine building. However, no specific legislative proceeding was identified in the record or mentioned in the pleadings, and there were no allegations or evidence that any statements were made in relation to the foreclosure proceeding involving the Peachtree Pine building.

Emory concedes that the complaint was "extremely vague" with respect to the underlying facts on which Metro based its claims, but it argues that Metro should not be allowed to circumvent the requirements of the anti-SLAPP statute through vague and evasive pleading. This argument lacks merit.

Although OCGA §9-11-11.1 (d) provides that all discovery and any pending hearings or motions in the action are stayed upon the filing of a motion to dismiss or a motion to strike based on a plaintiff's failure to file the verifications required by the anti-SLAPP statute, subsection (d) also provides that the trial court, upon motion, may lift the stay and "order that specified discovery or other hearings or motions be conducted." Thus, a party seeking to obtain additional facts or evidence to establish whether the anti-SLAPP statute applies could petition the court to do so.

The Court notes that, at the time of the hearing on its anti-SLAPP motion, Emory had a pending motion to dismiss for failure to state a claim or, in the alternative, for a more definite statement. However, Emory did not petition the trial court to lift the stay to obtain a ruling on this motion, nor did it seek to avail itself of the specified discovery provisions of OCGA §9-11-11.1 (d) "to obtain evidence for use in resolving [its] motion to dismiss pursuant to OCGA §9-11-11.1 (b)." Accordingly, Emory "cannot now raise this issue on appeal where it has failed to avail itself of this remedy in the trial court."

Our analysis of the applicability of the anti-SLAPP statute to the claims in this case was limited by the generalized averments of the complaint and the vagueness of the claims contained therein. Thus, we cannot make a threshold finding that the statements or acts alleged in the complaint were made in relation to some official proceeding. Accordingly, we find that the trial court did not err in finding that the anti-SLAPP statute did not apply in this case; thus, the trial court did not err in denying Emory's motion to dismiss or strike the complaint.

2. Emory contends that the trial court erred in denying the motion to strike Metro's voluntary dismissal of the complaint, arguing that Metro's right to voluntarily dismiss

its complaint is limited by the requirements of the anti-SLAPP statute. Based on our holding in Division 1, we find that Metro was authorized to voluntarily dismiss its complaint under OCGA §9-11-41 (a). We discern no error.

Case No. A12A1842

3. In light of our holding in Divisions 1 and 2 above, Metro's cross-appeal in Case No. A12A1842 is dismissed as moot.

QUESTIONS ABOUT THE CASE:

1 Although the lawsuit involves a suit under a specific statute and cross-appeals, the issue before the court is a simple one: verification. How does that issue arise in this case?
2 There is no dispute that Metro failed to include a verification and that this was required. Why, then, did the trial judge allow the suit to continue?
3 Emory requested that the appellate court rule that the trial court had committed error by not dismissing the case because of a lack of verification. How did the court address this issue?
4 Is this a case where a court is bending a rule to the point of breaking in order to assist a worthy cause?

Chapter Summary

There are many important considerations that go into creating a complaint in a civil case. First, the plaintiff must research the court's jurisdiction. Jurisdiction is the power of a court to enter judgments and compel parties. Before a plaintiff can file in a particular court, the plaintiff must establish that the court has both subject matter jurisdiction and personal jurisdiction. *Subject matter jurisdiction* refers to the power of the court to consider the specific issues raised in the case. Personal jurisdiction is the court's power to enter judgments against the parties involved. Some courts, particularly on the state level, are courts of general jurisdiction, meaning that they have broad power to hear a wide range of actions. Other courts, including all federal courts, are courts of limited jurisdiction. They are empowered to hear only specific types of actions. Federal courts are limited to considering cases involving federal questions, including the interpretation of the U.S. Constitution and U.S. statutes. In addition, the plaintiff must establish that there is diversity of citizenship between the parties and that the amount in controversy exceeds $75,000.

Whether a complaint is filed in federal or state court, it must have the same basic elements. All complaints have a caption or style that lists the names of the parties and the court. Complaints have internal requirements, including allegations concerning jurisdiction and the factual allegations that support the plaintiff's cause of action against the defendant. The plaintiff must have a prayer for relief, requesting damages to be assessed against the defendant.

Once drafted, a complaint must be served on the defendant, along with a summons directing the defendant to appear in court to answer the charges on a specific date and time. Service of process is often accomplished by law enforcement officers, although some states do allow service by private individuals.

SKILLS YOU NEED IN THE REAL WORLD

Creating an Evidence Chart

One item that helps in preparing a complaint is an evidence chart. Prepared for either the plaintiff or the defense, this chart shows all the elements of the claim, the evidence necessary to support that claim, and the identity of the witness or evidence that will prove the claim.

Obviously, the evidence chart will look different depending on which side prepares it. When the plaintiff prepares an evidence chart, the essential elements include all of the basic claims of the complaint. When the defense prepares an evidence chart, it focuses on disproving the essential elements of the plaintiff's claim by attacking particular pieces of evidence.

This is a sample evidence chart from a car wreck case. The allegations come directly from a complaint.

Allegation	Witness	Testimony (Summary)	Physical Evidence
That, on or about the 19th day of October, 2000, at approximately 9:40 a.m., plaintiff was operating a motor vehicle traveling west on Maple Street in Anytown, Mason County, State of Anywhere	Plaintiff: Jane Smith	That she was driving that day, on that street, and defendant ran red light and struck her car	Photographs: check foundation questions and make sure that she can answer them; model of the intersection; check foundation questions and make sure that witness can answer all
The defendant driver admitted at the scene that she did not see plaintiff's vehicle before pulling out into the intersection.	Officer John Doe	Taking the statement from defendant after being called to the scene	Possible hearsay objection; officer may have based his conclusions on secondhand info provided by witnesses, not his own observations

That plaintiff was operating her vehicle below the posted speed limit of 35 mph	Plaintiff: Jane Smith Accident reconstructionist: Dave Jones	Ms. Smith's testimony His study of the scene; skid marks, point of impact from glass shards	Possible hearsay testimony; photo issues, etc. Photographs, diagrams made by Dr. Jones, possible relevance objection: photos taken months after accident, does not fairly and accurately depict the scene as it appeared on the day of the accident; testimony based on hearsay

THE LIFE OF A PARALEGAL

Screening Cases

John Purvis is senior legal assistant at a firm that specializes in civil litigation. He has worked there for years and spends a great deal of his time concentrating on medical malpractice cases. "When it comes to med/mal," he says, "we handle strictly plaintiff work in medical malpractice cases." When the firm decides to accept a case, John's focus is investigation. "We have the client list every physician they have ever seen; we have them execute medical authorization releases. We take that information and immediately send out requests to all medical providers for complete copies of all their records, diagnostics, lab reports, that type of thing. Depending on the type of injury, we may also request actual copies of X-rays, MRIs, CAT scans—any diagnostic tool that may be useful in the ultimate evaluation and potential review by an expert."

At his firm, they use a team approach to litigation. "When we take a case to trial, we use two or three attorneys, letting [the opposition] know that we are bringing the full resources of the firm to a case."

John spends a large part of his day screening potential cases. "What usually happens is a possible client will call the office, and I or one of the other legal assistants will screen the call. There are a multitude of calls that you are going to get. Many people will call up complaining about something that a doctor did. Seventy-five percent of those are things that are not actionable as medical malpractice claims. When we are screening calls, if a case sounds like one with real merit, we then present it to one or all of the partners. We usually have a weekly meeting where we go over all of the pending cases, their status, and any potential statutes of limitations problems. The attorneys then vote on whether or not it's a case that they want to investigate. Then we have the person come in and have a sit-down meeting with them. At the meeting, there is at least one attorney and one legal assistant. We listen to what the person has to say about their medical treatment. Then we try to give them an overview of what is involved in bringing a medical malpractice case, what it takes to proceed on a case, and also inform them about the low likelihood of getting a recovery. The statistics show that only a small percentage of the medical malpractice cases that are brought are successful. If the client is willing to proceed and understand that there are risks associated with going forward, and that there will be expenses that they are going to incur in continuing with the action, then we agree to take the matter on an investigative review."

ETHICAL ISSUES FOR THE PARALEGAL

Cutting Corners in Complaints

When dealing with drafting and filing of complaints, there are important ethical issues to consider. For instance, we have already seen that there are important rules that must be followed in drafting the complaint and in the way that it is served on the defendant. Here, a tendency to cut corners or to make light of the rules can have drastic consequences for the client. If the complaint does not meet the minimum standards under your state's court rules, the judge may be authorized to strike some or all of the allegations. This would mean that your client would no longer have a legal recourse against the defendant. Of course, the client would have a legal malpractice against the firm, and that is something that should always be avoided. Strict adherence to the rules is not only a valuable ethical guideline but can also avoid some nasty and potentially devastating legal consequences.

Websites

- **Legal Information Institute**
  www.law.cornell.edu/

- **Law Guru — General Issues Surrounding Civil Litigation**
  www.lawguru.com/faq/9.html

- **U.S. Department of Justice — Tobacco Litigation**
  www.usdoj.gov/civil/cases/tobacco2/

- **U.S. Department of Justice — Statistics on Civil Cases**
  http://www.bjs.gov/
  See left-hand side for menu including civil cases.

Key Terms

Affidavit
Concurrent jurisdiction
Defendant
Domicile
Exclusive jurisdiction
Exhibit
In rem jurisdiction
Personal jurisdiction
Plaintiff
Prima facie
Removal
Special appearance
Standing
Subject matter jurisdiction
Verification

Review Questions

1. What are the terms that refer to the two main parties in a lawsuit?
2. How is a person defined as a "party" to a lawsuit?
3. What is personal jurisdiction?
4. What role does a paralegal have in drafting a complaint?
5. What is a forum, and what relation does it have to a court's jurisdictional power?
6. Compare and contrast obtaining personal jurisdiction through the defendant's presence in the forum and her domicile in the forum.
7. Explain how a forum can obtain personal jurisdiction over a defendant through minimum contacts under the *International Shoe* case.
8. Compare and contrast general jurisdiction courts with limited jurisdiction courts.
9. All federal courts are limited jurisdiction courts. Explain.
10. What is diversity of citizenship, and what impact does it have on jurisdictional issues in federal courts?
11. Explain "amount in controversy" and what it means to subject matter jurisdiction.
12. Compare and contrast pendent and ancillary jurisdiction.
13. What is "removal"?
14. Explain in rem jurisdiction.
15. What is capacity?
16. What is standing, and why is it a requirement in a lawsuit?
17. What is the "case or controversy" requirement?
18. Compare and contrast ripeness and mootness.
19. List and describe the basic elements of a complaint.
20. What is "notice pleading"?
21. Compare and contrast the jurisdictional questions raised in federal and state courts.
22. Why have courts moved to a "notice pleading" requirement in complaints? What purpose is served by such a requirement?

Applying What You Have Learned

1. Locate a recent news report of an automobile accident, and then prepare a legally sufficient complaint based on the report. Make sure that you make correct factual allegations and that you allege the jurisdictional basis and satisfy the other required elements of a complaint. Finally, locate your state court rules on notice pleading, and include copies of those rules with the final draft of your complaint.
2. Using the facts in Figure 4-12, create a complete complaint.
3. Using the facts set out in number 2 above, draft a letter to Mr. Baker explaining that your firm has decided not to accept Mr. Baker's case and that the statute of limitations for Mr. Baker's action appears to have passed. Your letter should detail the firm's conclusion that the case should not be filed, the meeting with Mr. Baker, and the facts as the firm has come to understand them.
4. Using the facts of Figure 4-12, draft a letter to the plaintiff declining representation on the grounds that the statute of limitations has run on the cause of action.
5. Last week, Mrs. Rivera's neighbor, Kurt, smashed her back windshield with a tire iron. It caused $920 in damages, and Mrs. Rivera wants to sue Kurt for the damages. Kurt is in high school and has had trouble with the law before. Mrs. Rivera knows, for instance, that Kurt spent time in a youth detention facility last year. What jurisdictional and other issues does this case raise?

Endnotes

[1]28 U.S.C. §1332.
[2]28 U.S.C. §1441(a).
[3]*Sun Pipe Line Co. v. Altes*, 511 F.2d 280 (8th Cir. 1975).
[4]*Walder v. Paramount Publix Corp*, 132 F. Supp. 912 (S.D. N.Y. 1955).
[5]*Kowalski v. Tesmer*, 125 S. Ct. 564 (U.S. 2004).
[6]*Elk Grove Unified School Dist. v. Newdow*, 124 S. Ct. 2301, 159 L. Ed. 2d 98, 188 Ed. Law Rep. 17 (U.S. 2004).
[7]*Lujan v. Defenders of Wildlife*, 504 U.S. 555, 112 S.Ct. 2130 (U.S.Minn.,1992).
[8]*Duke Power Co. v. Carolina Environmental Study Group, Inc.*, 98 S.Ct. 2620, 2630 (U.S.N.C.,1978).
[9]*Alons v. Iowa Dist. Court for Woodbury County*, 698 N.W.2d 858 (Iowa 2005).
[10]CA CIV PRO §422.30.
[11]West's Ann.Cal.C.C.P. §422.30.
[12]*Banakus v. United Aircraft Corp.*, 290 F. Supp. 259 (S.D. N.Y. 1968).
[13]*U.S. v. Forty-Five Thousand Nine Hundred Forty Dollars ($45,940) in U.S. Currency*, 739 F.2d 792 (2d Cir. 1984).
[14]*Xechem, Inc. v. Bristol-Myers Squibb Co.*, 274 F. Supp. 2d 937 (N.D. Ill. 2003).

The Defendant's Answer

5

Chapter Objectives

- **Explain the function of the defendant's answer**
- **Describe how an answer matches the allegations of the plaintiff's complaint**
- **Describe the minimum requirements of a legally valid answer**
- **Explain the process of raising affirmative defenses in an answer**
- **Define 12(b)(6) motions**
- **Explain counterclaims**
- **Discuss cross-claims**
- **Compare and contrast impleader with interpleader**
- **Discuss class action lawsuits**
- **Draft an answer containing a counterclaim**

I INTRODUCTION

In the last chapter, we explored the world of the plaintiff's complaint, where the plaintiff raises allegations against the defendant and seeks to build a case for compensation that should be paid by the defendant. In this chapter, we will examine all of the aspects of the defendant's answer, including admissions, denials, the consequences for failing to deny the plaintiff's allegations, counterclaims, cross-claims, and other elements of third-party practice. Before we can address those other issues, however, we must first consider the question of what exactly an answer is.

THE ANSWER

The answer is the defendant's response to the allegations raised by the plaintiff. Rule 7 of the Federal Rules of Civil Procedure requires that the defendant submit an answer to the plaintiff's complaint, as seen in Figure 5-1. The defendant must respond in writing to the complaint, and he must answer every one of the plaintiff's allegations. Answers frequently contain denials of the plaintiff's allegations.

FIGURE 5-1

Federal Rules of Civil Procedure, Rule 7. Pleadings Allowed; Form of Motions

(a) Pleadings. Only these pleadings are allowed:

(1) a complaint;
(2) an answer to a complaint;
(3) an answer to a counterclaim designated as a counterclaim;
(4) an answer to a cross-claim;
(5) a third-party complaint;
(6) an answer to a third-party complaint; and
(7) if the court orders one, a reply to an answer.

However, while Rule 7 creates the requirement for an answer, it is Rule 12 that frames the practical issues involved in drafting and filing the answer, including the time limits. We will discuss Rule 12 in greater detail when we consider the issues of defenses raised in answers. But first, we will examine the basic function of an answer.

A. THE FUNCTION OF THE ANSWER

The function of an answer is to allow the defendant to assert his defenses to the plaintiff's claims. Failure to do so results in a default judgment in the plaintiff's favor. But an answer serves more functions than simply providing the defendant with a forum to deny the plaintiff's claims. Answers contain denials, admissions, defenses, and counterclaims against the plaintiff.

B. THE MINIMUM REQUIREMENTS OF THE ANSWER

A defendant's answer must conform to certain minimum requirements. These are set out in Rule 8(b) (Fig. 5-2). Rule 8(b) requires short and plain terms in the answer. It also states that for each claim in the complaint, an answer must admit, deny, or allege that the defendant is without knowledge or information sufficient to form a belief as to the truth of the claim.

FIGURE 5-2

Federal Rules of Civil Procedure, Rule 8(b) Defenses; Form of Denials

(b) Defenses; Admissions and Denials.

(1) *In General.* In responding to a pleading, a party must:

(A) state in short and plain terms its defenses to each claim asserted against it; and

(B) admit or deny the allegations asserted against it by an opposing party.

(2) *Denials — Responding to the Substance.* A denial must fairly respond to the substance of the allegation.

(3) *General and Specific Denials.* A party that intends in good faith to deny all the allegations of a pleading — including the jurisdictional grounds — may do so by a general denial. A party that does not intend to deny all the allegations must either specifically deny designated allegations or generally deny all except those specifically admitted.

(4) *Denying Part of an Allegation.* A party that intends in good faith to deny only part of an allegation must admit the part that is true and deny the rest.

(5) *Lacking Knowledge or Information.* A party that lacks knowledge or information sufficient to form a belief about the truth of an allegation must so state, and the statement has the effect of a denial.

(6) *Effect of Failing to Deny.* An allegation — other than one relating to the amount of damages — is admitted if a responsive pleading is required and the allegation is not denied. If a responsive pleading is not required, an allegation is considered denied or avoided.

An answer will have three general components:

- A point-by-point response to each of the allegations raised in the complaint
- Affirmative defenses and counterclaims against the plaintiff
- A Rule 12(b)(6) motion (discussed later in the chapter)

C. DRAFTING THE ANSWER

The prime purpose of an answer is to either **admit** or **deny** the allegations in the complaint in such a way that it satisfies the requirements of Rule 8. If the defendant admits to the allegations contained in a particular paragraph, then those facts are deemed conclusively proven for purposes of further litigation between the parties. There is no requirement for a plaintiff to present evidence about contentions that the defendant has admitted. When a defendant denies a particular allegation, that frames the issues in the litigation. The plaintiff must present proof to substantiate allegations that the defendant has denied in her answer. If a defendant fails to properly deny an allegation, then it is deemed to be an admission and will carry the same weight, and have the same consequences, as if the defendant actually stated an admission in her answer (Fig. 5-3).

Admit
To agree or stipulate to the allegations presented in a complaint

Deny
To disagree with or contest the allegations presented in a complaint

FIGURE 5-3

Federal Rules of Civil Procedure, Rule 8(b) Effect of Failure to Deny

(6) *Effect of Failing to Deny.* An allegation — other than one relating to the amount of damages — is admitted if a responsive pleading is required and the allegation is not denied. If a responsive pleading is not required, an allegation is considered denied or avoided.

There is no requirement that a defendant be consistent in his denials. A defendant is not prohibited from offering different replies to different claims of the plaintiff's complaint, even if this puts the defendant in the position of pleading inconsistent or alternative defenses.

As you can see in Figure 5-4, a defendant can admit to the plaintiff's allegations, deny them, offer a partial admission and partial denial, or claim that she is without sufficient information to form a belief about the veracity of the claim. This last phrase effectively denies the plaintiff's allegations but is offered as a way to avoid a claim of bad faith or frivolous legal maneuverings that can open the defendant up to court-ordered sanctions. We will discuss those sanctions later in this chapter.

FIGURE 5-4

Possible Defense Responses in an Answer

Defendant hereby responds to the allegations contained in the complaint as follows:

1 **The allegations contained in paragraph 1 of the complaint are hereby admitted.**
2 **The allegations contained in paragraph 2 of the complaint are hereby denied.**
3 **The allegations contained in paragraph 3 of the complaint are admitted to the extent that the defendant admits that there was a collision on the second day of November, last year; as to all other allegations contained in this paragraph, denied.**
4 **As to the allegations contained in paragraph 4 of the complaint, defendant is without sufficient knowledge or information to form a belief as to the truth of the allegations and therefore denies each and every one contained therein.**

PRACTICE POINTER ▶ CAREFUL WORDING

When the legal team drafts the responses to the plaintiff's complaint, they must be precise and provide detailed responses, where appropriate. Denials should be specific, direct to the point, and not offer any argument. If there is some doubt about the wording of the corresponding paragraph in the complaint, then the denial should be phrased in such a way that there is no doubt about what is being denied. For instance, a complaint might contain the following language:

> 17. That the defendant did, on the day in question, recklessly drive his automobile, in disregard of the rules of the road, the good sense of man, and the established customs of worthwhile drivers.

This allegation contains some unusual statements. How should a defendant respond? One way is to offer the following:

> 17. (Defendant's answer.) The defendant denies that, on the day in question, he did operate his automobile in a reckless manner; he also denies that he disregarded the rules of the road. Defendant is unable to either admit or deny the additional allegations contained in this paragraph as he is without knowledge of their substance or relation to the facts alleged. However, these additional statements are deemed denied by the defendant.

1. DENYING CLAIMS

A defendant's denial of the allegations raised in the complaint serves to form the issues that will be litigated in the case. The defendant's admissions in the answer result in the parties taking as true the allegations made by the plaintiff in his complaint. Unlike the issues that the defendant admitted, however, the plaintiff must present proof about any allegation denied by the defendant. The allegations denied by the defendant force the plaintiff to present testimony and evidence at trial to sustain those allegations. For an example of a plaintiff's factual allegations in a complaint and a defendant's corresponding denials in an answer, see Figure 5-5.

FIGURE 5-5

The Defendant's Answer

STATE OF PLACID
DISTRICT COURT
LONDON COUNTY

Sherlock Holmes (Plaintiff) v. Professor James Moriarty, individually And as owner, operator of Moriarty Transport Trucking Co. (Defendant)	CIVIL ACTION 15-100 *ANSWER* (Jury Trial Requested)

COMES NOW, the defendants in the above-styled action and bring this their Answer to Complaint filed by Plaintiff Sherlock Holmes, hereafter referred to as Plaintiff. All responses are deemed made by Defendant James Moriarty (hereafter referred to as "Defendant") in his individual capacity and in his capacity as owner and operator of Moriarty Transport Trucking Company.

ANSWER BY DEFENDANT

1 The allegations contained in this paragraph are admitted.
2 The allegations contained in this paragraph are admitted.
3 The defendant denies that there is any cause of action in this case, either based in Baskerville, PL, or any other area in this state.
4 The allegations contained in this paragraph are admitted.
5 The allegations contained in this paragraph are admitted.
6 Defendant is without any information as to the cause of death of Irene Adler Holmes and therefore denies the contentions of paragraph 6.
7 Defendant has no information about the extent of the plaintiff's injuries nor the cause thereof and therefore denies the contentions of paragraph 7.
8 Denied.
9 Denied.
10 Denied.
11 Denied.
12 Denied.

13 Denied.
14 Denied.
15 Denied.

DEFENDANT's PRAYER FOR RELIEF

The defendant prays that the court:

1. Deny any compensation to the plaintiff.
2. Grant no award of damages to the plaintiff.
3. Make no award of costs to the plaintiff or plaintiff's attorney.
4. Dismiss the plaintiff's action for failure to state a ground upon which relief may be granted.
5. Grant the defendant's prayer for relief contained in Defendant's counterclaim, set out below.
6. Award the defendant a jury trial on all triable issues.
7. Award the defendant any and all damages, compensation, and other relief that justice may demand.

So submitted, this 19th day of December, 2015.

By: ____________________
Deborah Bolstridge

____
(PL. Bar No.)
Attorney for Defendant, James Moriarty

21 Robin's Wood Place
Bohemia, PL 28655
828-555-2121 (phone)
828-555-2123 (fax)

2. OTHER RESPONSES IN ANSWERS

Defendants are not limited to giving only admissions or denials in answers. There may be some allegations for which the defendant can neither admit nor deny. For instance, the defendant may have no information about a particular allegation or may be willing to admit a portion of the allegation but not the entirety. In such a situation, the defendant might admit part and deny the remainder of the allegation.

Consider the following example: Paragraph 12 of the plaintiff's complaint contains the following allegation:

> That, at the time of the collision, witness Nora Burke was an eyewitness to defendant's negligent driving and will testify thereto.

The defendant in this case is not sure how to respond to this allegation. How can the defendant say for sure what this witness saw or what she will testify to at trial? How does the defendant respond and still protect her legal interests?

Answer: The defendant will respond with the following phrase: "The defendant neither admits nor denies the allegations contained in paragraph 12; the defendant is without any information to form a belief as to the truth of the matter asserted."

As you can see in this example, when the defendant is presented with situations where he is unaware of the facts surrounding a particular allegation, the only proper response is for the defendant to state that he lacks information about the accuracy of the allegation and can neither admit nor deny it for purposes of the pleadings. In such a situation, the defendant's response would be deemed a denial, and the plaintiff would be required to present proof at trial to substantiate that claim.

3. BAD FAITH

A question about admissions and denials often arises when drafting complaints: Why wouldn't a defendant simply deny all of the allegations raised in the complaint? After all, by denying everything, the defendant is forcing the plaintiff to present proof for all of the allegations contained in the complaint. This would make the plaintiff's job harder at trial and might result in a favorable ruling for the defendant.

In order to answer this question, we must first look to the rules. Rule 11 provides that the judge can impose sanctions on parties who act in **bad faith**. This applies to both the plaintiff and the defendant. If the defendant interposes defenses or denies allegations out of bad faith or simply to harass or annoy the other party, the judge is authorized to impose sanctions, including:

Bad faith
A claim that a party to litigation is interposing legal claims or making other allegations not based on fact, but out of a desire to harass, intimidate, or otherwise waste the court's time

- attorneys' fees related to the litigation of the matter denied in bad faith;
- monetary sanctions against the attorneys involved; or
- other sanctions approved by the court, including dismissal of some of the defendant's denials (Fig. 5-6).

FIGURE 5-6

Federal Rules of Civil Procedure, Sanctions for Bad Faith in Pleadings. Rule 11

(c) Sanctions.

(1) *In General.* If, after notice and a reasonable opportunity to respond, the court determines that Rule 11(b) has been violated, the court may impose an appropriate sanction on any attorney, law firm, or party that violated the rule or is responsible for the violation. Absent exceptional circumstances, a law firm must be held jointly responsible for a violation committed by its partner, associate, or employee.

(2) *Motion for Sanctions.* A motion for sanctions must be made separately from any other motion and must describe the specific conduct that allegedly violates Rule 11(b). The motion must be served under Rule 5, but it must not be filed or be presented to the court if the challenged paper, claim, defense, contention, or denial is withdrawn or appropriately corrected within 21 days after service or within another time the court sets. If warranted, the court may award to the prevailing party the reasonable expenses, including attorney's fees, incurred for the motion.

(3) *On the Court's Initiative.* On its own, the court may order an attorney, law firm, or party to show cause why conduct specifically described in the order has not violated Rule 11(b).

(4) *Nature of a Sanction.* A sanction imposed under this rule must be limited to what suffices to deter repetition of the conduct or comparable conduct by others similarly situated. The sanction may include nonmonetary directives; an order to pay a penalty into court; or, if imposed on motion and warranted for effective deterrence, an order directing payment to the movant of part or all of the reasonable attorney's fees and other expenses directly resulting from the violation.

(5) *Limitations on Monetary Sanctions.* The court must not impose a monetary sanction:

(A) against a represented party for violating Rule 11(b)(2); or

(B) on its own, unless it issued the show-cause order under Rule 11(c)(3) before voluntary dismissal or settlement of the claims made by or against the party that is, or whose attorneys are, to be sanctioned.

(6) *Requirements for an Order.* An order imposing a sanction must describe the sanctioned conduct and explain the basis for the sanction.

(d) Inapplicability to Discovery. This rule does not apply to disclosures and discovery requests, responses, objections, and motions under Rules 26 through 37.

D. SERVING THE ANSWER ON THE PLAINTIFF

Under Rule 12(a), the defendant has 20 days from the date of service to file an answer, as seen in Figure 5-7. Calculating the actual due date is relatively simple. One must count all intervening days, including holidays and weekends, unless the final day falls on a weekend or a holiday. In that event, the actual deadline moves to the next business day that is not a weekend or holiday. Failure to file within the required time period will result in a default judgment against the defendant.

FIGURE 5-7

Federal Rules of Civil Procedure, Time Limits on Serving Answer Rule 12(a)

(a) Time to Serve a Responsive Pleading.

(1) *In General.* Unless another time is specified by this rule or a federal statute, the time for serving a responsive pleading is as follows:

(A) A defendant must serve an answer:

(i) within 21 days after being served with the summons and complaint; or

(ii) if it has timely waived service under Rule 4(d), within 60 days after the request for a waiver was sent, or within 90 days after it was sent to the defendant outside any judicial district of the United States.

(B) A party must serve an answer to a counterclaim or cross-claim within 21 days after being served with the pleading that states the counterclaim or cross-claim.

(C) A party must serve a reply to an answer within 21 days after being served with an order to reply, unless the order specifies a different time.

SEARCH SUGGESTION • LIMITING PARAMETERS

When researching issues related to answers, keep in mind that although the rules of civil procedure for your jurisdiction are important, the case law that applies and develops these rules is just as important. The rule may provide the basic parameters for a particular action, such as setting a time limit of 20 days to file an answer, but it is the case law that applies this rule that explains how the time periods are calculated and also provides answers for unusual situations, including federal holidays not recognized in the state and other situations where it is unclear from the wording in the rule exactly how a party should proceed.

E. FAILURE TO RESPOND TO THE COMPLAINT

If a defendant fails to respond to the complaint, the judge is authorized to enter a **default judgment** against her. In a default judgment, the judge takes as true all of the allegations in the complaint and awards whatever damages the plaintiff requested. Such a ruling can have obvious and devastating consequences for a defendant, which is one reason why attorneys who represent defendants insist on getting a copy of the complaint as soon as possible. Many make it a part of their practice to file the answer early, in order to avoid even the prospect of a default judgment. Of course, a default judgment is only authorized when the plaintiff can prove adequate service of process.

Default judgment
A judgment entered against a defendant who has failed to file an answer to the plaintiff's complaint

F. FAILURE TO RESPOND TO ALLEGATIONS IN THE COMPLAINT

As we have already seen, the defendant must respond to each allegation raised in the complaint. If he fails to do so, the Rules of Civil Procedure provide a single outcome: The facts, also known as *averments*, are deemed to be admitted. In this situation, the plaintiff's contention about a specific set of facts will be taken as true and deemed admitted by the defendant for all issues raised throughout the remainder of the litigation, as you can see in Figure 5-8.

(6) *Effect of Failing to Deny.* An allegation — other than one relating to the amount of damages — is admitted if a responsive pleading is required and the allegation is not denied. If a responsive pleading is not required, an allegation is considered denied or avoided.

FIGURE 5-8

Federal Rules of Civil Procedure, Effect of Failure to Deny. Rule 8(b)(6)

Consider the following hypothetical: Plaintiff's Complaint, paragraph 6, contains the following allegation:

> Defendant, did, on the 8th day of November, fail to keep a proper lookout and operated his car in a negligent manner to wit: operated his automobile too closely to the plaintiff's car, failed to maintain a safe distance, and failed to obey the rules of the road.

Defendant's answer to paragraph 6 contains the following statement:

> Defendant denies that he failed to keep a proper lookout on the day of the accident.

What effect does this language have on the other allegations contained in the complaint?

Answer: Because the defendant did not specifically deny each and every allegation in paragraph 6, a judge is likely to rule that the defendant has admitted that he (1) operated his car in a negligent manner, (2) operated his car too closely to the plaintiff's car, (3) failed to maintain a safe distance, and (4) failed to obey the rules of the road.

DEFENSES

Answers not only provide the defendant with a forum to admit or deny the allegations in a complaint, but they also offer a method for the defendant to assert defenses and counterclaims. A defense to an action is a legally recognized excuse. If proven, the defense would entitle the defendant to a verdict in her favor or provide that the defendant is not obligated to pay any judgment to the plaintiff. We will begin our discussion with affirmative defenses.

A. AFFIRMATIVE DEFENSES

Affirmative defense
A defense that the defendant must raise in an answer; it would entitle the defendant to a verdict in his or her favor, if proven

An **affirmative defense** entitles the defendant to judgment against the plaintiff for specific matters. Rule 8(c) sets out the general categories of affirmative defenses that a defendant can raise in a civil case (Fig. 5-9).

FIGURE 5-9

Federal Rules of Civil Procedure, Rule 8(c) Affirmative Defenses

(c) Affirmative Defenses.

(1) *In General.* In responding to a pleading, a party must affirmatively state any avoidance or affirmative defense, including:

- accord and satisfaction;
- arbitration and award;
- assumption of risk;
- contributory negligence;
- duress;
- estoppel;
- failure of consideration;
- fraud;
- illegality;
- injury by fellow servant;
- laches;
- license;

- payment;
- release;
- res judicata;
- statute of frauds;
- statute of limitations; and
- waiver.

A defendant raises affirmative defenses in the latter portion of his answer. The first part of the answer is dedicated to responding to every one of the allegations raised in the complaint. After that, the defendant is free to raise affirmative defenses, as in Figure 5-10. Suppose, for example, that the defendant wishes to raise the affirmative defense of laches. Under the doctrine of laches, a person may waive a legal right by failing to assert it within a specific time period. Such a defense is similar to raising the issue of statute of limitations. When a defendant raises the defense of laches, he is saying that the plaintiff is not entitled to any award of damages because the plaintiff has waited too long to raise objections to the defendant's actions. This defense is not assumed; it must be raised by the defendant in the answer.

FIGURE 5-10

Example of an Affirmative Defense

Defendant's First Affirmative Defense

Plaintiff's claim for personal injury against defendant is barred by the applicable statute of limitations. PL §5-2-13.

Defendant's Second Affirmative Defense

Plaintiff's claims against defendant are barred under the doctrine of assumption of risk. PL. §5-2-15(a).

Affirmative defenses provide the defendant with the mechanism to have the case dismissed. But there are situations in which the defendant actually has claims against the plaintiff. In that situation, instead of raising an affirmative defense, the defendant may actually seek damages from the plaintiff in the form of a counterclaim.

LEGAL LEGWORK ■ PERSONAL INJURY ACTIONS

One of the most common types of lawsuits in the United States today is a personal injury action, usually brought by an individual motorist against another individual motorist. Because we have seen that statute of limitations can be brought as an affirmative defense in any action, it is always important to determine what the statute of limitations is for a particular action. Research personal injuries arising from automobile collisions, and locate the statute in your state that provides exactly how long a plaintiff has to bring such an action before it is barred forever.

B. COUNTERCLAIMS

Counterclaim
A claim by the defendant against the plaintiff where the defendant seeks damages

Rule 13 sets out the basis for **counterclaims** and cross-claims. Under Rule 13, a counterclaim consists of "any claim which at the time of serving the pleading the pleader has against any opposing party, if it arises out of the transaction or occurrence that is the subject matter of the opposing party's claim and does not require for its adjudication the presence of third parties of whom the court cannot acquire jurisdiction."[1] This allows the defendant to bring a claim against the plaintiff. In many ways, a counterclaim resembles the original complaint, except that it is brought by the defendant against the plaintiff. What are some circumstances in which a defendant might have a counterclaim against the plaintiff?

Consider the following example: Maria is leaving work one day, and as she approaches an intersection, she notices that the traffic lights do not appear to be working. Motorists are attempting to cross through the intersection, but there is a great deal of confusion. Maria waits for an opportune moment and then proceeds through the intersection. William is driving a car that enters the intersection from Maria's right, and the two cars strike each other. A few days later, William drafts a complaint and serves it on Maria. She believes that William is responsible for the damages to her car and that he was at fault. In fact, she has been working with her attorney to draft a complaint against him. Because he filed his complaint first, he became the plaintiff in the action. Maria wishes to deny William's allegations of her negligence and to counterclaim against him for the damages that he caused to her car. In this situation, when Maria files her answer, she will include a counterclaim against William for the damages to her automobile.

1. COMPULSORY AND PERMISSIVE COUNTERCLAIMS

Compulsory counterclaim
A claim by the defendant against the plaintiff that must be raised in the case or it will be barred

Rule 13 recognizes two different types of counterclaims: compulsory and permissive. A **compulsory counterclaim** is one that arises from the transaction that forms the basis of the complaint and must be brought in the same action, or it will be barred forever. In the hypothetical involving Maria and William, Maria must bring her counterclaim against William for the damages done to her car because it arises out of the same transaction as William's complaint. If Maria fails to bring this counterclaim in her answer, then she has waived it. Under the rules of compulsory counterclaims, her failure to allege her counterclaim against William for the damages to her car would result in her being barred from bringing a separate action over this issue.

Permissive counterclaim
A claim by the defendant against the plaintiff that may be raised in the case; it may also be brought as a separate action

By contrast, a **permissive counterclaim** is one that is separate from the transaction that forms the basis of the complaint and may be brought in the same action or may be brought later as a separate action. In a permissive counterclaim, the defendant brings a claim against the plaintiff that is not related to the issues in the original complaint, simply because it would be convenient to resolve both issues in a single case. It is up to the judge's discretion whether to permit a permissive counterclaim to remain in a case. The judge's final decision will be based on several factors, including the potential confusion and additional time that proving the permissive counterclaim would add to the trial.

How do the courts determine when a counterclaim is compulsory or permissive? A compulsory counterclaim involves the same transaction that was raised by the plaintiff in the original complaint. In our hypothetical involving Maria and William, Maria's claim against William would be considered compulsory because it involves the same traffic collision. A court will insist that such a claim be brought in the original case in order to cut down on duplicative actions and also for the practical reasons that the same parties, witnesses, and issues are involved, and the court can dispense with two claims in one action.

PRACTICE POINTER ▶ WAIVING COUNTERCLAIMS

There are times when a defendant may decide that although she has the basis for a counterclaim against the plaintiff, she will waive it. Such a procedure, especially when it involves compulsory counterclaims, can result in a complete dismissal of one of the defendant's possible actions against the plaintiff. In such a situation, the legal team must ensure that the defendant is made fully aware of the consequences of failing to file a counterclaim. The best way to do this is in writing. Compose a letter to the defendant detailing exactly what the nature of the counterclaim is, what the firm's opinion is regarding its classification as compulsory or permissive, and the fact that if the claim is not raised in the answer, then the defendant may be waiving any right to bring the claim in the future. Some firms even go so far as to have the client sign an acknowledgment that she has been advised of the consequences and has voluntarily agreed to forgo the counterclaim.

2. RES JUDICATA

There is an important legal principle that applies in situations involving counterclaims. **Res judicata** is the principle that a legal finding on an issue in one case may be dispositive of that issue in another case. For instance, if the same parties are involved in litigation and a court makes a final determination that one of the parties is liable, that determination may be binding on related cases. The principle of res judicata is based on conservation of resources. If all parties were present and litigated the question to a resolution, it makes very little sense to relitigate the same issue in another case. Res judicata is important in compulsory counterclaims because if the issues in the counterclaim are resolved against the defendant, then he will be barred from bringing a new action challenging that finding. The court will rule that the issue is now res judicata and decided permanently, at least as it relates to the parties. Res judicata does not apply to other individuals who were not involved in the legal action; it only binds those who were named in the suit and had a chance to present evidence on the issue.

Res judicata
Latin for "the thing has been adjudicated"; the principle that a court's decision on a particular matter is binding on future litigation between the parties; sometimes referred to as *res adjudicata*

A different rule applies to permissive counterclaims. A permissive counterclaim is a claim that one party has against the other that does not arise out of the transaction involved in the original complaint. Suppose, in our earlier example, that Maria and William had, coincidentally, been involved in a business transaction together. Maria wishes to sue William for failure to comply with a business contract. This is a claim that could be brought separately, but because Maria is already involved in a suit against William, she decides to allege it in her answer involving the automobile collision. Because such a permissive counterclaim involves situations that are not related to the main case, the counterclaim might cause confusion and result in a protracted case. Thus, a judge might decide to sever Maria's claim for a business transaction out of the main case. In such a situation, Maria would be required to bring a separate complaint against William, and this would result in an entirely separate civil action, in which the principle of res judicata would not apply.

3. REPLIES TO COUNTERCLAIMS

Reply
The responsive pleading, provided in Rule 7, to a counterclaim

A **reply** is the pleading used to respond to the allegations of a counterclaim. The term *reply* is used to differentiate between this pleading and the answer, which the defendant uses to respond to the allegations made in the complaint. When a defendant serves a counterclaim on the plaintiff, the plaintiff responds with a pleading entitled, "Reply to Counterclaim." This pleading is very similar to an answer. It sets out the plaintiff's admissions, denials, and defenses to the counterclaim raised by the defendant. See Figure 5-11 for an example of a reply to a counterclaim.

FIGURE 5-11

Reply to a Counterclaim

STATE OF PLACID

DISTRICT COURT

LONDON COUNTY

Sherlock Holmes (Plaintiff) v. Professor James Moriarty, individually And as owner, operator of Moriarty Transport Trucking Co. (Defendant) CIVIL ACTION: 04-100	CIVIL ACTION 15-100 **REPLY TO DEFENDANT's COUNTERCLAIM**

COMES NOW Plaintiff Sherlock Holmes and files this, his reply to defendant's counterclaim.

1 The allegations contained in paragraph 1 of the defendant's counterclaim are denied.
2 The allegations contained in paragraph 2 of the defendant's counterclaim are denied.
3 The allegations contained in paragraph 3 of the defendant's counterclaim are denied.

Respectfully submitted, this 29th day of December, 2015.

By: ______________________

Neal Bevans

____

(PL. Bar No.)

Attorney for the plaintiff

Bevans & Bevans, P.A.
1001 Burkemont Avenue
Bohemia, PL 28655
828-555-1212 (phone)
828-555-1213 (fax)

IV RULE 12(b)(6) MOTIONS

The final aspect of the defendant's answer is not really a part of the pleading itself. A **12(b)(6) motion** is a separate motion from the actual answer. It is a motion that the defendant files that challenges the specific wording of the complaint, as in Figure 5-12.

12(b)(6) motion
A motion under the provisions of Rule 12 of the Rules of Civil Procedure that challenges the basis of the complaint for failure to state a claim upon which relief can be granted

"Paragraph 3 of the complaint fails to state a claim upon which relief can be granted."

"This court lacks subject matter jurisdiction over the action contemplated in this case as the plaintiff's allegations fail to allege a minimum monetary amount of damages in excess of $10,000."

FIGURE 5-12

Examples of a Rule 12(b)(6) Motion

A. PURPOSE OF THE RULE 12(b)(6) MOTION

The purpose of Rule 12(b)(6) is to provide the defendant with a mechanism to challenge the allegations raised in the plaintiff's complaint. A 12(b)(6) motion was never designed as a means to challenge the legal effect of the complaint. Instead, its primary purpose is based on the theory of notice pleadings. As we saw in our discussions of Rule 8 in Chapter 4, the plaintiff must make a short and plain statement of the claim against the defendant. When the defendant alleges that the complaint is confusing or fails to meet minimum notice requirements, she is entitled to file a 12(b)(6) motion in order to challenge the allegations in the complaint. A 12(b)(6) motion has a very narrow focus: It challenges the allegations by stating that the plaintiff's wording fails to set out a legally recognized action against the defendant. If the defendant can convince the judge that the plaintiff's complaint fails to rise to the minimum level required under the Rules of Civil Procedure, the judge would be authorized to dismiss some or all of the allegations. How does the court make this determination? The complaint must stand on its own. When a judge evaluates the complaint, he focuses on the language contained in that complaint, not any subsequent pleadings or other materials. Because of the potential benefit that a defendant would earn from such a ruling, it is routine for defendants in civil cases to file 12(b)(6) motions in all cases, whether or not they actually believe that the plaintiff's complaints are insufficient.

Sidebar

There are other motions authorized under Rule 12. However, a 12(b)(6) motion is one of the most common motions made in any civil case.

A 12(b)(6) motion was never designed to act as a corrective measure for poor choice of wording in a complaint. The rule does not require perfect pleadings, only pleadings that put the defendant on notice as to what the claim is against her. If the wording in the complaint is ambiguous or subject to different interpretations, a 12(b)(6) motion is not the appropriate way to challenge that language. Instead, the defendant would be authorized to bring a motion for more definite statement under the provisions of Rule 12(e), as seen in Figure 5-13. We will discuss these motions in greater detail in Chapter 8. If the defendant alleges that the complaint contains improper or redundant material, a 12(b)(6) motion is also not authorized. Instead, the defendant must file a motion under the provisions of Rule 12(f).

FIGURE 5-13

Federal Rules of Civil Procedure, Motion for More Definite Statement Rule 12(e)

(e) Motion for a More Definite Statement. A party may move for a more definite statement of a pleading to which a responsive pleading is allowed but which is so vague or ambiguous that the party cannot reasonably prepare a response. The motion must be made before filing a responsive pleading and must point out the defects complained of and the details desired. If the court orders a more definite statement and the order is not obeyed within 14 days after notice of the order or within the time the court sets, the court may strike the pleading or issue any other appropriate order.

B. WHEN CAN A DEFENDANT FILE A RULE 12(b)(6) MOTION?

Sidebar

12(b)(6) motions can be raised not only against complaints, but also against counterclaims, cross-claims, and third-party claims.

The most common method, and the one suggested by the rules, is for the defendant to file a 12(b)(6) motion contemporaneously with his answer. A strict interpretation of the rule would suggest that a 12(b)(6) motion should be filed before the responsive pleading, but it is common practice for defendants to file them at the same time. In such situations, the court will usually infer that the 12(b)(6) motion was filed prior to the answer. There is a practical reason why a defendant would file both pleadings at the same time: If a defendant's 12(b)(6) motion is denied, then the next item of business for the court to consider is whether the defendant filed his answer within the statutorily required time period. Rather than run the risk of having the 12(b)(6) motion dismissed and then losing the case on a default judgment, attorneys for the defendant will file both simultaneously.

If a party waits too long and files a 12(b)(6) motion after responsive pleadings, the court may still consider the issues but will view them as a motion for summary judgment instead of a 12(b)(6) motion. The conversion from a 12(b)(6) motion to a motion for summary judgment has important procedural aspects that we will discuss in Chapter 8.

Because answers must be filed within 20 days of service of process, the practical limitation on when a 12(b)(6) motion must be filed is also 20 days. However, the time periods can vary depending on the nature of the 12(b)(6) motion. For instance, if the motion is interposed on a counterclaim, then the time limit will be based on the time limits imposed on filing the reply to the counterclaim.

C. MOTIONS TO STRIKE

In addition to Rule 12(b)(6) motions, parties may bring several other motions under the authority of Rule 12 of the Federal Rules of Civil Procedure. For instance, it is quite common for a defendant to file a motion to strike some or all of a plaintiff's complaint based on Rule 12(f) (Fig. 5-14). Such a motion is referred to as a *motion to strike*, and a defendant may file such a motion when some portion of the plaintiff's complaint is impossible to understand, redundant, or inserts language that a court would deem to be scandalous. In a recent case, for example, a court struck a portion of the plaintiff's complaint that relied on improperly obtained communications between an attorney and his client.[2]

(f) Motion to Strike. The court may strike from a pleading an insufficient defense or any redundant, immaterial, impertinent, or scandalous matter. The court may act:

(1) on its own; or

(2) on motion made by a party either before responding to the pleading or, if a response is not allowed, within 21 days after being served with the pleading.

FIGURE 5-14

Federal Rules of Civil Procedure, Rule 12(f) Motion to Strike

V CROSS-CLAIMS

When a party has a claim against a co-party, she brings it as a **cross-claim**. The difference between counterclaims and cross-claims is that a counterclaim is brought against another party, such as a defendant against a plaintiff. A cross-claim, on the other hand, is brought against a co-defendant or a co-plaintiff. A party might bring a cross-claim against another party in order to allege that one party is more culpable in the action than the other. A co-defendant, for instance, might bring a cross-claim in order to seek reimbursement for any judgments she is compelled to pay out as part of the main action. See Figure 5-15 for a diagram of the differences between counterclaims and cross-claims.

Cross-claim
A claim by one party against another party on the same side of the action; for example, a plaintiff against another plaintiff or a defendant against a co-defendant

FIGURE 5-15

Difference between Counterclaims and Cross-Claims

Counterclaim	Cross-Claim
Brought by defendant against plaintiff	Brought by defendant against codefendant or plaintiff against co-plaintiff
Divided into two categories: compulsory and permissive	Only one class
Requires reply by plaintiff	Requires reply by co-party

A cross-claim must arise out of the same transaction or facts that form the basis of the original lawsuit. The theory behind cross-claims is very simple: If the court can dispose of several different actions within the context of the single civil case, it makes sense to do so. It will save time and resources to adjudicate related claims at the same time instead of forcing the parties to file multiple separate actions to litigate issues that are essentially based on a single occurrence. Because of this, courts have held that the rules about permitting cross-claims should be liberally construed in order to achieve the principle set out in Rule 13. However, even given the liberal approach under Rule 13, there are certain limitations on cross-claims, as seen in Figure 5-16. For one thing, a cross-claim is not authorized by someone who is not a party to the action. Only plaintiffs or defendants who are already involved in the litigation can bring cross-claims against one another. Also, unlike counterclaims, cross-claims are always permissive. This means that if a co-party does not bring a cross-claim in the main case, he may still be able to bring that claim in a separate action.

FIGURE 5-16

When Cross-Claims Are Allowed

Rule 13(g) allows cross-claims against a co-party in the following situations:

- When the claim arises out of the transaction or occurrence that forms the basis of the original complaint
- When the claim has the same subject matter as the original action
- When the claim is related to a counterclaim
- When the claim is related to property that is involved in the original action

The practical result of the limitations on cross-claim actions is that a party bringing a counterclaim has greater flexibility than does a party who seeks to file a cross-claim. A counterclaim, for example, can involve the main transaction alleged in the complaint but may also involve unrelated matters. Cross-claims, on the other hand, must involve the same subject matter as the original complaint and will be subject to dismissal if they do not.

Like the other pleadings involved in the case, the cross-claim must also contain a short and plain statement of the claim made against the co-party. Cross-claims, like all other pleadings, must conform to the requirements of Rule 8 of the Federal Rules of Civil Procedure. They are also subject to 12(b)(6) motions and therefore should be carefully crafted.

A. ANSWERS TO CROSS-CLAIMS

Just as we have seen with all previous pleadings, a party must respond to a cross-claim (Fig. 5-17). In some states, the reply to a cross-claim is referred to as a *reply*, the same terminology that is used to respond to a counterclaim on the federal level. In other instances, the responsive pleading to a cross-claim is referred to as an *answer*. Whatever the terminology, the response must meet the same requirements as any responsive pleading: It must admit or deny the allegations raised in the cross-claim.

(g) Cross-claim Against a Coparty. A pleading may state as a cross-claim any claim by one party against a coparty if the claim arises out of the transaction or occurrence that is the subject matter of the original action or of a counterclaim, or if the claim relates to any property that is the subject matter of the original action. The cross-claim may include a claim that the coparty is or may be liable to the cross-claimant for all or part of a claim asserted in the action against the cross-claimant.

FIGURE 5-17

Federal Rules of Civil Procedure, Rule 13 Cross-Claim against Co-Party

B. TIME LIMITS FOR CROSS-CLAIMS

Interestingly enough, Rule 13 does not impose a time limit for bringing a cross-claim. As such, the claim may be brought at any point in the litigation, although it is always up to the judge to allow it. The judge's decision will be influenced by the time and resources necessary to adjudicate the cross-claim, balanced against a general approach that seeks to avoid multiple lawsuits on the same issues.

VI THIRD-PARTY CLAIMS

So far, our discussion has centered on the claims brought by the original parties between and against one another. However, there are provisions that allow the addition of third parties to the action, individuals who were not originally parties to the litigation but whose presence may be necessary to bring about a final adjudication of all claims in the case. There are three methods that can be used to bring in third parties to a lawsuit. They include:

- impleader;
- interpleader; and
- intervention.

Sidebar

The standard for asserting a cross-claim is that the claim rests on issues that have strong relationship with the original action.

A. IMPLEADER

Impleader
The involuntary addition of a new party to the litigation, a party without whom all issues raised in the case could not be resolved

Impleader is authorized under Rule 14 of the Federal Rules of Civil Procedure. Also known as *third-party practice*, impleader is the process of bringing in a new party to the action. When a current defendant impleads a third-party defendant, this new party is added to the action as though she were one of the original parties. A defendant might implead a third-party defendant when she alleges that this third party is responsible for some or all of the plaintiff's claims against the original defendant, as in Figure 5-18.

FIGURE 5-18

Third-Party Complaint Form: Defendant Impleads a Third-Party Defendant

STATE OF PLACID
DISTRICT COURT
LONDON COUNTY

Professor James Moriarty, Individually and as owner, operator of Moriarty Transport Trucking Co. (Third-Party Plaintiff)	CIVIL ACTION 15-100
v.	**Third Party Complaint**
Dr. John Watson (Third-Party Defendant)	

Pursuant to PL Rules of Civil Procedure 14, James Moriarty, Defendant in Civil Action No. 15-100 (hereafter "Moriarty"), brings this Third-Party Complaint against Dr. John Watson, Third-Party Defendant (hereafter "Watson") and as grounds therefore shows the following:

1 Moriarty is named as defendant in the original complaint in this action.
2 Although Moriarty in no way admits to any extent of liability in the underlying complaint and answer, Moriarty shows that Watson is liable to Moriarty for all alleged liability and damages complained of by Plaintiff Holmes.
3 The presence of Watson in this suit is indispensable to the proper administration of justice in the underlying suit.
4 Third-party Plaintiff Moriarty has been served and has responded to a complaint filed in London County.
5 Moriarty has submitted to the personal and subject matter jurisdiction of this court.
6 On August 23, 2014, on or about 3:30 p.m., Watson was waiting for Plaintiff Holmes at the intersection of Carbuncle and Watson Street.
7 Watson flagged down the automobile operated by Plaintiff Holmes.
8 The automobile driven by Holmes came to an abrupt stop.
9 Plaintiff Holmes made no indications of his proposed stop.
10 Plaintiff Holmes was not responding to any traffic signs or signals.
11 Plaintiff Holmes's automobile blocked traffic in both lanes of traffic.
12 Upon seeing Moriarty, Watson drew a revolver and pointed it in Moriarty's direction.
13 Moriarty, in an attempt to avoid being shot, swerved into Plaintiff Holmes's vehicle.

14 Moriarty was severely injured in the crash and has incurred substantial medical bills.
15 Moriarty has been unable to return to his former employment as professor of mathematics at Oxford University.
16 Third-Party Defendant Watson was the sole, proximate, and legal cause of the injuries to both Moriarty and Plaintiff Holmes.

WHEREFORE,

Third-Party Plaintiff Moriarty prays that this court:

1 have judgment against third-party defendant Watson for damages in excess of $10,000.
2 order all necessary damages, equitable relief, and any other relief that the court may deem just and proper.
3 permit a jury trial on the issues raised by Third-Party Plaintiff on his Third-Party Complaint.

Respectfully submitted,

January 15, 2016

By: ______________________
Deborah Bolstridge

____
(PL. Bar No.)

Attorney for Defendant, James Moriarty

21 Robin's Wood Place
Bohemia, PL 28655
828-555-2121 (phone)
828-555-2123 (fax)

When a defendant brings in a third-party defendant, he does so with a third-party complaint. This complaint resembles the original complaint that initially began the case, but it is brought by a defendant against a person that the defendant claims is essential to resolve the issues in the main case. This third-party defendant has the right to file a third-party answer, alleging any defenses that any defendant would have, as well as cross-claims and counterclaims. As you can see, third-party practice can swiftly make the issues in the case very complicated. See this chapter's case excerpt for an example of issues involving third-party practice.

Although impleader originally required the trial judge's approval, modern practice allows a defendant to implead a third-party defendant within 10 days of the filing of the defendant's answer. The judge still retains the authority to strike the third-party complaint and to sever out the claim to be brought as a separate action.

Sidebar

Impleader is based on an old common law practice, first recognized in England, called "vouching to warranty." There, a defendant who was sued for the return of property could bring in a third party who had given the defendant warranty on the title to the property. The defendant could bring in this third party to prove that he had legitimate title to the disputed property.

B. INTERPLEADER

Interpleader
The deposit of contested funds with the court, followed by the removal of the filing party from other action in the suit

Interpleader involves an action where a party owes money to a party but is not sure to whom it should be paid. It applies to insurance proceeds, devises under wills, and other situations where there is no dispute about the fact that money is owed but no certainty about who should receive it. In such a case, the party who owes money would file an interpleader complaint and deposit the money with the court. The complaint must be as legally sufficient as any other and must also be served on all interested parties. However, interpleader is different in that once the party has deposited the contested funds with the court, her involvement in the case is essentially at an end. From that point onward, it is up to the court to decide who among the contesting defendants should receive the funds. Interpleader is governed by Rule 22 of the Federal Rules of Civil Procedure.

C. INTERVENTION

There are times when individuals who are not involved in the original action seek to interject themselves. In such a case, the party would comply with Rule 24 of the Federal Rules of Civil Procedure by filing a motion to intervene (Figs. 5-19 and 5-20). However, Rule 24 applies strict standards to those individuals who seek to enter into pending litigation. The party seeking to intervene must show one of the following elements:

- That a federal statute gives the party an unconditional right to intervene
- That the party claims interest in the litigation and that resolution of the case without the party's presence may affect his property rights.

FIGURE 5-19

Federal Rules of Civil Procedure, Intervention

Rule 24. Intervention

(a) Intervention of Right. On timely motion, the court must permit anyone to intervene who:

(1) is given an unconditional right to intervene by a federal statute; or

(2) claims an interest relating to the property or transaction that is the subject of the action, and is so situated that disposing of the action may as a practical matter impair or impede the movant's ability to protect its interest, unless existing parties adequately represent that interest.

(b) Permissive Intervention.

(1) *In General.* On timely motion, the court may permit anyone to intervene who:

(A) is given a conditional right to intervene by a federal statute; or

(B) has a claim or defense that shares with the main action a common question of law or fact.

(2) *By a Government Officer or Agency.* On timely motion, the court may permit a federal or state governmental officer or agency to intervene if a party's claim or defense is based on:

(A) a statute or executive order administered by the officer or agency; or

(B) any regulation, order, requirement, or agreement issued or made under the statute or executive order.

(3) *Delay or Prejudice.* In exercising its discretion, the court must consider whether the intervention will unduly delay or prejudice the adjudication of the original parties' rights.

(c) Notice and Pleading Required. A motion to intervene must be served on the parties as provided in Rule 5. The motion must state the grounds for intervention and be accompanied by a pleading that sets out the claim or defense for which intervention is sought.

FIGURE 5-20

Motion to Intervene

STATE OF PLACID
DISTRICT COURT
LONDON COUNTY

Sherlock Holmes (Plaintiff) and United States of America, Plaintiff-Intervenor v. Professor James Moriarty, individually and as owner, operator of Moriarty Transport Trucking Co. (Defendant) Professor James Moriarty, individually and as owner, operator of Moriarty Transport Trucking Co. (Defendant)	**CIVIL ACTION 15-100** **United States' Motion to Intervene as Plaintiff-Intervenor**

UNITED STATES' MOTION TO INTERVENE AS PLAINTIFF-INTERVENOR

COMES NOW the United States of America and for the reasons set out below, moves this court for an order permitting it to intervene as plaintiff in the above styled action, pursuant to Rule 24 of the Federal Rules of Civil Procedure. In support of this motion, the United States submits:

1 Plaintiff Holmes filed a complaint against Defendant Moriarty on November 18, 2015.

2 Plaintiff's allegations against Defendant include a demand for a jury trial and an award of damages for Defendant's alleged negligence.

3 On August 13, 2017, Defendant Moriarty entered the Federal Witness Protection under agreement to testify against alleged co-conspirators in federal indictment U.S. CR 124-47874.
4 On October 2, 2017, an attempt was made to murder Defendant in his home in London County.
5 Defendant's physical presence in or near the London County Courthouse to respond to the allegations of the plaintiff will jeopardize the physical activity of the defendant and hamper the government's ability to prosecute a serious criminal threat to the people of the United States.

WHEREFORE, the United States of America moves this court for an order dismissing the allegations of the Complaint by Plaintiff CV 15-100 or, in the alternative, to order that the trial of said case be postponed until the completion of the criminal action pending in Indictment U.S. CR 124-47874.

Respectfully submitted,

Elliott S. Ness, Assistant Attorney General
United States Department of Justice
601 D Street, N.W., Suite 4300
Washington, DC 20530
(202) 514-4092

Intervention
The voluntary insertion of a third party into a pending civil action, often to resolve issues directly related to the third party's interests

Although the first basis for **intervention**, reliance on a federal statute, is rare, the second is not. Various court decisions have determined that if a person has a direct, substantial, or significant property interest, that party will be allowed to intervene in the action.

Consider the following example: On April 6, 2014, Manny is driving home and fails to pay attention to the upcoming intersection. He applies his brakes too late and rear-ends the car in front of him. The driver, Earl, gets out of his car, rushes to Manny's car, and strikes him in the face. Natasha, who is standing at the intersection, sees the entire incident. She has an irrational fear of violence and especially of blood, and when she sees Manny's nose bleeding, she passes out, striking her head on the ground and suffering a concussion. When the police arrive, they cite Manny for following too closely and Earl for battery. Earl claims that he has severe pain in his neck and is transported to the hospital, where he incurs $3,256 in medical bills. Manny is also taken to the hospital, where they discover that his nose is broken. He undergoes surgery to repair it. The bill for his medical treatment is $4,590. Earl is behind on his child support payments, for a total of $11,435, and his ex-wife, Myra, learns that he has hired an attorney who is drafting a complaint against Manny based on the accident.

Which, if any, of these parties have cross-claims or counterclaims against one another? Should any of the parties be brought into the case through impleader? Are there any parties who might wish to interplead or intervene in the case?

Tech Topic

CASE MANAGEMENT SYSTEMS

Over the next few chapters, we will discuss various software packages that provide case, client, or litigation support (and some that provide all three). In this chapter, we will discuss Abacus Law (www.abacuslaw.com).

Many legal malpractice insurers now require law offices to have some kind of case management system to avoid the prospect of missing an important deadline, especially the running of the statute of limitations for a particular claim. Failing to file before the statute runs is a surefire way for an attorney to be sued for legal malpractice. Abacus Law is a case management program that allows a law office to create calendars showing when clients are scheduled to come to the office, when the attorneys must appear in court, and a wide variety of other activities. It also provides a platform for instant messaging to everyone on the network inside the office.

Abacus Law also allows individual users to check for conflicts of interest by reviewing current and past clients. It generates to-do lists and time lines and gives instant access to a broad range of client information. Like many case management programs, Abacus Law has its proponents and its critics. Some find that it suits their practice perfectly, while others prefer other programs. One of its best features is the broad database it provides, not only for clients but also for opposing counsel, paralegals, judge's secretaries, clerks, and many others whom a legal professional will deal with on a daily basis.

VII CLASS ACTIONS

There are provisions that allow dozens, even hundreds, of plaintiffs to bring suit against a defendant. Such a case is referred to as a **class action**, and before a court will allow a large group of plaintiffs to pool their resources in a suit against a defendant, the plaintiffs must meet four prerequisites, set out in Figure 5-21.

Class action
A lawsuit involving a large group of plaintiffs who have been certified by a court as having mutual interest, common claims, and a representative plaintiff who will pursue the action on the basis of the entire group

FIGURE 5-21

Federal Rules of Civil Procedure, Rule 23 Class Actions

(a) Prerequisites to a Class Action. One or more members of a class may sue or be sued as representative parties on behalf of all members only if:

(1) the class is so numerous that joinder of all members is impracticable;

(2) there are questions of law or fact common to the class;

(3) the claims or defenses of the representative parties are typical of the claims or defenses of the class; and

(4) the representative parties will fairly and adequately protect the interests of the class.

(b) Types of Class Actions. A class action may be maintained if Rule 23(a) is satisfied and if:

(1) prosecuting separate actions by or against individual class members would create a risk of:

(A) inconsistent or varying adjudications with respect to individual class members that would establish incompatible standards of conduct for the party opposing the class; or

(B) adjudications with respect to individual class members that, as a practical matter, would be dispositive of the interests of the other members not parties to the individual adjudications or would substantially impair or impede their ability to protect their interests;

(2) the party opposing the class has acted or refused to act on grounds that apply generally to the class, so that final injunctive relief or corresponding declaratory relief is appropriate respecting the class as a whole; or

(3) the court finds that the questions of law or fact common to class members predominate over any questions affecting only individual members, and that a class action is superior to other available methods for fairly and efficiently adjudicating the controversy. The matters pertinent to these findings include:

(A) the class members' interests in individually controlling the prosecution or defense of separate actions;

(B) the extent and nature of any litigation concerning the controversy already begun by or against class members;

(C) the desirability or undesirability of concentrating the litigation of the claims in the particular forum; and

(D) the likely difficulties in managing a class action.

Under Rule 23, before a group can bring a class action, it must first establish that the number of plaintiffs is so large that following a traditional civil case would be impractical. The plaintiffs must also show that there are questions of law or fact common to all of the plaintiffs, that the representative plaintiffs have claims and defenses that are similar to the entire class, and that the representative plaintiffs will be fair and adequately protect the interests of the entire group.

When the plaintiffs can establish these minimum requirements, the court will certify a class and allow the case to proceed as a class action. Once the class has been certified, all plaintiffs are grouped together as a single action. This has the advantage of resolving hundreds, and sometimes thousands, of cases in a single suit. Recent examples of major class action lawsuits include actions against Firestone Tire Company for producing defective tires and the manufacturers of breast implants for creating faulty products.

A class action case proceeds through the representative plaintiffs who act on behalf of the entire class. If the case is settled prior to trial, the judge must make a determination that the settlement is in the best interests of the class and what amount each plaintiff will receive to terminate the case.

Tech Topic
DICTATION SOFTWARE

Companies like Nuance have created dictation software that allows individuals, armed only with a microphone and a laptop, to reach typing speeds up to 100 words per minute. The software has come a long way from its origins when users were forced to dictate each word in a measured, beat for beat way. Now the software lives up to its hype by actually typing what you say. The programs have also gotten good enough to figure out words in the context of a sentence, being able to distinguish "witch" from "which" in a sentence such as, "He didn't know which person was responsible."

Besides being able to dictate at blinding speeds, many companies producing dictation software also allow users to use voice commands instead of mouse or keyboard entry. A user can enter command mode and tell the computer to print a page, pull up a particular website, or to format the document differently. These types of programs can improve a person's writing efficiency dramatically.

Case Excerpt

When does a party waive an affirmative defense? Must it be asserted immediately or can the party wait and bring it up later in the proceedings?

FLORES V. SKARO
2005 Tex. App. LEXIS 9162, 2005 WL 2885841
(Tex. App. Corpus Christi Nov. 3, 2005)

MEMORANDUM OPINION

Appellants, Rogelio Flores, individually and as representative of the estate of Teresa Flores, and intervenors, Teodoro and Elida Flores, individually and as next of friends of June Flores, appeal a summary judgment granted in favor of appellee, Ann Skaro, on a claim for breach of an employment contract. We affirm.

Background

On July 1, 1995, Rogelio Flores and his wife, Teresa, retained appellee, as legal counsel, under a contingency-fee agreement ("agreement") to represent them in a personal injury case, individually and as next of friends of their daughter, June Flores, for a medication error committed by a pharmacy, whereby the pharmacy erred in filling a prescription for a drug prescribed to Teresa. This error resulted in the hospitalization of Teresa and ultimately caused her untimely death on November 30, 1995.

After Teresa's death, Rogelio's parents, Teodoro and Elida, proceeding pro se, instituted a suit affecting the parent-child relationship, requesting that the court appoint them as joint managing conservators of June. Appellee had recommended that a change in conservatorship was advisable because Rogelio's behavior apparently was adversely affecting the potential settlement value of the case. In support of this allegation, appellee cites, inter alia, Rogelio's application for marriage to a seventeen-year-old minor, which occurred about five months after Teresa's death. After Rogelio and his parents agreed to a change in conservatorship and Rogelio signed a waiver of service and appearance the court entered an order appointing Teodoro and Elida as joint managing conservators on August 2, 1996.

In light of the conservatorship suit, on July 31, 1996, appellee and Rogelio also modified their agreement, which was changed to provide for appellee's representation of Teodoro and Elida Flores, as managing conservators and next of friend of June, in the personal injury case. Other than this change, the agreement remained the same — the parties agreed to pay appellee one-half (after litigation expenses) of "all monies, interest or property which may be recovered . . . ," in exchange for her representation in the personal injury case. Sometime after Teresa's death, appellee filed a wrongful death suit ("underlying suit") in the case on behalf of Rogelio, individually and as representative of the estate of Teresa Flores, and Teodoro and Elida, individually and as next of friends of June. Shortly before trial, appellee negotiated a $6.5 million settlement on her clients' behalf, which the court approved on April 30, 1997.

Approximately three years later, Rogelio sued appellee, asserting a single cause of action for breach of an employment contract on the basis that appellee extracted a fee in excess of the percentage distribution provided for by the parties' agreement. The record reflects that the $6.5 million settlement was distributed as follows:

Settlement	$6,500,000
less expenses	225,000
Balance	$6,225,000
less net amount apportioned to June	3,137,500 (50% or settlement)
Balance	$3,137,500 (50% remaining)
less attorney fees	2,823,700
less medical and funeral expenses	18,659
Net Balance allocated to Rogelio	$295,141

Under the settlement distribution, June's portion was structured in annuities and trusts, and Rogelio's portion was paid to him individually.

On April 30, 2003, in response to the allegations, appellee moved for summary judgment on both traditional and no-evidence grounds, asserting affirmative defenses of waiver, ratification, and estoppel. The trial court subsequently granted appellee's motion. However, it did not explain the basis for its judgment and did not specify whether it was granting appellee's motion on traditional or no-evidence grounds.

Issues on Appeal

Rogelio contends the court erred in granting summary judgment because appellee waived her affirmative defenses. As a preliminary matter, we first determine whether appellee waived her affirmative defenses. We will then consider whether summary judgment was improper in light of the evidence and pleadings before the court.

Waiver

Regarding his first issue, Rogelio argues that appellee waived her affirmative defenses because she failed to plead them in her original answer. In contrast, appellee argues that the defenses were not waived because the trial court granted her leave to amend her pleadings.

Generally, a trial court's ruling on an amendment to pleadings is reviewed for an abuse of discretion. Affirmative defenses must be pleaded to give the opposing party notice of defensive issues to be tried. A party waives an affirmative defense if it is not pleaded. However, Texas Rule of Civil Procedure 63 provides that parties may file amendments to their pleadings at such time as not to operate as a surprise to the opposite party, but that filing within seven days of the trial date or thereafter requires leave of court, which leave should be granted absent a showing of surprise by the opposite party. A summary judgment proceeding is a trial within the meaning of rule 63. 8 In considering the propriety of an amendment, appellate courts liberally construe rule 63.

During pre-trial proceedings, appellee failed to plead any affirmative defenses in her original answer. Nevertheless, appellee asserted the defenses of waiver, ratification, and estoppel in her motion for summary judgment. Rogelio filed a response arguing, inter alia, that appellee had waived the defenses because they were not pleaded in her original answer. Shortly thereafter, appellee filed a motion for leave to amend her pleadings to include the defenses, which the trial court granted that same day. On the next day, the court entered a final order granting appellee's motion for summary judgment. The order stated, in relevant part, that the "Court . . . after hearing the arguments of counsel and examining the pleadings and . . . evidence . . . finds that appellee is entitled to summary judgment in all respects."

In analyzing this issue, we note that the record does not contain a docket control order setting a submission deadline for pleadings, nor does it reflect that a hearing was held on appellee's motion for summary judgment. Consequently, we are unable to determine the precise deadline for amendments to the pleadings. The record, however, establishes that appellee received permission to amend her pleadings one day prior to the court's entry of its order. Although the order was issued on the following day, Rogelio's summary judgment response addressed each defense asserted by appellee. Specifically, the response presented concise arguments in opposition to each defense. The court's order also reflects that the pleadings, which included Rogelio's response, were considered by the court prior to entering its order.

Although Rogelio argues waiver, he does not claim surprise as a result of the amendment, nor does the record support a finding that the amendment operated as a surprise. Because rule 63 provides the court with discretion to allow a party to amend pleadings, and the record does not support a finding of surprise, we conclude the defenses were not waived, and that it was not an abuse of discretion to allow the amendment. Appellant's first issue is overruled.

Conclusion

Because the trial court's grant of summary judgment on traditional grounds was appropriate, we need not address the remaining issues on appeal. We affirm the trial court's grant of summary judgment in favor of appellee.

QUESTIONS ABOUT THE CASE:

1 The underlying case here involved a wrongful death claim, but the case on appeal has to do with a contract between the various parties. Specifically, the plaintiff claims that the defendant waived her affirmative defenses. What is the basis of the plaintiff's claim regarding waiver?
2 The appellate court clearly states that when a party fails to include affirmative defenses in an answer that these defenses are waived. Why was that not the case here?
3 If the defendant did not initially include her affirmative defenses in her answer, then how was the plaintiff put on notice of what these affirmative defenses were (thus satisfying the Texas rule regarding amending pleadings)?
4 Rogelio clearly argues that the defendant failed to submit affirmative defenses in her answer, but does he claim surprise or other damage because of this failure?

Chapter Summary

Once a complaint has been served on a defendant, she has a specific time period to file a response. This response is usually known as an *answer*. In most situations, the defendant has 20 days to file the answer and serve it on the plaintiff. An answer contains the defendant's response to each of the allegations raised by the plaintiff in the complaint. The answer must either admit or deny the contentions raised in the complaint. The defendant is also permitted to allege that she is without knowledge about a particular contention.

In addition to responding to the plaintiff's allegations in the complaint, the defendant's answer must also set out specific defenses. Some defenses, referred to as *affirmative defenses*, must be stated in the answer. Examples of affirmative defenses include accord and satisfaction, contributory negligence, res judicata, and statute of limitations, to name just a few. In addition to raising affirmative defenses, a defendant is also allowed to bring a counterclaim against the plaintiff for any injuries that the defendant claims were committed by the plaintiff. A compulsory counterclaim involves the same facts and circumstances as the complaint, while a permissive counterclaim is not factually tied to the complaint.

An answer may also raise other issues, including the provision for a 12(b)(6) motion. Such a motion challenges the actual wording of the complaint by claiming that it fails to state a claim upon which relief can be granted by a court.

Defendants also have additional options when it comes to pleadings. They can bring an action against a co-defendant by raising a cross-claim. They can bring other individuals into the suit through impleader. Individuals who want to insert themselves into the litigation, and who satisfy the legal requirements, are entitled to do so through intervention.

SKILLS YOU NEED IN THE REAL WORLD

Rules Concerning Answers and Other Claims

Locate copies of your state Rules of Civil Procedure concerning answers (especially the form of an answer), the rules concerning compulsory and permissive counterclaims, the rules concerning cross-claims, and the rules concerning third-party practice. Make copies all these rules, and place them in your trial notebook.

THE LIFE OF A PARALEGAL

Case Management Software and the Paralegal

Debra Holbrook is a paralegal at a firm that handles a wide variety of cases. "We do some real estate, some bankruptcy, criminal, business litigation, and corporate law." She finds that the variety keeps her stimulated. "Although it can be a little overwhelming, it's never boring." In addition to her duties of monitoring files, keeping up with clients, and scheduling, she has many other duties. "On any given day, you'll find me doing payables [tracking client fees]. I'm putting memos in the files, making sure that bills go out. In a small office, you never get bored, because there is always so much to do. I'm always involved in several different things at the same time. I don't have time to get bored. I'm kind of the office manager and the accountant and the investigator and the secretary all rolled into one."

Debra's firm uses Abacus Law as its case management system. "We use it to help keep track of client appointments. Using Abacus, you can link all of your various client documents together. You can look up clients by name, for instance, and find more information about them. We assign our client file number simply by year and number. As a paralegal, there is an awful lot of interaction with the client, and having all of your information in one place makes it a lot easier to dig out a telephone number or an address."

ETHICAL ISSUES FOR THE PARALEGAL

Bad Faith

As we have seen in this chapter, attorneys who interpose frivolous defenses or engage in bad faith in the claims raised in answers are subject to sanctions by the court. The sanctions include not only monetary fines, but also the possibility that a client's defenses may be struck from the answer. Such an action would have drastic consequences for the client and would no doubt result in a legal malpractice action against the attorney should the client lose the case. These are all excellent reasons to be familiar with the Rules of Civil Procedure for the jurisdiction in which you practice and also to avoid any pressure from the client to interpose frivolous or harassing claims in answers as part of a misguided attempt to seek revenge against or punish the other party. Such practices often misfire and have negative consequences for both the law firm and the client.

Websites

- **Texas Court System**
  www.txcourts.gov/

- **Wikipedia — Answers in Civil Cases**
  http://en.wikipedia.org/wiki/Answer

- **New Mexico — Judicial Education Center**
  http://jec.unm.edu/

Forms and Court Documents

Answer

This is the answer to the complaint found in Chapter 4.

STATE OF PLACID

DISTRICT COURT

LONDON COUNTY

Sherlock Holmes (Plaintiff) v. Professor James Moriarty, individually and as owner, operator of Moriarty Transport Trucking Co. (Defendant)	CIVIL ACTION: 15-100 **Answer of Defendant**

JURISDICTIONAL ALLEGATIONS

1. James Moriarty, hereafter referred to as "the defendant," hereby alleges that he is without information as to the plaintiff's residence, citizenship, or age.
2. James Moriarty is president, founder, and majority stockholder of Moriarty Transport Trucking Co. The remainder of the plaintiff's allegations in this paragraph are hereby ADMITTED.
3. Defendant denies that there is any cause of action; therefore this paragraph is deemed DENIED.

GENERAL ALLEGATIONS

4. The allegations in this paragraph are ADMITTED.
5. The allegations contained in this paragraph are admitted to the extent that defendant was the driver of a truck owned and operated by Moriarty Transport Trucking Co. The remaining allegations in this paragraph are DENIED.
6. Defendant is without sufficient knowledge to either admit or deny the allegations in this paragraph.
7. Defendant is without sufficient knowledge to either admit or deny the allegations in this paragraph.
8. Defendant is without sufficient knowledge to either admit or deny the allegations in this paragraph.
9. Defendant is without sufficient knowledge to either admit or deny the allegations in this paragraph.
10. Defendant is without sufficient knowledge to either admit or deny the allegations in this paragraph.
11. Defendant is without sufficient knowledge to either admit or deny the allegations in this paragraph.
12. The allegations contained in this paragraph are DENIED.
13. The allegations contained in this paragraph are DENIED.
14. The allegations contained in this paragraph are DENIED.
15. The allegations contained in this paragraph are DENIED.

REQUEST FOR JURY TRIAL

Defendant requests a trial by jury for all allegations raised in the pleadings by plaintiff and defendant.

AFFIRMATIVE DEFENSES

1. The plaintiff's allegations are barred by the statute of limitations.
2. The plaintiff's allegations are based on the plaintiff's own contributory negligence.
3. The plaintiff's allegations are based on fraud.
4. The plaintiff assumed the risk of any injuries he may have received on the date of the collision (as set out in the plaintiff's complaint) by undertaking a career as a self-proclaimed "investigative consultant."
5. The plaintiff's claims are barred by res judicata.

COUNTERCLAIM AGAINST PLAINTIFF

Counterclaim I

The defendant incorporates here by reference all previous paragraphs and further brings the following counterclaim against plaintiff:

1. That the plaintiff was, on the day of collision set out in paragraph 4 of the plaintiff's complaint, operating his automobile in an erratic manner.
2. That the plaintiff put his car in reverse as the defendant approached the intersection.
3. That the plaintiff caused the collision between the two vehicles by deliberating backing into the defendant's automobile.
4. That the defendant suffered personal injuries as a result of the plaintiff's negligent conduct.
5. That the defendant suffered property losses in excess of $10,000 by the plaintiff's conduct.

WHEREFORE, defendant prays:

1. That the plaintiff have and receive nothing from his claim against the defendant.
2. That the plaintiff be ordered to pay all of the defendant's medical, property, and other damages directly tied to the collision alleged in the plaintiff's complaint.
3. That the plaintiff be ordered to pay all costs, including defendant's attorney's fees, for the defense of this action.
4. That the defendant should receive whatever compensation, awards, and equitable relief that the court may deem just and proper.

Counterclaim II

The defendant incorporates by reference all previous paragraphs alleged by him in this Answer and Counterclaim. Defendant further brings this second counterclaim against the plaintiff, to wit:

1. That the plaintiff has, on numerous occasions, accused the defendant of unethical, immoral, and illegal conduct.
2. That the plaintiff has communicated these unethical, immoral, and illegal accusations to others, including police officers.
3. That the defendant's reputation has been damaged by the plaintiff's allegations.
4. That the allegations are untrue.
5. That the plaintiff has engaged in these statements as a result of malice and a generalized hatred of the defendant.

WHEREFORE, the defendant prays:

1. That the plaintiff have and receive nothing from his claim against the defendant.
2. That the plaintiff be assessed general and special damages for his slander of the defendant's reputation.
3. That the plaintiff be enjoined from issuing such statements in the future.
4. That the defendant should receive whatever compensation, awards, and equitable relief that the court may be deem just and proper.

PRAYER FOR RELIEF

Defendant requests:

1. That the plaintiff have and receive nothing from the defendant for any count alleged in plaintiff's complaint.
2. That the defendant's counterclaims be granted against the plaintiff.
3. That the costs of this action be assessed against plaintiff.
4. That the plaintiff be assessed for bad faith damages.
5. That the defendant's prayers for equitable relief should be granted.
6. That the defendant's prayers for monetary relief be granted.
7. That the court award any additional relief, award, equitable relief, sanctions, or other remedies in accord with its own findings and in the interests of justice.

Respectfully submitted, this the ____________ day of December, 2014.

____

B. B. Gershon

Attorney for Defendant
100 Treachery Lane
Placid City, Placid 10050
212-555-1212
State Bar No. 00666

Key Terms

12(b)(6) motion
Admit
Affirmative defense
Bad faith
Class action
Compulsory counterclaim
Counterclaim
Cross-claim
Default judgment
Deny
Impleader
Interpleader
Intervention
Permissive counterclaim
Reply
Res judicata

Review Questions

1 What is the purpose of the defendant's answer?
2 What are the minimum requirements for a legally sufficient answer?
3 What are the consequences of an admission in an answer?
4 What are the three possible statements that a defendant can give to the allegations in the plaintiff's complaint?
5 What are the consequences for the defendant when she fails to respond to an allegation in the complaint?
6 What are the consequences when a court determines that the defendant has acted in bad faith in drafting his answer?
7 What is the normal time limit for a defendant to serve an answer on the plaintiff?
8 What are affirmative defenses?
9 How does a defendant raise an affirmative defense?
10 What is a counterclaim?
11 What is the difference between a compulsory counterclaim and a permissive counterclaim?
12 What is res judicata?
13 What is a 12(b)(6) motion?
14 When is a defendant authorized to bring a 12(b)(6) motion?
15 What is a cross-claim?
16 Compare and contrast counterclaims and cross-claims.
17 What is impleader?
18 What is interpleader?
19 Explain intervention.
20 Explain how a court determines that a class is certified in a class action suit.
21 Explain the difference between compulsory counterclaims, permissive counterclaims, and cross-claims. How does the principal of res judicata interact with these various actions?

Applying What You Have Learned

1 For the complaint that you prepared in Chapter 4, prepare an answer that provides a legally sufficient response to each allegation raised. If the facts of your case suggest a counterclaim, include that as well.

2 Using the complaint you prepared in Chapter 4, draft an answer to the complaint. Also include in that answer a counterclaim against the plaintiff.

3 Review your state rules and case law on cross-claims and counterclaims, and then compare and contrast these two types of claims. When and where are they brought? What is the primary difference between a counterclaim and a cross-claim? What is the significance of permissive versus compulsory counterclaims? How do these claims relate to interpleader and impleader?

4 Allison rents an apartment and lives on the second floor of a unit owned by Landlord, Inc. One day, as she is leaving for work, the stairs give way beneath her; she falls through and is severely injured. She brings a complaint against Landlord, Inc. In her complaint, she alleges that recent repairs done to the stairway were incomplete and resulted in a dangerous condition. Acme Construction Company performed the work. Allison was also two months behind on her rent. Diagram out possible claims that these parties may bring against one another.

Endnotes

[1]Rule 13(a), Federal Rules of Civil Procedure.
[2]*Emmanouil v. Roggio*, 2006 WL 2927621, *2 (D.N.J.) (D.N.J., 2006).

6 Evidence

Chapter Objectives

- Describe the purpose of evidence
- Explain the consequences of a ruling of admissibility on evidence
- Discuss the differences between direct evidence and circumstantial evidence
- Explain how a judge determines admissibility of evidence
- Describe the process of laying the foundation of evidence
- Explain hearsay and its exceptions
- Describe the importance of demonstrative evidence
- Distinguish between physical evidence and documentary evidence
- Explain how the paralegal can be involved in gathering evidence
- Explain the best evidence rule

I INTRODUCTION

In this chapter, we will discuss the rules of evidence as they apply to civil pleadings and trials. Although we will base our discussion on the Federal Rules of Evidence, many states have used the Federal Rules as the template for enacting their own evidentiary rules. Learning these rules is important for all paralegals. However, not all of the complexities of evidentiary law can be expressed in a single chapter. There are huge, multivolume treatises written on the topic. Although attorneys spend their entire legal careers dealing with evidentiary issues, there are still many fine points that require them to engage in additional research. We will begin our discussion of evidentiary law by discussing how various types of evidence are used to support contentions in civil cases and then address important evidentiary rules, such as hearsay.

WHAT IS EVIDENCE?

Evidence
Any fact, testimony, or physical object that tends to prove or disprove allegations raised in a case

Evidence is any item that tends to prove or disprove any fact in contention between the parties. As such, evidence includes witness testimony, documentary evidence, physical evidence, oral testimony, and a wide variety of other items, all presented by the various parties at trial in order to support their contentions or detract from their opponents' claims.

The Federal Rules of Evidence bind all federal courts and obviously play an important role throughout the country, but the rules also serve as a template for the evidentiary rules in dozens of states. Each state has its own evidentiary code, and many have changed theirs over the years to follow the federal model. The advantages of using the Federal Rules as a model are that they provide a ready-made framework for the myriad of evidentiary issues and they allow practitioners to rely on well-considered decisions by appellate courts on the use of various kinds of evidence. Practitioners who routinely appear in federal courts can readily grasp the concepts of state evidentiary law when that law is based on federal rules. Practitioners in all states must be intimately knowledgeable about the rules that apply in their state or face disastrous consequences at trial.

In all states, evidence can be classified into three broad categories: direct, circumstantial, and documentary. Before it can be used, however, it must be shown to have three key characteristics:

- Relevance
- Competence
- Admissibility

PRACTICE POINTER ▶ APPELLATE CASES

Although it is always a good practice to read recent appellate decisions regarding evidence from both state and federal appellate courts, some opinions are more valuable than others. For instance, if you focus on litigation, then you might consider creating a separate reference that contains evidentiary opinions only. Any time a new appellate case discusses, amplifies, or changes an existing evidentiary rule, place a synopsis of this case in your reference. This could be a notebook containing print copies, an easily accessible computer file, or even a database cross-referenced to other material. Find a way that works for you. Inevitably, an issue will arise in a future case, and your ready access to the answer will prove invaluable.

Sidebar

Is evidence the same thing as "fact"? Although we tend to think of the terms evidence and fact as interchangeable, as far as the law is concerned, they are two separate entities. A fact is any data, whether admissible or not. Evidence is something that tends to prove or disprove allegations in a trial.

A. RELEVANCE

Just as all facts do not constitute evidence, not all evidence is admissible during a trial. Courts require that the party offering evidence satisfy some minimal criteria, the most important of which is **relevance**. Evidence is relevant if it tends to prove or disprove an allegation by the parties. Under this test, there are many different types of evidence that might be interesting to the parties but that would not be admissible.

Relevance
The characteristic of evidence that makes it tend to prove or disprove some fact or allegation in a case

Consider the following example: Maria has brought suit against a local newspaper for incorrectly placing a caption under her photograph as "Maria Collins, recently convicted of forgery." Maria's last name is not Collins, and she was not convicted of forgery. Unfortunately, the newspaper incorrectly switched photos of the real convicted felon with an article about winners of a recent pie contest. In Maria's suit for defamation of character against the newspaper, the attorney representing the paper has learned that Maria actually came in second at the pie contest, not first. Is this evidence admissible during Maria's trial for defamation?

Answer: No. The facts surrounding the pie contest are not under consideration in this case. If the attorney attempted to admit this evidence, the judge would likely rule that it had no relevance to the issues and would not allow the attorney to present it.

The Federal Rules of Evidence embody the concept of relevance in Rule 401 (Fig. 6-1). No matter what model is followed in a given state, however, all jurisdictions require that a party intending to present evidence at trial must establish that the evidence is relevant to the issues.

Sidebar

We tend to think of evidence as tangible objects — murder weapons, photographs, fingerprints, and DNA — but the legal definition is much more broad. Other examples of evidence include a person's testimony on the stand, a contract clause, and a medical analysis, among many others.

Evidence is relevant if:

(a) it has any tendency to make a fact more or less probable than it would be without the evidence; and
(b) the fact is of consequence in determining the action.

FIGURE 6-1

Rule 401. Test for Relevant Evidence

Example: Officer Baker is on the stand, being cross-examined about arriving at the scene of an accident. The plaintiff is alleging that the defendant was driving negligently and rear-ended her car.

Officer: I was dispatched to the scene of an accident. When I arrived, there were two cars in the middle of the intersection of Tango and Cash Streets. The front of the defendant's car was smashed in and so was the back of the plaintiff's car. I made sure that everyone was safe and asked if anyone needed medical attention, and then began taking statements.

Defense attorney: You've had family members who've been in trouble with the police, haven't you?

Plaintiff's attorney: Objection! Relevance.

How is the court likely to rule?

Answer: The judge will almost certainly rule that this question is not relevant to the proceedings and instruct the attorney to move on to a topic that has something to do with the allegations in the case.

B. COMPETENCE

In addition to a showing of relevance, the Rules of Evidence also require a showing of competency. In this regard, *competency* has a special meaning. It refers to the fact that the evidence presented tends to prove the facts in dispute and is not based on conjecture, guesswork, or mere speculation. Competent evidence must be based on a solid foundation and the witness's personal knowledge.

Consider the following example: Jane is on the stand and testifying under oath. She witnessed a car wreck last year, and the plaintiff's attorney asks her, "Did you see the color of the traffic light shortly before the defendant drove through that intersection?"

A: Yes, I did.
Q: What was the color of that light?
A: It was red for the drivers coming from the defendant's direction.

Confident of winning his case, the plaintiff's attorney then asks, "And how can you be so sure of the color of the light?"

A: Well, it had to be. The plaintiff was moving through the intersection, and she wouldn't have driven through a red light, so her light was green. Therefore, the defendant's light must have been red.

Is Jane's testimony competent?

Answer: No. Although it initially appeared that Jane based her testimony on her personal observations of the accident (which would have been competent evidence), she has revealed that her testimony is based on conjecture or guesswork. Such testimony is not admissible. If the defense attorney requests that the judge strike her testimony and instruct the jury to ignore it, the judge will probably comply.

In their testimony, most witnesses are limited to describing experiences that they actually perceived, not what they assume or guess must have happened. The practical result is that a witness is generally prohibited from testifying to facts and situations that he did not actually experience. There is at least one important exception to that rule: expert testimony. We will discuss that topic later in this chapter.

C. ADMISSIBILITY

Admissibility
A ruling on whether the jury will be allowed to view proffered evidence

A judge rules on the **admissibility** of evidence during the trial. If a judge rules that certain evidence is admissible, this means that the jury will be allowed to see or hear it. When the evidence consists of physical objects, such as weapons, a ruling of admissibility means that the evidence will go into the jury room with the jurors when they deliberate at the end of the case. They will be permitted to handle the evidence and examine it for themselves. However, a judge might rule that particular evidence is inadmissible, meaning that the jury will not be permitted to see or hear it. Evidence can be ruled inadmissible for a wide variety of reasons. The judge might decide that the evidence is not relevant to the issues in the case or that the evidence is too prejudicial and would result in an unfair trial if the jurors were to see it.

Consider the following transcript of testimony from a recent medical malpractice case:

Plaintiff's attorney: Doctor, I'm handing you what has been marked as "Plaintiff's Exhibit Number One." Would you describe it to the jury?

Witness: Yes. It appears to be a picture of the plaintiff when he was a child. He is smiling and being held by his mother.

Defense attorney: Objection! Relevance.

Judge: What is the relevance of this evidence?

Plaintiff's attorney: I'm attempting to show that the plaintiff had a nice childhood.

Judge: The plaintiff is 60 years old, Counsel. The issue is not relevant to a medical malpractice case.

Judge (to the defense attorney): Your objection is sustained.

In this example, the judge has ruled that the question is not relevant and will not be allowed. When the judge said that the objection was **sustained**, it meant that the judge was in agreement with the basis of the objection and had ruled in favor of the party who raised it. If the judge had decided for some reason to allow the testimony, then the judge would have said that the objection was **overruled**. If sustained, the objection would effectively preclude the party from asking further questions about the evidence. If overruled, the original party would be permitted to continue questioning the witness.

Sustain
A judge's ruling in agreement with the party who raised the objection

Overrule
A judge's ruling in disagreement with the party who raised the objection

III THE ROLE OF EVIDENCE

The purpose of evidence is clear: It is the way that the parties prove their allegations. When a plaintiff drafts a complaint, for instance, the plaintiff's attorney and paralegal must be mindful of the evidence that will be used to support each and every allegation contained therein. Without evidence to support the contentions, the claim will be dismissed. A plaintiff without evidence is a plaintiff without a case.

Another important point to keep in mind about evidence is that attorneys are not allowed to testify about the merits of their case. Attorneys cannot, for example, present evidence to the jury on their own. Instead, evidence must come through a sponsoring witness or some other source. This means that if the attorney wishes to introduce a photograph of the plaintiff's wrecked car, for example, the attorney must put a witness on the stand and ask that witness basic questions to establish relevance and competence, laying the proper foundation to prove that the photograph is admissible. Once that phase is complete, the attorney must then request that the judge rule on the admissibility of the evidence. All of these elements require attorneys and paralegals to be very knowledgeable about the use of evidence.

PRACTICE POINTER ▶ TALKING TO CLIENTS ABOUT EVIDENCE

You should always be prepared to explain to clients the importance of locating and retaining important evidence. Many paralegals take care of this point by incorporating it into the follow-up letter sent to the client after the initial meeting. They include a paragraph that might go something like this:

> As we discussed, it is absolutely essential to your case that we immediately take possession of any evidence in your case so that we may have it for safekeeping and retain it for any further purposes, including pretrial motions, settlement discussions, and possible admission at trial. If you know of any evidence that pertains to any issues in this case, whether it is in your possession or anyone else's, please notify us immediately so that we may begin the process of obtaining it. In some cases, it may be necessary to issue subpoenas to recover the evidence, so do not delay in listing all sources of medical and employment records, photographs, diagrams, or any other object that we touched on in our discussions when you came to our office.

A. LAYING THE FOUNDATION

Many attorneys view the process of presenting a case as analogous to building a house. In order to have a solid structure, the foundation must be properly constructed. Courts have often extended the construction metaphor to presenting evidence at trial. Before counsel can request that a judge rule on the admissibility of an item of evidence, the attorney must establish relevance and competence. These two items are the cornerstone of admissibility, and failure to properly lay the foundation could result in a ruling of inadmissibility.

Lay the foundation
The presentation of sufficient background material to establish the relevance and competence of a particular piece of evidence

In order to show that a particular fact has relevance and competence, the attorney must **lay the foundation** by asking specific questions of a witness. Because attorneys cannot testify about facts themselves, one of the few ways of presenting facts to the jury is by asking witnesses questions to show the relevance and competence of any particular piece of evidence.

Suppose that the plaintiff is testifying, and his attorney wants the jury to see a photograph of the intersection where the automobile collision at issue occurred. The attorney cannot simply walk over to the jurors and hand them a photo. Before the jury may see the photo, the attorney must prove that it is relevant and competent. How does the attorney accomplish this? She must question the plaintiff. That testimony might go something like this:

Plaintiff's attorney: Mr. Wilson, I'm handing you what has been labeled "Plaintiff's Exhibit Number One." What is it?

Plaintiff: It's a photograph.

Plaintiff's attorney: What does the photograph show?

Plaintiff: That's the intersection where the accident occurred. You can clearly see the traffic light and the gas station on the corner.

Plaintiff's attorney: Does that photograph accurately reflect how the intersection looked on the day of the accident?

Plaintiff: Yes, it does.

Plaintiff's attorney: Has that photograph been altered or changed in any way to change the actual appearance of the intersection?

Plaintiff: No, it hasn't been altered or tampered with.

Plaintiff's attorney: Is that how the intersection actually looked from your perspective as you were approaching it on the day of the collision?

Plaintiff: Yes.

Plaintiff's attorney: Your Honor, I move to admit Plaintiff's Exhibit Number One.

In the exchange between attorney and witness in this example, several important things have happened. First, the attorney asked open-ended questions. An attorney is not permitted to simply tell a witness what the evidence is. Instead, the attorney must draw the information from the witness. That accounts for the questions about what the exhibit is and what it shows. You will also notice that the attorney didn't simply start asking questions about the collision and how the photo proved something in the case. Before she can do that, an attorney must first prove that the photograph — or any piece of evidence — is relevant. In this example, the attorney does so by first establishing that the photograph shows the intersection where the collision occurred. The attorney then asks additional questions establishing that the photograph has not been altered in a way that emphasizes certain features at the expense of others. A photograph must accurately reflect the reality of the scene; if it has been altered, it is not admissible.

Photographs, like many other types of evidence, have specific types of foundation questions asked about them that have been established over the years. If the attorney were presenting another type of evidence, such as a videotape or the cast of a footprint, the attorney's foundation questions would have been different.

LEGAL LEGWORK ■ FOUNDATION QUESTIONS

It is always important to know what foundation questions are needed in order to admit different types of evidence. Locate your state's legal index, encyclopedia, and any other sources that will provide you with specific foundation questions to admit evidence such as audiotapes, videotapes, and photographs. What prominent cases provide the parameters for using this evidence? Are there cases that limit how new technology, such as computer animation, may be used at trial?

B. TENDERING EVIDENCE

In the preceding example, you will notice that after the attorney asked the witness what the attorney believed were sufficient questions to establish relevance and competence, he then requested that the court rule on the photograph. He did this by stating, "Your Honor, I move to admit Plaintiff's Exhibit Number One."

Tendering
The process of seeking admissibility of a particular item of evidence

This statement is referred to as **tendering** the evidence. What the attorney is doing here is asking the judge to rule on the admissibility of the evidence. The attorney could simply ask, "Judge, will you say that it is admissible?" But the traditions that have developed over centuries of trials require that the question be asked as it was in the example. Once the attorney makes this request, the judge will then refer to opposing counsel for any objections to the use of the evidence. Once all objections and arguments have been heard about the evidence, the judge rules on the admissibility of the item.

Consider this continuation of the previous example:

Judge: Ms. Hershey, do you have any objections to Plaintiff's Exhibit Number One, the photograph of the intersection?

Defense attorney: Yes, Your Honor, insufficient foundation.

Will this objection be sustained or overruled?

In order to answer this question, we must first decipher the nature of the attorney's objection. Essentially, the attorney's objection states that the plaintiff's attorney has failed to prove enough relevance or competence of the evidence. The shorthand way of stating this is to simply say, "insufficient foundation." Then the judge is left with the decision of whether to admit it.

Is there sufficient foundation for the photograph? The plaintiff's attorney has shown that the photo accurately shows the intersection as it appeared on the day of the collision, and the photo certainly seems to satisfy the requirements of relevance and competence. In this case, the judge will almost certainly overrule the defense attorney's objection. Most likely, the judge will make the following announcement:

Judge: Plaintiff's Exhibit Number One admitted over objection.

The protocol followed in admitting evidence always calls for the judge to refer to opposing counsel before admitting evidence. This gives the opposing attorney a chance to lodge an objection to the evidence and preserve the objection for appeal. In some cases, the objection may be properly raised and the judge may refuse to admit the evidence. In such a case, the plaintiff's attorney would be barred from referring to it in any way for the remainder of the trial.

SEARCH SUGGESTION • EVIDENTIARY SOURCES

Whenever you are researching evidentiary questions, keep in mind that there are several national treatises and publications on evidentiary issues that can provide you with valuable guidance. One such source is *American Law Reports.* Published by Thomson-West, this a continuing, multivolume set that analyzes every aspect of the law, especially recent case decisions and their impact on specific legal topics. *ALR* is also an excellent source for an overview of specific types of evidence and often provides foundation questions and other material that can be very helpful to a practitioner. *ALR*'s *Proof of Facts* provides specific foundation questions and checklists, and it details exactly what evidence must be admitted during the trial in order to conclusively prove a contested fact.

C. OBJECTING TO EVIDENCE

There are numerous objections that can be raised to evidence tendered to the court. The attorney may wish to object based on any of the following (offered only as a summary of the vast array of potential objections):

- Improper conclusion
- Relevance
- Prejudice
- Other issues

1. IMPROPER CONCLUSION

An attorney's objection about witness or other testimony on the basis that it calls for an "improper conclusion" is actually shorthand for an objection that is more extensive. In essence, this objection goes to the very heart of a jury trial. When attorneys present testimony, documentary evidence, or physical evidence to a jury, they are asking the jury to reach a conclusion about the impact of that evidence on the issues in the case. Because it is the jury's responsibility to allocate the importance of each piece of evidence into an overall cohesive conclusion about the case, it is improper for a witness to tell the jury the significance of any piece of evidence.

For instance, suppose that a witness testifies that the defendant's negligent driving was the cause of the accident. The attorney representing the defendant would object, pointing out that it is not for the witness to reach this conclusion but for the jury. In such a case, the judge would almost certainly sustain such an objection, direct the witness not to make such statements, and instruct the jury to disregard the witness' testimony. The judge might even go further and remind the jury that it is the responsibility of the individual jurors to determine the importance of each piece of evidence, not a witness.

In the next chapter, we will see that this rule has one important exception: Expert witnesses, once qualified, may give conclusions about specific facts in the case, primarily because the issues about which they testify are beyond the knowledge and training of the average juror.

2. RELEVANCE

An objection of relevance goes to the very heart of the purpose of evidence: It must bear on an issue pending in the case. When an attorney raises the objection of relevance, he is saying that the evidence sought to be admitted does not serve that critical function. If the judge rules that an item of evidence is not relevant, then the court is essentially denying the usefulness of the evidence to assist the jury in resolving any of the issues raised in the case.

3. PREJUDICE

An objection based on the prejudicial impact of evidence is one that may agree to the relevance of the evidence but objects because the evidence will have an effect on the jury that outweighs other evidence. Autopsy photos, for instance, may have relevance to the issues surrounding the decedent's injuries, but they are so gruesome that jurors will have a difficult time giving other evidence as much credence and attention. Although prejudice is an objection that can be raised for any evidence, it is often seen in the context of gruesome photos or other visual media, or concerning an individual's past actions, including conviction of a crime. These issues might tend to overly sway the jury and because of this, courts are reluctant to admit highly controversial evidence unless the party offering it can show that there is no other way to have the jury consider the facts.

4. OTHER ISSUES

There are so many other grounds for objection to evidence that entire books are written on the topic. Objections run the gamut from hearsay to impeachment to trade secrets. Paralegals should be aware of any potential objection to evidence that the legal team intends to use at trial. Simply because the opposition objects to the admission of specific evidence does not mean that the judge will sustain that objection. A paralegal who has thoroughly researched the legal issues surrounding the evidence intended to be used at trial can be an invaluable asset in helping the legal team convince a judge to rule in its favor.

IV TYPES OF EVIDENCE

Now that we have discussed how evidence is admitted at trial, we must address the various types of evidence that are used in civil cases. Evidence can be classified into three broad categories:

- Direct (real) evidence
- Circumstantial evidence
- Documentary evidence

A. DIRECT EVIDENCE

Direct evidence is also known as *real evidence.* Direct evidence is anything that is conclusive proof of a particular fact. Usually, it proves a point in contention between the parties. For example, suppose that in a personal injury lawsuit, the plaintiff offers evidence of the impact of the defendant's car with his own car. The plaintiff removes the car door from his car and brings it to court. Anyone can clearly see a terrible gash in the door, offering direct evidence of the damage to anyone looking at the door in the courtroom.

Direct evidence
Evidence that establishes a particular fact without resorting to other testimony or evidence

1. WHAT QUALIFIES AS DIRECT EVIDENCE

Bringing in direct evidence is sometimes neither practical nor possible. In those cases, such as when the car has been destroyed, the second best option would be to present a photograph of the car door. However, as we will shortly see, a photograph is not direct evidence; it is documentary evidence. Only the car door itself would be considered direct evidence. Another common example of direct evidence is eyewitness testimony (Fig. 6-2).

FIGURE 6-2

Examples of Direct Evidence

Eyewitness testimony
Photographs of plaintiff's injuries
Video or audiotapes of conversations
Objects relevant to issues in the case
Written statements
Documents

2. EYEWITNESS TESTIMONY

Both criminal cases and civil cases rely heavily on eyewitness testimony. There is something very compelling about hearing someone say, "I saw the defendant do it." Direct testimony offered on the stand is very convincing, and that explains why attorneys for both sides often try to find witnesses who can testify about their direct experiences. Suppose, for example, that the defense team in a car wreck case has located a witness who will testify that the plaintiff ignored the red light and actually caused the collision that he is now blaming on the defendant. When this witness takes the stand and testifies, his testimony is direct evidence that the plaintiff was at fault in the accident, which will be devastating to the plaintiff's case. We have all heard the old maxim, "Seeing is believing." This maxim applies indirectly to jury trials. There, the fact that the witness saw it is enough for the jury to believe it.

Many legal commentators, and average jurors, have a strong bias toward direct evidence. When in doubt, they would much prefer to be presented with eyewitness testimony or physical objects that substantiate the claims in the case. However, that is not always possible. Sometimes, the evidence presented falls into the category of circumstantial evidence.

B. CIRCUMSTANTIAL EVIDENCE

Circumstantial evidence Evidence that suggests a conclusion

If direct evidence is proof of a fact, then **circumstantial evidence** suggests a conclusion about a fact. Generations of law students have been presented with the famous example of finding a "a trout in the milk." In the example, a person finds a fish in a glass of milk. The conclusion? Someone put it there. The reason this qualifies as circumstantial evidence is that if this were your glass of milk, you could not conclusively say that you saw a person put the fish in the glass, but you could certainly draw the conclusion that someone must have done so.

Circumstantial evidence suggests a conclusion but does not directly prove it. The reason that circumstantial evidence is considered to be weaker than direct evidence is because circumstantial evidence is often open to interpretation.

Consider the following example: It's winter. Just before you fall asleep, you happen to look out your bedroom window and notice that the first snowfall of the season has started. In the morning, you look out your bedroom window and see footprints in the snow. When you get up and go to the kitchen, you see your child's boots next to the door, covered in snow. You draw a conclusion that your son got up early and went out to play in the snow before you woke up. Your conclusion is based on circumstantial evidence. After all, you didn't actually see your son playing in the snow, so you don't have any direct evidence, but it is a reasonable conclusion based on the facts at hand. This is circumstantial evidence because there are other possible explanations. For instance, someone else could have made the footprints and the snow dripping off your child's boots could have come from the front yard.

Simply because evidence falls into the category of circumstantial evidence does not mean that it is somehow defective. Entire cases can be constructed on circumstantial evidence. However, there is an important problem that arises in basing a case exclusively on circumstantial evidence: The conclusion suggested from the evidence must support the allegations. The more that the evidence is open to interpretation, the more likely it is that the judge and jury may draw a contrary conclusion.

In the real world of litigation, most cases are a blend of both direct and circumstantial evidence. In a personal injury case, for example, the damages to the plaintiff's automobile and her scarring from injuries received would qualify as direct evidence, while a witness's testimony about hearing a crash and then seeing the plaintiff climbing out of her car would be circumstantial evidence that a crash had just occurred.

Consider the following example: Ron is running late one day and fails to stop for a red light. He runs his car into the back of the car in front of him. Sue is at the wheel of the other car, and she sustains severe neck injuries. She is also knocked unconscious at the wreck and is later unable to testify about the facts immediately prior to the collision. There are no eyewitnesses. At trial, Ron claims that the light was green and that he never saw Sue's car. The damage to the front of Ron's car is extensive. There are also skid marks on the road from Ron's wheels.

What is the direct and what is the circumstantial evidence in this case? Sue's medical injuries are direct evidence of the extent of her injuries sustained in the car crash. Is there any circumstantial evidence in this case? As a matter of fact, there is. What about the skid marks from Ron's car? Taken by themselves, you could consider them as direct evidence that Ron put on the brakes. But this evidence is also circumstantial in that it suggests, but does not prove, a possible conclusion. What is that conclusion? If Ron claims that he never saw Sue's car, then there would have been no reason for him to hit the brakes and, therefore, he's not telling the truth. Circumstantial evidence in this case suggests that Ron saw Sue's car, hit the brakes, went into a skid, and plowed into the back of her car.

As you can see from this example, almost all cases have both direct evidence and circumstantial evidence in them. But there are also many cases that involve the third major classification of evidence: documentary evidence.

C. DOCUMENTARY EVIDENCE

The third broad category of evidence is documentary evidence. This is any evidence recorded in a medium. Evidence is classified as documentary when it records significant events but does not qualify as direct evidence itself. A contract is an example of documentary evidence. It records the details of the agreement between the parties but is not the agreement itself. A photograph is also documentary evidence. It records details and facts about a particular scene, but it is not the scene itself. It is a representation, in the same way that a drawing or cell phone picture is also a representation.

Documentary evidence raises several important considerations. Because this evidence is not direct evidence, it resembles circumstantial evidence. But classifying documentary evidence as circumstantial creates other confusion. After all, the wording of a document or the photographing of a scene would appear to represent a fact in itself, not open up the evidence for other possible considerations. As a result, documentary evidence falls into a middle ground. This accounts for the special rules involved in presenting it, such as the best evidence rule, discussed later in this chapter.

When a paralegal subpoenas documents, he should obtain a declaration from the custodian of the records that the records produced are complete and accurate. That way, the paralegal may have some indication that the request has been fully complied with and have proof that the documents can be classified as documentary evidence.

D. OTHER CATEGORIES OF EVIDENCE

In addition to direct, circumstantial, and documentary evidence, there are also several other classifications of evidence that are important in any civil case. They include:

- testimonial evidence;
- demonstrative evidence; and
- scientific (expert) evidence.

1. TESTIMONIAL EVIDENCE

Testimonial evidence
Oral statements made by a witness under oath

Testimonial evidence refers to statements made by witnesses from the witness stand while they are under oath. During the trial, a witness will be called to the stand by the attorney for either the plaintiff or the defendant and will be questioned in direct examination. The attorney will ask the witness questions about the incident in order to prove one or more allegations in the case. The witness may have been present when the incident occurred, may have additional information, may be an expert, or may even be the plaintiff or defendant. In every situation, the witness must give truthful testimony. When the attorney has finished asking questions, the witness is subject to cross-examination by the opposing attorney. Testimonial evidence carries the same weight as any other testimony but is often the most powerful evidence given at trial. After all, the jurors are far more likely to be swayed by the statement of a person than the words in a document. Because of the power of testimonial evidence, attorneys work very hard to locate as many witnesses as possible to help carry their burden of proving the elements in their pleadings.

2. DEMONSTRATIVE EVIDENCE

Demonstrative evidence
Any object, visual aid, model, scale drawing, or other exhibit designed to help clarify points in the trial

Attorneys and paralegals often prepare charts and diagrams to help them explain specific points to the jury. The question often arises, How is such a chart or diagram classified as evidence? Generally speaking, a visual aid prepared by one of the attorneys falls into the category of **demonstrative evidence**. This evidence can be used in the courtroom to help in the presentation of the party's case and can be relied upon by witnesses and even the attorney during a closing argument, but such evidence usually does not go out with the jurors when they deliberate on the case. Because the parties prepared it, it is not given the same weight as the direct, circumstantial, and documentary evidence presented at trial. After all, this evidence was prepared as an exhibit by one side in order to help prove its case and, as such, has inherent problems of bias and subjectivity.

Consider the following example: The plaintiff's attorney has asked a legal nurse consultant to go through all of the medical records in the case and prepare a chronology of medical treatment. This chronology lists every procedure carried out on the plaintiff after he was admitted to the hospital. The attorney has blown up the chronology so that it is now six feet tall and three feet wide. She has done this so that the jury can easily see it from the across the room. However, before the attorney can show it to the jury, she must establish relevance and have the judge rule that it is admissible.

The first issue that the attorney must resolve is which witness she will use to get the evidence admitted. She must use someone who knows about the exhibit and will be able to answer the foundation questions. Could she use the plaintiff? The problem with using the plaintiff is that he may not know the answers to some of the foundation questions. The attorney cannot give the questions and answers herself because she is barred from giving such testimony during the trial. So, whom should she call to the stand to testify about this medical chronology? The best choice is either a paralegal or some medical professional, such as the legal nurse consultant who actually prepared the chronology in the first place. The foundation questions for this demonstrative evidence will probably go something like this:

Plaintiff's attorney: Ms. Doe, did you prepare the medical chronology in this case?

Witness: Yes, I did.

Plaintiff's attorney: Would you tell the court how you prepared this medical chronology?

Witness: I sifted through all of the medical reports, bills, medical diagnoses, charts, nurses' notes, and the complete medical file, and then prepared a day-by-day account of what happened to the plaintiff from all of these various sources.

Plaintiff's attorney: Does this medical chronology fairly and accurately depict all of the plaintiff's treatment, procedures, and medicines administered, and all of the people who were involved in the plaintiff's treatment?

Witness: Yes, it does.

Plaintiff's attorney: Your Honor, I move to admit Plaintiff's Exhibit Number Two.

Has the attorney laid a sufficient foundation to have this evidence admitted at trial?

Answer: Yes. The attorney has laid sufficient foundation for this demonstrative evidence. When the judge admits it, the attorney can refer to it throughout the rest of the trial as a way of helping witnesses and the jury understand specific points in the case.

Tech Topic
COMPUTER-AIDED EVIDENTIARY PRESENTATIONS

In the age of the Internet and the widespread availability of computer-networked law offices, there are several companies that specialize in providing assistance to attorneys preparing to try a civil case. Visual aids are important for juries, whether it is simply providing the details of the accident site or laying out the complexities of a medical malpractice case. Today, there are companies that can offer a broad range of services, from simple aids to computer animation. Examples of companies that provide these services include Insight Legal Graphics and Animation (www.insightlegalgraphics.com) and High Impact Litigation, Inc. (www.highimpactlit.com), both of which specialize in helping attorneys prepare for trial by generating a wide variety of exhibits, diagrams, graphic design, computer animation, PowerPoints, and nearly every type of trial aid imaginable. Other companies, such as Power Graphics, Inc. (www.power-graphics.com), concentrate on taking the various evidentiary exhibits in a case and presenting them in as dramatic a way as possible. For instance, these companies can blow up an important photograph or diagram so that it is truly enormous—making it much easier for the jury to see all of the important details.

3. SCIENTIFIC EVIDENCE

There are times when the parties must present complicated, technical, or scientific evidence. In such a case, the parties will usually rely on the services of an expert witness. A person qualifies as an expert when she has knowledge that is beyond the normal experience and education of average jurors. Expert witnesses are permitted to reach conclusions and can base their testimony on conjecture, in direct opposition to the rules that prohibit similar tactics by lay witnesses. We will discuss expert witnesses in greater detail in the next chapter.

V SPECIFIC EVIDENTIARY RULES

Whenever we discuss the topic of evidence, there are specific evidentiary rules that always arise. Some of the most important of these rules concern the admissibility of original copies of documents, the use of hearsay at trial, and issues surrounding the authentication of the evidence used at trial.

A. THE BEST EVIDENCE RULE

Whenever an attorney must use a document at trial, such as a medical report, the Rules of Evidence require that the original must be presented. Copies are generally not admissible, unless the party can show that the original has been destroyed. The reason for the requirement of the original, also known under the slightly misleading name "the best evidence rule," goes back to the circumstances under which the document was created. The original document was the one actually handled by the parties and the one upon which the agreement was reached. In these days of nearly perfect copies, the best evidence rule continues to have important consequences. The original may bear handwritten notes or other modifications that a freshly printed document would not contain. See Figure 6-3 for a statement of the rule.

FIGURE 6-3

Rule 1002. Requirement of the Original

An original writing, recording, or photograph is required in order to prove its content unless these rules or a federal statute provides otherwise.

B. HEARSAY

The topic of hearsay can be very complicated. The basic definition of hearsay is an out-of-court statement offered to prove the matter asserted. Unfortunately, that definition fails to clarify exactly what hearsay is. At its simplest, hearsay consists of a statement repeated on the witness stand by someone who did not originally make it. The most common circumstance where hearsay arises is when a witness is asked a question while he is testifying in court and his answer encompasses a statement made by someone else.

Consider the following example: Rosario is on the witness stand testifying about a car collision. The plaintiff's attorney asks Rosario what happened immediately after the collision. Rosario testifies, "I got out of my car, and a man was standing there. He turned to me and said, 'That other guy ran the red light.'" At this point, the defense attorney objects that the statement is hearsay. Is it?

Answer: If hearsay consists of one witness testifying about what another person said, then this would qualify as hearsay. The Rules of Evidence would bar the use of this statement, and the witness's testimony about the other man's statement would be stricken from the record, although probably not from the jurors' minds.

The reason that hearsay is considered to be objectionable is that when one person repeats what another person has said, it is impossible to question the witness on the stand about the conditions under which that statement was made. For instance, the attorney cannot question the witness who repeated the statement about the other person's motivations, prejudices, or biases. The attorney cannot question the witness on the stand about what the other witness could or could not have seen. As a result, hearsay statements are considered to be inherently unreliable, and courts restrict their use. Rather than using a hearsay statement, courts much prefer the attorneys to produce the original witness who made the statement. When a statement qualifies as hearsay and an objection is raised, the court will instruct the witness not to repeat what someone else said.

Does the prohibition against hearsay mean that the witness can't repeat something that she said herself? No. If the witness made a statement and repeats it on the stand, then it does not qualify as hearsay. The person who made the statement can be questioned about it and the accuracy of the statement can be assessed because the person who made it is currently on the stand.

Sidebar

If the purpose of putting people up on the stand, swearing them in, and then asking them questions under oath is to get truthful testimony, then that whole process gets shot in the foot when the witness repeats what someone else said. How can you test the accuracy of a statement made by someone else? How can you be sure that the statement was repeated correctly? How can you be sure that the statement was ever even made?

1. HEARSAY IN DOCUMENTS

Hearsay is not limited to oral statements made by witnesses; it also applies to documents. When documentary evidence contains statements made by witnesses, it satisfies the definition of hearsay in the same way that a live witness would. That explains why documents such as police reports, medical narratives, and other records typically qualify as hearsay and cannot be used at trial, unless they fall under some exception.

Consider the following example: Terry was admitted to the hospital last year with classic symptoms of appendicitis: referred pain on the right side, fever, vomiting, and high white blood cell count. Unfortunately, he was incorrectly diagnosed with gastroenteritis. Later, his appendix burst and he had a severe case of peritonitis. He has brought a medical malpractice action against the doctor who originally saw him at the emergency room. You are working for the plaintiff's attorney. As you go through the file, you discover a note, made by the admitting nurse, that says, "Classic case of appendicitis." When it comes time for the trial, can the attorney simply use the nurse's note as evidence of the doctor's malpractice?

Answer: No. The note is hearsay. Nurses' notes, police reports, and other such documents are all technically classified as hearsay. Unless the note comes under an exception to the hearsay rule, it cannot be used. Instead, the nurse who made the notation must be called to the stand and questioned about it. Without that authentication, the note is inadmissible.

2. EXCEPTIONS TO THE HEARSAY RULE

Although we have seen that any out-of-court statement that is repeated on the stand or presented to the jury technically qualifies as hearsay, there are numerous exceptions to the hearsay rule that allow hearsay testimony to be used. In each of the exceptions, there are other indicators that the hearsay statement was made under conditions that give it some reliability; that is, they are based on the premise that a particular statement has a greater degree of credibility because of when it was made or who made it. This explains why statements made as excited utterances or as part of business records, or made in connection with medical diagnoses, are all admissible as exceptions to the hearsay rule.

The first exception to the use of hearsay statements is not really an exception at all. When a witness is testifying about what one of the parties to the case said, the hearsay rule does not apply. Suppose, for example, that a witness repeats what the plaintiff said at the time of the accident. Both the plaintiff and the defendant are present in the courtroom and can refute any such statement if it is untrue. Therefore, repeating statements made by parties to the case is not considered to be hearsay.

The Federal Rules of Evidence recognize 23 separate exceptions to the use of hearsay statements. They range from present sense impressions to civil judgments concerning family history. For the sake of clarity, we will address only the most commonly used exceptions, including:

- excited utterance;
- business records; and
- statements for purpose of medical diagnosis.

a. Excited Utterance

The basic premise behind not allowing hearsay statements to be repeated in court is that they are inherently unreliable. However, what if a person has no time or inclination to think up an unreliable statement? The premise behind the excited utterance exception is that when a person is confronted with a sudden, dangerous situation, anything that she might blurt out is probably not a lie. Under these circumstances, courts assume that the statement is probably true. As a result, it can be used at trial (Fig. 6-4).

FIGURE 6-4

Rule 803(2) Excited Utterance Exception to Hearsay

The following are not excluded by the rule against hearsay, regardless of whether the declarant is available as a witness:

. . .

(2) Excited Utterance. A statement relating to a startling event or condition, made while the declarant was under the stress of excitement that it caused . . .

In order to qualify as an excited utterance, the attorney seeking to use the statement must establish the conditions in existence shortly before the statement was made. The attorney must show that there was a sudden and unexpected event, one that shocked or surprised the speaker.

Consider the following example:

> Witness: The wreck had just happened, and I jumped out of my car. The passenger was sitting in one of the cars and said, "That guy should have been watching the road."

Ordinarily, the statement in this example would be hearsay and inadmissible at trial; however, because it is an excited utterance, it will be allowed into evidence.

b. Business Records

The premise behind the business records exception to hearsay is similar to that for the excited utterance exception (Fig. 6-5). When a person writes comments in business records, especially comments that are written before there is a lawsuit, the court may allow a witness to repeat what the business records contain. Again, because the statement is made in such a way as to be reliable, it is an exception to the general rule against the use of hearsay statements. In our previous example involving the nurse's note, would the notation "Classic case of appendicitis" be admissible as a business record? The answer is probably yes.

FIGURE 6-5

Rule 803(6) Business Records Exception to Hearsay

(6) Records of a Regularly Conducted Activity. A record of an act, event, condition, opinion, or diagnosis if:

(A) the record was made at or near the time by — or from information transmitted by — someone with knowledge;

(B) the record was kept in the course of a regularly conducted activity of a business, organization, occupation, or calling, whether or not for profit;

(C) making the record was a regular practice of that activity;

(D) all these conditions are shown by the testimony of the custodian or another qualified witness, or by a certification that complies with Rule 902(11) or (12) or with a statute permitting certification; and

(E) the opponent does not show that the source of information nor or the method or circumstances of preparation indicate a lack of trustworthiness.

c. Statements for Purpose of Medical Diagnosis

Another exception to the hearsay rule concerns statements made for the purpose of medical diagnosis. Here, again, the idea of inherent reliability makes the statement more likely to be true. After all, giving false information to a medical provider could have disastrous consequences. These statements — assuming that they are not protected by an evidentiary privilege — are admissible as an exception to the hearsay rule (Fig. 6-6).

FIGURE 6-6

Rule 803(4) Statements for Purposes of Medical Diagnosis or Treatment

(4) Statement Made for Medical Diagnosis or Treatment. A statement that:

(A) is made for — and is reasonably pertinent to — medical diagnosis or treatment; and

(B) describes medical history; past or present symptoms or sensations; their inception; or their general cause.

C. AUTHENTICATION

Authentication
Proof that evidence is what it is claims to be.

One issue that often comes up in presenting evidence at trial is how to authenticate the item. **Authentication** is actually a feature of competence but is often dealt with as a separate concern. We have already encountered a species of authentication in the best evidence rule. There, we saw that when a document is in dispute, the only way to prove its contents is to present the original. That is a form of authentication, or proof of the document's origin and provenance (Fig. 6-7). But what happens when the parties are faced with presenting facts that we all know to be true? Do the rules of authentication require witnesses to testify about those issues as well?

FIGURE 6-7

Rule 901 Requirement of Authentication or Identification

Rule 901. Authenticating or Identifying Evidence

(a) In General. To satisfy the requirement of authenticating or identifying an item of evidence, the proponent must produce evidence sufficient to support a finding that the item is what the proponent claims it is.

(b) Examples. The following are examples only — not a complete list — of evidence that satisfies the requirement:

(1) Testimony of a Witness with Knowledge. Testimony that an item is what it is claimed to be.

(2) Nonexpert Opinion About Handwriting. A nonexpert's opinion that handwriting is genuine, based on a familiarity with it that was not acquired for the current litigation.

(3) Comparison by an Expert Witness or the Trier of Fact. A comparison with an authenticated specimen by an expert witness or the trier of fact.

(4) Distinctive Characteristics and the Like. The appearance, contents, substance, internal patterns, or other distinctive characteristics of the item, taken together with all the circumstances.

(5) Opinion About a Voice. An opinion identifying a person's voice — whether heard firsthand or through mechanical or electronic transmission or recording — based on hearing the voice at any time under circumstances that connect it with the alleged speaker.

(6) Evidence About a Telephone Conversation. For a telephone conversation, evidence that a call was made to the number assigned at the time to:

(A) a particular person, if circumstances, including self-identification, show that the person answering was the one called; or

(B) a particular business, if the call was made to a business and the call related to business reasonably transacted over the telephone.

1. JUDICIAL NOTICE

So far, our discussions about evidence have revealed that the most common method for offering evidence is via a sponsoring witness or, as we will see in the next section, through a self-authenticating document. However, there are provisions that allow the parties to simply request the court to take **judicial notice** of a particular fact without the necessity of presenting proof to support it. When a court takes judicial notice of a fact, the fact is assumed to be true for purposes of the litigation and neither party must present evidence to prove it. Courts are limited in the ways that they may take judicial notice of facts. A court cannot, for example, take judicial notice of the fact that the defendant is liable to the plaintiff. Such a ruling would invade the province of the jury and would no doubt be overturned on appeal. Traditionally, trial judges are reluctant to take judicial notice of all but the most obvious facts. For instance, a court would be authorized to take judicial notice of the fact that a particular city is the state capital. It would be a waste of the court's time if the parties were required to present a live witness to testify about this fact when it is well known to everyone. Judicial notice, as seen in Figure 6-8, is generally limited to such obvious facts and rarely extended to the issue in contention between the parties.

Judicial notice
The authority of a judge to agree that certain facts are true without the necessity of proof

FIGURE 6-8

Rule 201(b) Judicial Notice

Rule 201. Judicial Notice of Adjudicative Facts

(a) Scope. This rule governs judicial notice of an adjudicative fact only, not a legislative fact.

(b) Kinds of Facts That May Be Judicially Noticed. The court may judicially notice a fact that is not subject to reasonable dispute because it:

(1) is generally known within the trial court's territorial jurisdiction; or

(2) can be accurately and readily determined from sources whose accuracy cannot reasonably be questioned.

(c) Taking Notice. The court:

(1) may take judicial notice on its own; or

(2) must take judicial notice if a party requests it and the court is supplied with the necessary information.

(d) Timing. The court may take judicial notice at any stage of the proceeding.

Consider the following example: During a trial involving medical malpractice allegations, the plaintiff's attorney requests that the judge take judicial notice of the fact that children have thinner bones than adults. The defense attorney objects to judicial notice on this fact and requests that the plaintiff present evidence to support it. How does the judge rule?

Answer: Because judicial notice is generally reserved for facts that are common knowledge, and the thickness of children's bones compared to adult bones is not a matter of common knowledge, the judge will most likely refuse to give judicial notice to the plaintiff's request and will require the plaintiff to present evidence to support the allegations.

2. SELF-AUTHENTICATING DOCUMENT

Self-authenticating document
A document, usually from the public record, that receives the benefit of special legislation that specifically avoids the necessity of requiring a witness to testify about the document's accuracy or competence

A **self-authenticating document**, also known as a *self-proving document*, is an official document that provides for its own authentication. Such documents are usually issued by the state and can be as simple as a certified copy. When the clerk of court issues a certified copy of a public document, the certification is authorized by law and avoids the necessity of issuing a subpoena to someone in the courthouse to testify that the document is a correct copy. Self-authenticating documents are often the product of special enabling legislation that specifically provides that documents bearing government seals do not require sponsoring witnesses (Fig. 6-9). At trial, the party with such a document may simply present it to the court, note the self-authentication feature, and move to admit it. As long as the document satisfies relevance, the judge must admit it.

FIGURE 6-9

Rule 902 Self-authentication

Rule 902. Evidence That Is Self-Authenticating

The following items of evidence are self-authenticating; they require no extrinsic evidence of authenticity in order to be admitted:

(1) Domestic Public Documents That Are Sealed and Signed. A document that bears:

(A) a seal purporting to be that of the United States; any state, district, commonwealth, territory, or insular possession of the United States; the former Panama Canal Zone; the Trust Territory of the Pacific Islands; a political subdivision of any of these entities; or a department, agency, or officer of any entity named above; and

(B) a signature purporting to be an execution or attestation.

(2) Domestic Public Documents That Are Not Sealed but Are Signed and Certified. A document that bears no seal if:

(A) it bears the signature of an officer or employee of an entity named in Rule 902(1)(A); and

(B) another public officer who has a seal and official duties within that same entity certifies under seal — or its equivalent — that the signer has the official capacity and that the signature is genuine.

. . .

(4) Certified Copies of Public Records. A copy of an official record — or a copy of a document that was recorded or filed in a public office as authorized by law — if the copy is certified as correct by:

(A) the custodian or another person authorized to make the certification; or

(B) a certificate that complies with Rule 902(1), (2), or (3), a federal statute, or a rule prescribed by the Supreme Court.

D. PRIVILEGES

In most situations, a person can be subpoenaed to the stand and questioned about his actions, including conversations that he had with other people. A witness can be asked what he said to another person, and he must divulge the contents of that conversation, even when the subject matter is embarrassing. However, there are certain classes of individuals who are protected from being forced to reveal the content of their communications with others. The ability to refuse to answer specific types of questions has long been referred to as a *privilege*.

Only certain individuals enjoy such a privilege. The idea behind protecting certain forms of communication is that, even though it might hurt a particular case, society as a whole is protected by making certain conversations off-limits. For instance, suppose that you visit a member of the clergy and discuss some personal problems. Later, this clergy member is called to the stand and asked to repeat that conversation. The clergy member can refuse to answer the question because she is protected by an evidentiary privilege. The judge cannot hold the witness in contempt for failing to answer the question, and no other court can compel the witness to discuss conversations that occurred within the bonds of that relationship.

Evidentiary privileges are granted only to specific professions and only under certain types of circumstances. The most commonly recognized evidentiary privileges include:

- husband–wife (known as *marital privilege*);
- attorney–client;
- physician–patient;
- clergyman–communicant;
- psychologist–patient;
- school counselor–student (in some states and only under certain circumstances);
- family therapist–patient; and
- social worker–client.

You will notice that only certain professions are listed here. For instance, most states do not recognize accountant–client evidentiary privileges. This means that, in most states, an accountant can be summoned to the stand and asked to repeat a conversation that he had with a party. However, if a party's attorney, physician, psychiatrist, or social worker is summoned to the stand, that person can refuse to answer any questions about confidential communications. This is a very powerful protection. The premise behind this privilege is that without it, a person might be reluctant to share vital information with the very person who can provide the best assistance. If a person believed that a conversation with a doctor might later be repeated, the person might not be willing to share enough information to receive proper treatment.

1. THE MARITAL PRIVILEGE

Marital privilege
The evidentiary privilege that prevents spouses from being compelled to testify against one another

The husband–wife privilege, or **marital privilege**, is one of the most misunderstood of all the evidentiary privileges. While it is true that legally married spouses cannot be compelled to testify against one another, this privilege only protects the spouse who has been called to the stand. A spouse cannot assert it to prevent her spouse from testifying. A wife is always free to testify against her husband, if that is her wish. This evidentiary privilege was created to prevent others from forcing a spouse to testify, not to prevent spouses from voluntarily doing so. The reason for the privilege is that society has determined that it is more important to respect the private communications between spouses than to force them to testify against one another, with devastating results to the marriage.

2. THE ATTORNEY–CLIENT PRIVILEGE

Attorney–client privilege
The evidentiary privilege that bars a court or other authority from compelling an attorney or a client to divulge the conversations that either had with the other

The **attorney–client privilege** has been called the most important aspect of the legal professional's role. The privilege is not only important for attorneys, but also for paralegals, legal assistants, and legal secretaries. When a client has a confidential meeting with her attorney, for instance, neither party can be compelled to reveal what was discussed. If the witness is asked about this conversation, she can invoke an evidentiary privilege that prevents any further questions. The attorney can also invoke this protection if she is subpoenaed to testify. This privilege against revealing any details of the conversation applies to any communication between a legal professional and a client, whether it is a telephone call, a face-to-face meeting, a letter, a fax, or an e-mail.

Tech Topic
ONLINE CLE AND WEBINARS

Whether gas prices rise, fall, or stay relatively static, it is clear that there is a trend away from traveling to and from seminars to obtain Continuing Legal Education Credits for attorney and paralegal certification. Instead, more seminars are going online as webinars. It is quite common for any number of continuing education credits to be offered through an online format with either asynchronous classes or live webinars. In the live webinar format, attendees can observe the presentation on their computers from either home or work—or in some cases traveling between the two. Attendees to live webinars can ask the presenter questions, usually in the form of typed questions in a chat room, and they can receive a response in real time. The advantages of such a system are obvious: it saves time and money.

Case Excerpt

When and under what circumstances is a judge "required" to take judicial notice?

JENKINS V. CACH, LLC
2014 Tex. App. LEXIS 9483 (Tex. App. Houston 14th Dist. Aug. 26, 2014)

Memorandum Opinion
This appeal arises from a debt collection action in which appellee CACH, LLC, the alleged assignee of appellant Franklin D. Jenkins' credit card debt, sued to recover on the debt. Following a bench trial, the trial court rendered judgment against Jenkins. On appeal, Jenkins complains that the trial court did not take judicial notice of adjudicative facts and challenges the trial court's overruling his hearsay objections to purported business records admitted at trial. Concluding that the trial court erroneously admitted hearsay evidence and that this error probably resulted in an improper judgment, we reverse and remand.

Background

CACH sued Jenkins for breach of contract based upon his failure to repay a debt under an agreement for consumer credit. According to the pleadings, FIA Card Services, N.A., a subsidiary of Bank of America, issued a credit card in Jenkins' name, and Jenkins used or authorized use of the card, thereby incurring charges that he failed to pay. The credit card was cancelled when Jenkins defaulted in making payments on the account. CACH alleges that it purchased the account with an outstanding balance of $10,121.88.

At trial, Jenkins stated his name and acknowledged his address. When asked whether he had received a credit card from Bank of America, he responded, "I have had many credit cards. I do not recall having a credit card from Bank of America." However, when presented with a Bank of America account statement, he admitted that it bore his name and address, although he still maintained that he did not recall receiving the credit card from or making payments to Bank of America.

CACH moved to admit into evidence a business-record affidavit signed by Tom Vigil of CACH. Vigil attested that he is an authorized agent for and a custodian of records of CACH and stated the following in pertinent part:

> (1) I . . . am familiar with CACH's business processes. Business records are kept and maintained in the ordinary course of CACH's business ("Records") concerning accounts like the account of Jenkins. The Records are made and maintained by individuals who have a business duty to make entries in the Records accurately at or near the time of the event that they record, or reasonably soon thereafter, by or from information transmitted by someone with personal knowledge of the event or act.
>
> (2) It is CACH's regular business practice to obtain, integrate, and rely upon documents prepared by the original creditor of the account at issue. In this particular action, CACH has obtained and integrated documents received from the original creditor, FIA CARD SERVICES, . . . a wholly owned subsidiary of Bank of America. . . . CACH relies upon the accuracy of such documentation in its day to day business activities and such documents are considered Records of CACH. The records consist of both hard copy

> information and electronic information that is generated, stored and maintained by the original creditor in accordance with generally accepted standards in the retail and financial industries by individuals that possess the knowledge and training necessary to ensure the accuracy and reliability of the records. I know from my experience in reviewing such records that they are made and maintained by individuals who have a business duty to make entries in the records accurately at or near the time of the event that they record. CACH relies upon the accuracy and reliability of said records in its day.

Thirty pages of records were attached to the affidavit, including the following:

> (1) a document entitled "Affidavit of Sale and Certification of Debt" signed by Justin S. Taro of FIA Card Services;
> (2) a document from Bank of America entitled "Exhibit C — Bill of Sale and Assignment of Loans" signed by Deborah L. Pellicciaro of FIA Card Services;
> (3) billing statements from Bank of America sent to Jenkins at his address reflecting payments and unpaid balances;
> (4) a "Federally Required Affiliate Marketing Notice" from Bank of America that is not addressed to a specific recipient;
> (5) a "Bank of America Privacy Policy" that is not addressed to a specific recipient; and
> (6) a "Credit Card Agreement" with "FIA Card Services . . . also known as Bank of America" that is not signed by Jenkins.

Following the Bill of Sale and Assignment of Loans is a heavily redacted document in different typeface that lists the disputed account, along with Jenkins' name, address, and the outstanding balance. There is no indication on this document that it was meant to be the loan schedule referenced in the Bill of Sale and Assignment of Loans.

Jenkins objected to the admission of the entire exhibit, arguing, in relevant part:

> (1) "The proffer of evidence does not meet the Business Records Exception Rule to hearsay."

The trial court overruled Jenkins' objections and admitted the exhibit in its entirety. The trial court ruled in favor of CACH and rendered final judgment ordering that CACH recover from Jenkins actual damages as well as attorney's fees, post-judgment interest, and court costs.

Discussion

Jenkins argues the trial court erred in overruling his objections to CACH's exhibit. When an appellant asserts multiple grounds for reversal of the trial court's judgment, we first should address any issues that would require rendition and then, if necessary, consider issues that would result in remand.

Abuse of Discretion in Overruling Hearsay Objections

In his first issue, Jenkins argues that CACH's exhibit failed to meet the business records exception to hearsay because it was not trustworthy for the following reasons, among others: (1) the Vigil affidavit contains hearsay because it includes out of court statements to prove the truth of the matter asserted concerning ownership of the subject account; (2) the Taro affidavit, which states that the account was sold on November 9, 2011, conflicts with the Bill of Sale and Assignment of Loans, which states that the account was sold on November 15, 2011; (3) the Taro affidavit was made nearly a year after the account was sold, indicating that it was not created in the regular course of business; and (4) the Bill of Sale and Assignment of Loans does not reference the subject account. CACH argues that the exhibit was admissible in its entirety under the business records hearsay exception.

> Hearsay is an out-of-court statement offered in evidence to prove the truth of the matter asserted and is inadmissible unless a statute or rule of exception applies. Tex. R. Evid. 801(d); 802. The proponent of hearsay has the burden of showing that the testimony fits within an exception to the general rule. Under the business-records exception, evidence that is otherwise inadmissible as hearsay may be admissible if the proponent of the evidence demonstrates that (1) the records were made and kept in the course of a regularly conducted business activity; (2) it was the regular practice of the business activity to create such records; (3) the records were created at or near the time of the event recorded; and (4) the records were created by, or from information transmitted by, a person with knowledge who was acting in the regular course of business. Tex. R. Evid. 803(6).

Except in those instances specified by statute or rule, affidavits are not evidence in contested cases. Id. Accordingly, when an ex parte affidavit presents evidence beyond the simple authentication requirements of Rule 902, the extraneous portions of the affidavit constitute inadmissible hearsay.

Vigil Affidavit. This affidavit contains the prerequisite authentication requirements of Rule 902. However, it also contains two paragraphs that are extraneous. Vigil attested:

> All credits and payments have been properly applied, Jenkins is not entitled to additional credits or offsets on the account of any kind, and the balance as set forth herein is currently due and owing. . . .
>
> I have reviewed CACH's file for the account at issue, including CACH's history for the account and Records for the account. Based on my familiarity with CACH's procedures regarding obtaining and integrating account documents and review of CACH's file and Records, I have personal knowledge of the account and the matters stated above are true.

In analyzing the contents of the attached business records and reaching conclusions based on that analysis, these statements contain information in addition to that required to authenticate business records under Rule 902 and thus constitute inadmissible hearsay.

Taro Affidavit. This affidavit was offered by CACH as a third-party document created by FIA Card Services that has become a business record of CACH. In the business-record affidavit, to which the Taro affidavit is attached, Vigil testifies that the documents from FIA Card Services are "maintained by individuals who have a business duty to make entries in the records accurately at or near the time of the event that they record." But the Taro affidavit is dated August 7, 2012, and asserts that FIA Card Services sold Jenkins' account to CACH on November 9, 2011. A record of a sale made nearly a year after a sale takes place is not "at or near the time of the event" that it purports to record. See id. at 631. Further, there is a notation at the bottom of the Taro affidavit that reads "CACH, LLC 8/6/2012." If those numbers refer to a date, it would be the day before Taro executed the affidavit, which suggests that he did so at CACH's request and not in the regular course of business. See id. Even assuming those numbers are not significant, the fact that the affidavit is dated three months before CACH filed suit and nearly a year after the alleged date of sale suggests that it was created in anticipation of litigation rather than in the course of a regular business activity, which casts doubt on its trustworthiness.

Bill of Sale and Assignment of Loans. This document, also offered by CACH as a business record created by a third party, purports to transfer FIA Card Services' "right, title and interest in and to each of the loans identified in the loan schedule . . . attached hereto." As set forth above, immediately following the Bill of Sale and Assignment of Loans is a heavily redacted document in different typeface that lists the disputed account, along with Jenkins' name, address, and the outstanding balance. However, there is no indication on the redacted document that it was meant to be the loan schedule referenced in the Bill of Sale and Assignment 16 of Loans. Moreover, the date of the assignment referenced in the Bill of Sale and Assignment of Loans — November 15, 2011 — conflicts with the date of assignment of the account attested to by Taro — November 9, 2011. Accordingly, the circumstances surrounding the Bill of Sale and Assignment of Loans and the redacted document do not indicate trustworthiness and the document does not fall within the business-records exception.

We conclude there is no legitimate basis upon which the trial court's overruling of Jenkins' hearsay objections can be supported. Having made that determination, we must determine whether the trial court's error resulted in an improper judgment. See id. Without the inadmissible evidence discussed above, there would be insufficient evidence to prove the assignment of the account to CACH and thus insufficient evidence upon which the trial court could have reasonably rendered a judgment in CACH's favor. Therefore, we conclude the judgment turned on the improperly admitted evidence and must be reversed. Because the trial court erroneously admitted hearsay evidence that was essential to the judgment, we sustain Jenkins' first issue.

Because we conclude that the trial court erred by admitting improper evidence upon which the judgment turned, we reverse the trial court's judgment and remand the cause for a new trial.

QUESTIONS ABOUT THE CASE:

1. How did CACH become a holder of over $10,000 it claims was owed by Jenkins?
2. How did CACH attempt to use the business records exception to the hearsay rule?
3. Why did Jenkins claim that the CACH's exhibit was not trustworthy and therefore not a proper exception to the hearsay rule?

Chapter Summary

An understanding of evidentiary law is extremely important for any legal profession. Evidence consists of physical items, testimony, documents, and other data presented to prove or disprove essential allegations in a case. The plaintiff must present evidence to support the claims made in the complaint, and the defendant will often present evidence in order to refute those same claims. Before evidence can be used at trial, it must be shown to be relevant and competent. An attorney who intends to present evidence must lay a proper foundation showing how the evidence is relevant and then must request a ruling on admissibility from the trial court judge before the jury will be allowed to see the evidence.

Evidence can be classified in any number of ways. The most common methodology used to classify evidence is in three categories: direct evidence, circumstantial evidence, and documentary evidence. Direct evidence consists of physical objects and testimony that can be used to unquestionably establish a specific fact. Circumstantial evidence, on the other hand, suggests a possible conclusion but is not definitive of that conclusion. Documentary evidence consists of written documents, photographs, and any other media that can be used to record information about a particular event. There are several important rules that govern evidence, including the best evidence rule. This rule requires that when the contents of a document are in dispute, the parties must present the original. Hearsay is another important rule. A hearsay statement is an out-of-court statement repeated by the witness on the witness stand. Hearsay statements are inherently unreliable and are therefore inadmissible. However, there are many important exceptions to hearsay, including statements made to medical professionals, statements against interest, business records exceptions, excited utterances, and many others. Paralegals are often involved in gathering evidence and preserving it for trial and must be aware of the evidentiary rules in order to make sure that none of them are violated, resulting in a ruling that the evidence is no longer admissible.

SKILLS YOU NEED IN THE REAL WORLD

Classifying Evidence

In a medical case, the firm has gathered a great deal of evidence. Classify each of the following as testamentary, documentary, or demonstrative. Do any of these items have potential hearsay issues?

- The doctor's narrative medical report
- Medical admission chart, showing injuries sustained by the plaintiff along with potential diagnoses
- The attending nurse's deposition concerning the treatment that the plaintiff received on specific days at the hospital
- The plaintiff's medical bills

- Photographs of the plaintiff's injuries
- A chart showing the care that the plaintiff received on each day
- A video showing an average day in the life of the plaintiff
- Oral statements by the plaintiff's family about the impact of the plaintiff's care on her current qualify of life

THE LIFE OF A PARALEGAL

Organizing Evidence

Cyndy Adams began her legal career 28 years ago at one of the largest firms in the state at that time. Her mentors were the firm's two senior members, both of whom were well-respected CPAs and attorneys. Since 1992, she has worked as a paralegal specializing in domestic law. While working as a paralegal, she also attended college and completed an associate's degree in Paralegal Studies in 2006. Her practical experience proved to be a great asset in her classes. "When other students were struggling with drafting pleadings in Civil Litigation I," she says, "I found the assignments easy. I often received e-mails from fellow students with questions about homework. With each semester that passed and with every class that I successfully completed, my level of confidence increased.

"My current and past bosses have both been extremely supportive of me during my time at college. I have recently been congratulated on my achievements by judges, clerks, fellow paralegals, attorneys, clients, my church, and my family. But in the end, nothing makes my day like being told by a client that I have done a good job for them or that I helped them through a difficult time in their legal situation. It is with a great sense of pride, commitment, and responsibility that I continue my career as a paralegal. A very wise attorney told me many years ago that I had 'found my niche in life,' and I do believe he was correct."

One aspect of Cyndy's job that she likes best is attending a trial with her attorney. However, before that can happen, a lot of work must go into the case. One of the most important aspects of the preparation is gathering and organizing the evidence.

"It is important to make a minimum of four copies of evidence to be presented, which is one for the court, one for your attorney, one for the opposing attorney, and one for the paralegal. If there is a jury, make additional copies for them. Never give the original of anything to your boss, though, because it may get introduced into evidence and become lost in the abyss. However, it is a good idea to have the original in the trial notebook, clearly labeled as such, in the event the court requires an original document. Keep a list of evidence introduced at trial, by number, description, date, and approximate time submitted.

"Place photographic evidence into clear sheet protectors for ease of handling, with notes made on the back of your attorney's copy as to the subject matter of the picture. If a PowerPoint presentation is used, review it numerous times before court, time it, and make sure that no typographical errors appear and that the flow of the slides is right. Take along a backup CD in case the first one gets scratched or becomes corrupted. Print an outline of the PowerPoint presentation, too, so that if the worst happens and the presentation, computer, or power fails, the attorney has something to rely on as a backup."

ETHICAL ISSUES FOR THE PARALEGAL

Preserving Attorney–Client Privilege

When an attorney advises a client about a legal matter, the substance of that conversation is legally protected by an evidentiary privilege. This privilege protects the client's privacy. An attorney who is called to the stand and asked to testify about a conversation with a client can legally refuse to answer any questions. The attorney cannot be held in contempt or otherwise prosecuted for failure to answer such questions. Are legal assistants and paralegals protected by a similar privilege? The answer is no. There are some jurisdictions that have held that the presence of a third party during an attorney–client discussion may actually waive or eliminate the privilege. However, other states have included paralegals under a kind of pseudo-protection, extending the attorney's privilege to the conversation because the paralegal or legal assistant is an integral part of the legal team. However, a paralegal might not be protected by the privilege in specific instances. If that is true, then the paralegal cannot refuse to answer questions about conversations with a client. Because the conversations between the attorney and the client are supposed to be private, you should make sure that they remain so. The best way to do this is to not discuss any client business away from the office. Unless given permission to do so, it is a good idea even to refuse to give out information that the attorney represents a particular person.

Websites

- **American Association of Law Libraries**
  www.aallnet.org/sis/lisp/research.htm

- **Cornell Law School — Overview of Evidence Law**
  www.law.cornell.edu/wex/index.php/Evidence

- **Obtaining and Admitting Electronic Evidence**
  www.justice.gov/sites/default/files/usao/legacy/2011/11/30/usab5906.pdf

- **California Evidence Code, Harvard Law School**
  www.law.harvard.edu/publications/evidenceiii/california.htm

Key Terms

Admissibility
Attorney–client privilege
Authentication
Circumstantial evidence
Demonstrative evidence
Direct evidence
Evidence
Judicial notice
Lay the foundation
Marital privilege
Overrule
Relevance
Self-authenticating document
Sustain
Tendering
Testimonial evidence

Review Questions

1. Explain admissibility of evidence.
2. Discuss how the jury uses evidence in reaching its conclusions in a civil case.
3. What is physical evidence?
4. Discuss the differences between documentary evidence and physical evidence.
5. Is witness testimony considered to be evidence? Explain your answer.
6. Explain circumstantial evidence.
7. Compare and contrast direct evidence with circumstantial evidence.
8. What is relevance?
9. Explain hearsay.
10. List and explain some of the exceptions to the hearsay rule.
11. Explain how paralegals can gather evidence.
12. What is demonstrative evidence?
13. Explain tendering of evidence.
14. What is laying the foundation?
15. What is the best evidence rule?
16. Explain the business records exception to the hearsay rule.
17. Explain the excited utterance exception to the hearsay rule.
18. Provide some examples of documentary evidence.
19. Explain privileges.
20. Federal and state Rules of Evidence recognize numerous exceptions to the hearsay rule. Have the exceptions essentially swallowed up the entire reason for the objection to hearsay in the first place? Explain your answer.
21. In the era of digital storage of media, does the best evidence rule continue to make sense? Why or why not?

Applying What You Have Learned

1. In one of the examples above, the plaintiff's attorney presented the doctor with a photograph of the plaintiff as a child. Is there a way that you could lay a proper foundation to have this photograph admitted? Would it be helpful to you if the

issues in the case involved a claim of botched plastic surgery? Can you create a scenario where such a photograph would be admissible?

2 Go through the complaint and answer in Chapters 4 and 5 and prepare an evidence chart listing the types of evidence that both the plaintiff and defendant must use in order to prove or disprove the allegations. Prepare an evidence chart listing each allegation and the type of proof necessary to sustain it.

3 Prepare a three-page, double-spaced paper discussing your state's rules of evidence, including the definition of relevance, the classification of different types of evidence, the hearsay rule, and important exceptions to the hearsay rule.

4 Go through the basic contentions of your complaint and answer created in Chapter 4, and classify the various types of evidence suggested in that factual scenario. Prepare a checklist showing the classification of each type of evidence and how it will be used. Then locate the two paragraphs in the complaint that contain hearsay statements. Do either one of those statements fall under the exceptions to hearsay rules? Explain your answer.

5 In a medical malpractice case, classify the following types of evidence:
- The doctor's narrative medical report
- The admission forms for the plaintiff's trip to the emergency room
- The attending nurse's testimony about the treatment that the plaintiff received
- The plaintiff's medical bills
- Photographs of the plaintiff's injuries
- A charge showing the comprehensive treatment received by the plaintiff during his illness, prepared by the plaintiff's attorney
- A video showing the impact of the plaintiff's injuries in his day-to-day activities
- Testimony by the plaintiff's family about how the plaintiff has changed since his illness

7 Discovery

Chapter Objectives

- Explain the purpose of discovery
- Provide a history of the development of discovery rules
- Describe the sequence normally followed in civil discovery
- Compare and contrast the use of depositions and interrogatories in civil discovery
- Prepare a deposition digest
- Explain how a paralegal participates in traditional discovery and e-discovery
- Describe the drafting of and responses to interrogatories
- Explain the sanctions available for parties who fail to comply with discovery
- Describe the use of protective orders in discovery

I INTRODUCTION

Once the pleadings have been filed and both sides have considered the evidence that they will need to prove the allegations in the case, the next phase in civil litigation is discovery. In the **discovery** phase, both sides can learn essentially everything about the case before going to trial. The parties will schedule depositions, exchange

Discovery
The exchange of information between the sides involved in a suit

interrogatories, and file additional discovery requests. Through this exchange of information, both sides can question witnesses, ask questions of the opposition, and demand production of critical documents relied upon by the opposition in proving its case. The modern approach to civil discovery is very liberal and requires the parties to produce nearly everything that they will rely upon in a trial. Discovery takes place months and sometimes years before a case is ever called for trial. This means that for attorneys in civil cases, there are few, if any, surprises during the trial. There are no unexpected witnesses, no undisclosed evidence, and no dramatic events. The discovery rules were drafted in such a way that they encourage the parties to know as much as possible about the case prior to trial. The reason for this is common sense: The courts reason that if both parties know everything about the case prior to trial, they might be less inclined to bring questionable cases to a jury. Whether or not that theory holds water is still an open question.

PURPOSE OF DISCOVERY

The basic purpose of discovery is to learn the facts of a case, but discovery actually serves several different functions, including:

- clarifying the facts;
- preserving testimony for later use;
- avoiding surprise at trial; and
- narrowing the issues.

A. CLARIFICATION OF THE FACTS

Although the plaintiff's attorney is required to conduct an investigation before filing the complaint, such an investigation is hardly exhaustive. Once the case has begun in earnest, it is time for the plaintiff to clarify every vital fact in the case. This includes pinning down witness testimony, questioning the defendant, and examining every pertinent document. Before the pleadings are filed, the plaintiff's legal team is limited in the depth of its investigation for the simple reason that many of the discovery tools are not available until the complaint and answer have been served.

Like the plaintiff, the defendant will also wish to conduct a thorough investigation and will actively participate in all phases of discovery. Obviously, the focus of each party is different. The plaintiff will seek out any and all evidence that supports the claims of the complaint, while keeping an eye out for negative or damaging facts. The defendant will attempt to learn as many details about the case as possible to attack the allegations raised in the plaintiff's complaint. The defendant will also stay alert to potentially damaging information that might push the case toward settlement instead of trial. For both parties, discovery is the vehicle to clarify all positive and negative facts in the case.

B. PRESERVATION OF TESTIMONY FOR LATER USE

Another important aspect of discovery is the preservation of witness testimony. In civil discovery, the parties are allowed to thoroughly question witnesses weeks or even months before the trial is scheduled. If a witness should become unavailable at the actual trial, the Federal Rules of Civil Procedure permit the parties to present the transcripts of that question-and-answer session instead of the live witness. Although presenting a live person is always better and more effective than simply reading a transcript to a jury, in some cases it is unavoidable. Preserving this testimony allows both parties to proceed to trial in the event that a witness is no longer available to testify.

C. AVOIDING SURPRISE AT TRIAL

We have all watched TV court dramas where a surprise witness suddenly appears and completely changes the dynamic of a case. Although this makes for exciting television, in the real world of civil litigation, such an event should be rare if not completely impossible. A party who conducts thorough discovery should know the names, addresses, and substantial testimony of all witnesses in the case. If not, then the failing is with the legal team, not the justice process. Although it takes much of the drama out of the trial, an attorney handling a modern civil case should have no surprises during the trial.

D. NARROWING THE ISSUES

Discovery is also a powerful tool that allows all parties to narrow the disputed issues prior to trial. By pinpointing the precise issues in contention and forcing parties to agree on others, discovery techniques bring out the main points in contention in the case and eliminate redundant or uncontested issues. At the conclusion of discovery, all parties in the case will be aware of exactly what the opposition claims are the facts in contention and, just as importantly, what they are willing to stipulate to. Here, a **stipulation** refers to facts, evidence, or testimony that a party is willing to adopt as true without the need for further proof.

Stipulation
An agreement between parties as to facts or an agreement between attorneys as to procedural matters

III SHORT HISTORY OF DISCOVERY

The rules governing discovery in civil cases have changed dramatically in the last 100 years. Prior to the creation of modern discovery statutes and rules, it was quite common for the opposing parties in civil cases to conceal evidence, hide witnesses, and engage in a wide variety of practices that modern practitioners would consider unethical (if not illegal). However, from an efficiency standpoint, such practices also committed the sin of wasting a considerable amount of the court's time. A surprise witness who debunks the plaintiff's entire case might make for an exciting spectacle, but such testimony should have been discovered long before the case ever came to trial. Proper discovery has much to do with saving time and resources by forcing the parties to learn as much as possible about the case before it is ever scheduled for a jury trial.

The modern approach to civil discovery took considerable time to get to and faced tremendous opposition. Parties were (and remain) reluctant to share damaging information in a civil case, knowing full well that it will be used against them. Many attorneys might be more than willing to learn as much about the opposing witnesses as possible, but they are considerably less enthusiastic about the opposition learning as much about their own.

Discovery rules, which began to be seriously reconsidered and redrafted in the middle of the 20th century, provided for more extensive exchange of information than had ever been seen before. In addition to requiring that the parties freely exchange witness names, documents, and all other evidence, the revised discovery rules also provided courts with the authority to impose sanctions against noncomplying parties, including striking provisions of pleadings, disallowing specific claims or defenses, and even dismissing the case in its entirety.

Under modern discovery rules, all parties have the duty to engage in the open exchange of information. This duty is continuous throughout the litigation. If a party receives updates on information, it must provide them to the opposition. Some states continue to require that the parties file copies of all discoveries obtained with the court, while other states have abolished this requirement.

Consider the following example: Carla is a witness for the plaintiff. She recently changed her address and moved out of state. If the defendant is not informed, he will attempt to serve a trial subpoena on Carla at the wrong address and she will not be located. In that case, Carla will not give testimony that is potentially harmful to the plaintiff. Does the plaintiff have a duty to provide Carla's new address to the defendant, even though he could conceivably find her himself?

Answer: The plaintiff must provide Carla's new address as soon as the plaintiff learns that she has moved. The discovery rules are clear on this point: A party has a continuous duty to update information prior to trial, and even though Carla's testimony is potentially damaging, failure to update her information would violate the discovery rules and could potentially open the plaintiff to court-ordered sanctions.

IV DISCOVERY IN MODERN CIVIL PRACTICE

Under the modern rules of discovery, attorneys routinely file discovery requests along with the initial pleadings. An attorney can request information and receive it even though it may not be admissible at trial. The opposing party must disclose the information, even though there may be a sound objection to it on the grounds of relevance, prejudice, or some other matter. Modern discovery rules provide that the parties may argue about admissibility at trial, but not during the discovery process. The premise behind current discovery rules is that nearly anything can be requested and produced, with a few important exceptions. This approach is most clearly enumerated in the Federal Rules of Civil Procedure.

A. RULES OF CIVIL PROCEDURE

In the Federal Rules of Civil Procedure, the discovery rules are found from Rule 26 through Rule 37 and govern issues as disparate as the duty of disclosure to the sanctions that a judge can impose for a party's failure to comply with discovery. Because so many states have adopted these rules, in whole or in part, we will rely on the federal discovery rules throughout the rest of this chapter.

SEARCH SUGGESTION • RULES OF DISCOVERY

Whenever there is an issue surrounding discovery, it is always best to begin with the rules of discovery, usually found in the Federal Rules of Civil Procedure. However, you must keep in mind that these rules may be supplemented, enacted, or otherwise modified by state statutes. You should review your state's rules, statutes, and case law in order to have a solid understanding of discovery issues.

B. SEQUENCE OF DISCOVERY

Once the pleadings in a civil case have been filed and served on opposing parties, the discovery phase begins. As we will shortly see, there are many different vehicles for discovering facts about a case (Fig. 7-1), but most practitioners follow a similar pattern based on the information that can be developed through the different discovery techniques. Many attorneys use the following sequence:

1. Interrogatories are filed on the opposing party.
2. Requests for production of documents are submitted, including e-discovery.
3. Witnesses are deposed.
4. Requests for physical examination are submitted.
5. Requests to admit are submitted.

FIGURE 7-1

Timing and Sequence of Discovery

Unless the court upon motion, for the convenience of parties and witnesses and in the interests of justice, orders otherwise, methods of discovery may be used in any sequence, and the fact that a party is conducting discovery, whether by deposition or otherwise, does not operate to delay any other party's discovery.

This sequence offers several advantages. The practitioner can learn specific answers to questions from interrogatories, follow up with requests to produce the documents upon which these answers are based, and then use both to question witnesses in the case. Following that, the attorney can decide if a physical examination is needed and finally pin down testimony that both sides can agree to through a request to admit.

Whatever the sequence used, both parties must agree to it before any steps are taken in the discovery phase. Under Rule 26(f) of the Federal Rules of Civil Procedure (Fig. 7-2), the parties in a civil suit must meet or otherwise arrange a plan of discovery that they will follow throughout this phase of the lawsuit. Among the items that they must arrange in this conference are:

- changes in the timing, sequence, or requirement of disclosure;
- subjects on which discovery may be needed;
- a schedule for completing all discovery; and
- what, if any, limitations should be imposed on discovery.

FIGURE 7-2

Federal Rules of Civil Procedure, Rule 26(f) Meeting of Parties; Planning for Discovery

(f) Conference of the Parties; Planning for Discovery.

(1) Conference Timing. Except in a proceeding exempted from initial disclosure under Rule 26(a)(1)(B) or when the court orders otherwise, the parties must confer as soon as practicable — and in any event at least 21 days before a scheduling conference is to be held or a scheduling order is due under Rule 16(b).

(2) Conference Content; Parties' Responsibilities. In conferring, the parties must consider the nature and basis of their claims and defenses and the possibilities for promptly settling or resolving the case; make or arrange for the disclosures required by Rule 26(a)(1); discuss any issues about preserving discoverable information; and develop a proposed discovery plan. The attorneys of record and all unrepresented parties that have appeared in the case are jointly responsible for arranging the conference, for attempting in good faith to agree on the proposed discovery plan, and for submitting to the court within 14 days after the conference a written report outlining the plan. The court may order the parties or attorneys to attend the conference in person.

C. SUPPLEMENTING DISCOVERY RESPONSES

As we have already seen, modern discovery rules allow parties to request and receive a wide variety of information, and they impose on the parties the obligation to supplement discovery responses as new information becomes available, as seen in Figure 7-3.

FIGURE 7-3

Federal Rules of Civil Procedure, Rule 26(e) Supplementation of Disclosures and Responses

(e) Supplementing Disclosures and Responses.

(1) In General. A party who has made a disclosure under Rule 26(a) — or who has responded to an interrogatory, request for production, or request for admission — must supplement or correct its disclosure or response:

(A) in a timely manner if the party learns that in some material respect the disclosure or response is incomplete or incorrect, and if the additional or corrective information has not otherwise been made known to the other parties during the discovery process or in writing; or

(B) as ordered by the court.

The rule about supplementation of information applies to witnesses — particularly expert witnesses — and discovery responses.

D. EXPERT WITNESSES IN MODERN DISCOVERY

Under the rules of discovery, an opposing party is permitted to learn the identity of any expert witness relied upon by the other side, as well as the pertinent details of this expert's proposed testimony (Fig. 7-4). A party must release the subject matter upon which the expert is expected to testify and the substance of the expert's testimony.

(2) *Expert Witness.* For an expert whose report must be disclosed under Rule 26(a)(2)(B), the party's duty to supplement extends both to information included in the report and to information given during the expert's deposition. Any additions or changes to this information must be disclosed by the time the party's pretrial disclosures under Rule 26(a)(3) are due.

FIGURE 7-4

Federal Rules of Civil Procedure, Rule 26(e) Discovery Rules Regarding Experts

Discovery rules essentially create two classifications of experts: those who will testify and those will not. For witnesses who will testify, the party must provide the following:

- The full name of the expert witness
- The address and telephone numbers of the expert
- The subject matter upon which the expert is expected to testify
- The substance of the expert's testimony, including the expert's ultimate opinion about the matters in contention
- A summary of the expert's conclusions

The rules change, however, when the expert is simply sought out for advice and will not be used at trial. In that situation, the party must simply identify the expert, and no further information is required.

E. ELECTRONIC "E-DISCOVERY"

Some studies show that up to 90 percent of all documents produced by businesses, law firms, and individuals are created on a computer. Traditional discovery has always focused on documents, especially those that reside in physical files; however, with modern technology, it is just as likely that an important memorandum or other writing resides on a computer hard drive. This is one reason why electronic discovery has become such an important part of any modern discovery phase. Attorneys and paralegals must adapt their discovery process to take into account the fact that some of the information they will need for trial will come from someone's computer. This forces legal professionals to think like computer forensic experts. However, before a paralegal can start sifting through computer files, it is important to realize that the legal team must first get access to those files, which isn't always a simple process. Unlike law enforcement officials who can simply seize computers and hard drives, civil litigants must use traditional discovery tools to retrieve advanced data. Whenever the attorney and paralegal have reason to believe that important information may be stored on a computer, the legal team should notify the person in possession that the drive may contain evidence that will be used in litigation. Such a letter may contain a demand that the person preserve the data intact and not seek to destroy it. Using various discovery techniques, including requests to produce, the legal team may then obtain access to the computer files and make backup copies of the data contained in those files.

In fact, Rule 34 of the Federal Rules of Civil Procedure provided specific guidance for the discovery of both physical or tangible objects, such as papers, photographs, and diagrams, as well as electronically stored media (Fig. 7-5).

FIGURE 7-5

Rule 34, Federal Rules of Civil Procedure

(a) In General. A party may serve on any other party a request within the scope of Rule 26(b):

(1) to produce and permit the requesting party or its representative to inspect, copy, test, or sample the following items in the responding party's possession, custody, or control:

(A) any designated documents or electronically stored information — including writings, drawings, graphs, charts, photographs, sound recordings, images, and other data or data compilations — stored in any medium from which information can be obtained either directly or, if necessary, after translation by the responding party into a reasonably usable form; or

(B) any designated tangible things; or

(2) to permit entry onto designated land or other property possessed or controlled by the responding party, so that the requesting party may inspect, measure, survey, photograph, test, or sample the property or any designated object or operation on it.

(b) Procedure.

(1) *Contents of the Request.* The request:

(A) must describe with reasonable particularity each item or category of items to be inspected;

(B) must specify a reasonable time, place, and manner for the inspection and for performing the related acts; and

(C) may specify the form or forms in which electronically stored information is to be produced.

The federal rules also provide a mechanism for the parties to respond to electronic discovery requests. In addition to dictating how a party may respond to discovery requests, the rules also give the party a method of lodging an objection to the discoverable material, whether it consists of tangible objects or electronic data (Fig. 7-6).

FIGURE 7-6

Federal Rules of Civil Procedure, Rule 34(b)(2).

(2) Responses and Objections.

(A) Time to Respond. The party to whom the request is directed must respond in writing within 30 days after being served or — if the request was delivered under Rule 26(d)(2) — within 30 days after the parties' first Rule 26(f) conference. A shorter or longer time may be stipulated to under Rule 29 or be ordered by the court.

(B) Responding to Each Item. For each item or category, the response must either state that inspection and related activities will be permitted as requested or state an objection with specificity the grounds for objecting to the request, including the reasons. The responding party may state that it will produce copies of documents or of electronically stored information instead of permitting inspection. The production must then be completed no later than the time for inspection specified in the request or another reasonable time specified in the response.

When the discovery request centers on electronic material, otherwise known as *e-discovery*, the party served must present the requested items, over objection. However, the question with electronic data is, How will it be presented to the requesting party? Will the party simply print off all electronic data and present it as a hard copy? Not only is that impractical given the sheer volume of electronic data that some companies have on hand, but also some data would appear confusing and nonsensical if presented in printed form, without the context of the software that created it. In such a situation, the parties must again resort to the Rules of Civil Procedure (Fig. 7-7).

FIGURE 7-7

Federal Rules of Civil Procedure, Rule 34(b)(2)(E).

(E) Producing the Documents or Electronically Stored Information. Unless otherwise stipulated or ordered by the court, these procedures apply to producing documents or electronically stored information:

(i) A party must produce documents as they are kept in the usual course of business or must organize and label them to correspond to the categories in the request;

(ii) If a request does not specify a form for producing electronically stored information, a party must produce it in a form or forms in which it is ordinarily maintained or in a reasonably usable form or forms; and

(iii) A party need not produce the same electronically stored information in more than one form.

V DISCOVERY METHODS

In civil cases, there are several different methods that parties can use in order learn more detail about the case. These include:

- interrogatories;
- requests for production of documents;

- depositions;
- requests for physical and/or mental examination; and
- requests to admit.

A. INTERROGATORIES

Interrogatories
Written questions posed by one side of a civil action to the other side

Interrogatories are official documents that ask a series of questions and are served on one party by another. The parties must then thoroughly answer all questions within a specific time period. The use of interrogatories is governed by Rule 33 of the Federal Rules of Civil Procedure (Fig. 7-8).

FIGURE 7-8

Federal Rules of Civil Procedure, Rule 33(a) Interrogatories to Parties

(a) In General.

(1) Number. Unless otherwise stipulated or ordered by the court, a party may serve on any other party no more than 25 written interrogatories, including all discrete subparts. Leave to serve additional interrogatories may be granted to the extent consistent with Rule 26(b)(1) and (2).

(2) Scope. An interrogatory may relate to any matter that may be inquired into under Rule 26(b). An interrogatory is not objectionable merely because it asks for an opinion or contention that relates to fact or the application of law to fact, but the court may order that the interrogatory need not be answered until designated discovery is complete, or until a pretrial conference or some other time.

Only parties to the suit are authorized to send or receive interrogatories. Witnesses cannot be served with interrogatories. The party to whom the interrogatories are sent must answer the questions in writing. Usually, the legal team works with the client to fashion answers and then takes responsibility for preparing them in their final form. Clients usually sign a verification that accompanies the interrogatory answers. The verification is the client's personal oath that the answers contain true and correct information (Fig. 7-9).

FIGURE 7-9

Interrogatory Verification

STATE OF PLACID

DISTRICT COURT

LONDON COUNTY

Sherlock Holmes (Plaintiff) **CIVIL ACTION: 15-100**

v.

Professor James Moriarty,
Individually and as owner,
Operator of Moriarty
Transport Trucking Co.
(Defendant)

To: Neal Bevans

Attorney for Plaintiff Sherlock Holmes

VERIFICATION

I hereby certify and attest upon my oath, that the following answers to Plaintiff's First Interrogatories are complete and truthful to the best of my knowledge.

____

Professor James Moriarty, Defendant

This, the _____________ day of February, 2016

1. LIMITATIONS ON INTERROGATORIES

A party can object to a question posed in an interrogatory on the basis of privilege. However, a party can also raise additional challenges to interrogatories, including:

- information sought is unreasonably cumulative or duplicative;
- discovery is unduly burdensome and expensive; and
- general grounds, including specific objections to individual questions.

a. Unreasonably Cumulative or Burdensome

As we will see later in this chapter, a party is always free to interpose the objection to a discovery device that it is unduly burdensome. When one party has already obtained the information or is simply posing questions in order to harass or wear down the other party, the other party can object to the judge. This objection can apply to the entire set of interrogatories.

b. Objections to Specific Questions

In addition to a general objection about the burdensome nature of the interrogatories, the party can also object to the issues raised in specific questions, again based on the burdensomeness of the question or because it infringes on some legally protected interest, such as privilege. See Figure 7-10 for the rule governing objections to interrogatories.

FIGURE 7-10

Federal Rules of Civil Procedure, Rule 33(b) Objecting to Interrogatory Questions

(4) Objections. The grounds for objecting to an interrogatory must be stated with specificity. Any ground not stated in a timely objection is waived unless the court, for good cause, excuses the failure.

2. DRAFTING INTERROGATORIES

The best place to start when drafting interrogatory questions is with the complaint. This document sets out the main issues raised by the plaintiff and therefore will serve as a good starting point for both parties. The plaintiff will ask questions related to proving the elements of the complaint, while the defendant will pose questions attempting to disprove them. After that, the parties who are drafting interrogatories will review the answer. Together, the complaint and the answer will provide the issues in the case and serve as bedrock for the interrogatory questions that must be posed to both the plaintiff and the defendant.

These days, it is very common for law offices to have forms of interrogatories ready to go at the click of a mouse (Fig. 7-11). However, simply because there is a computer-generated form does not mean that the form will comply with the facts of the case. Forms can provide a good starting point, but they are no substitute for clear thinking and processing information provided in a specific case.

FIGURE 7-11

Caption Page of an Interrogatory

STATE OF COLUMBIA

COUNTY OF BURNETT

IN THE GENERAL COURT OF JUSTICE

SUPERIOR COURT DIVISION
FILE NUMBER: ____________

ALVIN REGINALD,

Plaintiff	)	INTERROGATORIES
vs.	)	
COLUMBIA RAILWAY LINES,	)	
Defendant	)	

To: ____________

I herewith serve upon you the following written interrogatories under the provisions of Rule 33 of the Rules of Civil Procedure.

You are required to answer these interrogatories separately and fully in writing under oath and to serve a copy of your answers on the undersigned within 30 days after service hereof.

These interrogatories shall be continuing in nature until the date of trial, and you are required to serve supplemental answers as additional information may become available to you.

1. State the name and address of each person whom you expect to call as an expert witness at trial, and state the subject matter on which the expert is expected to testify, and for each such expert identified, state the following:

(a) The substance of the facts and opinions to which the expert is expected to testify, and a summary of the grounds for each opinion;

(b) The identity of any and all documents submitted or supplied to the expert in connection with his or her opinions and testimony; and

(c) The qualifications of each such expert, listing the schools attended, years of attendance, degrees received, experience in any particular field of specialization or expertise, and all publications authored, including the title of work and the book or journal in which it was published and the date of publication.

In addition to relying on the pleadings and forms, legal practitioners who draft interrogatories also refer to form books, similar files, and even recent appellate cases. All of these will provide guidelines for the types of questions that should be asked. However, it is always good to keep in mind the unique features of the individual case and to tailor questions to meet those demands. See Figure 7-12 for a list of topics frequently used in interrogatories.

FIGURE 7-12

Frequent Topics in Interrogatories

- Identity of the person answering the interrogatories
- Identity of witnesses
- Information about expert witnesses
- Information about documents relied upon in the case
- Complete details of the other parties' version of the facts
- Specification of the amount/type of damages
- Insurance coverage and liability amounts

Many states impose numeric limitations on interrogatories, such as restricting a practitioner to 25 to 50 questions in total. For purposes of counting the questions, a sentence that ends with a question mark might constitute more than one question. For example, the following question might easily be construed as three questions instead of one: "Was there anyone else in the car with you; how fast were you going; and did you see anyone who was a witness to the collision between your car and the plaintiff's?"

Because these three questions cover three separate topics, a party might contest the number of interrogatories by asking the court to rule that this single question qualifies as three, and thus that the total number of the party's interrogatories exceeds the permissible limit. In such a case, the court might rule that the party is only required to answer a certain number of questions and that the others are deemed withdrawn. Different jurisdictions deal with this issue in a variety of ways, and you should be aware of such possible complexities in drafting interrogatory questions.

3. ANSWERING INTERROGATORIES

When a party answers interrogatory questions (Fig. 7-13), he must provide a verification or post that the answers provided are truthful. Dishonesty or deceit in answering interrogatory questions can have disastrous consequences for that party.

FIGURE 7-13

Federal Rules of Civil Procedure, Rule 33(b) Answering Interrogatories

(3) *Answering Each Interrogatory.* Each interrogatory must, to the extent it is not objected to, be answered separately and fully in writing under oath.

In general practice, it is very common for attorneys and paralegals to give the client an artificially early due date for her response to the interrogatories, usually a week to 10 days prior to the actual due date. Because many people tend to procrastinate, giving the client an artificially early date gives the law firm sufficient time to collate the answers, type them up, and serve them on the requesting party. Obviously, the client must respond to all questions, and if there are any gaps or omissions in the answers, these must immediately be called to the attention of the attorney.

4. TIME LIMITS ON INTERROGATORIES

If filed by the plaintiff along with the complaint, the defendant has 45 days to respond to an interrogatory. Otherwise, once served, a party has 30 days to respond (Fig. 7-14). Failure to serve answers within the time limit will subject the party to sanctions, which we will discuss later in this chapter.

FIGURE 7-14

Federal Rules of Civil Procedure, Rule 33(b) Time Limits on Interrogatory Answers

(2) Time to Respond. The responding party must serve its answers and any objections within 30 days after being served with the interrogatories. A shorter or longer time may be stipulated to under Rule 29 or be ordered by the court.

B. REQUESTS FOR PRODUCTION OF DOCUMENTS

Another discovery method is to serve a **request for production of documents** on the opposing party. This is a request that asks for copies of all relevant documents in the case, including photographs, videotapes, and any other evidence. When this request has been filed, the other party must produce the evidence or risk sanctions by the court.

Request for production of documents
A request by one party to another in a civil case for copies of all documents relevant to that case

One of the best sources to determine the existence of critical documents about the case is the client. The legal team should always thoroughly question the client about any potential photographs, written reports, or other documents that might serve as the basis for any contention in the case. The legal team can then file a request for production on the opposing party. The Federal Rules of Civil Procedure do not require the party to give a reason for the request (Fig. 7-15). Once the request is made, the opposing party must either comply or raise an authorized objection to producing the documents. The request can also be fashioned in such a way as to allow the parties to inspect physical items that are impossible to either move or reproduce in some other form. In fact, the rules even allow the parties to enter onto real estate to examine specific items.

FIGURE 7-15

Federal Rules of Civil Procedure, Rule 34(a) Request for Production of Documents

(a) In General. A party may serve on any other party a request within the scope of Rule 26(b):

(1) to produce and permit the requesting party or its representative to inspect, copy, test, or sample the following items in the responding party's possession, custody, or control:

(A) any designated documents or electronically stored information — including writings, drawings, graphs, charts, photographs, sound recordings, images, and other data or data compilations — stored in any medium from which information can be obtained either directly or, if necessary, after translation by the responding party into a reasonably usable form; or

(B) any designated tangible things; or

(2) to permit entry onto designated land or other property possessed or controlled by the responding party, so that the requesting party may inspect, measure, survey, photograph, test, or sample the property or any designated object or operation on it.

In many ways, a request for production of documents resembles — and is often served along with — the interrogatories in the case. However, where interrogatories request answers, requests for production require physical objects. A request for production should specify a date, time, and location for inspecting or copying the requested material, as seen in Figure 7-16. In large lawsuits, production of documents is a huge undertaking that may require thousands of man-hours and a team of clerical assistants to help gather and copy documents. Before documents are turned over to the opposition, the legal team must review them to make sure that information of a confidential or privileged nature is not included.

FIGURE 7-16

Federal Rule of Civil Procedure, Rule 34(b) Procedure for Request for Documents.

(b) Procedure.

(1) Contents of the Request. The request:

(A) must describe with reasonable particularity each item or category of items to be inspected;

(B) must specify a reasonable time, place, and manner for the inspection and for performing the related acts; and

(C) may specify the form or forms in which electronically stored information is to be produced.

PRACTICE POINTER ▶ PROTECTING ORIGINALS

As the paralegal featured in this chapter's "The Life of a Paralegal" suggests, it is always a good idea to protect the original of any document or other evidence to be used at trial. There are many times when the court will allow the parties to use a copy of a document, but only when it has been clearly established that the original is available or that there is a good explanation for the disappearance of the original. Sloppy record keeping is not considered to be a good excuse. Many paralegals protect original documents by placing them in plastic protectors or storing them where they are accessible but not readily so. If a person must work to obtain the original, there is less of a chance that the original will be used as scratch paper for notes or simply misplaced in a pile of other papers.

Subpoena duces tecum
A court order commanding a witness to produce documents or physical evidence for presentation to a judge

Although frequently discussed within the context of a request for production of documents, a **subpoena duces tecum** is a court order compelling a witness to appear at a certain date and time and to bring specific documents and other evidence with them. Such a subpoena can be used within the context of a civil trial, but it differs in important ways from a request for production of documents. A request for production of documents compels one party to serve documents and evidence on another party, while a subpoena duces tecum requires a witness to bring items to court and present them to the judge.

C. DEPOSITIONS

Deposition
Oral questions asked of a witness, under oath, by an attorney and later preserved in a transcript

Court reporter
A person who is empowered to administer oaths and records oral testimony, usually by stenography

A **deposition** is a face-to-face session between the attorneys in the case and a witness. The witness is sworn in and then asked general questions about the issues surrounding the litigation. The questions and answers are taken down by a **court reporter** and later printed off in a transcript. If the witness becomes unavailable to testify during the trial, the transcript of the deposition can be read instead. Although depositions are common in civil cases, they are rarely used in criminal cases. In criminal cases, the defendant has the right to face his accusers, and therefore depositions are of little use. In a civil deposition, however, attorneys for both sides can ask broad-ranging questions, not only about the issue under contention but also about any potential bias on the part of the witness or any other matter related to the case.

The Federal Rules of Civil Procedure provide for two different types of depositions: oral and written. Depositions upon written questions are relatively rare and consist of one party sending written questions to witnesses in the case. Oral depositions are far more common. These depositions are governed by Rule 30 and its various subparts (Fig. 7-17).

FIGURE 7-17

Federal Rules of Civil Procedure, Rule 30 Deposition Upon Oral Examination

(a) When a Deposition May Be Taken.

(1) Without Leave. A party may, by oral questions, depose any person, including a party, without leave of court except as provided in Rule 30(a)(2). The deponent's attendance may be compelled by subpoena under Rule 45.

(2) With Leave. A party must obtain leave of court, and the court must grant leave to the extent consistent with Rule 26(b)(1) and (2):

(A) if the parties have not stipulated to the deposition and:

(i) the deposition would result in more than 10 depositions being taken under this rule or Rule 31 by the plaintiffs, or by the defendants, or by the third-party defendants;

(ii) the deponent has already been deposed in the case; or

(iii) the party seeks to take the deposition before the time specified in Rule 26(d), unless the party certifies in the notice, with supporting facts, that the deponent is expected to leave the United States and be unavailable for examination in this country after that time; or

(B) if the deponent is confined in prison.

1. PREPARING FOR A DEPOSITION

In many ways, a deposition is similar to the testimony that a witness will give at trial. The witness will be asked questions on direct examination, and the opposing attorney also has the right to cross-examine the witness. However, the similarities between trial testimony and deposition testimony end there. Depositions are much more relaxed affairs than trial testimony. For one thing, they are rarely held in courthouses. The most common place to conduct a deposition is at one of the attorneys' offices, although almost any venue will serve. Before questioning can begin, the attorney must prepare. Preparation for a deposition includes a close review of all relevant facts of the case, the pleadings, other witness statements, and any other source that can provide details. Many attorneys also rely on general question forms to make sure that they ask sufficient questions. There are some basic guidelines that most attorneys adhere to in fashioning questions for witnesses in a deposition, including:

- the questions must be clear;
- the attorney should avoid questions that require yes/no answers; and
- the attorney should ask the witness to specify the information source for her replies.

2. SETTING A DEPOSITION

In theory, setting a deposition can be as simple as issuing a Notice of Deposition for a specific date and time and waiting for the witness and other attorneys to appear. However, in the real world of litigation, things are more complicated. Attorneys often attempt to work out the time and place of a deposition around their schedules and those of the opposing attorneys. This is considered to be common courtesy among professionals. The job of coordinating the date and time of the deposition usually falls to the attorney's paralegal, who may need to call the other attorney's offices several times before arriving at a mutually convenient time. Generally, the witness is not given such a courtesy.

The Notice of Deposition, also called a *Notice of Examination*, is a simple form that sets the date, time, and place for a deposition (Fig. 7-18). In some states, it may be issued in conjunction with a witness subpoena to appear for a deposition. In any event, the notice serves to alert all parties that a deposition has been set and that they should attend if they want the opportunity to question the witness thoroughly. Rule 30(b) of the Federal Rules of Civil Procedure governs such notices (Fig. 7-19).

FIGURE 7-18

Notice of Deposition Form

STATE OF PLACID

DISTRICT COURT

LONDON COUNTY

Sherlock Holmes
(Plaintiff) **CIVIL ACTION: 15-100**

v.

Professor James Moriarty, individually
and as owner, operator of Moriarty
Transport Trucking Co. (Defendant)

TO: Mrs. Joan Hudson
221 B Baker Street
London, PL 28655

PLEASE TAKE NOTICE that at 9:00 a.m. on April 10, 2017, at the offices of Deborah L. Bolstridge, Attomey at Law, 21 Robin's Wood Place, Bohemia, PL 28655, the Plaintiff in the above-entitled action will take the videotaped deposition of Madge Manager, as witness upon oral examination, pursuant to Rule 30 of the Placid Rules of Civil Procedure, before a Court Reporter or before some other person authorized by law to administer oaths. The oral examination will begin at 9:00 a.m. and will continue from day to day until completed. The oral examination will be videotaped. You are invited to attend and cross-examine.

This the 6th day of March, 2017.

FIGURE 7-19

Federal Rules of Civil Procedure, Rule 30(b) Notice of Deposition

(b) Notice of the Deposition; Other Formal Requirements.

(1) Notice in General. A party who wants to depose a person by oral questions must give reasonable written notice to every other party. The notice must state the time and place of the deposition and, if known, the deponent's name and address. If the name is unknown, the notice must provide a general description sufficient to identify the person or the particular class or group to which the person belongs.

(2) Producing Documents. If a subpoena duces tecum is to be served on the deponent, the materials designated for production, as set out in the subpoena, must be listed in the notice or in an attachment. The notice to a party deponent may be accompanied by a request under Rule 34 to produce documents and tangible things at the deposition.

(3) Method of Recording.

(A) Method Stated in the Notice. The party who notices the deposition must state in the notice the method for recording the testimony. Unless the court orders otherwise, testimony may be recorded by audio, audiovisual, or stenographic means. The noticing party bears the recording costs. Any party may arrange to transcribe a deposition.

(B) Additional Method. With prior notice to the deponent and other parties, any party may designate another method for recording the testimony in addition to that specified in the original notice. That party bears the expense of the additional record or transcript unless the court orders otherwise.

(4) By Remote Means. The parties may stipulate — or the court may on motion order — that a deposition be taken by telephone or other remote means. For the purpose of this rule and Rules 28(a), 37(a)(2), and 37(b)(1), the deposition takes place where the deponent answers the questions.

PRACTICE POINTER ▶ CONFIRMING LETTERS

On a daily basis, a paralegal will find that he spends a great deal of time on the telephone speaking with other legal professionals, many of whom represent opposing parties in pending cases. Most of these individuals are honest, hardworking, and perfectly reputable. However, there will be times when you encounter legal professionals who are not as scrupulous as you might like. In response, many attorneys and paralegals make it a habit to follow up any verbal communication with a confirming letter and an e-mail. In fact, setting up the template for a letter is remarkably easy given the availability of word-processing programs. By sending both an e-mail and a letter, the paralegal has two methods to prove that the other party was notified. A hard copy of the e-mail should be placed in the file after it has been sent and acknowledged. The follow-up letter can be as simple as confirming the details of a telephone call, but it can have dramatic effects on the case. Suppose, for instance, that the attorney in this chapter's case excerpt had listed the April 4 report as part of what he was providing to the opposing party. He might easily have avoided paying $1,750 in fines. Here is a sample confirming letter:

Allison Attorney, Attorney at Law
100 Maple Street
Placid City, PC 00550

June 5, 2015

Re: *Calvin Client v. Darrell Defendant*
Case No. 07CV9786

Laura Lawyer
1020 Legal Place
Placid City, PL 00550

Dear Ms. Lawyer,

This will confirm our conversation today in which you kindly agreed to our request to schedule the deposition for our client on a Thursday or Friday afternoon in the next two weeks. As I understand our conversation, you will need to check with Judge Roberts to see if you are scheduled for trial next week, and if you are not, then we will schedule the deposition of our client, Calvin Client, at your office either Thursday, June 11, or Friday, June 12, anytime between 1:00 p.m. and 5:00 p.m. If those dates are not convenient, we will then schedule the deposition for Thursday, June 18, or Friday, June 19.

Thank you for your cooperation in this matter. If I have misstated any portion of our conversation, please contact me at 555-1212 to discuss the matter.

Sincerely,
Paul Paralegal
Legal Assistant for Allison Attorney, Esq.

3. CONDUCTING THE DEPOSITION

The rules provide that any person can be deposed, whether the person is a witness or a party. In a civil case, both the plaintiff and the defendant will be deposed, as well as any other witness with information about any aspect of the case.

a. Opening Stipulations

When the day of the deposition arrives, the attorneys usually meet beforehand to work out some stipulations (Fig. 7-20). For a deposition, the parties might enter into several stipulations regarding the admissibility of the testimony, including the following:

- Any question or answer deemed objectionable shall be reserved for argument at trial.
- The parties have not waived attorney–client privilege.
- The witness waived her right to review the transcript of the deposition.

Unless the court orders otherwise, the parties may stipulate that:

(a) a deposition may be taken before any person, at any time or place, on any notice, and in the manner specified — in which event it may be used in the same way as any other deposition; and

(b) other procedures governing or limiting discovery be modified — but a stipulation extending the time for any form of discovery must have court approval if it would interfere with the time set for completing discovery, for hearing a motion, or for trial.

FIGURE 7-20

Federal Rules of Civil Procedure, Rule 29 Stipulations Regarding Discovery Procedure

b. Reserving Objections

Because the deposition is taken weeks or months before the trial, attorneys routinely reserve the right to object to the questions offered during a deposition (Fig. 7-21). Because the rules about deposition questions are so liberal and essentially allow the attorneys to ask any question, whether relevant or not, the attorneys generally begin the deposition by reserving their right to challenge testimony at a later date. Simply because an attorney can ask about a matter during a deposition does not mean that that same testimony will be admissible during the trial. By reserving an objection, the attorney ensure that she will be able challenge the testimony before the jury hears it.

(2) Objections. An objection at the time of the examination — whether to evidence, to a party's conduct, to the officer's qualifications, to the manner of taking the deposition, or to any other aspect of the deposition — must be noted on the record, but the examination still proceeds; the testimony is taken subject to any objection. An objection must be stated concisely in a nonargumentative and nonsuggestive manner. A person may instruct a deponent not to answer only when necessary to preserve a privilege, to enforce a limitation ordered by the court, or to present a motion under Rule 30(d)(3).

FIGURE 7-21

Federal Rules of Civil Procedure, Rule 30(c) Schedule and Duration; Motion to Terminate or Limit Examination

c. Permissible Questions

The rules about questions in a deposition are extraordinarily liberal. Essentially, the attorneys can ask the witness anything, while recognizing that some of the answers may not be admissible later at trial. Attorneys are free to ask questions only tangentially connected to the case, as seen in Figure 7-22. The only exception is when a question crosses into privileged matters.

(b) Discovery Scope and Limits.

(1) Scope in General. Unless otherwise limited by court order, the scope of discovery is as follows: Parties may obtain discovery regarding any nonprivileged matter that is relevant to any party's claim or defense and proportional to the needs of the case, considering the importance of the issues at stake in the action, the amount in controversy, the parties' relative access to relevant information, the parties' resources, the importance of the discovery in resolving the issues, and whether the burden or expense of the proposed discovery outweighs its likely benefit. Information within this scope of discovery need not be admissible in evidence to be discoverable.

FIGURE 7-22

Federal Rules of Civil Procedure, Rule 26(b) Scope of Questions in Depositions

A witness cannot be compelled to answer questions protected by the attorney–client privilege or any other legally recognized privilege. If such a question is asked, the witness may simply refuse to answer it. Unlike other refusals that may lead to court sanctions, a witness who refuses to reveal privileged information cannot be punished for doing so. Recognized privileges include:

- attorney–client privilege;
- pastor–penitent privilege;
- marital privilege; and
- doctor–patient privilege.

d. Cross-Examining a Witness During the Deposition

The opposing attorney is also permitted to question the witness during the deposition (Fig. 7-23). Technically, this qualifies as cross-examination and can, in some instances, become quite heated. The attorney for the opposition has the same latitude in questioning the witness as the other attorney, and cross-examining a witness during a deposition makes a great deal of sense. It is better to pin down all possible points at this stage rather than wait for surprises at trial.

FIGURE 7-23

Federal Rules of Civil Procedure, Rule 30 Cross-Examination at Deposition

(c) Examination and Cross-Examination; Record of the Examination; Objections; Written Questions.

(1) Examination and Cross-Examination. The examination and cross-examination of a deponent proceed as they would at trial under the Federal Rules of Evidence, except Rules 103 and 615. After putting the deponent under oath or affirmation, the officer must record the testimony by the method designated under Rule 30(b)(3)(A). The testimony must be recorded by the officer personally or by a person acting in the presence and under the direction of the officer.

(2) Objections. An objection at the time of the examination — whether to evidence, to a party's conduct, to the officer's qualifications, to the manner of taking the deposition, or to any other aspect of the deposition — must be noted on the record, but the examination still proceeds; the testimony is taken subject to any objection. An objection must be stated concisely in a nonargumentative and nonsuggestive manner. A person may instruct a deponent not to answer only when necessary to preserve a privilege, to enforce a limitation ordered by the court, or to present a motion under Rule 30(d)(3).

e. Use of Exhibits

Attorneys and witnesses can use exhibits during the trial, including photographs, diagrams, and anything else to help illuminate the witness's testimony. When the deposition has been concluded, the court reporter will include the exhibit with the transcript.

4. PERSONS PRESENT AT THE DEPOSITION

Whenever a deposition is scheduled, there are always several people present. They include the:

- witness;
- attorneys;
- court reporter; and
- parties.

a. The Witness

The witness, or **deponent**, is always present at the deposition. Although there are provisions that allow attorneys to conduct depositions over the telephone, the most common practice is for all parties to be physically present.

Deponent
The person questioned during a deposition

b. The Attorneys

Attorneys are the persons who request the deposition; therefore, they are present in order to ask questions. Generally, a legal representative for each party in the case will be present. Both the plaintiff's and the defendant's attorneys are permitted to ask questions during the deposition, with the attorney who set the deposition beginning the questioning and then turning the witness over to the opposing attorney for cross-examination.

c. The Court Reporter

A court reporter is a person who has been trained to record testimony, usually on a stenograph machine. A court reporter takes down everything said at the deposition, no matter who is speaking (Fig. 7-24). Modern stenograph machines come with computer hardware and software programs that allow the court reporter to convert shorthand script into readable English. The court reporter is also the person who swears in the witness before the deposition begins.

FIGURE 7-24

Federal Rules of Civil Procedure, Rule 30(b) Court Reporter

(5) Officer's Duties.

(A) Before the Deposition. Unless the parties stipulate otherwise, a deposition must be conducted before an officer appointed or designated under Rule 28. The officer must begin the deposition with an on-the-record statement that includes:

(i) the officer's name and business address;
(ii) the date, time, and place of the deposition;
(iii) the deponent's name;
(iv) the officer's administration of the oath or affirmation to the deponent; and
(v) the identity of all persons present.

(B) Conducting the Deposition; Avoiding Distortion. If the deposition is recorded nonstenographically, the officer must repeat the items in Rule 30(b)(5)(A)(i)–(iii) at the beginning of each unit of the recording medium. The deponent's and attorneys' appearance or demeanor must not be distorted through recording techniques.

d. The Parties

The parties are also permitted to be present when others are being deposed. However, in most cases, the attorney will suggest that the party not attend the deposition. The client may need to work or have other conflicts, and sometimes having the client present is more of a distraction to the attorney than a help.

5. DURATION OF THE DEPOSITION

The Federal Rules of Civil Procedure limit the duration of a deposition to seven hours over one day, as seen in Figure 7-25. If an attorney needs additional time, he must petition the judge for an extension. There are times when it is reasonable for a deposition to last longer than a single day. Consider the issues raised in class action lawsuits or highly complicated civil actions. In those cases, attorneys routinely request additional time to conduct depositions of the main witnesses in the case.

FIGURE 7-25

Federal Rules of Civil Procedure, Rule 30(d) Time Limits on Depositions

(d) Duration; Sanction; Motion to Terminate or Limit.

(1) Duration. Unless otherwise stipulated or ordered by the court, a deposition is limited to 1 day of 7 hours. The court must allow additional time consistent with Rule 26(b)(1) and (2) if needed to fairly examine the deponent or if the deponent, another person, or any other circumstance impedes or delays the examination.

6. AFTER THE DEPOSITION

Once the deposition has been completed, the court reporter gathers together all notes and records and prepares a transcript. Preparing the transcript sometimes takes days or weeks, even in this era of computer stenograph machines. This is because the court reporter must go through the entire transcript and ensure that there are no errors. Once completed, the transcript is sent to the attorneys who attended the deposition and the witness who was questioned. Figure 7-26 shows a sample transcript.

FIGURE 7-26

First Page of Transcript

STATE OF COLUMBIA COUNTY OF HALEY	IN THE GENERAL COURT OF JUSTICE SUPERIOR COURT DIVISION
CHARLES REGINALD, Plaintiff, vs. COLUMBIA RAILWAY LINES RAILWAY COMPANY, TOWN OF CLING, and STEVE W. BLUE, Defendant.	FILE NUMBER: 98 CVS 1001

DEPOSITION OF BENNIE HALL

March 29, 2014

APPEARANCES:

For the Plaintiff:	I. M. Lawyer DEWEY, EATHAM AND HOWE, P.A. 89 N. Montford Street Morganton, NC 28655 (704) 438-6153
For the Defendants:	Rip Offe Offe & Going 800 Spruce Street Cling, NC 28777 (704) 555-1000
	Hugh Burpe Eaten, Swallow & Burpe 900 Apple Tree Street Asheville, NC 28801 (704) 555-9999

The Rules of Civil Procedure allow a witness to review the transcript of the deposition and to make changes in the wording, but only in limited contexts (Fig. 7-27). The witness cannot, for example, change the substance of the testimony but can correct typographical errors or words that were transcribed incorrectly. The rules provide a 30-day time period for a witness to correct the transcript once it has been completed. After that time, the witness is not permitted to make any changes.

FIGURE 7-27

Federal Rules of Civil Procedure, Rule 30(e) Review by Witness; Changes; Signing

(e) Review by the Witness; Changes.

(1) Review; Statement of Changes. On request by the deponent or a party before the deposition is completed, the deponent must be allowed 30 days after being notified by the officer that the transcript or recording is available in which:

(A) to review the transcript or recording; and

(B) if there are changes in form or substance, to sign a statement listing the changes and the reasons for making them.

(2) Changes Indicated in the Officer's Certificate. The officer must note in the certificate prescribed by Rule 30(f)(1) whether a review was requested and, if so, must attach any changes the deponent makes during the 30-day period.

Deposition digest
Also known as a *deposition summary*; a document that summarizes the important points of a deposition transcript by cross-referencing topics with page numbers

Once the transcript has been generated, it usually falls to the paralegal to prepare a **deposition digest**. This is a document that summarizes the critical points raised in the deposition and cross-references them by the page number on which they appear in the transcript. Deposition digests are useful tools in helping attorneys and others understand the important points in a witness's testimony, without having to read the entire transcript to ferret them out. You will find an example of a deposition digest in Figure 7-28.

FIGURE 7-28

Deposition Digest

Deposition Summary
Howell v. Howell
11-6-14

DIGEST TO DEPOSITION OF **Ruth Bowles Lee** October 28, 2014

Page #:	Testimony:
3-4	Witness resides at 6 Bluebird Road, Morganton, NC; she is married to lawyer Phil Lee and is self-employed. She runs a business called Appraisers, Inc., for personal property appraisals, and rents a space in an antique mall. She has a second business, Antique Estimates, Inc.; she has a partner, and has operated this business for 22 years doing estate auctions and estate sales.
4	She has been in the appraisal business almost 23 years. Twelve years previously, she took the exam for the American Society of Appraisers and passed it. When she took the exam, she had already been in business 10 years.
5	She has to be recertified with 100 classroom hours every five years and standard examinations; she was recertified in February 2014. She also keeps current with periodicals, trade journals, etc. She keeps current publications for American/English antiques and popular collectibles and orders new publications as her business requires.
6	Discussion of her exam to be certified in antiques, decorative arts, and residential contents.
7	She is certified in all these areas.
7	On July 20, 2014, she appraised personal items at 10 Beaver View Court, Morganton; some items, boxed, in the garage she did not appraise.
7-9	Discussion of review of home contents with Mrs. Howell and access; also, her written report.
9-10	Discussion of first three items, Franklin Mint Plate through Danbury Mint Plates. She has valued these kinds of items many times. Although these producers publish catalogues discussing values of their items, she knows from her experience that the items are a "hard sell" and the value deflates terrifically after purchase. The values the publications would show are not "real world" values.

Tech Topic
VIDEO DEPOSITIONS

Although this chapter discusses the more traditional approach to depositions—oral questions taken before a court reporter or stenographer—there is a growing trend toward using video depositions. There are companies all over the United States that specialize in providing professional video deposition services. Companies such as Affordable Video Solutions (www.affordablevideosolutions.com) and Video Resources (www.videoresources.com) specialize in setting up, recording, and then indexing video depositions. A deposition recorded in this manner has several distinct advantages over the traditional method. For one thing, if the witness is unavailable, the party seeking to admit the testimony can simply play the video for the jury. Under the old system, the only way to get the absent witness's testimony before the jury would be to have the attorney or someone else read it aloud. No matter how well a person reads a transcript, the jurors become quickly bored. When they can actually see the person as he appeared at the deposition, they pay closer attention. Video depositions also help capture a witness's demeanor, allow the witness to present visual aids, and give the attorney the option of a dramatic presentation during the trial. These days, companies offer a video service and the possibility of indexing various videos, recording them in digital format for quick retrieval, and even juxtaposing one video segment with another (such as showing how the witness contradicted her own previous testimony).

D. REQUESTS FOR PHYSICAL AND/OR MENTAL EXAMINATION

A request for a physical and/or mental examination is often raised in situations where the condition of one of the parties is a central issue in the case. A request for a physical examination can be made by the defendant in a personal injury case to have the plaintiff evaluated by the defendant's doctors in order to determine the extent of the plaintiff's physical injuries. Mental examinations are less frequent under the rule but are also permissible (Fig. 7-29). Before such an examination will be authorized, the parties must show good cause to require it. Physical and mental evaluations are not a common feature in all cases but are used when a party's condition is a central point of the case, especially in medical malpractice or personal injury cases.

FIGURE 7-29

Federal Rules of Civil Procedure, Rule 35(a) Request for Physical or Mental Examination

Rule 35. Physical and Mental Examinations

(a) Order for an Examination.

(1) In General. The court where the action is pending may order a party whose mental or physical condition – including blood group – is in controversy to submit to a physical or mental examination by a suitably licensed or certified examiner. The court has the same authority to order a party to produce for examination a person who is in its custody or under its legal control.

E. REQUESTS TO ADMIT

In every case, there are always certain facts that are beyond dispute between the parties. The function of a request for admission of facts allows the parties to stipulate to these undisputed facts and then concentrate their time and resources on the contested issues (Fig. 7-30). A request to admit facts helps the parties focus on the important issues raised in the case. Examples of issues that are commonly raised within the confines of a request to admit are set out in Figure 7-31.

FIGURE 7-30

Federal Rules of Civil Procedure, Rule 36. Requests for Admission

(a) Scope and Procedure.

(1) Scope. A party may serve on any other party a written request to admit, for purposes of the pending action only, the truth of any matters within the scope of Rule 26(b)(1) relating to:

(A) facts, the application of law to fact, or opinions about either; and
(B) the genuineness of any described documents.

(2) Form; Copy of a Document. Each matter must be separately stated. A request to admit the genuineness of a document must be accompanied by a copy of the document unless it is, or has been, otherwise furnished or made available for inspection and copying.

FIGURE 7-31

Undisputed Facts That Are Commonly Raised in Requests to Admit

- Date of the incident
- Location of the incident
- Location of corporate headquarters

VI OBJECTIONS TO DISCOVERY REQUESTS

As we have already seen in several contexts, a party or witness can object to discovery requests on the grounds of privilege or some other legally recognized excuse. We have already seen examples of the use of the attorney–client privilege usurping a discovery request. However, there are additional grounds for objections to discovery requests:

- Work product
- Unduly burdensome, cumulative, and/or expensive
- Constitutional rights
- Trade secrets
- Protective orders

A. WORK PRODUCT

Work product refers to the mental impressions, conclusions, strategies, opinions, and legal theories about the case put together by the parties' attorneys. This material is not discoverable because it reflects the essence of what the attorney does for the client, using her talents and skills to provide the best possible outcome. In many ways, the work product objection is an offshoot of the attorney–client privilege. The very substance of what an attorney does is reflected in work product, and requiring a party to give the other party a complete overview of the legal team's theory of the case would be unreasonable and would substantially damage the relationship between attorney and client.

Work product
An attorney's notes, impressions, charts, diagrams, and other material used to prepare strategy and tactics for trial

B. UNDULY BURDENSOME, CUMULATIVE, AND/OR EXPENSIVE

We have already seen examples of a party interposing an objection of unduly burdensome, cumulative, or expensive in responding to interrogatories and requests for production of documents. If a party believes that the opposition's discovery request falls into any of these categories, it can petition the court for relief. The party cannot, however, simply ignore the discovery request and hope the court will eventually rule in its favor. Such actions would doubtless result in court-ordered sanctions for failure to comply with discovery requests.

C. CONSTITUTIONAL RIGHTS

There are times when a person may refuse to respond to discovery requests because the information requested infringes on a Constitutionally guaranteed right. A party might refuse to answer certain questions because they cause the person to incriminate himself, in violation of the Fifth Amendment.

Consider the following example: Anne is being deposed about a car wreck last year. The allegation is that Anne was intoxicated at the time, crossed the centerline, and had a head-on collision with the plaintiff. Anne was cited for driving under the influence, but her case has not yet been adjudicated. At her deposition, Anne is asked:

Q: How many drinks had you had that night?
A: I refuse to answer on the grounds that the answer might tend to incriminate me.

Is Anne's failure to answer grounds for sanctions, or is she protected?

Answer: She is protected under the Fifth Amendment.

Several months after the first deposition, attorneys again question Anne. This time, she has entered a plea of guilty to one count of driving under the influence. As part of a guilty plea, Anne waived her Fifth Amendment rights. When she is questioned at the deposition, she again raises the same objection. Is Anne still protected by the Constitution from having to answer this question?

Answer: No. Anne waived her Fifth Amendment protections when she pled guilty. She can now be questioned thoroughly about the incident and must answer those questions.

D. TRADE SECRETS

In addition to interposing objections to discovery requests on the basis of privilege, work product, or Constitutional rights, a party may also object to discovery requests that demand information about trade secrets. Revealing such secrets could provide competitors with everything that they need to launch a similar product. As a result, courts generally guard trade secrets and prevent parties from requesting this information in a civil suit.

E. PROTECTIVE ORDERS

In situations where a party believes that the opposition is acting in bad faith or that she has a legally recognized interest in protecting certain information, the party can move for a discovery protective order that bars the opposition from receiving specific information. In order to receive such a protective order, the party who is subject to the request must file a petition with the court, and the judge must make specific findings before invoking the order. A court may issue a discovery protective order in situations where the opposition's request is overly broad or irrelevant or the opposition is requesting material it has already received; where the material requested is protected by trademark or other legal provision; or where the discovery request is designed to be abusive or harassing. See Figure 7-32 for a list of requests that would justify such an order.

FIGURE 7-32

Examples of Requests Justifying a Discovery Protective Order

- Information requested is protected under trademark or copyright.
- Discovery request is too broad.
- Discovery request is designed to harass or annoy the other party.
- The information requested would unnecessarily delay the proceedings.
- The discovery request is overly expensive or time-consuming.
- The request would endanger the health of the party (physical examination).

Some states have held that an attorney's request for a protective order (Fig. 7-33) or sanctions against the opposing side will not be upheld when the attorney has failed to exercise the courtesy of advising opposing counsel of his intention not to appear at a deposition or to comply with discovery requests.

FIGURE 7-33

Motion for Protective Order

STATE OF COLUMBIA

COUNTY OF BURNETT

IN THE GENERAL COURT OF JUSTICE

SUPERIOR COURT DIVISION
FILE NUMBER: ____________

ALVIN REGINALD,
Plaintiff) Motion for Protective Order
vs.)
COLUMBIA RAILWAY LINES,)
Defendant.)

Now comes Darrell Defendant, pursuant to Rule 26 and 45 of the State Rules of Civil Procedure, and hereby moves the court for order of quashing the subpoena attached hereto as Exhibit a, and also for a protective order from the court prohibiting the plaintiff from obtaining the discovery sought in the subpoena, and an order specifying that all parties cannot be questioned nor shall be required to answer questions regarding the material presented in Exhibit a and in support of this motion Darrell Defendant hereby respectfully shows the court that the documents and records requested are not relevant to any matter in this action, that the material requested cannot reasonably lead to the discovery of any other relevant material, that the materials requested are privileged under the attorney-client relationship, that the material requested is also protected under the work product rule, and that the request is designed to harass, intimidate, and annoy the defendant.

WHEREFORE, Darrell Defendant requests that the court issue an order quashing the subpoena in this case, and also entering a protective order specifying that the plaintiff, the plaintiff's attorney, and any party associated with the plaintiff is hereby prohibited from requesting, demanding, posing questions regarding, or otherwise using discovery rules to request information contained in Exhibit a. Defendant also requests that the costs of this action be assessed against the plaintiff, including reasonable attorney's fees that were incurred in researching, preparing, and presenting this motion to the court, and for such other and further relief as the court may deem appropriate and just.

This the 12th day of October 2014.

____
Attorney for Darrell Defendant

VII FAILURE TO RESPOND TO DISCOVERY REQUESTS

The Rules of Civil Procedure provide a broad range of sanctions against a party or witness who fails to comply with discovery requests (Fig. 7-34). If a witness fails to appear for a deposition, for instance, she can be required to pay all reasonable fees incurred by the party who set it, including attorneys' fees. Other sanctions that a court can impose for failure to comply with discovery include:

- an order by the court taking as truth facts alleged by the opposing party in its pleadings;
- a court order prohibiting the noncomplying party to present evidence to support its case;
- a court order striking all or a portion of the noncomplying party's pleadings;
- a court order prohibiting the party from presenting a particular defense;
- dismissal of the action; and
- default judgment against the party.

FIGURE 7-34

Federal Rules of Civil Procedure, Rule 30. Depositions by Oral Examination

(g) Failure to Attend a Deposition or Serve a Subpoena; Expenses. A party who, expecting a deposition to be taken, attends in person or by an attorney may recover reasonable expenses for attending, including attorney's fees, if the noticing party failed to:

(1) attend and proceed with the deposition; or
(2) serve a subpoena on a nonparty deponent, who consequently did not attend.

LEGAL LEGWORK ■ SANCTIONS

According to your state's rules of civil procedure, what sanctions are available to a trial court for violations of discovery rules? Can judges in your state impose monetary fines as the court does in this chapter's case excerpt? What other sanctions are courts in your state authorized to impose?

VIII COMPELLING DISCOVERY

A party who believes that the opposing party is acting in bad faith in failing to respond to discovery requests is also entitled to file a motion to compel discovery (Fig. 7-35). Such a motion lists the specific failures of the opposing party to comply and requests that the court impose sanctions against the noncomplying party (Fig. 7-36).

FIGURE 7-35

Federal Rules of Civil Procedure, Rule 37. Failure to Make Disclosures or to Cooperate in Discovery; Sanctions

(a) Motion for an Order Compelling Disclosure or Discovery.

(1) In General. On notice to other parties and all affected persons, a party may move for an order compelling disclosure or discovery. The motion must include a certification that the movant has in good faith conferred or attempted to confer with the person or party failing to make disclosure or discovery in an effort to obtain it without court action.

(2) Appropriate Court. A motion for an order to a party must be made in the court where the action is pending. A motion for an order to a nonparty must be made in the court where the discovery is or will be taken.

FIGURE 7-36

Federal Rules of Civil Procedure, Rule 37(a) Sanctions for Failure to Comply with Discovery

Rule 37. Failure to Make Disclosures or to Cooperate in Discovery; Sanctions

(b) Failure to Comply with a Court Order.

(1) Sanctions Sought in the District Where the Deposition Is Taken. If the court where the discovery is taken orders a deponent to be sworn or to answer a question and the deponent fails to obey, the failure may be treated as contempt of court. If a deposition-related motion is transferred to the court where the action is pending, and that court orders a deponent to be sworn or to answer a question and the deponent fails to obey, the failure may be treated as contempt of either the court where the discovery is taken or the court where the action is pending.

(2) Sanctions Sought in the District Where the Action Is Pending.

(A) For Not Obeying a Discovery Order. If a party or a party's officer, director, or managing agent — or a witness designated under Rule 30(b)(6) or 31(a)(4) — fails to obey an order to provide or permit discovery, including an order under Rule 26(f), 35, or 37(a), the court where the action is pending may issue further just orders. They may include the following:

(i) directing that the matters embraced in the order or other designated facts be taken as established for purposes of the action, as the prevailing party claims;
(ii) prohibiting the disobedient party from supporting or opposing designated claims or defenses, or from introducing designated matters in evidence;
(iii) striking pleadings in whole or in part;
(iv) staying further proceedings until the order is obeyed;
(v) dismissing the action or proceeding in whole or in part;
(vi) rendering a default judgment against the disobedient party; or
(vii) treating as contempt of court the failure to obey any order except an order to submit to a physical or mental examination.

IX SOFTWARE THAT ASSISTS IN DISCOVERY

Given the sheer bulk of documents and other material that can be generated in contemporary litigation, it is no wonder that some companies have designed litigation software packages specifically targeted at lawyers and paralegals. These programs, such

Tech Topic
USING SOFTWARE TO SIFT THROUGH DIGITAL MOUNTAINS OF DATA

Although we commonly think of using e-discovery software in large cases, often involving tens of millions of dollars, it is becoming more and more common for all cases, even small personal injury or medical practice cases, to have a great deal of digital information. Consider how often a person uses her phone to send texts, receive and send photos, and do other things online. If a defendant were online or sending a text at the moment of the car collision, that is an important fact to note. But if witnesses are discussing the case—or worse, coordinating their stories—and doing it through texts or e-mails, then that is information that the party should turn over during the discovery phase. The problem with software that is meant to sift through digital media is that most of these programs were designed with large law firms and mountains of data in mind. Scalability is often an issue with such software. A program that was designed to sort through millions of words, thousands of documents, and hundreds of other records is not often easily used in much smaller cases. The other issue with some of this software is cost. Large firms can absorb the yearly flat fees and processing fees of as high as $200 per gigabyte of data. If a small case has as much as 1,000 GB (or 1 terabyte) of information, then the cost for sifting through that data could easily take up the entire budget set aside to handle the entire case.

There are companies that produce small and more cost-effective e-discovery packages, including:

- dtSearch Desktop: www.dtsearch.com
- Acrobat Legal Edition: www.adobe.com
- Digital WarRoom Pro: www.digitalwarroom.com
- Discovery Cloud: www.discoverycloud.nextpoint.com

as Summation and Concordance, among many others, allow attorneys and paralegals to scan, organize, label, and categorize the hundreds or even thousands of documents that can be produced in a single lawsuit. This software even allows the legal team to cross-reference documents with deposition transcripts, motions, and other discovery to produce a coherent picture of the facts supporting particular points in the complaint or answer.

Case Excerpt

When can a court impose monetary sanctions for violating discovery rules?

MAYNARD V. NYGREN
332 F.3d 462 (C.A.7 [Ill.] 2003)

Cudahy, Circuit Judge.

Corrections officer Harry Maynard sued his former employer, the McHenry County Sheriff, alleging a violation of the Americans with Disabilities Act (ADA), 42 U.S.C. §§12101-213. On February 14, 2002, the district court, finding discovery violations,

Fed.R.Civ.P. 37(c), granted the defendant Sheriff's motion to dismiss and assessed monetary sanctions against Maynard and his counsel, attorneys Dennis Favaro and Patricia Jochum and the firm of Favaro, Buzek & Groman, Ltd. Maynard and his counsel appeal on the ground that the trial court failed to make a finding of a discovery violation sufficient to sustain the sanction of dismissal. The appellants also claim that part of the monetary sanctions were improper and that there was insufficient cause to sanction counsel. The appellants ask us to vacate the district court order and remand to a different district judge under 28 U.S.C. §455(a). The Sheriff cross-appeals, requesting additional attorney's fees from the appellants. We affirm in part and reverse in part and remand for reconsideration.

I.

Harry Maynard began working as a corrections officer at the McHenry County Sheriff's Department in 1992. In February 1996, Maynard was hospitalized and diagnosed with multiple sclerosis. Following his hospital stay, he presented his supervisor, Chief Maire, with a report (dated March 4) from his doctor, David Martinez, allowing him to return to work. However, Maynard was told by Maire that he would not be allowed to return to work because the report stated that he could have recurrent episodes of weakness and unsteadiness. Maynard met with Dr. Martinez to discuss Maynard's displeasure with the content of the March 4th report, and they arranged for Maynard to meet with a neurologist. On March 25, Benjamin Nager, a neurologist, wrote to Dr. Martinez confirming that Maynard should not be released back to work without restrictions. Based on this letter, Dr. Martinez wrote a second report on April 4, stating that Maynard was not then able to perform the functions of his job, but that he might become able within ninety days. Where this April 4th report ended up, and did not end up, lies at the root of Maynard's troubles; what is known is that the Sheriff was not given a copy of this report until this lawsuit was well underway.

The Sheriff's lawyer wrote Maynard in November 1996 to advise him that, as an alternative to releasing his medical records (something he was not legally obligated to do), Maynard could submit himself to an examination by an Independent Medical Examiner in order to determine his ability to return to work. In January 1997, Maynard met with Dr. Pradip Sethi, who confirmed that there was no guarantee that Maynard would be symptom-free or that he could perform all his job functions at all times. Based on Dr. Sethi's reports, the Sheriff terminated Maynard. This lawsuit alleging refusal to provide a reasonable accommodation under the ADA followed.

The Complaint and the Amended Complaint in this action failed to mention the existence of the second, April 4th, report of Dr. Martinez. Nor did the April 4th report appear during discovery, although Maynard's counsel forwarded to the Sheriff what was supposed to be all of Maynard's medical records from Dr. Martinez's file. The Sheriff finally learned of the April 4th report and received a copy of it from Dr. Martinez in January 2002, shortly before the trial date. The Sheriff then filed an emergency motion seeking involuntary dismissal and sanctions under Fed.R.Civ.P. 37(c)(1) for Maynard's failure to disclose the document. The trial judge held an evidentiary hearing to explore exactly what had happened to the April 4th report.

At the hearing, Dr. Martinez testified that he had prepared the April 4th report at Maynard's urgent request. Jeanne Gannon, Dr. Martinez's assistant, testified that she had typed the report and left it hanging in a public area of the office to be picked up. While she did not witness Maynard picking up the report, she concluded that the report had been picked up since the original was not returned to Maynard's medical file. On the other hand, there was no note in Maynard's chart showing that he had requested such a report (as there ordinarily would be), and Maynard denied that he had requested or received the report. Cynthia Kroncke, Dr. Martinez's former medical assistant, also testified. She said that she had copied the entire Maynard file and had sent copies to Maynard's counsel in February 1999. In view of Dr. Martinez's testimony that a copy of the April 4th report was in the file in 2002, it appeared that Maynard's counsel had received the April 4th report during discovery, but somehow had failed to forward it to the Sheriff's counsel.

Judge Reinhard found that Maynard's denials were not credible, and that he had intentionally withheld the April 4th report. Judge Reinhard also noted that Maynard had lied in his Amended Complaint and in an affidavit by stating that Dr. Martinez would not change the original, March 4th report. Am. Compl. at 4, para. 18 ("Maynard tried unsuccessfully to obtain a different release, but the physician would not change the wording from the original release"); Maynard Aff., Pl.'s Resp. to Def.'s Emergency Mot. for Involuntary Dismissal Ex. G, at 1 ("I had never seen Dr. Martinez's April 4, 1996 letter until January 25, 2002 when it was provided to me by my counsel"). The judge dismissed Maynard's suit, awarded the Sheriff attorney's fees and costs incurred in bringing the emergency motion and assessed a fine of $3500 payable to the court for the time spent on the motion. Judge Reinhard also found that the April 4th report had been provided to Maynard's counsel, but he did not believe that counsel had deliberately withheld the letter, positing instead that the letter was either lost in the office or removed from the office, possibly by Maynard. Nonetheless, the monetary sanctions were divided evenly between Maynard and his counsel because the judge felt that the situation could have been avoided had counsel been more careful with the discovery documents or more diligent in investigating their client's testimony.

The court enters the following sanctions against plaintiff/his counsel: (1) This case is dismissed with prejudice for discovery violation; (2) Defendant is awarded reasonable attorney fees, expenses, and costs incurred in bringing this emergency motion (1/2 to be paid by the plaintiff and 1/2 to be paid by plaintiff's counsel); and (3) an additional sanction of $3,500 to be paid to the Clerk of Court for the court's time incurred on this emergency motion (1/2 to be paid by plaintiff and 1/2 to be paid by plaintiff's counsel).

II.

Discovery sanctions are reviewed for abuse of discretion. Under this standard, we uphold any exercise of the district court's discretion that could be considered reasonable, even if we might have resolved the question differently. However, a district court by definition abuses its discretion when it makes an error of law, and, while factual findings are generally reviewed only for clear error, findings which are tainted by the application of an inapposite standard are subject to fuller review. In cases of mixed questions of law and fact the standard is oftentimes clear error (or abuse of discretion), though plenary review may be used when certain factors indicate it is warranted or needed.

We must first clarify the law of this circuit on the weight of evidence necessary to support dismissal as a discovery sanction. Then, we will consider the appropriateness of the other sanctions ordered by the district judge.

A.

Of all possible sanctions, dismissal is considered "draconian," and we must be "vigilant" in our review. Because of its severity, we have circumscribed the range of cases in which dismissal may be used as a sanction. Looking at the case law, we find two different standards for determining whether a case can properly be dismissed. Some of our cases have held that actions can be dismissed "when there is a clear record of delay or contumacious conduct, or when other less drastic sanctions have proven unavailing." This appears to be the standard used when cases are dismissed for want of prosecution or failure to comply with orders of the court, Fed.R.Civ.P. 41(b). A slightly different requirement — a finding of willfulness, bad faith or fault — comes into play when dismissals are used specifically as a discovery sanction under Fed.R.Civ.P. 37. That is, even without "a clear record of delay, contumacious conduct or prior failed sanctions," a court can apply the sanction of dismissal for Rule 37 violations with a finding of willfulness, bad faith or fault, as long as it first considers and explains why lesser sanctions would be inappropriate.

We have not yet answered the question of what burden of proof is necessary to sustain a Rule 37 dismissal based on willfulness, bad faith or fault. For Rule 41(b) dismissals, the record of delay, contumacious conduct or prior failed sanctions must be "clear." Is there a similar requirement for the evidence supporting a finding of willfulness, bad faith or fault? The Sheriff argues that a preponderance of the evidence suffices, while Maynard argues that there must be clear and convincing evidence before a case is dismissed for a discovery violation. We agree with the appellants that, considering the severe and punitive nature of dismissal as a discovery sanction, a court must have clear and convincing evidence of willfulness, bad faith or fault before dismissing a case.

Working without the benefit of a clear pronouncement from this court on the appropriate burden of proof, the district judge did not specify which standard he was applying. We are left to deduce from the record which standard was applied. We agree with the appellants that the district court may have applied a preponderance standard. This belief is grounded principally on the portions of the ruling which deal with Maynard's counsel's culpability. On two occasions, the district judge noted that it was "more likely" than not that the April 4th report was sent to counsel. We also note the circumstantial nature of much of the evidence, which makes this perhaps a closer case than some. While we cannot conclude with certainty that a preponderance, rather than a clear and convincing, standard was applied, the absence of any assurance that the higher burden of proof was considered advises us to assume for the purpose of this appeal that the lower threshold was used.

The Sheriff argues now that, regardless of the standard used below, the evidence is in fact clear and convincing, and that we should affirm the dismissal. And the evidence does appear to support the Sheriff's positions and the district court's conclusions quite strongly. The court reasonably relied on the persuasive testimony of Dr. Martinez and his staff in finding that Maynard had acted in bad faith in concealing evidence during pleadings and discovery. However, especially because factual determinations such as these are the special province of the trial judge, we must defer to the trial judge and allow him to reconsider the evidence in light of the standard announced here. In remanding the case, we do not find appropriate the recusal of Judge Reinhard, and are confident that he will approach this determination without preconception. Nothing in the record persuades us otherwise.

B.

Even if the district court upon reconsideration declines to dismiss this lawsuit — and we make no recommendation on the matter — there remain the other, non-dismissal sanctions, which are generally permissible even without clear and convincing evidence. The monetary sanctions imposed by the district judge included both attorney's fees to the Sheriff and a $3500 fine for the court's time. Half of these amounts was to be paid by Maynard and half by Maynard's counsel. The appellants argue that the $3500 fine was an abuse of discretion, as was any sanction against counsel.

As to the $3500 fine, the appellants provide no case law that supports their argument. On the contrary, there is ample case law validating the use of fines, especially where they are "remedial" and correspond to some real cost (here, the court's time at $500 per hour). While fines are not specifically included in the non-exclusive list of sanctions in Rule 37(b)(2), they are among the tools available to trial courts to remedy the harms of discovery violations. Such a fine was within the discretion of the district judge.

The second question demands more analysis. We see two potential bases for upholding the district court's sanction against Maynard's counsel: the Federal Rules of Civil Procedure and the inherent powers of the court. Reading the transcript of the proceedings below, it is not clear on which the district court was basing the sanctions; thus, we consider whether the sanctions against Maynard's counsel would have been permissible under either authority.

We agree with the appellants that *Insurance Benefit Administrators v. Martin*, 871 F.2d 1354, 1360 (7th Cir.1989), does not permit the imposition of Rule 37(c) sanctions on attorneys. In IBA, we held that attorneys can be sanctioned for failure-to-disclose violations only under Rule 26(g)(3), which authorizes sanctions against attorneys who certify discovery disclosures in violation of the rules. In the case at hand, because the court found that counsel had no knowledge that the discovery response was inadequate, there is no ground for a sanction under Rule 26(g), which applies only to knowing violations of the rules. Any sanction against Maynard's counsel based on Rule 37(c) or 26(g) was improper.

The district judge's finding of no willfulness also precludes any sanction against counsel under the inherent powers of the court. While generally the inherent powers of the court can extend beyond those powers granted in the Federal Rules of Civil

Procedure, the assessment of fees against counsel under the inherent powers of the court is permitted only when there is a finding of willful disobedience or bad faith. Here, however, the district judge found explicitly that counsel did not willfully withhold the document — the judge blamed the document's disappearance on negligent mishandling. There is no authority under the Rules or under the inherent powers of the court to sanction attorneys for mere negligence, and so sanctions must be reversed as applied to Maynard's counsel.

III.

The Sheriff cross-appeals, arguing that he should have been awarded all his attorney's fees, and not merely those incurred in bringing the successful motion for dismissal. The Sheriff argues that such full reimbursement is required by the text of Rule 37. However, Rule 37 supports only the reimbursement of fees resulting from the discovery violation. As long as the suit as a whole was not frivolous, and we have no reason to believe that it was, the remaining attorney's fees would have been incurred even without the discovery violation; thus, the causality requirement was not met. The Sheriff also argues that attorney's fees are required under Rule 41, under which a dismissal not otherwise grounded "operates as an adjudication on the merits." However, the American Rule is generally that prevailing parties are not entitled to fees, even where a full adjudication on the merits has taken place. The Sheriff's claim under the ADA, 42 U.S.C. §12205, also fails since there was no finding that Maynard's claim was frivolous, unreasonable or without foundation. None of the bases for cross-appeal are therefore valid.

IV.

For the foregoing reasons, the judgment of the district court is REVERSED in part and AFFIRMED in part.

QUESTIONS ABOUT THE CASE:

1. Explain the significance of the second letter by Dr. Martinez about Maynard's condition.
2. What is the basis of the suit by Maynard against the sheriff?
3. According to the trial court, why was it likely that Maynard had intentionally withheld the April 4 report?
4. Why were both Maynard and his attorney fined?
5. What view does the appellate court take of dismissing a civil action? Why?
6. According to the appellate court, is it proper for a trial court to impose monetary fines for abuse of discovery?

Chapter Summary

Discovery is the exchange of information between opposing sides in a civil case. Although the historical approach to discovery was to limit information exchange between the parties, modern approaches to discovery rules have liberalized the process and require parties to exchange as much information as possible prior to trial. The modern discovery rules are based on the premise that the parties should know everything about the case before the trial ever begins. Discovery methods include interrogatories, requests for production of documents, depositions, requests for physical and/or mental examination, and requests to admit. Interrogatories are written questions posed to parties of the case that must be answered within a specified time period. Requests for production of documents require opposing parties to produce any written document that will form the basis of any contention raised in the case. Depositions are the oral questionings of witnesses, taken under oath. A request to admit facts is posed by one party to another, requesting that the party stipulate to an undisputed fact, thus freeing the party from the necessity of presenting evidence to support it. Discovery requests must be reasonable, and the party who receives a request may move for a protective order if the information requested is excessive, overly broad, or infringes on a privilege, such as the attorney–client privilege.

SKILLS YOU NEED IN THE REAL WORLD

Visiting the Courthouse

One of the important aspects of working as a legal professional is knowing where and how to find information. Although most court records are available online, that is not always the case. Eventually, almost all public records will be available to anyone, anywhere, and for free, but that day is not quite here. Until then, paralegals must know how to search through physical files in the clerk's office, the deed room, the tax office, and any other public record facility in order to locate specific information. The courthouse is a great resource for discovery information on what a person owns, whether she has been sued previously, and whether this person has financed a car, boat, or trailer. There is a great deal of other information available there, and actually visiting the courthouse in person is still necessary to get at some information until the day arrives when it is available online in every county in every state of the Union.

THE LIFE OF A PARALEGAL

Discovery

Jane Huffman has been working as a paralegal for several years. "I enjoy working in the legal field," she says. "In fact, now that I've gotten my bachelor's degree, I actually teach part-time at the college where I originally got my associate's degree. You never know what doors will open to you once you enter the law." She works on all facets of a case, from the initial meeting with the client, to preparing and reviewing discovery materials, to preparing settlement brochures. "The law can be very consuming. Some days, you'll look up and say, 'What happened to the day?' I guess that's a good thing. I've worked in jobs where you just watch the clock. There's always plenty to do in a law office."

One of Jane's favorite parts of a civil case is going through discovery materials. "When I organize discovery, I dig through everything that we've received. I pull out every relevant document produced and go through it with a fine-toothed comb. I make four copies of everything: one for the attorney, one for the judge, one for the opposition, and one for the witness. I organize our attorney's copies first. I put them in an order that makes sense. I like to have a clean set of discovery. The attorneys tend to make notes on their copies, so I always keep a clean set that hasn't been marked. It's a lot harder to get a document admitted at trial if it's got handwritten notes across it.

"Once I've gone through the discovery, I start working the file to get it ready for trial. You can't start too soon for that. I put together a list of the evidence that we'll be using at trial and put it in a notebook. That way, when the witness is on the stand, we can just hand them the notebook, or even leave it on the witness stand and just ask them to turn to a specific page."

After the first round of discovery, there is usually a follow-up. "It's what I call the second round of discovery. I follow up on the stuff we get in the first round. I review what the other side has given us for completeness and objections. If they've raised an objection and I don't think it's legitimate, we'll point it out and cite a statute or case law showing how the objection isn't legitimate."

ETHICAL ISSUES FOR THE PARALEGAL

Hiding Damaging Information

Individuals have a natural tendency to conceal personal information from others. This is especially true during the discovery phase of a civil case. Many times, clients will wish to conceal or at least "spin" details about their personal lives, work history, or the incident that forms the basis of the civil suit. The problem with all of these approaches is that when a client conceals information in the discovery process, it can have dire consequences for the case. The opposing attorney may use this concealment to show that the client is unworthy of belief or even to move for sanctions. Legal professionals must be ready to explain to clients the benefits of being forthright and honest, even when this involves revealing details that may be embarrassing. The modern rules of discovery place a high premium on complete disclosure, and courts are always ready to impose sanctions against parties who fail to live up to that standard. This chapter's case excerpt is a prime example of the dangers of concealing or withholding damaging evidence.

Websites

- **Federal Rules of Discovery — Cornell Law School**
  www.law.cornell.edu/rules/frcp/

- **'Lectric Law Library — Discovery Sanctions**
  www.lectlaw.com/def2/s113.htm

- **Federal Rules of Civil Procedure**
  www.federalrulesofcivilprocedure.org/

- **Litigation — Cornell University Law School**
  www.law.cornell.edu/wex/litigation

Key Terms

Court reporter
Deponent
Deposition
Deposition digest
Discovery
Interrogatories
Request for production of documents
Stipulation
Subpoena duces tecum
Work product

Review Questions

1. What is the purpose of discovery?
2. Explain the historical approach to discovery and how that has changed over time.
3. What approach do the Federal Rules of Civil Procedure promote in revealing information to opposing sides?
4. Is there a typical sequence followed in civil discovery? Explain.
5. What are depositions?
6. What are the two types of depositions that are permissible in civil cases?
7. What are interrogatories?
8. What is a deposition digest?
9. Explain how a deposition is conducted.
10. What is the time limit imposed on answering interrogatories?
11. What sanctions can be imposed against a party who fails to comply with discovery?
12. What are requests for production of documents?
13. What are requests to admit?
14. What types of objections can a party raise to a discovery request?
15. What is a discovery protective order?
16. What individuals are normally present at a deposition?

17 Explain the type of information that must be revealed about expert witnesses in civil discovery.
18 Create a time line of the civil process, beginning with the service of the complaint and continuing through discovery.
19 How has the modern approach to civil discovery changed the process of exchange of information in civil cases?
20 Have the discovery rules increased the chance that civil cases will be settled prior to trial? Explain your answer.

Applying What You Have Learned

1 Please locate a deposition online, and prepare a deposition digest of that testimony.

2 Suppose that you have been handed a case involving a typical automobile accident. Defendant B rear-ended Plaintiff A at a red light. Compose 20 interrogatory questions that the plaintiff should serve on the defendant, making sure they abide by your state's limitations on interrogatories and that they do not request privileged information.

3 Our client, Joe Doe, and his wife, Flo, were driving through their hometown on their way to go out to dinner. The restaurant was on the other side of the railroad tracks that run through the town. As they approached the intersection of the track with the road, Joe thinks he looked both ways and didn't see anything but isn't sure because of his injuries.

> It is undisputed that just as Joe began crossing the tracks, his car was struck by a southbound train, owned and operated by Columbo Railway. The force of the impact impaled Joe's car on the front of the engine, and the car was dragged 242 feet down the track before falling off to the side.
>
> Flo was killed at the scene, and Joe was severely injured, requiring hospitalization for four months before he was released, in a wheelchair, never to walk again. Joe came to our firm, wanting to sue, because the trees that grow next to the track block anyone's view and everybody in town knows it.
>
> We have filed a wrongful death action on behalf of Flo and a separate action for damages for Joe's injuries. We are now at the stage where interrogatories are to be filed. Draft up 10 questions for the railroad company.

4 Review your state's discovery rules and then prepare a paper discussing the following:
- When, where, and who may be deposed?
- What issues can and cannot be raised in interrogatories?
- What can be produced through requests to produce?
- What privileges protect the production of materials through any type of discovery device?
- What cases expand or limit the use of depositions, interrogatories, and requests to produce in civil cases?

5 Visit your local courthouse, and locate a civil case. What discovery is available in the file? Have there been motions to compel discovery or to move for sanctions for discovery violations? If so, what was the outcome of those motions?

6 Wally Whistleblower was fired last year by Spurious, Inc. Wally alleges that he was fired when he brought the company's questionable accounting practices to the attention of the shareholders. He has brought a wrongful termination suit against Spurious, Inc. Wally's attorney, Laura Litigator, is questioning a Spurious employee at a deposition. Also present at the deposition is Barry Barrister, representing Spurious, Inc. Laura asks the following question:

Q: At any point in your employment with Spurious, did you ever observe any accounting practices that you thought were questionable, unethical, or illegal?

A: Well, I would have to say—

Mr. Barrister: Objection. This question goes into privileged matter. I direct the witness not to answer this question.

Is this question objectionable? What privilege could Mr. Barrister be asserting in this case? Is this a legitimate objection, or could it be subject to a motion for sanctions under the discovery rules?

Motions Practice

8

Chapter Objectives

- Explain the importance of motions in civil practice
- Describe how a motion is prepared
- Define how a motion is served on opposing parties
- Compare and contrast a notice of motion with a certificate of service
- Explain the role of the judge in granting or denying motions
- Describe the function of a motion for summary judgment
- Explain the significance of a motion for more definite statement
- Describe the significance of a judgment on the pleadings
- Define the role of a 12(b)(6) motion
- Explain how attorneys use motions to clarify the issues in a civil case

I INTRODUCTION

Motions practice is as critical to a legal practitioner as the ability to draft legal pleadings and to prepare for trial. At its simplest, a motion addresses a specific issue and clarifies it for trial. There are several different types of motions, from those directed at specific evidence to those that seek to dismiss the entire case. We will address all of these motions in this chapter.

BRINGING A MOTION

A party may file a motion in a civil case for any number of reasons. The plaintiff might bring a motion to prevent the defense from presenting prejudicial and inflammatory evidence during the trial. A defendant might move for summary judgment, requesting that the case be dismissed for failure of the plaintiff to state a legally recognized claim. Other motions may be more narrowly focused on specific legal or evidentiary issues.

Consider the following example: In a personal injury case, the defendant does not want the jury to hear that he has been involved in other litigation. The defendant's attorney believes that if the jury should hear about the defendant's contentious divorce, the jury might be more inclined to rule against him. In order to avoid anyone bringing up such evidence, the defense attorney files a motion with the court, seeking an order directing all parties to refrain from mentioning the defendant's divorce.

When the judge receives this motion, she confers with all parties and enters an order doing precisely what the defense attorney requested.

A. CONSTRUING THE LANGUAGE IN A MOTION

The rules about how to interpret the language in a motion are very broad. In previous centuries, a party's motion might be denied for failure to apply the correct formulation of words, but such rulings have fallen by the wayside. These days, courts liberally interpret the language of a motion and, as long as the intent can be discerned, do not require specific legal language before considering the merits of the motion.

The legal test used to determine the intent of a motion is whether the wording puts the opposing party on notice about the claims being raised and the action requested. If a motion satisfies these two conditions, the court will consider it. Whether or not the motion is granted, however, is an entirely separate issue.

Sidebar

In previous decades, a motion might be dismissed because of a technical failure to allege the appropriate wording or by a failure to include the correct formulation of words. That approach is no longer followed.

B. DRAFTING A MOTION

Once the party conceives of an issue that would be appropriately dealt with through a motion, the next step is to draft it. Drafting a motion might be as simple as a one-sentence request (Fig. 8-1).

FIGURE 8-1

Plaintiff's Motion

STATE OF PLACID IN THE SUPERIOR COURT
COUNTY OF BURKE FILE NUMBER: 06 CV 2121

INGRED SVENSON)
Plaintiff,)
vs.)
JANE MARPLE)
Defendant.)
)

The plaintiff hereby requests that the parties be allowed to adjourn at 4:30 PM each day of the trial, in order to give counsel sufficient time to notify witnesses to appear for the following day's testimony.

Respectfully submitted, this the 6th day of June, 2015.

Laura Lawyer
Attorney for Plaintiff

Although drafting a motion may be as simple as presenting a request to adjourn at a specific time each day, many motions require extensive legal research and keen attention to drafting. A motion for summary judgment, for example, might require several days' attention before it is ready to be served on the opposing side.

LEGAL LEGWORK ■ LOCAL RULES

Some court systems have statewide rules regarding motions and "local rules" governing the filing of motions and related activities. Does your court system have local rules? If so, what do they provide for filing motions or for summary judgment motions? For instance, do your local rules require that an affidavit supporting the motion be filed with the motion? Do the local rules make any other changes to the general requirements under your state's rules of civil procedure?

C. SERVING A MOTION

Once drafted, the next step for the party seeking court intervention is to serve a copy of the motion on the opposition. All parties, including co-defendants and co-plaintiffs, must be served with a copy of the motion. Service can be accomplished by having the motion hand-delivered to the offices of the attorneys who represent the various parties, or it can simply be mailed. In either event, the party presenting the motion proves service by creating a certificate of service to accompany the motion.

1. CERTIFICATE OF SERVICE

Certificate of service
A party's verification that a copy of a pleading or necessary document was served on the opposing party, either through the U.S. postal system or by personal hand delivery

A **certificate of service** is the party's proof that a copy of the motion was served on all parties. Whether the motion was hand-delivered or mailed, the party will sign the certificate of service indicating exactly how the other parties were served and when this service took place. The purpose of the certificate of service is to document the actions taken by the attorneys in the case. A certificate of service is considered to be sufficient proof that the service took place as alleged, and such certificates are rarely challenged. Obviously, an attorney or other legal professional who creates fraudulent certificates of service is violating ethical rules.

Whenever an attorney creates a motion or other pleading, it must be served on the opposing attorneys as well as filed in the courthouse. The failure to complete either step may render the entire motion null and void. A court may, for instance, refuse to consider a motion filed by one party that has not been served on the other party— or that the moving party cannot prove was served on the opposition. This is why certificates of service can be pivotal in deciding issues in a case even before the court considers the merits of the actual motion. See Figure 8-2 for a sample certificate of service.

FIGURE 8-2
Certificate of Service

This is to certify that the undersigned has, on the date set out below, served a copy of this Motion for Summary Judgment on the plaintiff's attorney, to wit:

Linda Lawyer
200 Elm Street
Placid City, PL 25360

By depositing same, postage prepaid, in the United States Mail.

This the 9th day of May, 2015.

____

Clarence D. Arrow
Attorney for Defendant
100 Maple Avenue
Placid City, PL 25360
(555) 555-1212
State Bar No. 004562

2. ATTACHING AFFIDAVITS TO THE MOTION

Affidavit
A written document containing the statement of a person who then swears that the contents are true and correct to the best of his knowledge

In addition to the actual motion, a party might also include exhibits to accompany the motion. The most common exhibit is an **affidavit** by a party or a witness attesting to the facts raised in the motion. Attaching an affidavit in this situation helps the party prove the facts associated with its request. In some circumstances, the accompanying affidavit may serve as verification for the facts and claims contained in the motion. In addition to an affidavit, a party may, in some jurisdictions, be required to file additional supplementation, including a memorandum of the legal points raised in the motion, the legal authority that supports the motion, and the movant's theory about how those facts and legal authorities support its position. See Figure 8-3 for a sample affidavit and Figure 8-4 for the relevant section of the Federal Rules of Civil Procedure. The person providing the affidavit must set out that the facts alleged in the affidavit are within the affiant's personal knowledge (and not acquired secondhand).

Sidebar

If the facts supporting the motion are already a matter of record, there may be no requirement to file a supporting affidavit.[1]

FIGURE 8-3

Affidavit

STATE OF PLACID IN THE SUPERIOR COURT
COUNTY OF BURKE SUPERIOR COURT FILE
NO. ________

JANE DOE,) AFFIDAVIT
Plaintiff)
vs.)
NICHOLAS CHARLES,)
Defendant.)

Date: ____________

Affidavit of Nicholas D. Charles

Nicholas D. Charles, having been duly sworn, says:

1 Affiant is the defendant in the above action and makes this affidavit based upon personal knowledge.
2 Affiant has personally reviewed plaintiff's complaint filed in the above action and is familiar with its content.
3 Affiant was not personally involved nor did affiant participate in the alleged acts and/or omissions which form the factual basis for plaintiff's complaint in the above action.
4 Affiant was not present at the date and time alleged by the plaintiff as the occurrence for the underlying action in this case.
5 Affiant, if called to testify as a witness, will give sworn testimony to the points raised in paragraphs numbered 1-4.

____
Affiant

Subscribed to and sworn before
me on ____________

____
Notary Public
My commission expires: ____________

FIGURE 8-4

Federal Rules of Civil Procedure, Rule 56. Summary Judgment

(c) Procedures.

(1) Supporting Factual Positions. A party asserting that a fact cannot be or is genuinely disputed must support the assertion by:

(A) citing to particular parts of materials in the record, including depositions, documents, electronically stored information, affidavits or declarations, stipulations (including those made for purposes of the motion only), admissions, interrogatory answers, or other materials; or

(B) showing that the materials cited do not establish the absence or presence of a genuine dispute, or that an adverse party cannot produce admissible evidence to support the fact.

(2) Objection That a Fact Is Not Supported by Admissible Evidence. A party may object that the material cited to support or dispute a fact cannot be presented in a form that would be admissible in evidence.

(3) Materials Not Cited. The court need consider only the cited materials, but it may consider other materials in the record.

(4) Affidavits or Declarations. An affidavit or declaration used to support or oppose a motion must be made on personal knowledge, set out facts that would be admissible in evidence, and show that the affiant or declarant is competent to testify on the matters stated.

D. FILING A MOTION

Once served on all parties, the motion is then filed with the court. Filing may be as simple as presenting the document to the clerk of court and having it inserted in the file. Most attorneys bring at least two copies to the courthouse, one for the clerk's file and one that can be date- and time-stamped so that they have independent proof that the motion was correctly filed. As we will see later in this chapter, federal courts require motions and other pleadings to be filed electronically, using its PACER program.

Unlike pleadings, a motion generally does not require a response. After all, the motion is the written embodiment of the party's request for a judge to take some action and assumes that the points of the motion will be discussed at a hearing. At this hearing, the opposing party will have the right to contest the issues, raise additional points, and even present evidence in opposition to the motion. As a result, unless specifically ordered to do so by the trial court, the opposing side is not required to file a written motion in opposition to the original motion.[2] However, many practitioners often feel that providing a written explanation of their opposition to the motion gives the judge something to review and something that will remind her of the opposition's points if she chooses to review written materials before coming to a decision.

Tech Topic
AUTOMATING DOCUMENTS

In this chapter, you will find discussion of how to create your own "motions bank." By taking copies of motions created in other cases and storing them in a central location, you can often save time when it comes to creating similar documents in the future. However, there are also companies that offer the same process. Companies such as Word Automation (www.wordautomation.com) and Thuriam (www.thuriam.com) allow users to create templates for a huge variety of documents, including legal pleadings and motions. Instead of copying and pasting from old documents, automated documents pull up the basic structure of the proposed motion and ask you for details, often by requesting you to fill in material in a discussion box. Once completed, the program then fills in the rest of the information, generating all of the standard language and preparing a completed form in seconds. The advantage of word automation programs is that they also generate ancillary documents, including certificates of service, affidavit forms, court cover sheets, and any other forms required. Then you can print all this material from the programs. In a few seconds, you can produce everything you need to file and serve a motion, right down to the envelope and signature pages for attorneys. However, you should always keep in mind that no matter how great a program is at taking the drudgery out of drafting, serving, and filing motions, there is still no substitute for thought and analysis in deciding to bring one.

E. ARGUING A MOTION

Simply serving a motion and filing it does not complete the motion process. In order to have the judge rule on the motion, the attorney must usually request a court hearing to formally present the motion to the judge and to seek a ruling on the issues it contains. Although some courts routinely set aside a specific date for the argument of all motions pending in the case, many attorneys must contact the court administrator and specifically request such a hearing in order to make sure that the motion is heard.

Once the hearing date is set, the attorney notifies all other parties about the day and time that the motion will be heard. The right of parties to have an opportunity to appear and argue a motion is considered one of the central rights in a civil or criminal case.[3] The most common way of alerting other parties to the motion hearing date is by a notice of motion (Fig. 8-5).

FIGURE 8-5

Notice of Motion

IN THE SUPERIOR COURT
BURKE COUNTY
STATE OF PLACID
SUPERIOR COURT DIVISION
FILE NUMBER: ___________

JANE DOE,	)	
Plaintiff,	)	
vs.	)	NOTICE OF MOTION
NICHOLAS D. CHARLES	)	
Defendant.	)	
______________________	)	

TO: Linda Lawyer
200 Elm Street
Placid City, PL 25360

THIS MATTER having been brought before the court on its Motion for Summary Judgment by Clarence D. Arrow, attorney for defendant, for an order dismissing the plaintiff's complaint by and through a Motion for Summary Judgment filed by Defendant Nicholas D. Charles, hereinafter referred to as "Defendant" and notice having been given to all parties, the Defendant's Motion for Summary Judgment is set for argument on the 8th day of July, 2015, at 1 p.m. in Courtroom 1A, Burke County Superior Court, 100 Courthouse Lane, Placid City, PL before Judge Hancock.

PLEASE TAKE notice that attorney for the defendant has requested oral argument on his Motion for Summary Judgment.

PLEASE TAKE FURTHER NOTICE that, in support of his motion, defendant will rely on Plaintiff's First Interrogatories to Defendant, and Defendant's Response to Plaintiff's First Interrogatories to Defendant, Defendant's Request for Admission to Plaintiff, and Plaintiff's Response to Defendant's Request for Admission to Plaintiff.

This the 19th day of June, 2015.

Respectfully submitted,

____
Clarence D. Arrow
Attorney for Defendant
100 Maple Avenue
Placid City, PL 25360
(555) 555-1212
State Bar No. 004562

On the day of the hearing, the party who initially filed the motion has the burden of presenting arguments and perhaps even testimony to support his contentions. Attorneys can simply argue many motions, but sometimes attorneys are required to present live testimony to bolster their position. We will discuss the details of how specific motions are argued later in this chapter.

F. RULING ON A MOTION

The ultimate ruling on a motion is always left up to the judge. Juries are not allowed to consider motions for the simple reason that the jurors are the final arbiters of the facts of the case, while the judge has the final say about legal issues.

G. WRITTEN MOTIONS

The rules governing motions, specifically Rule 12 of the Federal Rules of Civil Procedure, and case law interpreting those rules provide that motions be made orally or in writing, but most courts prefer written motions. Although modern courts allow greater latitude in how the written motion may be presented, most prefer that any motion raising substantive issues or affirmative defenses be written, served on opposing counsel, and filed with the court. However, that is not to say that there are no provisions for oral motions.

H. ORAL MOTIONS

There are many circumstances in which an oral motion is permissible. A party may bring such a motion within the context of a hearing, while arguing another motion, and during the trial itself. A **motion in limine**, for example, is usually an oral motion made at the commencement of the trial. Such a motion might request a ruling on a particular item of evidence sought to be admitted later in the trial by one of the parties. In addition to motions in limine, it is common practice for defense attorneys to use an oral motion to request a JNOV ruling at the conclusion of the plaintiff's case. (We discuss such motions in Chapter 8.)

Motion in limine
A motion at the conclusion of a trial, often made orally, that may request a wide variety of forms of relief, including a ruling on evidentiary matters

III ISSUES THAT CAN BE ADDRESSED IN A MOTION

Motions can be used to address a wide variety of issues, from correcting errors in the original pleadings to requesting that the entire case against the defendant be dismissed. Under the Federal Rules of Civil Procedure, Rule 12 governs the issues that can be raised in motions (Fig. 8-6):

- Motion for summary judgment
- Motion for partial summary judgment
- Judgment on the pleadings
- Affirmative defenses

- 12(b)(6) motion
- Motion for more definite statement
- Motion for default judgment

FIGURE 8-6

Federal Rules of Civil Procedure, Rule 12(b) Presenting Motions

Rule 12. Defenses and Objections: When and How Presented; Motion for Judgment on the Pleadings; Consolidating Motions; Waiving Defenses; Pretrial Hearing

. . .

(b) How to Present Defenses. Every defense to a claim for relief in any pleading must be asserted in the responsive pleading if one is required. But a party may assert the following defenses by motion:

(1) lack of subject-matter jurisdiction;
(2) lack of personal jurisdiction;
(3) improper venue;
(4) insufficient process;
(5) insufficient service of process;
(6) failure to state a claim upon which relief can be granted (emphasis added)
(7) failure to join a party under Rule 19

Dispositive motion
A motion that resolves some or all issues in pending litigation

The general purpose of Rule 12 is to provide practitioners with the vehicle through which they can dispose of a case early in the litigation process when it is clear that a legal element is missing from the pleadings. As a result, Rule 12, which has been the template used by many states, provides a number of grounds that parties can raise on a motion that may dispose of all issues pending in the case. This is one reason why motions under Rule 12 are commonly referred to as **dispositive motions**. It is important to keep in mind that the burden of proof is always on the party bringing such a motion. The party who files a motion for summary judgment or any other motions that may be brought in a case has the burden of proof and the burden of persuasion. The first requires satisfying the court of the merits of the legal claim while the second requires the party to persuade the court of the rationale for bringing the motion.

A. MOTION FOR SUMMARY JUDGMENT

Motion for summary judgment
A written motion filed by a party requesting a ruling in its favor and dismissal of the opposition's claims

A **motion for summary judgment** is a request by one party for a complete disposition of the case without ever taking it to trial (Fig. 8-7). A party who moves for a summary judgment alleges that, taking all facts as true, the opposing party is not entitled to any legal relief. If the party can show that there are no disputed material facts, the party can argue that there is no need for a jury to intervene in the case. The jury's function is to determine the facts, and if the important details of a case are not contested, then there is no need for a jury. The stated purpose of a motion for summary judgment is to eliminate the expense and drain on resources for trials where there are no contestable issues between the parties. Parties routinely file motions for summary judgment when they believe that the opposition has raised frivolous claims. Because such claims are not based on legally recognized issues, a judge would be authorized to dismiss the case. However, simply because a party moves for summary judgment does not mean the party will actually have the motion granted. Unlike other motions we will discuss in this chapter, a motion for summary judgment falls under the jurisdiction of Rule 56 of the Federal Rules of Civil Procedure.

FIGURE 8-7

Motion for Summary Judgment

Federal Rules of Civil Procedure, Rule 56. Summary Judgment

(a) Motion for Summary Judgment or Partial Summary Judgment. A party may move for summary judgment, identifying each claim or defense – or the part of each claim or defense – on which summary judgment is sought. The court shall grant summary judgment if the movant shows that there is no genuine dispute as to any material fact and the movant is entitled to judgment as a matter of law. The court should state on the record the reasons for granting or denying the motion.

There is a huge body of cases that stand for the proposition that granting a summary judgment is a drastic action that should only be taken when the court has determined that the original claim is frivolous or that there are no genuine issues to be determined in the case, or when the claim is brought for the purposes of harassing or annoying the other party. Courts are required to be cautious before granting a summary judgment because such an order removes a party's right to seek compensation in a case.[4] The purpose of a motion for summary judgment is to resolve questions of law, not fact. Essentially, a party requesting a motion for summary judgment states that, taking all of the facts raised by the opposition as true, that party is still entitled to win.[5] When there are no factual disputes for the jury to resolve, it becomes the judge's duty to rule on the legal issues. If the judge finds that the law is squarely on one side's favor, then she is obligated to rule in conformance with that legal authority. For an example of a motion for summary judgment, see the "Forms and Court Documents" section at the end of this chapter.

Because the ultimate decision in a motion for summary judgment may be the dismissal of a party's case, judges should act with caution in ordering it. Many court decisions have also held that a trial judge must strictly comply with the provisions of the law, especially Rule 56, in granting such a motion.[6]

PRACTICE POINTER ▶ MOTIONS BANK

Given that attorneys often concentrate on certain areas of litigation, there is a strong potential for the legal team to face the same legal issues over and over. A firm that specializes in medical malpractice defense, for example, may find itself filing motions for summary judgment on statute of limitations issues in nearly all of its cases. As a result, both defenses' and plaintiffs' firms maintain a "motions bank." This is a file containing motions filed in other cases. In the days before computers, it actually was a file, often an overstuffed manila file folder with copies of old motions. These days, it is far more common to find the files in digital form. Once drafted, a motion can be redone with relatively minor work and put to use in a current case. Of course, given the fact that no case is ever identical to another, it is a good idea to use this practice with caution. Every motion filed in every case should be closely reviewed, not only from the standpoint of whether it is justified by the law, but also by the standard of whether it is a legitimate motion or simply "filler."

B. MOTION FOR PARTIAL SUMMARY JUDGMENT

When a party moves for partial summary judgment, he requests a ruling on a specific issue in the case and does not seek disposition of the entire case. A motion for partial summary judgment is usually addressed at a specific contention in the complaint or answer. The movant requests the court to dismiss the allegation and in support of the motion shows that there is no genuine dispute about the facts surrounding that issue. If the court grants a partial summary judgment, then a particular claim will be struck and the jury will not consider it at trial.

C. JUDGMENT ON THE PLEADINGS

Judgment on the pleadings A motion that alleges that if all of the allegations raised in the pleadings are true and correct, the movant would still be entitled to a ruling in his favor and a dismissal of the opposition's pleadings

A **judgment on the pleadings** is a motion filed by either party that essentially requests the judge to make a ruling that even if the court takes all of the opposition's allegations as true, the party has failed to allege any legally recognized injury. This motion falls under the jurisdiction of Rule 12(c) of the Federal Rules of Civil Procedure. A motion for judgment on the pleadings is usually reserved for cases where legally recognized defenses are not pled. A party facing the prospect of having the pleadings dismissed because of an obvious omission can move under Rule 15 of the Federal Rules of Civil Procedure to amend the pleadings to correct the error.

The essence of a motion for judgment on the pleadings is that the issues in contention are so defective that even if taken at face value, they do not make out a case for the legal liability of the other party. Motions for judgment on the pleadings are often mentioned in conjunction with motions for summary judgment for the simple reason that they are linked by the express working of Rule 12(c) and by the fact that the point of the motion is to attack the basis of a party's contention. When one party challenges the legal sufficiency of the other side's claim, that action begins to resemble the legal definition of a motion for summary judgment. As you can see from reading Rule 12(c) (Fig. 8-8), a motion for judgment on the pleadings can easily convert to a motion for summary judgment, but only when issues and evidence not expressly provided in the pleadings are to be considered.

FIGURE 8-8

Judgment on the Pleadings

Federal Rules of Civil Procedure, Rule 12. Defenses and Objections: When and How Presented; Motion for Judgment on the Pleadings; Consolidating Motions; Waiving Defenses; Pretrial Hearing

. . .

(c) Motion for Judgment on the Pleadings. After the pleadings are closed — but early enough not to delay trial — a party may move for judgment on the pleadings.

D. AFFIRMATIVE DEFENSES

In addition to motions for summary judgment and a motion for judgment on the pleadings, parties are also entitled to raise various affirmative defenses in motions. Under Rule 12 of the Federal Rules of Civil Procedure, parties may raise affirmative defenses in their responses to pleadings or by motion. Among these affirmative defenses are:

- lack of jurisdiction over the subject matter;
- lack of jurisdiction over the person;
- improper venue;
- insufficiency of process;
- insufficiency of service of process;
- failure to state a claim upon which relief can be granted (Rule 12(b)(6)); and
- failure to join a party under Rule 19.

1. LACK OF JURISDICTION OVER THE SUBJECT MATTER

If the court lacks subject matter jurisdiction, it is not empowered to hear any of the issues raised in the complaint and answer. As a result, if a party can successfully claim lack of subject matter jurisdiction, the court has no option but to dismiss the case or to transfer it to a court that does have appropriate jurisdiction.

2. LACK OF JURISDICTION OVER THE PERSON

A motion under Rule 12(b)(2) makes an allegation similar to lack of jurisdiction over the subject matter. In this situation, the party alleges that the court has no jurisdiction over one or both parties involved in the case, and the court is therefore unable to enter a legally binding decision. If a court determines that it lacks personal jurisdiction over the parties, the court must again dismiss the case or remove it to the appropriate forum.

3. IMPROPER VENUE

Venue refers to the locale where the trial occurs. Like personal jurisdiction and subject matter jurisdiction, the trial must occur in an appropriate venue. Venue is determined by state statute. If the court determines that the trial is located in the incorrect county, the action must be transferred to the appropriate venue.

4. INSUFFICIENCY OF PROCESS AND SERVICE OF PROCESS

These defenses under Rule 12 are directed toward two different aspects of the same action. Insufficiency of process refers to some error or defect that occurred in drafting the summons that accompanied the complaint. On the other hand, insufficiency of service of process refers to some error that occurred in actually serving the defendant with a copy of the summons and complaint.

5. FAILURE TO JOIN A NECESSARY PARTY UNDER RULE 19

Rule 19 of the Rules of Civil Procedure provides that all parties who have an interest in the litigation must be joined as plaintiffs or defendants in the action. Interested parties are often described as "necessary parties" and must be parties to the action. If they are not, the original parties or the interested parties may file motions to have them added to the case.

You may have noticed that we skipped Rule 12(b)(6). A motion under this subpart to Rule 12 deserves separate treatment.

E. 12(b)(6) MOTION

It is very common for a party to file a 12(b)(6) motion. In fact, it is one of the most commonly filed motions and goes to the very heart of the issues raised in the case. Many defense attorneys make it part of their routine motions. The purpose of such a motion is to challenge the basis of the complaint by stating that it fails to allege a legally recognized wrong and should therefore be dismissed. Although this motion is common, actually succeeding on the motion is rare. Because most states have adopted notice pleading as the basis for all of their civil actions, the question often arises: What makes a complaint so vague or lacking in factual detail that it fails to state a claim upon which relief can be granted? For instance, if the defendant alleges that the allegation lacks sufficient detail to put her on notice of claim, the appropriate vehicle to challenge the wording of the complaint is a motion for a more definite statement. The standard that courts use in evaluating a 12(b)(6) motion is to consider the facts pled by the plaintiff as true and to determine if, given the veracity of those facts, the plaintiff's claim alleges a legally recognized wrong. Another way to approach a 12(b)(6) motion is to ask whether, taking all of the plaintiff's allegations as true, the complaint fails to allege sufficient grounds to entitle the plaintiff to a recovery. Examples of deficiencies that would authorize a court to grant a 12(b)(6) motion are set out in Figure 8-9.

FIGURE 8-9

Grounds for Granting a 12(b)(6) Motion

- The complaint sets out no valid legal theory to support the plaintiff's request.
- The complaint fails to allege an essential fact, required for the court to rule in the plaintiff's favor.
- The complaint contradicts its own allegations by providing a bar to the plaintiff's claim. Example: The complaint clearly alleges that the claim is barred by the statute of limitations.

F. MOTION FOR MORE DEFINITE STATEMENT

Motion for more definite statement
A motion that cites specific deficiencies in a pleading and requests a court order that the judge force the opposition to provide additional detail to support the claim

If the defendant believes that the complaint is so vague or ambiguous that it fails to place the defendant on adequate notice about the nature of the plaintiff's claim, the defendant is authorized to bring a **motion for more definite statement** under Rule 12(e) (Fig. 8-10). That rule provides that a party may request the opposing party to supplement the wording of its pleading with additional details that the party claims are specifically lacking. See Figure 8-11 for a sample motion for more definite statement.

FIGURE 8-10

Federal Rules of Civil Procedure, Rule 12(e) Motion for More Definite Statement

Rule 12. Defenses and Objections: When and How Presented; Motion for Judgment on the Pleadings; Consolidating Motions; Waiving Defenses; Pretrial Hearing

(e) Motion for a More Definite Statement. A party may move for a more definite statement of a pleading to which a responsive pleading is allowed but which is so vague or ambiguous that the party cannot reasonably prepare a response. The motion must be made before filing a responsive pleading and must point out the defects complained of and the details desired. If the court orders a more definite statement and the order is not obeyed within 14 days after notice of the order or within the time the court sets, the court may strike the pleading or issue any other appropriate order.

FIGURE 8-11

Sample Motion for More Definite Statement

IN THE SUPERIOR COURT
BURKE COUNTY
STATE OF PLACID

SUPERIOR COURT DIVISION
FILE NUMBER: ___________

JANE DOE,)
Plaintiff,)
vs.)
NICHOLAS D. CHARLES)
Defendant.)
______________________)

Motion for More Definite Statement

Defendant, by counsel, pursuant to PL R Civ P 8(e), moves the court to grant its motion requiring the plaintiff, Jane Doe, to file with the court and serve on the defendant a more definite statement, based on the following reasons:

1 Plaintiff's complaint is so vague and ambiguous that it fails to comply with the court rules in the following respects:

a. It violates PL Rules of Civil Procedure, Rule 8, in that it fails to contain an affidavit by a third party establishing that the party heard or had communicated to it a slanderous statement supposedly made by the defendant concerning the plaintiff.

b. It violates PL ST. ANN. 23-21-06, in that it fails to allege that the statements supposedly made by the defendant concerned the plaintiff's professional status, a crime involving moral turpitude, a sexually transmitted disease, or the plaintiff's mental incompetence.

Defendant requests that this court enter an order requiring plaintiff to file and serve a more definite statement.

This the 9th day of May, 2015.

Respectfully submitted,

____

Clarence D. Arrow
Attorney for Defendant
100 Maple Avenue
Placid City, PL 25360
(555) 555-1212
State Bar No. 004562

G. MOTION FOR DEFAULT JUDGMENT

A plaintiff is also authorized to move for a default judgment when the defendant fails to respond to the complaint. A motion for default judgment is commonly raised when the defendant fails to file an answer or fails to appear for a scheduled court date. In such a case, the plaintiff would win the case by default and could then request the court to award damages.

PRACTICE POINTER ▶ COORDINATING MOTIONS

Although it is possible for one party in a civil case to unilaterally schedule a motion by use of a notice of motion, it is far more common for the parties to work with one another and the judge's office to schedule the motion at a convenient time. People who are unfamiliar with the legal profession are often surprised by how much opposing sides in a civil case accommodate one another with issues such as scheduling discovery and hearing motions. Setting a date to argue a series of motions may involve a lot of telephone calls between the parties in order to find a time that is convenient. Although this isn't always possible, especially if the court has a rigid schedule about when it hears motions, it is always good practice to work with the opposing legal team as much as possible. Much of this prefiling communication is usually only documented in memoranda to the file. Only the final agreement is written up in a confirming letter.

IV THE JUDGE'S ROLE IN CONSIDERING MOTIONS: MOTIONS FOR SUMMARY JUDGMENT

So far, we have discussed the role of the parties in bringing and arguing motions, but it is just as important to understand the role of the judge in the process. We have already seen that a motion for summary judgment assumes that certain facts are true and that, given these facts, the plaintiff is not legally entitled to win. What, exactly, does that mean? Are there situations where the judge can take all of the plaintiff's allegations as true and still rule for the defendant?

Consider the following hypothetical: Two years ago, John Doe sought medical treatment from Dr. Medico. Unfortunately, Dr. Medico did not follow the prescribed standard of care, and Doe's original injury was aggravated. Eventually, John had to undergo surgery on the affected area and was left with a terrible scar. Doe has brought suit against Dr. Medico, alleging medical malpractice. Dr. Medico answers the complaint, denying any responsibility. There is some brief discovery in the case, and then Dr. Medico files a motion for summary judgment, alleging that the statute of limitations for such an action is one year and that Doe's complaint is thus barred. Will the judge grant the motion for summary judgment?

In order to answer the question posed in the example above, we must address the basic issue of the contested facts in the case of *Doe v. Medico*. What Dr. Medico is saying in his motion for summary judgment is that there are no contested facts in this case. Dr. Medico does not challenge Doe's version of the facts and even, for purposes of the motion only, will agree that they are valid. However, the defendant states that the law on this issue is clear: The plaintiff must bring a claim of medical malpractice within one year of the injury.

When a trial judge is presented with a motion for summary judgment, the first question that must be answered considers the contested facts. If there are any genuine issues of fact to be resolved, the judge is barred from making a ruling on the motion. If the judge were to make a ruling when the facts were not clear, the judge would be invading the authority reserved for the jury. It is for the jurors to determine which party's version of the facts is the more reasonable, and judges are usually more than willing to let them carry out this function. Even more importantly, at least from the judge's perspective, if a judge does invade the **province of the jury**, then the judge is likely to be overturned on appeal. The judge must, therefore, determine if there are contested facts in this case. However, because parties can always find some facts upon which they disagree, the law establishes a standard that the trial judge must apply to the motion for summary judgment: Are there genuine issues concerning material facts?

Province of the jury
An issue that must be determined by a jury, not a judge

A **material fact** is one that is so vital to the allegations that the case will fail without it. When a court considers a motion for summary judgment, the judge makes this determination by reviewing the written motions filed by the parties and all accompanying information, including affidavits and excerpts from discovery. If a judge finds that there are genuine issues about the important facts in the case, then he must deny the motion and allow it to go to trial, where the jurors will consider all of the evidence and reach their own conclusions. On the other hand, if there are no genuine issues, then the only remaining points in the case involve interpretations of the law, and that is the exclusive province of the judge.

Material fact
A contested fact in litigation; a fact that, if different, might alter the entire outcome of the case

Questions of law are resolved by the judge, not by juries. It is not for the jurors in the case of *Doe v. Medico* to say whether the statute of limitations applies. The trial judge makes that determination. If the judge rules that the defendant's motion for summary judgment is valid and that there are no triable issues left in the case, then the judge must grant the motion.

Consider the following continuation of the *Doe v. Medico* case: Does John Doe have any possible defense to the claim that the statute of limitations has run? On its face,

Dr. Medico seems to have a solid case. The statute provides that Doe must have brought his case within one year, and it was actually brought two years later. However, the law on the statute of limitations, especially when it involves medical malpractice cases, is rarely so black and white. For one thing, most states have provisions in their statutes allowing a tolling (or temporary suspension of the running of the time limit) of the statute until the patient becomes aware of the condition or by reasonable procedures would have become aware of the condition. In such a situation, Doe's claim may not be barred by the statute of limitations.

V USING MOTIONS TO CLARIFY ISSUES IN LITIGATION

Given the fact that various motions can resolve or even completely dismiss a pending case, it should come as no surprise that parties in civil cases routinely file many motions. Whether requesting a default judgment, a dismissal of the case, sanctions for improper activities during discovery, or partial summary judgment, motions are important for any number of issues in a case. Civil practitioners also use motions as a way of honing their cases. By filing a wide variety of motions, the parties can help shake loose any minor issues and force the court, and later the jury, to focus on a few specific points. When a judge grants a motion for partial summary judgment, for example, the issues addressed in that motion will never be presented to the jury. The parties can then present testimony and evidence on the remaining issues. Attorneys often file a broad spectrum of motions with this endgame in mind: By resolving many of the issues prior to trial, the motions will help clarify the remaining issues in the case, saving on time and resources.

VI PRETRIAL, TRIAL, AND POST-TRIAL MOTIONS

One way of categorizing motions is by grouping them in terms of when they are likely to be brought during the course of litigation. For instance, if we were to arrange motions into the broad categories of pretrial, trial, and post-trial motions, we might easily come up with the headings found in Figure 8-12.

FIGURE 8-12

Motion Categories

Pretrial motions:

- Summary judgment
- Partial summary judgment
- Judgment on the pleadings
- Affirmative defenses
- 12(b)(6)
- More definite statement
- Default judgment

Trial motions:
- Continuance
- In limine

Post-trial motions
- JNOV
- Directed verdict
- New trial

We have addressed both pretrial and trial motions, but we have not considered the issues surrounding post-trial motions. For instance, one motion that is frequently brought at the conclusion of a jury trial is a JNOV motion.

A. JNOV MOTIONS

The abbreviation **JNOV** stands for the Latin phrase *judgment non obstante verdicto*, or "a judgment not withstanding the verdict." When the jury returns its verdict, the losing party is permitted to file a JNOV motion requesting that the jury's decision be overturned and replaced with a verdict in favor of the moving party. The losing party might justify this request on the grounds that no reasonable jury hearing the evidence presented in the case could rule as the present jury had done. The party might also claim that the verdict is against the weight of both law and facts and ask that the judge reverse the jury's verdict. Although this motion is made at the conclusion of many civil trials, it is rarely granted. In order to justify reversing the jury, the trial judge must reach the conclusion that the jury's findings were not supported by the evidence and that no reasonable jury could reach such a conclusion. Given the hotly contested nature of most civil suits, there is usually more than sufficient grounds for the jury's decision in favor of either party.

JNOV
Also known as a *judgment notwithstanding the verdict*; a motion filed by a party at the conclusion of a trial asking the judge to overturn the jury's decision and rule in favor of the unsuccessful party

B. MOTION FOR DIRECTED VERDICT

Another motion that is commonly brought at the conclusion of one or more phases of a trial is a **motion for directed verdict**. This motion may come at the conclusion of the plaintiff's case in chief and may be renewed at the conclusion of the trial. Here, a party moves the court to enter a verdict in its favor without resorting to jury deliberations. A defendant might move for a directed verdict at the conclusion of the plaintiff's case when the plaintiff has failed to prove some essential element of her case. The defendant is also free to renew the motion at the end of the trial. The plaintiff, too, is permitted to move for a directed verdict against the defendant, especially when the defendant has filed counterclaims and failed to present any evidence to support them. Directed verdicts can also be granted for specific issues, while leaving others for the jury's consideration.

Motion for directed verdict
A motion which, if granted, takes the case away from any consideration by the jury and enters a judgment in favor of one party over the other

C. MOTION FOR NEW TRIAL

Although we discuss motions for new trial in greater depth in Chapter 12, a word about them here is also helpful. Let us suppose that at the end of a trial, the jury finds

Motion for new trial
A motion requesting a new trial, made by a party who has received an unfavorable ruling; often the first step in bringing an appeal

for the plaintiff and assesses damages against the culpable defendant. In such a situation, the defendant would file a **motion for new trial**, alleging any possible improprieties that may have occurred during the trial. If the judge grants the motion, which is rare, then the parties must retry the case before a different jury. If the judge denies the motion, then that denial allows the defendant to begin the appellate process.

PRACTICE POINTER ▶ MOTIONS AND APPEALS

In this chapter, we discussed the fact that a motion makes certain assumptions. For instance, in a motion for summary judgment, the opposing party claims that taking all of the movant's contentions as true, the law still requires that the judge rule in the opposing party's favor. However, simply because a judge grants a motion does not automatically mean that the case will be appealed. There are many instances where the judge may make a ruling and the case will continue to trial on other issues. When there are remaining issues in the case, the parties are prevented from taking the case up on appeal. However, when a motion for summary judgment dismisses all pending issues in the case, then the losing party is entitled to bring an appeal. This why you will often find cases brought on appeal on the grounds of "an order granting appellant's motion for summary judgment."

Tech Topic
ONLINE ACCESS TO FEDERAL CASES

The federal judiciary has been a leader in developing online filing procedures. In an effort to both create better efficiency and reduce the sheer amount of paper involved in federal civil cases, the judiciary authorized the creation of the Case Management/Electronic Case Files (CM/ECF) system, which permits users to file, monitor, and review pleadings, motions, petitions, and any other document pending in a case. The case files can be accessed from anywhere on the Internet and dramatically cuts down on the paper needed to be served, filed, documented, and recorded in federal cases. Not everyone gets free or unlimited access to CM/ECF. Passwords are given to attorneys who have pending federal cases—or who request a password. Others who are given open access are bankruptcy trustees. In limited circumstances, persons who bring their case pro se are also given a login and password. Part of the judicial initiative is PACER—Public Access to Court Electronic Records. This database allows the public and approved users to access case and docket information. Users have the ability to locate federal appellate, district court, and bankruptcy courts and to use PACER to file pleadings, including motions. The database gives users access to bankruptcy, U.S. District Court, and appellate courts. Users can look up pending cases and can also file pleadings in their own pending cases. One of the great features of PACER is that a user can look up a party to see if the party has any pending federal litigation anywhere in the United States.

Case Excerpt

When is an expert witness required in legal malpractice cases and when and how does this rule impact a motion for summary judgment?

NIEPSUJ V. DOE
2015-Ohio-3864, 2015 Ohio App. LEXIS 3752
(Ohio Ct. App., Summit County Sept. 23, 2015)

Opinion

TIMOTHY P. CANNON, P.J.

This appeal is from a final judgment in a legal malpractice case before the Summit County Court of Common Pleas. Appellant, Vincent Niepsuj, contests the trial court's decision granting summary judgment for appellee, Attorney Susan B. Vogel, on his sole claim for relief. Specifically, appellant asserts that the trial court erred in ruling that he could not proceed on his malpractice claim because he could not find an expert witness to testify on his behalf. For the following reasons, the trial court's holding is affirmed.

In April 2011, appellant's former spouse filed a petition for a civil protection order against him in Summit County domestic relations court. After issuing a temporary civil protection order, the trial court scheduled the matter for a full hearing before a court magistrate on April 13, 2011. According to the allegations in appellant's complaint, one day prior to the scheduled date, appellant contacted appellee and requested that she represent him at the full hearing. Appellee accepted, and she met with him approximately one hour before the hearing to discuss the case for the first time. Although appellant continued to contact appellee about the case after the hearing, her representation of him soon ended.

Fifty days after the hearing, the court magistrate issued a form judgment granting a civil protection order against appellant. Acting pro se, appellant submitted objections to the magistrate's decision and a Civ.R. 60(B) motion for relief from the civil protection order. However, the domestic relations court overruled each submission and upheld the magistrate's decision.

Approximately thirteen months after the termination of their attorney-client relationship, appellant instituted his first malpractice action against appellee. Ultimately, he chose to voluntarily dismiss that action under Civ.R. 41(A). One year later, though, appellant initiated the underlying case, again alleging that appellee had committed legal malpractice in representing him at the April 2011 "civil protection order" hearing. In his amended complaint, he set forth eighteen different allegations of malpractice under his sole claim for relief.

In the caption of his amended complaint, appellant referred to appellee as "Unnamed Susan Doe Attorney." However, in all of appellee's various filings throughout the case, her own counsel referenced her using her complete proper name.

Once appellee answered the amended complaint, the trial court held a pretrial conference. After that proceeding on June 5, 2014, the court issued a judgment that scheduled various deadlines in the case. In relation to the disclosure of expert witnesses, the judgment ordered that appellant had until September 5, 2014, to inform appellee of the names of all such expert witnesses "with reports" he intended to call at trial.

The judgment further provided that the failure to comply with that order or any other court order could result in the dismissal of the case.

On September 6, 2014, appellant filed a notice with the trial court, stating that he had been unable to secure an expert witness to testify on his behalf. As part of this notice, appellant gave an explanation concerning the steps he had taken to obtain an expert. As a separate point, he also argued that he should not be required to have an expert in order to proceed because appellee's legal errors were so obvious that a lay person did not need assistance in finding that malpractice had occurred.

Four days after the submission of appellant's notice, appellee moved the trial court to dismiss the case pursuant to Civ.R. 12(B)(6) and Civ.R. 41(B)(1). As the primary basis for the motion, she maintained that appellant failed to comply with the court's scheduling order by not obtaining an expert witness with report by the required date. She further maintained that dismissal of the entire case was warranted because, without an expert, appellant would not be able to establish a breach of duty.

In responding to the motion to dismiss, appellant moved the trial court for a temporary stay of the proceedings. He asserted that a stay was necessary because (1) he needed more time to locate an exhibit that had been introduced into evidence during the hearing in the "civil protection order" case; and (2) he was waiting for a ruling on a new motion he had filed in the "civil protection order" case. As to the need for an expert witness, he only stated that he was still taking steps to try to find an attorney who would testify on his behalf.

Appellee moved to convert her motion to dismiss to a motion for summary judgment. As part of the motion to dismiss, she attached as an exhibit a copy of appellant's September 6, 2014notice to the trial court on the "expert witness" issue. Notwithstanding the fact that the notice had already been filed as part of the record, appellee evidently concluded that her motion had to be one for summary judgment because she had submitted an exhibit. In a separate judgment, the trial court granted the motion to convert and ordered that a copy of the judgment be sent to appellant.

On October 22, 2014, the trial court issued its final determination granting summary judgment in favor of appellee on the sole count of legal malpractice. After noting that appellant had failed to comply with its scheduling order by not identifying an expert witness by September 5, 2014, the trial court reviewed his malpractice allegations and held that he would need expert testimony in order to demonstrate a breach of duty.

In appealing the summary judgment decision, appellant has asserted only two assignments of error for review:

1. The trial court erred in granting summary judgment when the material issue of fact or of law concerning the need for a legal expert was not certainly established, given that several of the allegations could be easily understood by a lay (jury) person as equating with care well short of that needed to defend a father in a fleeting, preponderance burden of proof, CPO hearing.
2. The trial court in granting summary judgment when there was a pending motion for stay filed by the plaintiff/appellant almost 1 month earlier on September 23, 2014 and a pending motion for leave to respond to plaintiff's revised request for admissions filed by the defendant/appellee 4.5 hours before the court granted summary judgment.

Under his first assignment, appellant challenges the trial court's ruling that he needed an expert witness before he could prove that appellee acted negligently in representing him during the proceeding for the civil protection order. He contends that no expert was necessary because many of his malpractice allegations were so simple and straightforward that a lay person could understand them without further explanation.

A claim for legal malpractice can be predicated upon negligence, breach of contract, or both. To prevail on such a claim, a plaintiff must prove three elements: (1) the existence of an attorney-client relationship giving rise to a professional duty; (2) a breach of that duty by the attorney; and (3) damages which were proximately caused by the breach.

"Generally, expert testimony is required to support a claim of attorney malpractice." Accordingly, in many instances, "an affidavit from the defendant attorney is a legally sufficient basis upon which to grant a motion for summary judgment absent an opposing affidavit of a qualified expert witness for the plaintiff."

The Supreme Court of Ohio has recognized one exception to the "expert witness" requirement: i.e., a legal malpractice claim can be established notwithstanding the lack of expert testimony when the alleged breach of professional duty falls within the common understanding of a lay person. *McInnis v. Hyatt Legal Clinics*, 10 Ohio St.3d 112, 113, 10 Ohio B. 437, 461 N.E.2d 1295 (1984). In *McInnis*, the client hired the law firm to represent him in a divorce action. As part of their preliminary discussion, the client told one of the attorneys that he did not want the filing of the action to be cited in a local newspaper. Even though the attorney assured the client that no publication was necessary, the law firm subsequently used a newspaper to obtain service of the complaint. In rejecting the firm's contention that the client could not prevail on his malpractice claim without presenting any expert testimony, the McInnis court held that no expert was necessary when the nature of the breach was such that it falls within the ordinary knowledge of the jury. Id.

As noted above, appellant's amended complaint listed eighteen different allegations of malpractice by appellee. However, in his appellate brief, he has focused upon three basic points. First, he maintains that appellee was not properly prepared for the April 13, 2011 hearing. In support of this point, he emphasizes that appellee failed to obtain a mental health expert to testify, did not submit any exhibits, did not know who the opposing witnesses were and did not adequately question them, did not move for a continuance, and appeared to be confused about the exact facts of the case. Second, appellant submits that appellee improperly chastised him before the domestic relations magistrate concerning a telephone call he made to a local minister. Third, he contends that appellee did not properly contest or object to a finding made by the magistrate as to whether he had engaged in behavior that traumatized his sons.

Regarding appellant's "preparedness" allegation, this court would note that he expressly alleges in his amended complaint that he did not contact appellee about representing him in the "civil protection order" action until one day before the scheduled hearing. He also alleges that they first met about the case for one hour prior to the hearing. Given these circumstances, expert testimony would absolutely be needed to establish the degree or quality of representation a client could legitimately expect when the attorney has been afforded such a short time to prepare. For example, a lay person would not know whether an attorney could realistically be expected to submit exhibits or call any witnesses on such short notice.

As to the "chastisement" allegation, appellee's decision to admit fault on a particular factual point could have been part of her trial strategy; accordingly, an expert would be needed to show whether the strategy was legitimate. Concerning the failure to object to the "trauma" finding, expert testimony would be necessary to show whether any logical objection could be made in light of the evidence heard by the magistrate.

In *McInnis*, the nature of the alleged attorney negligence was such that a person did not need any legal background to understand why the attorney's acts had fallen below the applicable standard of care. This cannot be said of the allegations cited by appellant in his appellate brief or of the other allegations contained in his complaint. At a minimum, in order to adequately evaluate appellee's actions during the April 2011 hearing, a person would need general knowledge of the procedure governing a domestic violence civil protection proceeding. Clearly, an ordinary lay person would not have that knowledge.

After the passage of the September 5, 2014 deadline for identifying his expert witness, appellant filed a notice in which he specifically stated that, although he had made a serious effort to secure an expert, he had been unable to do so. Given that the underlying case had been pending for eight months by that date, and the fact the case was previously filed and ultimately dismissed when appellant could not find an expert, the trial court could justifiably conclude that appellant was simply unable to find an attorney who would be willing to testify that appellee had acted negligently. Under such circumstances, the granting of the motion to dismiss for failure to comply with the court's order or summary judgment was warranted because, in the absence of any expert testimony, appellant would not be able to satisfy the "breach" element of his malpractice claim. For this reason, his first assignment is without merit.

Under his second assignment, appellant argues that the trial court erred in going forward on appellee's summary judgment motion without first issuing a ruling on his motion to stay the trial proceeding and appellee's motion for leave to respond to his requests for admissions. In essence, he contends that if appellee had been given more time in which to respond to his discovery request, he may have been able to submit evidentiary materials that could have created a factual dispute as to a material fact.

As to this point, this court reiterates that the trial court's decision to grant judgment in favor of appellee was not based upon the lack of a dispute as to any material fact, but instead was based solely upon appellant's failure to obtain an expert witness prior to the September 5, 2014 deadline. Appellant had been repeatedly told by the trial court, in the prior case and in this refiled case, that he needed an expert and a written report of that expert. Appellant was either unable to locate an expert or ignored the trial court's order. Either reason would justify the trial court granting judgment in appellee's favor. Appellant has failed to show or argue how he could have used appellee's discovery response to establish he did not need an expert.

In this case, the motion to stay would properly have been overruled. The trial court, under these circumstances, was justified in bringing this case to a conclusion. Because the merits of appellant's motion to stay and appellee's motion for leave were rendered moot by the trial court's granting of summary judgment, and are considered overruled, the court's failure to rule upon the two motions did not adversely affect the outcome of the action. As a result, appellant's second assignment is also not well taken.

The judgment of the Summit County Court of Common Pleas is affirmed.

We order that a special mandate issue out of this Court, directing the Court of Common Pleas, County of Summit, State of Ohio, to carry this judgment into execution. A certified copy of this journal entry shall constitute the mandate, pursuant to App.R. 27.

Immediately upon the filing hereof, this document shall constitute the journal entry of judgment, and it shall be stamped by the Clerk of the Court of Appeals at which time the period for review shall begin to run. App.R. 22(C). The Clerk of the Court of Appeals is instructed to mail a notice of entry of this judgment to the parties and to make a notation of the mailing in the docket, pursuant to App.R. 30.

Costs taxed to appellant.

QUESTIONS ABOUT THE CASE:

1. Why does the appellant claim that he doesn't need an expert in his legal malpractice action?
2. Why is an expert required in this case?
3. According to the court, what are the two bases on which a claim of legal malpractice can be made?
4. What are the three elements that a client must prove to establish legal malpractice?

Chapter Summary

A motion is a party's request to a trial judge for a specific ruling. Motions can be raised for a wide variety of issues. Parties may file motions in order to exclude evidence from the trial, request accommodations, or even dismiss the entire case. A motion in limine is usually an oral motion made during the course of the trial that requests the court to make a specific evidentiary ruling, usually to exclude evidence. A motion for summary judgment, on the other hand, is normally made prior to trial and is filed by the defendant. This motion requests that the judge dismiss the entire case because there are no genuine issues of fact remaining for a jury to consider. In addition to filing a motion for summary judgment, a party may also move for partial summary judgment. Such a motion requests dismissal of a specific count of the complaint. Parties may also request courts to order the opposing party to clarify its wording in its pleadings through the vehicle of a motion for a more definite statement. A motion for judgment on the pleadings is similar to a motion for summary judgment in that the party alleges that there are no genuine issues of fact remaining in the case and that one side is entitled to a verdict in its favor. A 12(b)(6) motion is a motion based on Rule 12 of the Federal Rules of Civil Procedure. This motion alleges that the plaintiff has failed to state a legally recognized claim in his complaint and that the defendant is therefore entitled to a dismissal of the action. Although motions can be filed as separate documents, many modern practitioners also include motions in their responsive pleadings.

SKILLS YOU NEED IN THE REAL WORLD

Preparing a 12(b)(6) Motion

Using your state's version of FRCP 12(b)(6), draft a motion to dismiss the case, using the fact scenario set out in this chapter's libel case, found under "Forms and Court Documents."

THE LIFE OF A PARALEGAL

The Importance of Organization

Carmen Brown has always wanted to be an attorney. Several years ago, she decided to start by obtaining a degree from a paralegal program. "Attending a paralegal program would allow me to gain the foundation of law that would inevitably help me in law school," she said. Completing the program was no easy matter because she worked full-time, but she completed her associate's degree in two years. The program offered her a chance to work as an intern at the local courthouse. "This opportunity allowed me to gain a lot of useful knowledge in the field of law. [It] allowed me to actually have hands-on experience, which to me is the best. It also allowed me the opportunity to meet people within my field of interest. The internship was a very valuable experience."

Carmen now works full-time as a paralegal, specializing in personal injury cases. But she also finds herself working on other types of cases, including domestic and medical malpractice cases. "I love my job! Being a paralegal is a lot of work, but it is very interesting work."

Carmen believes that two things are essential to the day-to-day work of a paralegal: organization and attention to detail. "The largest amount of work done in a law firm is done by the paralegal. It is critical that the paralegal invest all of his or her attention to every aspect of a client's file, not just the document at hand. This is where good organization is a must. Organization within a file eliminates time wasted and allows one the ability to quickly answer any question posed regarding the file. Organization is critical!

"A paralegal's daily tasks vary from day to day. I may come in to work and be prepared to work on a certain file and may or may not get to work on [it]." On any given day, a paralegal might help draft a complaint, compile documents for a settlement brochure, prepare interrogatories, or research issues related to motions in the case."

ETHICAL ISSUES FOR THE PARALEGAL

Bad Faith Affidavits

The Federal Rules of Civil Procedure, and the various state rules modeled closely on them, permit trial judges to impose a wide variety of sanctions against parties who file affidavits in bad faith or affidavits that simply delay the court's procedures. In such a situation, the court is empowered under Rule 12(g):

> Should it appear to the satisfaction of the court at any time that any of the affidavits presented pursuant to this rule are presented in bad faith or solely for the purpose of delay, the court shall forthwith order the party employing them to pay to the other party the amount of the reasonable expenses which the filing of the affidavits caused the other party to incur, including reasonable attorney's fees, and any offending party or attorney may be adjudged guilty of contempt.

Under this rule, the judge can assess attorney's fees against the party who filed or participated in the filing of the bad faith affidavit. The court's power also includes contempt powers, which can result in monetary sanctions or even a finding that a party's willful acts deserve a few days in jail. As a result, it is important for all legal professionals to be aware of and to discourage clients from attempting to file bogus or disingenuous affidavits. A party might wish to harass or annoy the other party, but using court procedures or sworn affidavits to do so can result in harsh actions by the trial judge.

Websites

- **'Lectric Law Library: Motion for Summary Judgment**
  www.lectlaw.com/def2/m043.htm

- **Tech Law Journal: Motion for Summary Judgment**
  www.techlawjournal.com/glossary/legal/summary.htm

- **Motion for Default Judgment — Federal Court, filing instructions**
  www.deb.uscourts.gov/content/rule-7055-1-default

- **Cornell University — Motion for More Definite Statement**
  www.law.cornell.edu/uscode/html/uscode26a/usc_sec_26a_00000051 — 000-.html

Forms and Court Documents

Motion for Summary Judgment

IN THE SUPERIOR COURT
BURKE COUNTY
STATE OF PLACID

SUPERIOR COURT DIVISION
FILE NUMBER: ___________

JANE DOE,)
Plaintiff,)
vs.)
NICHOLAS D. CHARLES)
Defendant.)
)
______________________________)

Motion for Summary Judgment

COMES NOW the defendant, hereinafter referred to as Defendant Charles, and files this his motion for summary judgment pursuant to PL R Civ P 56 and as grounds therefore shows that there is no genuine issue as to any material fact and Defendant Charles is entitled to judgment as a matter of law. Defendant Charles respectfully shows the court the following in support of his motion:

1. This is an action for slander.
2. Interrogatories served and filed by plaintiff Doe and answers filed by Defendant Charles establish the following facts:

(a) Interrogatory No. 12
Question: List any incident in which you referred to the plaintiff in any manner to any third person.
Answer to Interrogatory No. 12
"Defendant has, to his knowledge, never referred to, mentioned, or otherwise discussed the plaintiff in any manner. Defendant denies any knowledge of the plaintiff's existence prior to the filing of this action."

(b) Interrogatory No. 33
Question: List any communications between yourself and third parties, including, but not limited to, newspaper reporters, journalists, writers, and television reporters concerning the plaintiff.
Answer to Interrogatory No. 33
"Defendant has, to his knowledge, never discussed the plaintiff with any other person, including the list promulgated by the plaintiff. Defendant denies any knowledge of the plaintiff prior to the filing of this action."

3. Requests for admissions were filed by defendant and served on plaintiff on March 3, 2015, and answers to admissions were filed by plaintiff on April 4, 2015, admitting the following facts:

    (a) Request for Admission No. 2
    The plaintiff is unable to produce any witness, other than herself, to substantiate the slanderous statements allegedly made by the defendant.
    Response to Request for Admission No. 2
    "Plaintiff has not located any witness, to date, who can substantiate the defendant's slanderous comments about the plaintiff. However, plaintiff's investigation is proceeding."

Plaintiff is, as a matter of law, unable to meet the elements of slander in that she is unable to produce a third party who overhead or had communicated any supposedly slanderous statement by defendant. Defendant Charles requests that the court enter judgment in his favor, together with the costs of this action.

This the 9th day of May, 2015.

Respectfully submitted,

____

Clarence D. Arrow
Attorney for Defendant
100 Maple Avenue
Placid City, PL 25360
(555) 555-1212
State Bar No. 004562

Key Terms

Affidavit
Certificate of service
Dispositive motion
JNOV
Judgment on the pleadings
Material fact
Motion for directed verdict
Motion for more definite statement
Motion for new trial
Motion for summary judgment
Motion in limine
Province of the jury

Review Questions

1 What is the purpose of a motion?
2 How do parties prepare motions?
3 What is a notice of motion?

4 What is a certificate of service?
5 Explain the function of motions for summary judgment.
6 What is a motion for partial summary judgment?
7 Explain the purpose of a motion for more definite statement.
8 What is a judgment on the pleadings?
9 What is a motion in limine?
10 Explain the function of affidavits when they are included with a motion.
11 Explain how a party argues a motion before the court.
12 What is the judge's role in considering a motion?
13 How might a party seek to clarify issues in the case through the use of motions?
14 What are some of the issues that can be addressed through motions?
15 Explain the affirmative defenses that can be brought through a motion.
16 Why is it important for a legal professional to avoid allowing a client to file an affidavit in bad faith?
17 What basic holding can you describe from this chapter's case excerpt?

Applying What You Have Learned

1 Please review the complaint in Chapter 4 and prepare a 12(b)(6) motion requesting that the court dismiss counts one, two, and three of that complaint. Your motion must include a certificate of service and a notice of hearing or notice of motion, setting a day in the future when the motion will be argued.

2 Prepare a table, with the first column containing a list of the motions authorized under your state's rules of civil procedure, and then summarize what each motion does.

3 Based on the materials found in the Baker file, including the depositions, affidavits, and pleadings, prepare a motion for summary judgment requesting that the plaintiff's count one be dismissed.

4 Prepare a series of motions on behalf of the plaintiff in the Apple case, including a motion in limine to restrict the defense witnesses from referring to the plaintiff's prior and unrelated marital trouble and the filing of charges involving domestic violence, a motion for partial summary judgment alleging that count two is legally insufficient, and a judgment on the pleadings for the entire complaint.

5 Prepare a notice of motion, based on the form provided in this chapter, to argue a motion for summary judgment in the Apple case for the first Tuesday of next month. Remember to include a time and location for the argument of the motion.

6 In the case of *Smith v. Gonzalez*, Mr. Smith is representing himself. One afternoon, the attorney representing Ms. Gonzales receives a handwritten document from Mr. Smith that states:

> The plaintiff, being sui juris and independent of any governmental authority and acting pursuant to his rights granted by birth in a free nation and is therefore a

person with sufficient qualities recognized under the legal preeminence of the United States, hereby requests that the defendant's Answer be struck and replaced with the allegations found in the plaintiff's complaint. This motion is made under authority of the Rules of Civil Procedure, which the plaintiff refers, but does not adhere, to.

This the 10th day of June, 2014.

This document was also filed at the courthouse and includes a notice of motion for the first Monday in August. How should Ms. Gonzalez's attorney respond?

Endnotes

[1]*Muller v. Reagh*, 173 Cal. App. 2d 1, 343 P.2d 135 (1st Dist. 1959).
[2]*Driver v. Driver*, 148 Vt. 560, 536 A.2d 557 (1987).
[3]*Craver v. Craver*, 298 N.C. 231, 258 S.E.2d 357 (1979).
[4]*Venti v. EDS*, 236 F. Supp. 2d 264 (W.D. N.Y. 2002).
[5]*Dalton v. Camp*, 353 N.C. 647, 548 S.E.2d 704 (2001).
[6]*Manchester Memorial Hospital v. Whitney*, 6 Conn. Cir. Ct. 212, 269 A.2d 300 (App. Div. 1969), petition denied, 158 Conn. 667, 259 A.2d 648 (1969).

9

Preparing for and Conducting the Trial

Chapter Objectives

- Explain how legal professionals prepare for trial
- Explain the role of the trial paralegal
- Discuss how the case file is organized prior to trial
- Explain the function of the trial notebook
- Discuss the ethical concerns in preparing witnesses to testify
- Describe the various phases of the civil trial
- Explain the difference between direct examination and cross-examintion
- Discuss the importance of the charge conference
- Explain the role of suggested pattern jury instructions
- Describe the process through which a jury determines its verdict

I INTRODUCTION

Trials are some of the most dramatic events in law. Television viewers tune in almost every night to see depictions of civil and criminal trials. There is something electric about that moment when the bailiff steps into the courtroom and announces, "The jury has a verdict!" At that moment, everything seems to kick into high gear. The judge returns to the bench. The jury returns to the jury box. The parties return to the courtroom and take their seats. It is time for the jury to announce its verdict. This is the moment where the parties find out if all of their hard work has paid off.

Trial work is stressful for everyone involved. Witnesses are scared about testifying. Attorneys — even those who have done trial work for years — are usually tense and nervous before a trial starts. Paralegals who may have been working in the field for their entire career will also be anxious both before and during the trial.

In this chapter, we will examine the various phases of a trial and will emphasize the paralegal's increasingly vital role in helping to prepare for and participate in the presentation of a civil case. A growing number of attorneys are relying on litigation-trained paralegals to assist them during the trial, and a paralegal with a broad knowledge of the trial process and a specific knowledge of the case can be a tremendous asset at trial. We will also discuss the fact that as a paralegal, you may be the main contact point for clients and witnesses who need information about the trial, including when they are scheduled to testify and how they should act when they are on the witness stand.

PREPARING TOOLS FOR THE TRIAL

Thorough preparation is always a requirement for both sides of a civil case. Attorneys who represent the parties must know every aspect of the case in order to ensure that there are no surprises and that they give their clients the best possible representation. The paralegals who work with these attorneys should know the case file, evidence, and witness statements as well as the attorneys who have prepared the case for trial.

Some of the work that goes into preparing for a trial casts paralegals in the role of private detectives. In big cases, the firm will often retain a real private detective, but in smaller cases, there may not be sufficient resources to justify the expense. In that situation, the investigative work often falls to the trial paralegal. You must be able to locate witnesses and track down judgments, criminal histories, and any other important information. In modern trial practice, both attorneys and paralegals should know how to do some basic investigation.

In addition to assisting the attorney with gathering evidence, researching legal issues, tracking down witnesses, and preparing documentation for trial, the work of a trial paralegal sometimes involves unusual activities, such as reconnaissance work. As we saw in an earlier chapter, you may need to go to the scene of the accident or locate a witness. Part of your reconnaissance work may involve a trip to the courthouse to examine the courtroom where the trial will be held. This trip may be necessary so that you can tell witnesses where they will be sitting, make sure that there is enough seating for the parties, and even ensure that there are sufficient electrical outlets for the attorneys' laptops, projectors, and other electrical equipment.

Many paralegals who specialize in litigation are drawn to the work because of the excitement and the element of unexpected developments. Trial work can be very exciting; it can also be very draining. There is a rush of adrenaline as the attorneys and paralegals adjust to sudden changes in testimony, witness availability, and adverse rulings. Trial attorneys and paralegals must be able to think quickly on their feet. They must be able to readjust their plans, rethink their strategy, and work closely with one another to ensure that the case goes smoothly.

A. THE ATTORNEY'S ROLE

The attorney's role in preparing for trial consists of reviewing all pleadings, discovery, and witness statements and preparing a strategy to win the case. The plaintiff's attorney must build the case from the bottom up, using witness testimony and evidence to support every contention in the complaint. Without such support, the case will fall apart. On the other side, the attorney representing the defendant will engage in a similar process, but with a different orientation. That attorney will attempt to show that the plaintiff's allegations are groundless and will attempt to use testimony and evidence to destroy the plaintiff's case. If the defendant also has counterclaims against the plaintiff, then the defense attorney will attack the merits of the plaintiff's case while proving the defendant's counterclaims. All of this requires a great deal of time and energy. Attorneys must know every piece of evidence, every witness transcript, every pleading, and every item produced through discovery. In a large case, this can be a daunting task. Later, we will see that software developers have attempted to take some of the drudgery out of the process by creating ways for attorneys to track all of this information. But it is important for paralegals to understand that an attorney facing trial will be completely wrapped up in a case. It is often the only way to learn everything that the attorney needs to know in order to be successful at trial.

Added to this burden is the very real possibility of losing the trial. For the plaintiff's attorney, a loss means that all of the time and energy put into the case will have been for nothing. For the defense attorney, a loss is also painful. The defendant may have to pay a hefty monetary judgment to the plaintiff, in addition to the money that the defendant will pay to his attorney.

For all attorneys, participating in a trial is a lot like acting in a play, except that there is no script and the other actors are working against her. Although trial attorneys frequently find the process of trying a case to be stimulating and exciting, there is no question that trials are stressful. Stress brings out both the good and the bad in people — more often the bad. A paralegal must be aware of the fact that in addition to having to handle the intensive preparation and concentration necessary to prepare for trial, an attorney may also be anxious or worried about participating in the trial. People suffering from anxiety are not always the easiest individuals to be around.

B. THE PARALEGAL'S ROLE

Attorneys are not the only professionals devoting tremendous time and energy to prepare for a trial. For a trial paralegal, intensive preparation is also the order of the day. Most paralegals follow a standard pattern when they begin preparing a case for trial, which we will outline in this section. In general, a trial paralegal starts trial preparation by first going through the pleadings and then every item of discovery produced by all parties, including the party being represented by the paralegal's firm. Trial paralegals sift through all of these documents and create several aids for the trial, including:

- chronology of events;
- master index;
- issue table;
- witness cross-reference;
- witness summaries;
- trial timetable;
- organized client file;
- trial notebook; and
- exhibits.

1. CHRONOLOGY OF EVENTS

One of the best ways to start organizing a case for a trial is to prepare an overall chronology of the events in the case. A chronology is useful because it frames the case by explaining exactly what happened, step-by-step, from beginning to end. Because this is the way that most people tell stories to one another, a detailed chronology can help the entire legal team see the case as a whole. A chronology has other advantages as well. By meticulously reviewing the case for each event and putting it in its proper sequence, the legal team can quickly see when specific areas have been neglected and develop additional information to explain gaps in the time line. Many paralegals begin creating a case chronology as soon as the complaint and answer have been filed in the case. The chronology will then help guide the discovery process and will help the legal team prepare for the trial.

Creating a chronology requires careful review of all documents and testimony in the case. A paralegal must review the deposition transcripts, statements, affidavits, interrogatory answers, pleadings, and any other evidence in the case to be able to create a detailed and understandable chronology of events. See Figure 9-1 for an example of a case chronology.

FIGURE 9-1

Chronology of Events: *Brown v. Dangerous*

Collision between Mary Brown and Danny Dangerous

Date of collision: May 15, 2015
Location: Intersection of Burnett and Burke Streets (Elizabeth County, Placid)
Civil File No.: 06-1007

May 15, 2015

Time	Summary of Activity
9:15 a.m. (approx)	Plaintiff Mary Brown (P) leaves her home to drive to grocery store. She is alone in car.
9:20 a.m. (approx)	P heads west on Burke Street, approaches traffic light at Burke and Burnett, and stops for red light. She is first in line. There is a car behind her and some traffic in oncoming lane.
9:21 a.m. (approx)	Red light on Burke Street changes to green; she slowly proceeds into intersection.
9:21 a.m. (approx)	D runs red light on Burnett Street and hits passenger side of P's car. P's car is rammed across intersection and into light pole. P briefly loses consciousness.
9:25 a.m.	Officer Mark Williams receives call of accident at Burke and Burnett and logs call.
9:32 a.m.	Officer Williams arrives at scene. Finds P trapped in her car. D is standing next to his truck. Sees that P is trapped in her car and calls for med/vac and fire & rescue.
9:41 a.m.	Fire & rescue arrives, begins working on P's car door to free her.
10:14 a.m.	P freed from her car by fire & rescue; placed on spine board and transported to Memorial Hospital emergency room.
10:18 a.m.	P evaluated in ER, intubated, sedated. Dr. Wade is on-call physician. Begins her assessment. Notes broken ribs, dislocated shoulder, facial bruising, concussion. P sent to surgery to drain fluid from base of brain.
May 15–18	P in intensive care.
May 18	P's status changed from critical to serious. Moved to private room.
June 1	P discharged from hospital.

When you create a chronology, there are some simple rules to keep in mind. First, the chronology must be accurate. If it is impossible to know a specific fact absolutely, then the entry should reflect this fact. In Figure 9-1, the plaintiff was not sure about the time that she left her house for her trip to the grocery store, so the time entry is listed as "approximate." Second, the chronology should be simple and not overloaded with details. What a chronology records are events, not all of the issues surrounding those events. Finally, a chronology must list every important detail in the case. Obviously, the date, time, and place of the accident are important, but in a case where the plaintiff is suing for physical injuries, specific details about her treatment, including admission into the critical care unit and finally being released to go home, are important points for a chronology.

Tech Topic
CREATING TIME LINES

There are numerous programs available to assist you in creating a realistic time line. Internet search engines offer dozens of programs that can provide simple to highly complex time lines, permitting entries for each second or dragging the time line out to cover decades. However, there is nothing that says that preparing a chronology requires expensive software. Many word-processing programs provide templates that can just as easily serve the purpose. Even if you do not choose to use these ready-made templates, the simplest way to create a chronology is by using a table. A simple two-column table will serve as a rudimentary time line. Consider the following example:

Time	Event

Here you can add, edit, or delete events as you gather information. Done correctly, you can even add the details as you discover them and then use the table sort feature to track the dates and times for you.

2. MASTER INDEX

A master index is a general guide to all of the major points to be found in the client's file. A master index should direct the reader to the location of all important documents, discovery, pleadings, orders, and other materials. There are several ways to create a master index. A paralegal might simply bind all documents in the case together, number them consecutively, and then prepare an index similar to a table of contents for a book. See Figure 9-2 for a sample using this technique.

FIGURE 9-2

Master Index

Complaint	1–14
Answer	15–32
Plaintiff's First Interrogatories to Defendant	33–56
Defendant's Answers to Plaintiff's First Interrogatories	57–94
Plaintiff's First Request for Production of Documents to Defendant	95–99
Defendant's Response to Plaintiff's First Request for Production of Documents to Defendant	100–256

The "table of contents" approach to a master index suffers from specific drawbacks. If additional material must be added, the page numbers may be altered, or the paralegal may need to add letters to the numbers, such as 32a, 32b, 32c, and so on, to reflect additional materials.

Another approach to creating a master index to a file is to create clearly marked tabs for all important information. The tab method allows anyone reviewing the file to quickly locate specific material, without having to refer to a list with corresponding page numbers. It also frees the plaintiff from the drudgery of numbering consecutive pages for documents that were originally created independently of one another.

3. ISSUE TABLE

An "issue table" goes by many different names. Some attorneys refer to it as an *issue breakdown* or *count-by-count summary.* No matter what the name used, the purpose of an issue table is to summarize each of the key issues in the case by the evidence and testimony to support or detract from it. By focusing on specific issues, the legal team can evaluate the possibilities of proving (or disproving) the claim at trial. In Figure 9-3, you will find an issue table for the proof of the plaintiff's financial losses in an automobile accident.

FIGURE 9-3

Issue: Plaintiff's Financial Damages

Item	Proof
How much did plaintiff earn in previous years?	Plaintiff's W-2; income tax returns from 2001, 2002, 2003, 2004, 2005
How much did plaintiff earn after accident?	W-2 for 2006; return for 2006
What insurance and other benefits did plaintiff receive following accident? (Collateral source)	Copies of checks from Everyone State Insurance Company
Property damages to plaintiff's car?	Photographs P's testimony Expert witness T. Holden, fair market value of car after accident = $0
Effect of her injuries on ability to earn future income	Dr. Marshall's testimony re: long-term prognosis
Future medical treatments, costs	Dr. Marshall

An issue table is one way for the legal team to double-check each issue in the case and make sure that there is sufficient evidence to prove it. Without a system of double-checking the issues and related proof, the legal team might easily fail to gather sufficient evidence to prove the point at trial.

4. WITNESS CROSS-REFERENCE

As a paralegal prepares a case for trial, it is important to focus on specific issues raised by the various witnesses and to compare what each witness has to say about that specific point. Suppose, for example, that your firm is representing the plaintiff in an automobile accident case. The allegation is that the defendant ran a red light and rammed into the plaintiff's car. Obviously, the issue about the color of the traffic light when the defendant passed through it is going to be a key issue in the case. A witness cross-reference sheet compares the testimony of all relevant witnesses to this one issue. The process of creating one involves going through police reports,

Sidebar

If you ever have a situation where two or more witnesses agree point by point in the description of an event, then you should be cautious. Identical testimony almost always means that someone has rehearsed the witnesses in what they will say, and that smacks of witness coaching, which is unethical and may also be illegal. (See this chapter's "Ethical Issues for the Paralegal.")

statements, and deposition transcripts. What you are looking for in a witness cross-reference are discrepancies between the witnesses or even discrepancies by individual witnesses. Compare times, dates, and events to see how each witness stacks up against the others. When you compare the recollections of different people about the same event, the one thing you can be sure of is that they will all be different. It is axiomatic that no two people remember an event in exactly the same way. What you are looking for when you create a witness cross-reference is the extent of the difference.

Consider the following example: Last year, Mary Brown was involved in a traffic accident. According to her, she was stopped at a red light, and when the light changed, she pulled out into the intersection and was struck by a car driven by defendant Darryl Dangerous. Mary says that it was about five seconds between the time that the light changed and when she pulled into the intersection. This refutes some claims that she was traveling at speed when she approached the intersection and ran a red light herself. We need to know what the other witnesses say about the time delay between the light change and the impact. See Figure 9-4 for a sample witness cross-reference sheet for this situation.

FIGURE 9-4

Witness Cross-Reference Sheet

Time delay between light change for plaintiff and defendant hitting plaintiff's car.

Summaries marked in **bold** indicate discrepancy between witnesses.

Witness	Testimony	Transcript X-Ref
John Doe	That he was sitting across intersection in oncoming lane, saw defendant's car from left, driving at high speed; that his light turned green and defendant kept coming; **about ten seconds between light change and the collision,** saw D's car hit P on passenger side.	Doe, pp. 4–9, 23, 27, 28-34
Jane Roe	That she was behind P, going in same direction; that the light turned green and P pulled out; didn't actually see collision but looked up immediately after; **not sure of time interval between light change and collision, maybe two seconds;** that D said, **"I'm so sorry; I knew it was red. I just couldn't stop."**	Roe, pp. 2–7, 13–17
Officer Mark Williams	That he arrived on scene approx. 15 minutes after collision; that **D refused to give a specific answer about color of light;** that P was definite that light was green for her (hearsay); that John Doe was in far right lane, about to turn in same direction as D was coming; that D was charged with failure to yield.	Williams, pp. 4–6
Plaintiff	That she was stopped at red light, first in line; that Jane Roe was behind her; that John Doe was across intersection facing her; that D came from right, failed to stop; **less than five seconds between light change and collision;** effects of crash, terrible pain, taken from scene in ambulance, questioning by police, consistent statement at the scene as now.	P, pp. 3–23, 42, 45, 71–73, 86–101

When creating a witness cross-reference sheet, it is often helpful to select the landscape page orientation, as the result is much easier to read. You should create a witness cross-reference sheet or chart for every major issue in the case. That way, the legal team can quickly cross-check the testimony of every witness with every critical point in the case. This also makes it easy for the team to see what points are weaker than others. These weak points may require additional investigation or development before the trial begins.

As a paralegal prepares a witness cross-reference sheet, he will go through deposition digests prepared from transcripts. Important pages from the transcripts should be copied off and attached to the witness cross-reference sheet for future reference.

5. WITNESS SUMMARIES

A witness summary provides a general overview of what a witness will say in the trial. It is left deliberately general and is created simply as a quick reference guide to double-check the purpose that the witness will serve in the trial. Many paralegals create a general witness summary, listing each witness and what the witness will testify to at trial. See Figure 9-5 for an example.

FIGURE 9-5

Witness Summary

Witness	Summary
Plaintiff	That she was involved in an automobile accident; that she was stopped for a red light; that D ran the red light; that she was taken to the hospital; that she suffered pain and financial loss as a result; that bills were paid.
John Doe	That he witnessed the collision; that D ran the red light.
Jane Roe	That she was behind P; that they were both stopped at a red light at intersection of Burnett and Burke; that D made statement that he had run a red light.
Officer Mark Williams	That he was dispatched to scene; that he diagrammed scene; that he took photos of the damage to both cars; that he has been trained as an accident reconstructionist; that it is opinion that D was traveling at 45 mph when he came through the intersection; that P was traveling 5 mph.
Dr. Marshall	P's injuries; P's prognosis; P's ability to work in the future.

6. TRIAL TIMETABLE

Another important entry in the client's file is a summary of the important dates and deadlines in the case. This is usually a one-page sheet that details specific events in the case and their concomitant dates (Fig. 9-6). This helps remind the legal team about looming deadlines in the case.

FIGURE 9-6

Trial Timetable

Mary Brown v. Darryl Dangerous

Civil File No.: 06-1007

(All dates calculated in accordance with Rule 23-12, Placid State Rules of Civil Procedure)

Event	Date
Complaint filed and served	June 12, 2015
Discovery scheduled to end (6 months after complaint filed):	November 12, 2015
Motions deadline	December 1, 2015
Pretrial conference scheduled	January 23, 2016
Trial date	Not yet set
Final pretrial order due (10 days prior to trial date)	*
Final attorney conference (at least 20 days prior to trial date)	*
All exhibits, evidence exchanged (no later than 30 days prior to trial date)	*

7. ORGANIZED CLIENT FILE

Organizing a file for trial is a process that varies considerably depending on the type of case, the amount of evidence, and the personal preferences of the attorneys involved. Some attorneys organize their case by using manila file folders, each containing information specific to a particular issue or witness. Other attorneys rely on trial notebooks that contain internal sections reserved for evidentiary issues, witness transcripts, evidence, pleadings, and discovery. Some general categories will appear in nearly every case, including pleadings, correspondence, and discovery. Beyond that basic file structure, there are as many methods for organizing files as there are attorneys. An important tip for any paralegal is to learn the method used by the attorney with whom you work and follow it. There is nothing more frustrating for an attorney than to look for a crucial document or pleading at a crisis point in a trial and be unable to locate it in the section where the attorney believes it should be.

8. TRIAL NOTEBOOK

A trial notebook is a handy reference guide that is filled with all of the legal topics and questions that an attorney will need at trial. We use the term *notebook* here broadly.

Some attorneys use a system of file folders containing all of the information that they will need for trial, while others actually use a series of three-ring binders. The benefit of the binder system is that the pages can be securely fastened inside the cover. Manila file folders have a tendency to become lost, almost always when they are needed most. Trial notebooks help attorneys stay focused and organized over the course of a trial. A good trial notebook should contain:

- jury materials, including voir dire questions;
- motions in limine;
- trial briefs;
- notes for the opening statements;
- witness list;
- direct or cross-examination points to be raised with specific witnesses;
- evidence to be admitted during the direct examination of specific witnesses, along with any foundation questions required for specific evidence;
- evidence list;
- exhibit list;
- foundation questions for specific types of evidence;
- relevant pleadings, including the complaint, the answer, any counterclaims, and any cross-claims;
- witness deposition excerpts and summaries;
- medical summaries and crucial medical records;
- relevant case law, usually about issues that the attorney anticipates will arise during trial; and
- equipment.

Many attorneys have a standard format for a trial notebook. This format may be unique to the particular attorney, so a trial paralegal should always take the extra time to learn the attorney's system. For instance, some attorneys might group discovery responses under a general "Discovery" heading, while others might associate them with witness statements and other evidence in the case.

It is usually helpful to have all of the items contained in a single notebook. Large documents, such as lengthy depositions, can be held in separate files. The crucial points of a deposition transcript can be copied off as single pages and placed under the heading for that witness.

9. PARALEGAL TRIAL NOTEBOOK

In addition to the attorney notebook, a paralegal should have a trial notebook as well. If you are attending the trial with the attorney, your focus will be slightly different than that of the attorney. You are there to provide logistical support and to anticipate problems; a paralegal trial notebook is built on the premise of avoiding problems at trial or being able to handle them as expeditiously as possible. Trying a case is a stressful event, and it often brings out the worst (though sometimes the best) in an attorney. Anything that you can do to eliminate complications will help alleviate that stress and make you that much more valuable to the attorney.

Your notebook should contain the following:

- Contact information: witness telephone and cell phone numbers (for those occasions when you must contact that witness immediately)
- Basic information about the case: case file number, important filing dates, and unmarked copies of the complaint and answer as well as your own highlighted copy of both documents
- Evidence checklist, cross-referenced by witness and foundation questions
- Jury charts, juror questions, and a section listing improper questions that may be asked by the opposing counsel, with the cases that clearly state such questions are improper
- Order of witnesses who will testify and the evidence that should be admitted during each witness's testimony
- Telephone numbers, cell phone numbers, and e-mail addresses of opposing counsel and opposing counsel's paralegal/legal assistant/legal secretary (they usually know how to get in contact with the attorney better than anyone else); name of the judge's secretary, law clerk, and other staff, and their direct-dial numbers (sometimes it is easier to contact these people with a cell phone call in the courthouse hallway than trying to talk to them personally); client's work, home, cell, and any other telephone number where she can be reached, including e-mail address and contact numbers for friends and relatives (you never know to whom you may have to speak to track down a missing client)
- Names, addresses, and telephone numbers for special witnesses, such as expert witnesses and investigators
- Names and contact information for any support personnel, such as FedEx or UPS, court reporters, computer technicians, network administrators, and even the attorney's laptop manufacturer (remember Murphy's law: anything that can go wrong, will go wrong and at the worst possible moment)
- Home telephone numbers of all trial team members, including attorneys, paralegals, runners, and anyone else who might be useful
- Complete list of all equipment needed for the trial, as well as a checklist showing that each piece of equipment has been tested and confirmed working; backup lightbulbs for projectors; dark-colored duct tape (for emergency patches and to hold down pesky wires and electrical cords)
- Diagram of the courthouse, showing the location of bathrooms, vending machines, and water fountains (and designated smoking areas for clients who smoke)

10. PREPARING EXHIBITS

Preparation of exhibits is one of the most important aspects of trial preparation. In recent decades, the importance of exhibits has become more and more obvious. Attorneys often rely on charts, diagrams, scale models, and a wide range of other exhibits to help bring home certain key points during the trial. The availability of reproduction technology has made it far easier to get certain documents blown up to emphasize a particular aspect. It is also a great deal easier to blow up photographs and diagrams to a size where jurors can easily see them. These days, exhibits are not just limited to drawings, models, and enlarged photographs. Computer-generated animation has also become a feature in many civil cases. These programs allow the parties to use video to create a mini-movie that describes the party's version of what happened in the case. Such evidence can have a tremendous impact on the jury. Visual aids are always important. You should consider using diagrams and models to explain any aspect of the case that might be difficult for the jurors to understand.

In addition to the tried-and-true methods of creating exhibits, such as enlarging photographs or hiring artists to render the scene of an accident, commonly available software packages are now making it possible for paralegals to perform a great deal of exhibit preparation right on their office computers. For instance, any drawing program will allow a paralegal to create diagrams, often to scale. Video-editing software can even turn a paralegal into a video production team, editing together various videos to present to the jury. There are also relatively inexpensive methods to scan in thousands of pages of documents and then reproduce them on a computer projector, thus saving a lot of time shuffling through stacks of documents during the trial.

III PREPARING WITNESSES FOR THE TRIAL

Preparing a witness for testifying at trial is one of the most important aspects of trial preparation and should never be skipped. Witnesses are often very nervous about testifying. They are afraid of looking foolish in front of a large group of strangers. They are afraid that the opposing attorney will yell at them or try to confuse or embarrass them. Make sure that the witness has a copy of his deposition transcript before he testifies. Tell him to read through the transcript, even if he claims to remember the event clearly. The deposition was given much closer in time to the event than the witness's testimony will be, and a witness will invariably forget some minor points — and sometimes even some major ones. However, the process of preparing a witness to testify at trial does raise some potential ethical issues, as you can see in this chapter's "Ethical Issues for the Paralegal."

A. REVIEW DEPOSITION TESTIMONY

The first place that many paralegals start when they prepare a witness for trial is the deposition transcript. If this person is going to testify in a civil trial, she should have been deposed. Have the witness read over the deposition transcript. This is a great way to remind her about her testimony and all the big and little facts in the case, because it may have been months (or even years) since she last spoke about the case.

B. DOUBLE- AND TRIPLE-CHECK DOCUMENTATION

Once the witness has read the deposition transcript, go over the documentation. If the witness is someone who prepared notes to accompany the medical file, go back over those notes with the witness. Double-check the dates and times with him. Make sure that you both have a solid understanding of exactly what happened and when. Cross-reference the documentation with the deposition transcript. Does everything jibe? If it doesn't, you can bet that the other side has picked up on it, too. How does your witness explain any discrepancies? Once you've double-checked the documentation, triple-check it. Wait a couple of days and go over it with the witness again. You'd be surprised how much detail will bubble to the surface of a person's mind once he has started thinking about the case again. Take advantage of this phenomenon.

C. WHAT TO TELL WITNESSES ABOUT TESTIFYING

Witnesses always want to know what to expect. They don't like surprises. Sometimes it helps calm a witness down simply to visit the courtroom before the trial starts. You can take the witness there on a non-court day and let the witness take in the entire layout. Tell the witness where she will be sitting. If the courtroom is vacant, take her to the stand and have her sit in the box. This simple process can help alleviate many of the anxieties that witnesses have about taking the stand. Of course, they will still be nervous, but they may be a little less nervous after they've seen the courtroom and have some idea of what to expect.

Besides being able to tell witnesses about the layout of the courtroom, your early reconnaissance work will also help you tell witnesses where they should park. Remember to tell them where the bathrooms are; people always need to go to the bathroom right before they testify.

When you are working with expert witnesses, you will not be required to spend this extra time calming them down and helping with their anxieties. Expert witnesses have done this kind of thing dozens of times before, and they are professionals. However, with all other witnesses, you should take them through a list of dos and don'ts, like the one found in Figure 9-7.

FIGURE 9-7

Dos and Don'ts for All Witnesses

Do:

- Review the file
- Dress professionally
- Make eye contact with the jurors
- Be polite
- Tell the truth

Don't

- Guess
- Get angry or use sarcasm
- Take notes to the stand

1. DO: REVIEW THE FILE

Witnesses should always review the file. It helps them remember the facts, and it makes them feel a little more comfortable about testifying. However, the witness should never take the file to the witness stand. If the witness has given more than one statement, he should review them all. The witness should compare statements made in a deposition with statements contained in other documents. Are there discrepancies? Can these discrepancies be explained? Reviewing the file helps the witness anticipate the questions that the attorneys will ask and how he will answer them.

2. DO: DRESS PROFESSIONALLY

Always tell witnesses to dress professionally. It isn't always a successful strategy to tell witnesses to dress as though they were going to a wedding or a religious event because dress codes for these events can vary drastically. Instead, tell witnesses that a courtroom is a very formal place and that they should dress accordingly.

3. DO: MAKE EYE CONTACT

Witnesses should make eye contact with the most important people in the courtroom: the jury. When they are answering questions, they should address their answers to the jury. We all tend to pay closer attention to someone who is making eye contact with us, and jurors are no exception.

4. DO: BE POLITE

It isn't always easy for a witness to be polite during a trial, especially when she is being cross-examined by opposing counsel. You should tell witnesses that they should try to remain calm and polite, even when the other attorney is being rude. When a person is polite in the face of rude tactics, the jury naturally sides with the polite person. Tell witnesses to remain polite even when they would rather snap at the opposing attorney. A witness should also never show any disrespect to a judge. Besides the fact that the judge has the power to throw a witness in jail for contempt, the jury takes its cues on how to behave from the judge. If the judge rebukes a witness, the jury may discount anything that witness has to say.

5. DO: TELL THE TRUTH

This piece of advice to witnesses is also the first thing they should hear: No matter what, tell the truth. The witness is testifying under oath, and knowingly giving false testimony is perjury. Even when the facts are not that flattering, a witness should always tell the truth. Evading, shading, or outright lying will invariably be found out, and the witness's credibility will be destroyed. Once the witness is proven to be untruthful about one point, the jury tends to discredit anything else that person has to say.

6. DON'T: GUESS

Just as important as telling witnesses what they should do is telling them what they should not do. For instance, witnesses should always avoid guessing to answer a question. If the opposing attorney asks, "Just how far is it from the witness stand to the back of the courtroom?" and the witness does not know, the best answer is to say, "I don't know." We all have a natural tendency to please, and saying, "I don't know," makes us feel that we are creating a bad impression. But this is a trial, not a social gathering. Guessing can get a witness into a lot of trouble, especially when the witness guesses wrong.

7. DON'T: GET ANGRY OR USE SARCASM

Angry people say stupid things. Attorneys know this, and it is a time-honored technique for an attorney to try to anger a witness. Tell your witnesses to work hard at maintaining their composure. Tell them that once they get off the stand, they can express their anger outside the courthouse, but they should try to remain as calm as possible on the stand.

8. DON'T: TAKE NOTES TO THE WITNESS STAND

Witnesses are always surprised when they hear that they should not take notes or files with them to the stand. We all want something to hide behind, and a big piece of paper is as good as anything else. But if a witness takes notes to the stand, then the opposing attorney has the right to take them away, read them, and even question the witness about them. Suppose that the witness has a note that reads, "Don't forget: Light was red!" The attorney can do a lot with a statement like that.

Consider the following example: Andrew is a witness in a case involving the defendant running a red light. He takes some notes with him to the stand and handles direct examination quite easily. However, cross-examination goes differently:

> Attorney: I noticed that you've been referring to some notes in your hands. May I see them?
> Witness: Yes.
> Attorney: It says here, "Don't forget: The light was red!" Is that what this note says?
> Witness: Yes.
> Attorney: You mean that without this note, you wouldn't have remembered that the light was red? Did someone tell you to say this on the stand today?

IV PREPARING FOR THE TRIAL: ROLE OF THE PARALEGAL

So far, our discussion has focused on preparing the witnesses for the impending trial. But it is just as important to prepare yourself for the trial. Preparing the file, going through the documentation, and summarizing depositions will give you a feel for the case, but a trial is about more than technical points. In this section, we will discuss how a paralegal prepares for the activities associated with the trial.

A. RECONNOITER THE COURTROOM

As it becomes more and more likely that a particular case is actually going to go to trial, it is time for you to get into "trial mode." If you think of a trial as if it were a battle (and in many ways, it is), you should do what military professionals do: reconnaissance work. Go to the courthouse and find out which courtroom is reserved for your case. If the courtroom is locked, ask courthouse personnel to open it for you. Explain to them that you are there getting ready for trial.

Once you are inside the courtroom, draw a basic diagram of the room. Locate the witness stand, the judge's bench, and the attorney tables. The plaintiff usually has the table closest to the jury box. Sit in the jury box and look at the room from the jurors' perspective. If you have a friend with you, have the friend talk in a normal tone of voice from the witness stand. Can you hear her? If not, is there a microphone? These are the things that you can tell witnesses later.

Next, locate electrical outlets. These days, attorneys and paralegals often bring laptop computers, overhead projectors, and even printers into the courtroom. Are there enough plugs to accommodate all of these devices? If not, will you need a power strip or extension cords? Will you need to tape the cords down so that people won't trip on them?

If the attorney wants to write out notes for the jury during an opening or closing argument, is there a chalkboard, a whiteboard, or an easel available? Even if something is available, make sure that you have backup supplies. Do not rely on courthouse personnel to supply you with a dry-erase marker, for instance, when the one in the courtroom goes dry just as the attorney is starting his closing argument.

B. REHEARSE YOUR EQUIPMENT

According to Murphy's law, anything that can go wrong will go wrong, and at the worst possible moment. Keep this in mind if your team is going to be using any equipment during the trial, such as an overhead projector. Do a dry run with the device shortly before the trial. If it is a digital projector, does it actually work with the attorney's laptop? Do you have backup lightbulbs and the right cable connectors? If possible, rehearse the presentation right in the courtroom. Is there a screen for the projection? If not, where will the attorney beam the projection so that the jury can see it? These are all questions that should be answered long before the trial starts.

C. LEARN THE LAYOUT OF THE COURTHOUSE

As part of your reconnaissance work at the courthouse, don't neglect the layout of the building outside the courtroom. If you are unfamiliar with the building, draw a map of the facility. You are going to have witnesses waiting around to testify. Where are they going to sit? What if they need to go to the bathroom or want to get a quick snack? If you know where the restroom and the snack bar are, you can direct them — and you'll also know where to look for them if they disappear.

D. MASTER THE TRIAL NOTEBOOK OR THE CASE FILES

By the time the case is actually about to go to trial, you should know the case file as well as the attorney does, if not better. Test yourself: Can you find any particular medical record, bill, summary, or doctor's note in less than 10 seconds? If you can, you know the file; if you can't, you have more work to do.

At some point in the trial, something unexpected will happen and the attorney will need a document that the team hadn't anticipated would be needed. Can you find it immediately? There is nothing more frustrating (or nerve-wracking) than floundering in the middle of a cross-examination because a particular document is lost.

E. GET READY FOR STRESS

If you are good at handling stress, then you are in the right business. Unfortunately, most people aren't. Trials are stressful events. The stress you'll feel will be different from the stress that attorneys will feel. In many ways, you will find yourself constantly trying to anticipate where the case is going so that you can be ready with the right thing at the right time. There are ways that you can reduce the stress — such as by following the tips set out here — but there is no way to get rid of it completely.

Because you know that both you and the attorney will be under a great deal of stress, prepare ways to deal with it. If you like to exercise, don't neglect it during the trial. At least take a break at the end of the day and take a walk or do something else that you find enjoyable. Unfortunately, too many stressed-out people turn to alcohol or food or some other unhealthy diversion. Over time, these short-term "stress relievers" take their toll. The longer the trial, the more stress on everyone involved. It is not wise to stay up late every night of the trial, going over items. Regular sleep is one of the best ways to maintain physical and mental health, and anyone who neglects it — especially during a trial — is only asking for trouble.

F. ANTICIPATE PROBLEMS

Anticipating a problem is different than worrying. An anticipated problem can be dealt with and resolved; a worry can never be. One way of anticipating problems is by visualizing the trial, step-by-step. What exhibits will the attorney need for each witness? Are those exhibits available? By tracing out each phase of the trial and working out the details associated with each, many potential problems can be solved before they ever rear their heads.

V MOCK TRIALS

Many attorneys use juror simulations or mock trials to help prepare for the trial. Some attorneys are reluctant to use the actual witnesses to testify at a mock trial, reasoning that if the witness makes a statement contrary to a statement already provided to the opposing side, then this new statement might also have to be provided to the opposing side through discovery. As we saw in a previous chapter, an attorney has a continuing obligation to update witness statements, and a contradictory statement at a mock trial would probably qualify under that rule. Instead, many attorneys use actors to portray key witnesses or show the videotaped deposition of crucial witnesses at the mock trial. The jurors are selected from the community at large, usually from the juror lists of dismissed panels from two or three court sessions before. Because these individuals have already completed their jury duty, the attorney can be confident that this group of people will not be called for jury duty in the present case.

At the mock trial, the attorneys present their case to a jury and then gauge the jurors' reactions. This can be a very effective tool for trying out a risky trial strategy or for assessing how well, or how poorly, the real jury may receive the attorney's case. Attorneys sometimes use the results of a mock trial to encourage their clients to settle a case. This is far easier to do when a mock jury has rendered a verdict against the client. We will discuss other aspects of settling a case in Chapter 11.

VI PHASES OF THE TRIAL

In this section, we will discuss the various stages of a civil trial, beginning with the pretrial conference and ending with the jury's verdict and the entry of a judgment against one party by the presiding judge.

A. PRETRIAL CONFERENCE

Pretrial conferences are scheduled so that the judge can meet with all parties and discuss the basic framework of the action and settle some of the ground rules for the later trial. Rule 16 of the Federal Rules of Civil Procedure governs pretrial conferences. That rule authorizes a judge to direct the attorneys for the parties to appear before him for a conference to consider numerous issues. Some of these issues include discussions about simplifying or streamlining the issues in the suit, whether pleadings should be amended, and the possibility of obtaining admissions of fact to help narrow the issues that need to be proven at trial. In addition to these issues, the judge will also inquire about the number of witnesses and their potential areas of testimony. The judge will often attempt to boil issues down at a pretrial conference and thus limit the overall number of witnesses, especially expert witnesses who often testify for lengthy periods of time.

Pretrial conference
A conference between the judge, plaintiff, and defendant before the trial commences; the parties discuss witness issues and evidence and finalize their agreements in a pretrial order

At the pretrial conference, the attorneys for the parties will often exchange witness and exhibit lists. The matters resolved will be reduced to writing in a **pretrial order** (Fig. 9-8).

Pretrial order
An order, prepared by the trial judge with the input of the parties, that summarizes key issues in the case, including witness order, evidence, and other critical concerns

FIGURE 9-8

Pretrial Order

STATE OF PLACID IN THE SUPERIOR COURT
COUNTY OF BURKE SUPERIOR COURT FILE NO. __________

JANE DOE,) Pretrial Order
Plaintiff)
vs.)
NICHOLAS CHARLES,)
Defendant.)

Order on Final Pretrial Conference Between Plaintiff and Defendants

Pursuant to the provisions of PL R Civ P 16, and Rule 7 of the Placid General Rules of Practice, a final pretrial conference was held in the above-entitled cause on April 1, 2015. Allison Attorney (PL Bar # 9999) appeared as counsel for the plaintiff; Clarence D. Arrow (PL Bar # 1999) appeared as counsel for defendant, Nicholas Charles.

(1) It is stipulated that all parties are properly before the court, and that the court has jurisdiction of the parties and of the subject matter.

(2) In addition to the other stipulations contained in this order, the parties stipulate and agree with respect to the following undisputed facts:
 a) Ms. Doe was severely injured in an automobile accident on May 15, 2014, in Placid City, PL.
 b) The weather was clear.
 c) Nicholas Charles owned and operated the 2005 Ford Spitfire involved in the accident.
 d) Nicholas Charles was driving on the day of the collision.
 e) Ms. Does was the sole occupant and driver of her automobile.
 f) Ms. Doe was driving her car south on Burke Street and Nicholas Charles was coming from the east.
 g) Mr. Charles's car struck Ms. Doe's car on the passenger side of Ms. Doe's car.
 h) Before the accident, Ms. Doe worked as a supervisor at Knight Manufacturing Co.
 i) Ms. Doe has not been able to return to work since the accident.

(3) A list and description of all known exhibits plaintiff Doe may offer at trial are attached and marked as plaintiff Doe's pretrial exhibits. It is stipulated and agreed that opposing counsel has been furnished a copy of each exhibit listed by the plaintiff.

(4) It is stipulated and agreed that each of the exhibits identified by plaintiff Doe is genuine and, if relevant and material, may be received in evidence without further identification or proof.

(5) A list and description of all known exhibits defendant Nicholas Charles may offer at trial are attached and marked as defendant Nicholas Charles's pretrial exhibits. It is stipulated and agreed that opposing counsel has been furnished a copy of each exhibit listed by defendant, except:
 (List exceptions)

(6) It is stipulated and agreed that each of the exhibits identified by defendant Nicholas Charles is genuine and, if relevant and material, may be received in evidence without further identification or proof, except:
 (List exceptions)

(7) A list of the names and addresses of all known witnesses plaintiff Doe may offer at trial is attached and marked as plaintiff Doe's proposed witnesses. A list of names and addresses of all known witnesses defendant Nicholas Charles may offer at trial is attached and marked as defendant Nicholas Charles's proposed witnesses. Counsel shall immediately notify opposing counsel if the names of additional witnesses are discovered after the preparation of this order.

(8) There are no pending motions, and neither party desires further amendments to the pleadings, except:
  a) Motion for More Definite Statement by defendant, Nicholas Charles.
  b) Motion to Strike by defendant, Nicholas Charles.

(9) Additional consideration has been given to a separation of the triable issues, and counsel for all parties are of the opinion that a separation of issues in this particular case would not be feasible.

(10) The plaintiff Doe contends that the contested issues to be tried by the jury are as follows:
  a) Defendant, Nicholas Charles, is negligent for failing to maintain a proper lookout.
  b) Defendant, Nicholas Charles, was negligent for failing to abide by the rules of the road.
  c) Defendant, Nicholas Charles, was negligent for failing to stop for a red light in his line of travel at the intersection of Burke and Burnett Streets.
  d) These instances of negligence by the defendant were the cause of the automobile accident and of Ms. Doe's injuries.

(11) The defendant, Nicholas Charles, contends that the contested issues to be tried by the jury are as follows:
    (List contested issues)

(12) Counsel for the parties announced that all witnesses are available and the case is in all respects ready for trial. The probable length of the trial is estimated to be one week.

(13) Counsel for the parties represent to the court that, in advance of the preparation of this order, there was a full and frank discussion of settlement possibilities. Counsel for the plaintiffs will immediately notify the clerk in the event of material change in settlement prospects.

(14) Plaintiff Doe's Exhibits
  a) Photos of intersection of Burke St. and Burnett St.
  b) Diagrams of the intersection.
  c) Accident reports.
  d) Medical bills and reports.
  e) Photographs of plaintiff's injuries.
  f) "Day in the Life" video detailing plaintiff's daily activities following the collision.

(15) Plaintiff Doe's Witnesses
  a) Mr. Warren Green, West Placid, PL
  b) Dr. Expert, Raleigh, PL
  c) Clara Hodges, West Placid, PL
  d) Steve Blue, Asheville, PL
  e) Officer Law, West Placid, PL

By: ___________

Neal Bevans
PL Bar # 9999
Attorney for Plaintiff

By: ____________

Clarence D. Arrow
PL Bar #1999
Attorney for Defendant Nicholas Charles

Approved, ordered, and filed:
This the 4th day of November, 2015

Hon. A. Clayton Powell
Court Judge Presiding

In many jurisdictions, judges now require that attorneys appear at the pretrial conference with a draft of the pretrial order in their possession. Some even go so far as to require that the attorneys have the proposed order in both print and digital media. This makes the job for the judge's secretary considerably easier: The secretary can simply copy and paste the relevant parts into the final order. In creating a proposed pretrial order, the judge will require each party to prepare the portions relevant to their presentation.

LEGAL LEGWORK ■ PRETRIAL ORDERS

What are the rules about the preparation, timing, and final presentation of pretrial orders in your state?

B. CALENDAR CALL

Calendar call
A mandatory court hearing where the judge inquires about the readiness of the parties to go to trial; also known as a *docket call*

Conflict letter
A letter sent by an attorney to the judge explaining that the attorney has several different appearances scheduled for the same date and detailing which courts the attorney will go to first

Following the pretrial conference, the next stage in the litigation is scheduling the case for trial. Parties must appear to find out exactly when their cases will be called for trial. On the first day of the week reserved for trials, judges have what is referred to as a **calendar call** or a *docket call*. This is a hearing in which the parties in all pending cases are made to appear to give a status report. If a plaintiff fails to appear for the calendar call, the judge may dismiss the suit. This makes calendar calls very important. If the attorney representing the plaintiff has more than one courtroom to be in on the same day (a common experience), then the attorney will file a **conflict letter** with the court listing the various court appearances and requesting permission to report later in the day.

When the parties announce that they are ready for trial, the judge often schedules them to appear later that week. Suppose that there are 60 cases on the current calendar. Obviously it would be impossible to hold trials in all 60 cases in just one week. However, by requiring the parties to appear for the calendar call, the judge can exert some subtle (and sometimes not so subtle) pressure on the parties to settle the case.

C. JURY SELECTION

Once the case has been called and both parties have announced that they are ready for trial, the next step is jury selection. In the American legal system, it is inaccurate to say that a jury is selected. What actually happens is that a group of citizens is brought in, and members of the group are eliminated until 12 remain. Those 12 will sit on the jury and consider the issues raised in the case.

Panel
A group of people who have been called for jury duty; the final jury will be selected from this group; also known as *venire*

Before we can discuss the details of jury selection, it is important to emphasize some of the terminology used during this process. For instance, when citizens are called in for jury duty, they appear in court as part of a **panel** or *venire*. Panel members are removed until 12 people remain. Those 12 people are then called **jurors**. The process of carrying out jury selection is often referred to as **voir dire**.

Jurors
Those people who have been selected to sit on a jury; they will consider the evidence and reach a verdict in the case

Voir dire
(French) To look, to speak; the process of questioning jurors about their potential biases in the case

During the voir dire process, the various members of the panel are questioned about their life experiences, their knowledge of the case and the parties, and any other relevant issues. The attorneys then evaluate these answers to decide which members of the panel should be removed or challenged.

1. TRIAL PARALEGALS AND JURY SELECTION

A well-trained trial paralegal can be an invaluable asset during jury selection. A paralegal can assist the attorney by keeping track of panel members' responses to questions, noting unusual or interesting information about particular panel members, and even doing the little things such as noticing the facial expressions of panel members when they think that they are not being observed.

When it comes time to actually select the jury, the attorneys are permitted to use jury strikes or challenges to remove panel members until 12 remain. There are two types of jury challenges: peremptory and cause.

2. PEREMPTORY JURY STRIKES

Both sides in a jury trial have a minimum number of **jury strikes** or *challenges* that they may use to remove panel members. Suppose, for example, that in a civil case both the plaintiff and the defense have 10 strikes. If the panel consists of 32 persons and both sides use all their strikes, then the result will be a 12-person jury. Such strikes are called **peremptory jury strikes** because the sides may use them in any manner they see fit to remove panel members. The number of strikes the parties may use varies depending on the type of case. In some cases, the parties have equal numbers of strikes, but in other jurisdictions the plaintiff may have a slight numeric advantage.

Jury strike
The removal of a jury panel member, also known as a *jury challenge*

Peremptory jury strike
The removal of a jury panel member for any legally permissible reason

In the past, there were no limitations on the use of peremptory strikes. However, in recent decades the U.S. Supreme Court has begun limiting a party's ability to use peremptory strikes, especially when the strike is based on race.

3. CHALLENGES FOR CAUSE

There is a second method that parties can use to remove panel members. When a party makes a **challenge for cause**, it means the party is requesting that the judge remove the

Challenge for cause
When a panel member is removed because he or she cannot sit on the jury

Sidebar

In some jurisdictions, peremptory removal of a juror is called a strike, while in other jurisdictions it is called a challenge. The terms are used interchangeably throughout this chapter.

panel member. A party might make this request for several reasons. For example, if a panel member has stated in open court that she will not obey the court's orders or will not actively participate in the jury deliberations or has religious objections to being seated on a jury, a party might make a challenge for cause. If the judge accepts the challenge, the panel member is removed and the removal is not assessed against any side's number of peremptory strikes.

Once a jury has been selected to serve on the case, the next step is opening statements.

D. OPENING STATEMENTS

An opening statement is a brief speech made by the attorneys for the plaintiff and the defendant wherein they outline what will happen in the case and what evidence the jury can expect to see. The purpose of an opening statement is to provide some framework for the jurors. After all, the jurors have no independent knowledge of the case; thus, the attorneys can use the opening statement to explain the issues to them. Attorneys use opening statements as a roadmap of where the trial will go and what witnesses will testify. Although opening statements are often depicted on television as dramatic presentations where attorneys forcefully argue major points in their cases, the reality is that opening statements are usually dry and formal. Attorneys are barred from arguing points; the best they can do is to provide a foretaste of what will happen in the course of the trial.

In a civil case, the plaintiff's attorney presents an opening statement first. The reason for this is simple: The plaintiff is the person who brought the allegations and must now prove them. Once the plaintiff has given an opening statement, the defendant is permitted to address the jury. Although a defense attorney may wait to give his opening statement until after the plaintiff's case has been presented, the common practice is for both attorneys to address the jury shortly after jury selection. Once the opening statements have been given, the next phase is the presentation of the plaintiff's case.

E. PRESENTATION OF THE PLAINTIFF'S CASE

The plaintiff has the burden of going first in a civil case. The plaintiff presents her case through two primary methods: witnesses and evidence. Attorneys are not allowed to address the jury and tell them directly about pertinent evidence or to offer opinions about the legal position of their client. Instead, the attorneys must prove their case and introduce evidence through witnesses.

1. WITNESSES

We have all seen movies and television dramas where witnesses testify. Although some of the fictional accounts may be overly dramatic, the basics are usually correct. When a witness testifies, he is called to the stand, sworn in, and then asked questions. This is called *direct examination.*

a. Direct Examination

When the plaintiff's attorney calls a witness to the stand and questions her about the plaintiff's allegations, it is called **direct examination**. The witnesses who testify on direct examination are usually friendly to the plaintiff, or at least neutral about the outcome of the case.

Direct examination
The questioning of a witness by the side that called the witness to the stand

Consider the following example: Maria was injured in a car wreck when the defendant, Jonathan Journeyman, ran a red light and struck Maria's car broadside. Maria brought suit against Jonathan, and the trial has now begun. After giving her opening statement, Maria's attorney calls her first witness. In this case, there was another driver at the intersection that day who saw the entire incident. Maria's attorney, Lucy Lawyer, calls Wanda Witness to the stand and begins asking her questions. The direct examination might go something like this:

> Lawyer: Please state your name for the record.
> Witness: My name is Wanda Witness.
> Lawyer: Ms. Witness, were you present at the intersection of Elm Street and First Street in this city on May 1 of last year?
> Witness: Yes, I was.
> Lawyer: What, if anything, did you see that day?
> Witness: I saw the defendant fail to stop at the red light and strike the car driven by that lady over there.
> Lawyer: Let the record reflect that the witness has identified the plaintiff in this case. Ms. Witness, how can you be so sure that the defendant ran the red light that day?
> Witness: Well, I was in the car right behind him, and I saw the light turn red. I turned to my daughter, who was in the car with me, and I said, "That guy's crazy. He's running a red light."
> Lawyer: What happened after the defendant ran the red light?
> Witness: He slammed into that lady's car, and both cars sort of rolled sideways.
> Lawyer: What did you do then?
> Witness: I parked my car and ran to the lady's car. I asked her if she was okay. That man, the defendant, had already gotten there.
> Lawyer: Did the defendant say anything to you?
> Witness: Yes, he said that he should have been paying attention and that he hoped he hadn't killed someone.

You will notice that the way the attorney phrases questions on direct examination is different from the way that a person would question the witness on the street. The lawyer uses stilted questions such as, "What, if anything, did you see that day?" The reason that attorneys phrase questions that way is that direct examination has strict limits. For one thing, attorneys are not allowed to testify for the witness; the witness must tell his own story. If the attorney puts words in the witness's mouth (called "leading" a witness), the other attorney may object.

When the plaintiff's attorney has asked the witness all the questions she thinks are necessary, the plaintiff's attorney turns the questioning over to the defense attorney. This is called cross-examination.

PRACTICE POINTER ▶ WITNESSES

One of the most important things you, as a trial paralegal, can do immediately before and during a trial is to maintain contact with your various witnesses. Tell the witnesses what is happening and when they are likely to be needed. Don't commit yourself to an absolute time, explaining that no one can ever be sure exactly when a witness will take the stand; however, by keeping them advised of the proceedings, you lessen some of their anxiety. By staying in contact with them, you also make sure that you can reach them, should you need to do so at a moment's notice. Don't forget to call the witnesses when the case is over and tell them what happened. You never know when you might deal with that person again, and witnesses are always curious to know what happened — and if their testimony assisted in resolving the case.

b. Cross-Examination

Cross-examination
The questioning of a witness to show bias, prejudice, or lack of knowledge

Cross-examination occurs after direct examination and is always done by the other side's attorney. The rules about asking questions on cross-examination are much more liberal than the rules governing attorneys on direct examination. During cross-examination, attorneys are allowed to ask leading questions, such as, "You weren't even looking at the light, were you?" Attorneys are also allowed to be more confrontational with witnesses on cross-examination. Cross-examination is more dramatic, and this is probably why you are more likely to see it depicted on television courtroom dramas than direct examination.

Attorneys are allowed to explore a witness's potential biases or lack of knowledge on cross-examination. The attorneys can also impeach a witness by showing that the witness is not someone who should be believed. Impeachment can occur through a demonstration that the witness has no knowledge of the event, such as the fact that the witness was not at the scene on the day of the accident or that the witness has been convicted of a crime involving dishonesty, such as perjury.

c. Paralegal Assistance during the Testimony Phase of the Trial

A paralegal who has mastered all of the other skills that a trial paralegal needs must also work to develop a sixth sense about trial work. You must stay alert for the little things that could prove to be important later.

Consider the follow example: Mary testifies that her husband kept her locked up in a room for 12 hours and wouldn't let her leave. The attorney has painstakingly gone through the entire episode, proving all of the elements and establishing the husband's pattern of abuse. At the end of direct examination, he turns to his trial paralegal with the question that attorneys often ask of their assistants: "Anything else?" Fortunately for this attorney, the trial paralegal has been involved in the case from the outset and has been paying attention. She scrawls a quick note on a piece of paper and hands it to the attorney. The note reads: *When did she go to the bathroom?* The attorney shrugs and asks the question. The witness explains that she had had to urinate in a bottle in the room.

Later, when they'd won the case, the attorney spoke with the jurors. The foreperson said, "I wasn't sure about the case until you asked about going to the bathroom. When I heard that, I knew she was telling the truth."

PRACTICE POINTER ▶ TRIALS

Throughout this chapter, we have examined the issues surrounding the presentation of a trial. It is one thing to talk about a trial and quite another to actually participate in one. One of the best things you can do, if you plan on a career in litigation, is to take the time to watch others present a trial. The local courthouse will have trials scheduled constantly. Find a case and sit in on the proceedings. The public is allowed to attend nearly all trials, and this can be an invaluable learning tool. Try to watch every phase of the trial and see how the attorneys, witnesses, paralegals, judges, bailiffs, and others interact with one another. This type of hands-on experience will serve you well in the future, when you are standing on the other side of the bar.

2. RESTING THE CASE

The plaintiff's attorney will proceed through his case, calling witnesses and presenting evidence, until he believes that all allegations against the defendant have been proven. When finished, the attorney will announce, "Your Honor, the plaintiff rests."

This announcement informs the court that the plaintiff does not plan on presenting any additional witnesses or evidence and that the plaintiff is finished with her side of the case. At this point, the focus turns to the defendant, who is free to present evidence and witnesses. However, before the defendant begins her case, it is common for the defense attorney to raise a motion.

3. MOTION FOR DIRECTED VERDICT

A **motion for directed verdict** comes at the end of the plaintiff's case, shortly after that party has announced that it rests. When a defendant brings a motion for directed verdict, he is saying that the plaintiff has failed to prove all of the allegations raised in the complaint. Because the plaintiff has failed to prove his case, the defendant is entitled to a verdict entered by the judge that essentially dismisses the case and ends the trial. Motions for directed verdict are routine in civil cases. Defendants raise these motions because there is no reason not to. If the defendant brings the motion and the judge denies it, the defendant is in no worse position than he was before. However, if the judge sustains the motion, the trial will end and the defendant will win. Given that situation, it is little wonder that defense attorneys routinely bring a motion for directed verdict at the conclusion of the other side's case.

Motion for directed verdict
A motion by the defense that asks the court to enter a verdict in the defendant's favor because the plaintiff has failed to prove all material allegations against the defendant

When the plaintiff has rested her case, the defendant is permitted to present her own case. The rules for the defendant's case are identical to those that bind the plaintiff. The defendant can present witnesses and testimony to attempt to disprove the plaintiff's allegations.

F. PRESENTING THE DEFENSE

Although the defense is under no obligation to present a case in a civil case, most defense attorneys do. The defense reasons that if the jurors hear only the plaintiff's version of the case, they will probably reach a verdict favorable to the plaintiff. The defendant will thus present witness testimony and evidence that tends to disprove or mitigate the defendant's liability.

1. DEFENSE WITNESSES

Like plaintiff's witnesses, the defendant must also present oral testimony from witnesses to prove his allegations or to attempt to disprove the plaintiff's allegations. Just as we saw in the plaintiff's case, the defendant will call witnesses and conduct a direct examination. Afterward, the plaintiff's attorney is free to conduct a cross-examination of the defense witnesses.

2. RESTING THE DEFENSE CASE

Once the defendant has presented her case, she also makes the announcement, "The defense rests." This signals that the defendant has no additional testimony or witnesses. The trial will now move into its final phase. At this point, the jury is usually sent back to the jury room or given a recess while the court conducts a charge conference.

G. CHARGE CONFERENCE

A charge conference is a meeting between the judge and the attorneys for both sides where they discuss the type of instructions that will be given to the jury. As we will see, the judge always gives the jurors instructions about what they should do as they deliberate in the case and how they should announce that they are finished. The charge conference is where the judge gives the attorneys for both sides the opportunity to suggest specific types of instructions for the jury.

Attorneys know that in addition to the judge's instructions about what they should do in the jury room, the judge will also instruct the jurors about what the law is on particular topics. The attorneys will research different cases, hoping that the judge will use language in his instructions to the jury that might slightly favor their side over the other. Consider the following jury instruction:

Plaintiff's Suggested Jury Charge #1

Ladies and gentlemen of the jury, I charge you that the defendant has been impeached by proof of a crime of dishonesty. Impeachment suggests that the witness is not capable of being believed. How much weight you give to that testimony is for you to decide.

Consider the defendant's suggested jury charge on the same topic:

Defendant's Suggested Jury Charge #1

Ladies and gentlemen of the jury, I charge you that whether or not a person has been impeached in this case is solely a matter for you to decide.

You will notice that although both suggested jury charges state the same basic idea, the way that the defendant has worded the charge lessens the impact on the testimony, while the plaintiff's suggested charge focuses attention on the defendant's testimony. The difference may be simple semantics, but attorneys do not take anything for granted. The entire case may hinge on how the jury considers this one issue.

The judge is free to accept or reject any of the parties' proposed jury charges. Once the court has considered all suggested jury instructions (Fig. 9-9), the judge will call for the jury to return and announce that closing arguments may commence.

FIGURE 9-9

Suggested Jury Charge Cover Sheet

STATE OF PLACE COUNTY OF BURKE	IN THE SUPERIOR COURT SUPERIOR COURT FILE NO. ___________
JANE DOE, Plaintiff vs. NICHOLAS CHARLES, Defendant.	Jury Charge

PLAINTIFF's REQUESTS TO CHARGE NUMBER 1 THROUGH 4

Comes now the Plaintiff, Jane Doe, by and through Allison Barrister, Attorney for Plaintiff, and submits the attached requests to charge number 1 through ___________.

Respectfully submitted, this 10th day of April, 2016.

____

Allison Barrister
Attorney for Plaintiff Jane Doe

PLAINTIFF's REQUEST TO CHARGE NO. 1

All drivers must obey traffic signs and electronic devices.
P.C.A. section 16-5-40.

PLAINTIFF's REQUEST TO CHARGE NO. 2

A driver who is cited for violation of a traffic device is presumed negligent, *Brown v. Simms*, 132 Pl. App. 399, 208 S.E. 2d 183 (1974).

PLAINTIFF'S REQUEST TO CHARGE NO. 3

The plaintiff has the burden of proof in a civil case and when the plaintiff presents a preponderance of evidence, the burden shifts to the defendant to disprove the material allegations of the complaint.

Helton v. Plate, 166 Pl. App. 662, 305 S.E. 2d 592 (1983).

PLAINTIFF'S REQUEST TO CHARGE NO. 4

A defendant has the obligation of proving the counterclaims raised in the answer and if the defendant fails to do so, the jury is authorized to find for the plaintiff on each and every unproven counterclaim.

P.C.A. section 16-5-23

H. CLOSING ARGUMENT

In a closing argument, the attorneys summarize their cases and show the jury why they should win. Unlike opening statements, in closing arguments attorneys are free to engage in the full range of dramatic presentations to sway the jury to their side. Attorneys can appeal not only to logic, but also to emotion. They can argue that the verdict they want is good for their clients and for society in general. Closing arguments in real cases have come to resemble their fictional counterparts on television, with attorneys pulling out all the stops to convince the jurors that they should win. Unlike fictional trials, however, most real closing arguments last a lot longer than the few seconds that they take on television. In many cases, attorneys have an hour or more to sum up their cases. In previous decades, attorneys might take several days to complete closing arguments.

Just as we saw with opening statements, the plaintiff goes first in presenting a closing argument. When the plaintiff is finished, the defense gives its closing argument.

I. JURY INSTRUCTIONS

Jury charge
Oral instructions given by the judge to the jury about how they should deliberate and what law they should follow

When the closing arguments are complete, the judge then reads the **jury charge**. Among other things, the charge instructs the jury what they must do in the jury room. For instance, a judge might read, "Once you have retired to the jury room, your first task will be to select one member of the jury to act as foreperson. This person will act as the jury spokesperson for any questions the jury might have and any communications, such as requests for breaks or meals, that the jury might need to make to the court."

In addition to instructing the jury about the practical matters about how to deliberate, the judge also instructs the jury about the law. The judge might instruct the jury about the burden on the plaintiff to prove the case against the defendant and that if the jurors feel that the plaintiff has failed to prove the case, they should vote a verdict for the defendant.

A jury charge in a complex case could easily last for several hours. The court must go over procedural matters, such as where the jurors should write their verdict, as well as the full range of legal issues that have arisen in the case.

SEARCH SUGGESTION • JURY INSTRUCTIONS

We have seen that jury instructions are often prepared prior to trial. Although there are publications that contain jury instructions, this is not the only way to find them. In fact, one of the best ways of coming up with jury instructions about specific points in a case is to research the case law in your state or federal jurisdiction for recent appellate decisions on specific issues. A court's holding on an issue can serve as the basis for a very effective jury instruction.

J. JURY DELIBERATION

When the jury charge is complete, the jurors are led from the courtroom to the jury room, where they can finally discuss the case among themselves. Jury deliberations are private; no one other than jury members is permitted to be inside the jury room while they deliberate. How does a jury actually deliberate on a case? The most common approach is for the jurors to discuss the case and then vote, often by secret ballot, which side they believe should win. The foreperson collects the ballots and then tabulates them. In most cases, the final verdict must be unanimous, so if the majority votes for one party and two or three people vote for the other, the majority will then spend some time trying to talk the minority over to their side. This process can take minutes, hours, or even days. Although the length of the trial is an indication of how long the jury will deliberate (longer trials usually result in longer deliberations), there are no rules when it comes to juries. Any trial attorney who has been involved in numerous trials will be quick to tell a client that there are no guarantees with jurors. This is why many trial attorneys refer to jury deliberations as "rolling the dice."

When the jurors finally reach a unanimous verdict, the jury spokesperson will knock on the jury room door and tell the court bailiff that they are ready to make their announcement. The bailiff will not ask about the verdict. Instead, he will conduct the jury back into the courtroom, where the judge will ask about the final verdict.

Sidebar

If the jurors are unable to reach a unanimous verdict, the judge will declare a mistrial. The jury will be referred to as a "hung jury," and the case will be tried again before a different jury.

K. VERDICT

In civil cases, when the plaintiff wins, the jury's announcement will be, "We find for the plaintiff." If they have decided that the defendant should win, their verdict will be, "We find for the defendant." If the jury has decided to make a monetary award, the jury spokesperson will then announce the amount and the party to whom it is awarded.

Tech Topic
METADATA

Metadata is the term used to describe how information contained in a file describes the contents, including origination time, date, and even the author. Attorneys and paralegals use metadata as a way of confirming when a file was created and by whom. At its best, metadata can answer complex questions such as when a party knew a particular fact and what that party did with the information. Metadata originated out of the need to organize digital files in such a way that they could be retrieved, cataloged, and then stored for later reuse. In its simplest form, such as when an attorney uses metadata to cross-examine a witness, the attorney can point to metadata that identifies who authored the particular file and when it was prepared. A witness who claims on direct testimony that she did not know about the plaintiff's request for medical leave can be shown to be untruthful on cross-examination when the attorney points to a memo prepared on her office computer that refers directly to the plaintiff's request, denies it, and then insists that the plaintiff should be "forced out" in order to avoid further medical costs. Most people know that a digital file, once created, can be quite difficult to delete. Even an individual who types up such a memo and then erases it cannot be confident that the file won't resurface through other means. This is the very core of e-discovery. Because so much of our lives occur through devices as diverse as telephones, computers, and even GPS systems in our automobiles, it may only be a matter of time before metadata for information can be retrieved from even supposedly erased hard drives that can directly conflict with a person's oral testimony.

L. JUDGMENT

Judgment
A court's conclusion about a specific issue in controversy

After the jury has announced its verdict, the judge officially enters that verdict as the final outcome in the case. This is referred to as the **judgment**. The jurors are released from jury duty and are now free to discuss the case with anyone they wish. Entering judgment has several important consequences. For one, the entry of judgment gives the winning party in a civil case the right to collect the amount awarded by the jury. It also gives the losing party the right to file an appeal.

M. ENFORCING THE JUDGMENT

Once the case has concluded and the judge has entered judgment against one party, the other party may use various means to enforce that judgment. If the final judgment is that the defendant is liable to the plaintiff for specific damages, the plaintiff can use the judgment to enforce payment and can even use the judgment to compel the defendant to sell off assets to pay the judgment.

Case Excerpt

When can an attorney receive punishment from one state's bar when the attorney has already been sanctioned by another state's bar for improper procedures in civil cases?

IN RE LOWELL
14 A.D.3d 41, 784 N.Y.S.2d 69 (N.Y.A.D. 1 Dept., 2004).

Per Curiam.

Respondent Melinda E. Lowell was admitted to the practice of law in the State of New York by the Third Judicial Department on June 26, 1980, under the name Melinda Eilene Lowell. From 1996 to the present, she has maintained an office for the practice of law within the First Judicial Department. Respondent was also admitted to the bar in New Jersey in 1981, and at all relevant times herein, maintained an office for the practice of law there.

The Departmental Disciplinary Committee now seeks an order, pursuant to 22 NYCRR 603.3, suspending respondent for three years predicated upon similar discipline issued by the Supreme Court of New Jersey by an order filed November 25, 2003, imposing a three year suspension, retroactive to May 30, 2002. In the alternative, the Committee seeks an order sanctioning respondent as this Court deems appropriate. Respondent does not object to the imposition of reciprocal discipline but urges that such discipline should be coterminous with the disciplinary term imposed in New Jersey.

The New Jersey District II-B Ethics Committee served respondent with two separate disciplinary complaints and an amended complaint charging 48 counts and violations of various Rules of Professional Conduct. Most of the counts involved the charging of excessive fees. The remaining charges alleged that respondent engaged in a course of misconduct over a period of several years which included creating false documents which she then submitted to a court; counseling a client to lie in a certification and to disobey a court order; directing an employee to work on a client's case and charge the client after the client had discharged her; eliciting false testimony from a witness during trial; making misrepresentations to clients, the court and third parties; failing to refund the unearned portion of a retainer; failing to file a motion for pendente lite relief as requested by a client; failing to notify her adversary of the submission of an insertion made to a stipulation; directing a paralegal in her employ, who formerly worked for respondent's adversary in a pending case, to work on that case, even questioning the paralegal about her adversary's litigation strategy; and billing clients for work done by paralegals at the higher attorney billable rate.

Respondent answered the complaints and six days of hearings, between July 6, 2000 and August 8, 2000, were held before a Special Master at which respondent, represented by counsel, testified.

While the Special Master did not sustain all of the charges against respondent, he sustained 14 of them. In sustaining these charges, the Special Master reported that:

> I find that (respondent) has no appreciation of the inappropriateness of her conduct. I find that her testimony throughout the hearing was evasive and not credible. She neither

> expressed remorse nor did she accept any responsibility for her conduct. She attempted to challenge each of the allegations of misconduct by blaming others, including employees and associates of her firm or her adversaries. I find that her inability to recognize neither the nature nor the severity of her actions to be an aggravating factor.
>
> The Special Master recommended a three-year suspension.

Upon a de novo review of the matter, the Disciplinary Review Board issued a lengthy decision dated October 26, 2001, recommending respondent's disbarment. This sanction was imposed after the Review Board thoroughly discussed the charges and findings against respondent.

Respondent represented the husband in a matrimonial matter. The Disciplinary Review Board found that by submitting to the court an order concerning a psychological exam of the parties' children without notifying the wife's attorney of its terms, she deliberately tried to circumvent the court rules so that her adversary could not object to the order, thereby violating Rules of Professional Conduct 3.4(c) (knowingly disobeying an obligation under the rules of a tribunal). Although respondent was not charged with violating Rules of Professional Conduct 8.4(d) (engaging in conduct prejudicial to the administration of justice), the Disciplinary Review Board nevertheless found that her conduct violated this rule and amended the complaint to conform to the proof.

Also in this matrimonial action, respondent employed a paralegal who had formerly worked for the law firm which represented the wife. The Disciplinary Review Board found that by requiring the paralegal to work on this case and even questioning her about her adversary's litigation strategies, respondent breached the "screen" between the paralegal and the legal matter in violation of Advisory Committee Professional Ethics Opinion 665. This opinion requires the creation and maintenance of a "Chinese wall" separating the paralegal from any association with the matrimonial matter while in respondent's office.

In another matrimonial case, respondent added a sentence to a stipulation signed by her adversary and directed another attorney who worked for her to sign the stipulation containing the addition and to file it with the court, without advising the adversary of the addition. Respondent's associate refused, and the Disciplinary Review Board found that respondent attempted to pressure the associate to alter the stipulation and file it and, but for her refusal, it would have been filed with the court. Therefore, respondent violated Rules of Professional Conduct 8.4(a) (knowingly assisting or inducing another to violate the Rules of Professional Conduct) by her attempt to violate Rule 8.4(d).

In another matter, respondent stipulated and the Disciplinary Review Board concluded that by having her secretary sign her paralegal's name on a certification and then filing the certification with the court without the paralegal's consent respondent violated Rules of Professional Conduct 3.4(c).

In 1996, a client paid respondent $5,000 to file a divorce complaint in New York and move for pendente lite support. Respondent never filed a pendente lite motion and was discharged in July 1996. The Disciplinary Review Board found that after her discharge, respondent instructed her paralegal to draft a pendente lite motion, place it in the file and deliver it to the client. Respondent then billed her former client for 15.4 hours of work including four hours for a "draft" of that motion and "review of financials." The Disciplinary Review Board concluded that respondent's conduct violated Rules of Professional Conduct 8.4(c) (conduct involving dishonesty, fraud, deceit or misrepresentation), that her failure to file the motion despite her client's request violated Rule 1.3 (lack of diligence), and by failing to return the unearned portion of the retainer she violated Rule 1.16(d) (failure to return unearned retainer on termination of representation).

In 1991, respondent filed an application for pendente lite relief for another client alleging that the client's father had lent her some $110,000, and attached six promissory notes to that effect. The husband claimed the notes were shams and the money was given to the couple as gifts. The Disciplinary Review Board found that respondent had her client sign fraudulent promissory notes and false certifications which respondent then filed with the court. In addition, respondent elicited false testimony from the wife's father at the divorce trial that the funds were loans and not gifts. By the foregoing conduct, the Review Board found that respondent violated Rules of Professional Conduct 1.2(d) (counseling or assisting a client in conduct the lawyer knows is illegal, criminal, or fraudulent), Rule 3.3(a)(1) (knowingly making a false statement of a material fact to a tribunal), Rule 3.3(a)(4) (offering evidence known to be false or failing to take remedial measures after learning that false evidence has been offered), Rule 8.4(c).

On a separate issue, although the court had issued an order restraining the parties from transferring or dissipating assets, respondent assisted her client in cashing bearer bonds in order to pay her legal bill. The Disciplinary Review Board found respondent violated RPC 8.4(d).

While representing the wife in another matrimonial action, respondent filed a complaint in May 1997 against the husband seeking unpaid support. The husband was in the process of selling his house and respondent sent a letter to the broker stating that she represented the wife in a pending action and advised the broker that all proceeds from the sale must be held in escrow. However, there was no court order requiring that the proceeds be escrowed and respondent's subsequent application for such an order was denied. The Disciplinary Review Board concluded that respondent's conduct violated RPC 4.1(a)(1) (making a false statement of material fact or law to a third person) and Rule 8.4(c).

While the Disciplinary Review Board did not sustain 38 counts of charging clients with excessive fees, it did find that respondent billed various clients for work performed by paralegals at the higher attorney rate. The Review Board characterized this conduct as "misrepresentations" on clients' bills in violation of Rule 8.4(c) (engaging in conduct involving dishonesty, fraud, deceit, or misrepresentation).

Respondent did not present any evidence in mitigation.

In initially recommending disbarment, the Disciplinary Review Board found respondent's conduct "so egregious" that her "pervasive pattern of deceit and deficiency of character" warranted the most severe discipline. Specifically, the Review Board wrote in its report that:

> (respondent) displayed an alarming lack of probity in these matters. Furthermore, she showed no appreciation for the basic trust that must exist between opposing counsel. The record is clear that, even at the ethics hearing, (respondent) displayed an arrogant,

> discourteous attitude toward the presenter, the witnesses and even the district ethics committee that docketed the grievances.

The Review Board also agreed with the Special Master that respondent had no appreciation of the inappropriateness of her behavior, failed to accept responsibility for her actions by blaming everyone but herself, and relentlessly browbeat her employees until they agreed to do things they otherwise would not have done.

Accordingly, the Disciplinary Review Board found that respondent had violated at least 10 provisions of the Rules of Professional Conduct as well as an Advisory Committee Opinion and recommended disbarment.

Thereafter, respondent moved to supplement the record with a report from her treating psychiatrist, letters from family members, attorneys and clients attesting to her reputation and character. In particular, respondent wished to address the Review Board's statements that at the hearing she was "arrogant" and "discourteous" and showed no appreciation that her behavior was inappropriate. The New Jersey Supreme Court granted respondent's motion and remanded the matter back to the Disciplinary Review Board for reconsideration of the record as supplemented. In addition, the court permitted the Office of Attorney Ethics to make its own submissions. The court also directed respondent, who had represented that she was not practicing law, to refrain from doing so until further order of the court.

Specifically, respondent's psychiatric expert explained in his report that at the time of respondent's hearing (summer 2000), she was on five different large doses of medication since she was suffering from "major depressive disorder, recurrent" and, as of the spring 2002, her major depressive disorder was in "partial remission." Respondent's doctor opined that respondent's medications and condition contributed to the way she projected to others during the hearing. While the psychiatric expert retained by the Office of Attorney Ethics shared the same diagnosis, he concluded that respondent's behavior during the hearing "were manifestations of (her) style of advocacy and presentation as an attorney, and not inevitable and invariable manifestations of her underlying psychiatric disorder."

The Disciplinary Review Board made no finding that respondent's mental condition caused any of the underlying misconduct. Rather, it was offered only to explain her behavior at the hearing before the Special Master and her then apparent lack of appreciation for her wrongdoing or acceptance of responsibility.

Upon reconsideration and by supplemental decision dated October 8, 2003, the Disciplinary Review Board did not modify its decision as to liability. However, with no new evidence submitted with respect to her conduct relating to the underlying charges, the Review Board nevertheless changed its sanction recommendation from disbarment to a three-year suspension. In recommending the reduced sanction, the Review Board considered these factors: respondent had failed to present any mitigating circumstances when the matter was first before the Review Board, the character letters submitted, the evidence of respondent's "severe psychiatric and emotional problems during the ethics hearing," and the Office of Attorney Ethic's recommendation of a three year suspension. Given these factors, the Review Board was no longer convinced that respondent could never again conform her conduct to the high standards required of an attorney, but that her misconduct warranted a lengthy suspension and that, prior to reinstatement, she should submit proof of her mental fitness.

Upon receipt of the Disciplinary Review Board's Supplemental Decision, the New Jersey Supreme Court issued an order, retroactively suspending respondent for three years from May 30, 2002.

The Departmental Disciplinary Committee now seeks an order finding respondent guilty of misconduct pursuant to 22 NYCRR 603.3(c) based upon the findings of misconduct made in the New Jersey disciplinary proceeding. Respondent was provided with sufficient notice that the Departmental Disciplinary Committee was seeking "an order, pursuant to 22 NYCRR 603.3, suspending (respondent) predicated upon similar discipline issued by a foreign jurisdiction, or, in the alternative, sanctioning respondent as this Court deems appropriate, or granting any other and further relief that is just and proper." She submitted a response in which she concedes none of the defenses enumerated in 22 NYCRR 603.3(c) are available to her and does not object to the imposition of reciprocal discipline. The findings of misconduct are supported by the record and are accepted by this Court. However, we cannot agree that the sanction New Jersey has imposed is appropriate under these circumstances.

We recognize and support the generally accepted and well reasoned principle that the jurisdiction where a respondent lives and actively practices law at the time of the offense has the greatest interest in the issue and the public policy considerations relevant to such disciplinary actions (see Matter of Yagman, 263 A.D.2d 151, 698 N.Y.S.2d 224 (1999); Matter of Reiss, 119 A.D.2d 1, 505 N.Y.S.2d 604 (1986)). However, while we respect this long standing policy and tradition, and we always or virtually always impose a reciprocal sanction, we most respectfully — and indeed with some reluctance to deviate from our consistent adherence to the sound policy of reciprocal discipline — must decline to follow the doctrine of reciprocal discipline in this particular matter (see Matter of Gilbert, 268 A.D.2d 67, 707 N.Y.S.2d 394 (2000) (Committee's petition for more severe sanction of six months suspension rather than three months imposed in New Jersey granted). Rather, we find ourselves in complete agreement with the original sanction which the New Jersey Disciplinary Review Board imposed because it is completely in accord with our own precedent in matters involving such egregious patterns of violations of legal and ethical obligations (see Matter of Heller, 9 A.D.3d 221, 780 N.Y.S.2d 314 (2004), lv. denied 3 N.Y.3d 607, 785 N.Y.S.2d 25, 818 N.E.2d 667 (2004) (11 counts of professional misconduct involving conduct prejudicial to the administration of justice, falsely testifying at a deposition, falsely submitting to the Supreme Court a post-trial affidavit, and intentionally engaging in conduct involving fraud, dishonesty, deceit and misrepresentation warranted disbarment over Committee's recommendation of suspension); Matter of Weinstein, 4 A.D.3d 29, 772 N.Y.S.2d 275 (2004), lv. denied 3 N.Y.3d 608, 785 N.Y.S.2d 26, 818 N.E.2d 668 (2004) (professional misconduct which included converting and failing to return client funds, drafting and filing false petitions and affidavits, engaging in improper solicitations and charging and collecting excessive fees, despite otherwise unblemished record and character evidence, warranted disbarment); Matter of Gadye, 283 A.D.2d 1, 726 N.Y.S.2d 401 (2001) (where attorney neglected numerous client matters, engaged in bad faith court filings, failed to comply with court orders, failed to advise clients of conflict of interest issues, and committed acts of fraud, dishonesty, and misrepresentation, disbarment appropriate sanction); Matter of Brooks, 271 A.D.2d 127, 708 N.Y.S.2d 22 (2000), lv. dismissed 95 N.Y.2d 955, 722 N.Y.S.2d 468, 745 N.E.2d 388 (2000) (attorney who neglected legal matters, engaged in dishonesty involving clients, fabricated three orders and a bond, neglected numerous client matters, repeatedly failed to comply with court orders and directives, advancing claims he knew were unwarranted, filing documents with false information and false notarization was disbarred); Matter of Feldman, 252 A.D.2d 76, 682 N.Y.S.2d 204 (1998) (attorney disbarred when, over course of seven years involving four separate matters, he neglected legal matters entrusted to him and engaged in acts of misrepresentation, deceit and forgery in attempting to conceal behavior); Matter of Goffe, 209 A.D.2d 124, 624 N.Y.S.2d 592 (1995) (under doctrine of reciprocal discipline, attorney disbarred where he was found to have engaged in conduct involving dishonesty, fraud, deceit and misrepresentation, conduct prejudicial to the administration of justice, proffered fabricated or altered evidence to the IRS and the United States Tax Court and lied under oath before the Tax Court).

Respondent had the opportunity to put in evidence at the original hearing and again thereafter at the supplemental proceeding. Based on the record respondent developed, we find that the higher sanction is appropriate (see Matter of Gilbert, supra; Matter of Dinhofer, 257 A.D.2d 326, 690 N.Y.S.2d 245 (1999); Matter of Aschheim, 224 A.D.2d 149, 647 N.Y.S.2d 221 (1996)). In reaching this determination, we note that the evidence respondent submitted to supplement the record does not address the underlying conduct giving rise to the charges of professional misconduct. Rather, it was offered only to explain her negative behavior at the hearing. As such, it cannot serve to lessen the sanction for an underlying pattern of conduct as egregious and dishonest as was otherwise established against this respondent. We add and emphasize that we have reached this conclusion only with the greatest regard for our sister state's disciplinary system on the one hand, but with a sincere, profound and respectful disagreement with its supplemental decision reducing respondent's sanction from disbarment to a three year suspension.

Accordingly, the Committee's petition should be denied to the extent that it seeks to impose a sanction of a suspension of three years and granted to the extent that it seeks findings of misconduct and an alternate sanction, and respondent should be disbarred and her name stricken from the roll of attorneys.

Respondent's name was stricken from the roll of attorneys and counselors-at-law in the State of New York, effective December 9, 2004.

QUESTIONS ABOUT THE CASE:

1 Although there are numerous charges of misconduct against the attorney in this case, explain the allegations concerning falsifying court documents and eliciting false testimony from a witness at trial.
2 The attorney in this case also tried to get her paralegal to engage in several unethical practices. What were they?
3 The court refers to the fact that the attorney lacked a basic understanding of the trust that must exist between an attorney and her clients. Explain what the court means by this statement.

4 Does the fact that the attorney here was suffering from depression and was on medication mitigate her actions? Why or why not?
5 How would you, as a paralegal, conduct your own affairs if you had found yourself working for this attorney?

Chapter Summary

The trial is the culmination of months or even years of preparatory work that has included discovery, investigation, and drafting of pleadings. Preparing for a trial is absolutely necessary in order to ensure that both parties have the evidence and witness testimony they need to proceed on their claims. The actual trial begins with jury selection. Parties are given a specific number of peremptory jury strikes that they may use to remove panel members for any reason. If a juror indicates that she is unable to follow the court's directions, she may be removed for cause. After the jury is selected, the parties proceed to opening statements, where they outline facts in the case and what they intend to prove at trial. Once opening statements have concluded, the plaintiff presents his case, proceeding from witness to witness and offering evidence until the plaintiff believes that he has presented sufficient proof to prove the allegations in the complaint. At the conclusion of the plaintiff's case, the defendant is permitted to move for a directed verdict. If the judge grants this motion, it means that the plaintiff's case will be dismissed and the judge will enter a verdict in the defendant's favor. If the motion is denied, the defendant is free to present his own case, including witness testimony and evidence. At the conclusion of the defense case, the parties meet in a brief charge conference where they discuss the instructions that the jury will receive at the conclusion of the case. Following the charge conference, the parties will engage in closing arguments, which summarize their perspectives on the case and request the jury to vote in their favor. At this point, the judge will read jury instructions and then release the members of the jury to confer with one another in the jury room. The jury's decision is the verdict. When the jury announces its verdict, the judge imposes the jury's decision on the parties through a judgment.

SKILLS YOU NEED IN THE REAL WORLD

Preparing Witnesses to Testify

It is often extremely helpful to prepare a small demonstration of how the direct and cross-examination of a witness is most likely to proceed. Go over the questions with the witness to let her know what will be asked on direct examination and what kinds of questions she can expect on cross-examination. Take the witness to the actual courthouse several days before the trial begins and show her where the courtroom is and how it is laid out. Show her where she will be seated and how to speak into the microphone, if one is provided. Witnesses who go through this process are often a great deal less anxious about testifying. Courthouse personnel are typically accommodating and will allow access to the courtroom when court is not in session if you call ahead and ask for permission.

Trials are often rescheduled at the last moment. It is common for a trial to be continued until the next week or month. You must be adept at shifting gears at a moment's notice and be able explain this to witnesses and clients.

Many people respond to anxiety with unreasonable demands and anger. You must be able to recognize that these mood swings are in direct response to the growing anxiety about the upcoming trial. Working with witnesses is often a challenge to your people skills, but if handled well, it can make the difference between winning and losing a case.

THE LIFE OF A PARALEGAL

Preparing for Trial

Cheryl Jones has worked as a paralegal for over 11 years, primarily for a prominent attorney in a small community. "I specialize primarily in domestic law and criminal law. My personal motto has always been: The attorney (or firm) is only as good as his or her paralegals. When the paralegal's work is below par, the attorney's reputation and business may suffer. Let's face it—clients interact more often with the paralegal than the attorney. I strive for perfection or pretty darn close in every task I tackle, whether answering the phone or assisting in trial. I believe the quality and professionalism of my work assisted me in obtaining and maintaining respect and a personal yet professional rapport with the judges, court personnel, attorneys, and other paralegals. A great paralegal should exude confidence as well as knowledge and should learn how to professionally complement the attorney.

"In my experience, it is imperative that new paralegals familiarize themselves with and know the Local Rules of Court. In my experience, I have learned that attorneys generally know the Rules of Civil Procedure, but most depend on their paralegals to thoroughly know the Local Rules of Court and procedures to enforce the Local Rules of Court."

When Cheryl prepares for trial, she does her homework. "I believe the most important aspect in assisting at trial happens before the trial. All paralegals should know the contents of the file, especially discovery. While in trial, I have developed the art of intense listening while multitasking. My goal is to listen to my attorney's line of questioning and predict where his questioning is going—doing this makes you and your attorney appear competent and professional in the eyes of a jury. About 99.9 percent of the time, I know the direction my attorney is taking the witness during direct or cross-examination and know what document or exhibit to pull out of the file for his use before he asks for it. Some attorneys and prosecutors pre-label exhibits and follow outlines, but my attorney does everything 'off the cuff,' which makes my job crucial.

"Another important aspect of being a litigation paralegal is effective legal research skills. On one occasion, I had to leave the courtroom and travel back to the office to pull supporting case law. When I returned to the courtroom and handed the cases to my attorney, he asked if the cases were in our favor, and I gave him an affirmative nod. Because of his confidence in my abilities, he was able to hand the court and opposing counsel copies of the case law without fully reviewing it first."

ETHICAL ISSUES FOR THE PARALEGAL

Preparing Witnesses for Trial

One of the issues that always arises when working with witnesses who will testify at trial concerns the difference between coaching a witness and preparing a witness. Coaching a witness is telling the witness what she should say and is not only unethical but also may fall under the crime of tampering with a witness. Preparing a witness is not considered to be an ethical or a legal violation. The question often arises, What is the difference? A legal professional coaches a witness by taking that witness through questions that will likely be asked at trial and telling the witness how she should respond. Legal professionals are sometimes tempted to take these issues into their own hands, especially when they are dealing with reluctant or overly shy witnesses. But attorneys and paralegals are barred from providing witnesses with their answers. Preparing a witness involves asking the witness questions that she might be asked at trial and then determining how the witness will respond. In the first example, the legal professional is providing the answers; in the second, the legal professional is noting what the witness's responses will be. The best approach to take with witnesses is to advise them to tell their own story truthfully. Witness coaching often backfires on the legal team when the witness suddenly reveals that one side scripted her responses. The jury will usually disregard the witness's entire testimony, and the judge will probably contact the state bar.

Websites

- **Bureau of Justice Statistics — Search for Statistics on State and Federal Civil Trials**
  www.bjs.gov

- **The Ten Commandments of Cross-Examination**
  www.thefederation.org/documents/Pratt-SP03.htm

- **Nolo.com — Direct Examination**
  www.nolo.com/dictionary/direct-examination-term.html

- **American Bar Association — Preparing Witnesses for Trial, What You Can and Can't Do**
  www.abanet.org/litigation/programs/cle_052506.html

Key Terms

Calendar call
Challenge for cause
Conflict letter
Cross-examination
Direct examination
Judgment
Jurors
Jury charge
Jury strike
Motion for directed verdict
Panel
Peremptory jury strike
Pretrial conference
Pretrial order
Voir dire

Review Questions

1. Explain the importance of preparing for trial.
2. What role can a paralegal play in trial preparation?
3. Explain how exhibits can be used in a trial.
4. Why is it necessary to organize the case file prior to trial?
5. What is a trial notebook?
6. What is a charge conference?
7. Explain a motion for directed verdict.
8. Describe how a juror would be struck for cause.
9. Describe peremptory jury strikes.
10. List the various phases of a civil trial.
11. Describe the process of selecting a jury.
12. What is the purpose of an opening statement?
13. Compare and contrast direct and cross-examination.
14. Why would an attorney conduct a mock trial before the actual trial?
15. Explain the function of the closing argument.
16. What are jury instructions?
17. What is a verdict?
18. Compare and contrast verdicts and judgments.
19. Are all of the various phases of a civil trial actually necessary? Is there a way to streamline or even eliminate some of these phases? Explain your answer.

Applying What You Have Learned

1. Prepare an issue table for the major issues presented in the case you created in Chapters 4 and 5.

2. Review the pleadings from Chapters 4 and 5, and then prepare at least 10 possible jury charges that the plaintiff would most likely submit to the judge.

3. Discuss the important activities that a paralegal would carry out, from the initial meeting with a client to the day before a jury trial.

4. Prepare a chronology of events in the case you created in Chapters 4 and 5.

5 Next week, your firm has a case that is likely to go to trial. The plaintiff is a young man who was struck by a delivery truck owned by the national corporation Get It There Deliveries. You have just met with the plaintiff and two of the people who were in the car with him at the time of the accident. During his deposition, several months ago, the plaintiff claimed that the delivery truck driver came up to him after the accident and admitted fault, saying that he failed to yield and thus caused the accident. When Al Able and Billy Better were originally deposed, they said they had not heard any statement by the delivery truck driver. Before your firm's meeting with the three men, you saw them talking with another attorney who has only recently come to work for the firm. During the meeting, Al and Billy suddenly change their story and say that they had heard the deliveryman make a statement. You and your supervising attorney separate the men and ask them about this statement. In both circumstances, the men make identical statements, saying, "The driver came up to the car and said, 'Hey, I was at fault. I should have yielded. I'm to blame.'"

What, if anything, should you do about new evidence?

Damages

10

Chapter Objectives

- Explain the difference between compensatory damages and punitive damages
- Compare and contrast general damages with special damages
- Create a list of specific types of damages and categorize them
- Describe how attorneys present damages to juries
- Describe how to measure future lost income
- Explain how attorneys prove damages at trial
- Define the importance of fair market value in property loss
- Explain the collateral source rule
- Describe the doctrine of mitigation of damages
- Define a court's equity power

I INTRODUCTION

In any civil case, the plaintiff must prove that the defendant is liable for the plaintiff's loss and the extent of that loss. **Damages** refer to the monetary, property, or personal losses suffered by the plaintiff. The point of an award of damages is to restore the plaintiff to the condition he was in prior to the injury, when possible. Damages are

Damages
The amount of money that the plaintiff requests of the defendant in a civil suit

also designed to punish the defendant for his willful actions or wanton disregard for the safety of others. Because civil damages serve so many functions, we will begin this chapter with a general discussion of what damages are and then address the specific types of damages available in civil cases. For the sake of clarity, we will refer to damages that are tied to tort law. There are also damages available in breach of contract, breach of warranty, and other civil actions. These damage actions are proven differently as we will see when we address equitable remedies later in this chapter.

Requiring one party to pay for the injuries she inflicts on another is not a new idea. As far back as the Old Testament, there were provisions that a person who injured another must pay a fee. This fee varied according to the type of injury, with loss of hand valued higher than loss of finger. Rather than continuing to impose an eye for an eye, societies realized that it made more sense — and caused much less violence — to impose a monetary fine for the negligent behavior of others.[1]

In the last few chapters, we have outlined the various steps involved in bringing and proving a suit. Now we shall address the concept of proof of damages: In a basic civil suit, the plaintiff files a complaint and alleges a loss that might be financial, physical, or emotional and alleges that the defendant is responsible for that loss. Proof of the defendant's proximate cause for that loss is only the first step. Next, the plaintiff must establish that he has suffered a legally recognized wrong. According to the Restatement of Torts, damages are defined as "a sum of money awarded to a person injured by a tort of another."[2] This definition provides an excellent summary of the purpose of awarding damages. If the jury determines that the defendant is liable, then the jury is empowered to award damages to the plaintiff. On the other hand, if the jury determines that the defendant is not liable, then there is no consideration of damages. Determining the type of damages and how best to prove these at trial are the main functions of the attorneys for both the plaintiff and the defendant. While the plaintiff's legal team will focus on how best to show the jury that the plaintiff has suffered a legal wrong, the defendant's attorney will focus on any evidence that tends to mitigate or completely cancel out the defendant's responsibility for paying such damages.

II TYPES OF DAMAGES

The damages available in civil cases are often classified into three broad categories:

- Compensatory damages
- Punitive damages
- Nominal damages

A. COMPENSATORY DAMAGES

Compensatory damages An award by the jury (or judge) designed to compensate the plaintiff for physical or financial losses

Compensatory damages are designed to do exactly what their title suggests: compensate the victim for losses caused by the defendant's negligent conduct. The stated purpose of compensatory damages is to place the plaintiff in the condition she was in prior to the injury. Of course, that is often impossible. In situations where returning the plaintiff to her original condition is impossible, compensatory damages are designed to compensate the plaintiff for the change in her condition. Some jurisdictions define compensatory damages as the monetary assessments paid by the defendant to "make the plaintiff whole" again.

When the plaintiff's injuries are financial, the jury's award of money is designed to put the plaintiff back in the situation he was in before the defendant's actions. When the plaintiff's injuries are physical, money is seen as a form of compensation for aggravation, pain and suffering, and other losses, even when these conditions are not easy to assess on a monetary scale. The plaintiff can recover for all harm: past, present, and future. Compensatory damages are usually broken into two separate categories: general damages and special damages.

1. GENERAL DAMAGES

General damages are those payments made by the defendant to the plaintiff that are most closely associated with the defendant's act. General damages are difficult to quantify. One example of general damages is pain and suffering. Just how much is a person's pain and suffering worth? Obviously, different people will have different answers to this question, and any of the plaintiff's requests that fall into this category of subjective injury usually qualify as general damages. In such cases, the jurors are often called upon to rely on their own life experiences in determining an amount.

General damages
A monetary award by a jury (or judge) that is closely tied to the defendant's actions but has no preset or easily quantifiable amount[3]

a. Calculating Damages

Although calculating such damages is difficult and varies considerably from jury to jury or even region to region, there are some basic guidelines. The more severe the injury, the more money the jury is likely to award. A scar on a person's face will justify a much larger award than a similar scar on a person's leg. However, because the very nature of general damages is so subjective, these awards have come under increasing criticism. The fact that similar cases can have such divergent results is often seen as one of the primary weaknesses of the American civil justice system. Further complicating the issue is the fact that most jurisdictions do not require the plaintiff to state a specific amount sought for general damages. Instead, plaintiffs leave the final determination up to the jury.

Sidebar

The Restatement of Torts defines general damages as those injuries that result so frequently from most negligence and other tort actions that their existence can be assumed and their amount can be proven at trial.

PRACTICE POINTER ▶ ORGANIZING DAMAGES

When organizing a case for trial, keep a separate section for the damages. All medical bills, payment stubs, expert analyses, lost wages, and the dozens of other documents related to proof of damages at trial should be categorized, recorded, and calculated. You should also include a master list of all these items so that you can double-check with the client that all bills have been listed.

b. Pain and Suffering

One of the most hotly contested issues in civil cases concerns the issue of the plaintiff's claim for compensation for pain and suffering. What precisely qualifies under this definition? The law is vague, perhaps deliberately so. Most jurisdictions follow a formula that allows the jury to assess a sum that a "reasonable person" would find acceptable to compensate the plaintiff for the constant pain and suffering caused by an injury. Of course, the very vagueness of the definition often results in widely divergent jury awards.

Because general damages are, by their very nature, difficult to quantify, attorneys have developed several different presentation styles to sway the jury to award pain and suffering to plaintiffs. For example, an attorney might make a **per diem** argument.

Per diem
Latin for "by the day," or daily

A per diem argument is based on a simple calculation: How much would it be worth to a person, on a daily basis, to forgo specific pain? An attorney might argue that any reasonable person might be willing to pay $5 a day not to have the persistent ache from the injury in a car wreck or from a botched medical procedure. Applying the $5 per day formula for 365 days in a year equals $1,825. The best estimates show that the plaintiff might live as long as 30 additional years. Multiplying the per diem by that life span equals an award of $54,750. The attorney would then argue that the only reasonable award in this case would be an award in excess of $50,000 for the plaintiff's suffering, in addition to any other awards that the jury might make.

Of course, there is nothing predetermined about the attorney's argument. The defense attorney might easily argue that the plaintiff is not entitled to any pain and suffering, let alone a daily charge for the rest of the plaintiff's life to put up with pain that has already faded away. There is no state that imposes a per diem formula in any personal injury case.

2. SPECIAL DAMAGES

Special damages
Damages, such as lost wages or medical bills, that can be calculated with specificity

Special damages are those damages that are usually easier to quantify because they have specific amounts. Examples of special damages are items such as the plaintiff's total medical bill for the injuries sustained in a car wreck, the additional fees that the plaintiff was charged by other doctors to repair the damage in a medical malpractice case, or even the total time that the plaintiff lost from work while recuperating from her injuries. Plaintiffs routinely plead the specific amounts of medical bills and other special damages in their complaints. At trial, the plaintiff will be required to present proof of the amount of her special damages before the jury will be authorized to make an award.

a. Lost Wages

A prime example of special damages is lost wages. When the plaintiff alleges that the injuries caused by the defendant's actions resulted in the plaintiff's lost time from work, the plaintiff must present something more than the bald assertion of how much he would have made if he had worked. As we will see later in this chapter, actually proving losses can involve complicated testimony. Lost wages are an excellent example of how detailed the plaintiff's attorney must get in order to successfully plead this issue to the jury.

In order to prove the plaintiff's lost wages, the plaintiff's attorney must present tax returns, paycheck stubs, affidavits from employers or clients, and other information, including IRS forms and similar items. The plaintiff's paralegal is usually the person responsible for gathering and organizing all of this information for use at trial.

PRACTICE POINTER ▶ GATHERING MATERIAL TO PROVE DAMAGES

Because gathering all of the material together to prove civil damages can be a time-consuming project, it is important for you to communicate with the client the necessity of tracking down every bill. Unfortunately, clients aren't always as organized as we would like them to be. You may send home questionnaires and checklists, but some clients lack the diligence to complete them. In the end, you may find that your attempts to communicate the importance of finding all of the bills fall on deaf ears. In some cases, you may find yourself going through the client's records yourself, just to be absolutely sure that all documents required to prove the damages at trial have been produced.

b. Medical Bills

Medical bills are another example of special damages. In personal injury and medical malpractice cases, the client may have amassed enormous medical bills and will request that the defendant pay all of the ones directly related to the defendant's negligence. Plaintiffs are often anxious about pending medical bills. They may be receiving telephone calls from bill collectors and letters in the mail from medical providers demanding payment. The best practice is for the plaintiff's attorney to intercede on the client's behalf and contact all medical providers to inform them that the case has gone to litigation. This often results in the creditors waiting until the resolution of the case before making additional demands. In modern practice, it is usually the paralegal who must meet with the client, sort through the medical bills, and then organize them to make sure the plaintiff is requesting payment for every bill. These amounts will then be listed in the complaint.

c. Future Losses

A plaintiff is permitted to seek recovery for future medical services that are "reasonably certain" to be needed for the plaintiff's future care. The award for future losses is designed to anticipate all reasonable expenses connected to future medical care, including charges by doctors, nurses, therapists, and medical suppliers. The plaintiff is also entitled to compensation for being required to hire someone else to perform her job while she is incapacitated. However, a plaintiff is not legally entitled to compensation for lost "time" — that is, the time she lost from leisure activities while recuperating from injuries.

At the end of the trial, the jurors will be instructed that before they can determine an amount of future lost income, they must calculate the difference between what the plaintiff's future income would have been before he was injured and what it will be now that he has been injured. Proving lost future income usually involves expert testimony. The expert will calculate future lost income based on complicated formulas involving the plaintiff's past income, education, likelihood of promotion, probable life span, and a wide range of other factors.

d. Emotional Distress

The rules about suing for emotional distress vary from state to state. Although most states allow some claim for the emotional and mental impact of the injuries sustained by the defendant's actions, not all of them allow a plaintiff to recover for purely psychological injuries. In those jurisdictions, the emotional impact must be coupled with some physical impact. For instance, in these jurisdictions, a plaintiff could not request damages when the defendant's actions cause the plaintiff to lose sleep or to feel anxious but there was no physical injury. In many other jurisdictions, this requirement of physical trauma has either slowly eroded away or been replaced entirely with actions allowing recovery for purely emotional or psychological injuries.[4] An award of damages for emotional distress, or mental anguish, can include the plaintiff's sufferings in the past and any mental distress the plaintiff is likely to endure in the future.[5]

e. Loss of Consortium

Loss of consortium
A claim filed by the plaintiff's spouse for the loss of companionship in the marriage, caused by the injuries

Another type of damage that falls into a special category is a **loss of consortium** claim. This is a claim raised by the injured plaintiff's spouse. This claim states that when the plaintiff was injured, the marital relations between the plaintiff and the spouse were also injured. In all jurisdictions, the spouse is entitled to file some form of loss of consortium claim. The spouse is entitled to damages for the loss of companionship, affection, sexual relations, and other losses that frequently occur when one spouse is incapacitated. At trial, the plaintiff's legal team will be required to present evidence to support the spouse's claim. This often comes in the form of the oral testimony of the spouse, who takes the stand and discusses the marital relationship prior to the injury and the state of the relationship postinjury. Some of this testimony will involve intimate details about the couple's sexual history before and after the incident.

With recent developments in the law of marriage, it is currently an open question if a loss of consortium claim could be sustained by a gay married couple or individuals who have entered into a civil union.

f. Bad Faith Damages

Often confused with punitive damages (discussed later), bad faith damages generally do not involve the facts of the case. Instead, bad faith damages involve a specific party's conduct during the litigation. For instance, if a plaintiff brings a lawsuit solely for the purpose of harassing the defendant, the plaintiff may be subject to bad faith damages. In such a situation, the court might order that the plaintiff pay the costs of the action and the defendant's attorney fee. Normally, the losing party in a suit is not required to pay the fees of the opposing attorney. However, when a party files frivolous claims or has engaged in unethical or unfair tactics, a judge is authorized to make such an award.[6] Bad faith damages are not seen in all cases and are actually awarded in a minority of cases, but they have become important in recent decades and are certainly more prevalent than they were 25 years ago.

B. PUNITIVE DAMAGES

Punitive damages Monetary assessments by the jury against a party that are designed to punish or make an example of the party for others

Punitive damages are a separate category of damages from the compensatory damage issues we have addressed so far. All compensatory damages are designed to serve the same function: to reimburse the plaintiff for losses, even when those losses are difficult to quantify. But punitive damages serve a completely different purpose. If requested by the plaintiff, an award of punitive damages against a defendant is the jury's way of punishing the defendant for particular actions. They are awarded in addition to compensatory damages. Punitive damages are sometimes called *exemplary damages* or *vindictive damages* or even *smart money* damages. When the jury awards punitive damages, the jurors are sending a message to the defendant and the rest of society that the defendant's conduct in the case was unacceptable. A jury might award punitive damages when it is obvious that the defendant acted in wanton disregard for the safety of others or engaged in willfully dangerous conduct that caused injury to others. Because the jury in a civil case is not empowered to request jail time for the defendant, the only real punitive action the jury can take is financial.

Many states have passed so-called tort reform statutes that usually target punitive damages. In these states, it is common for a statute to limit the total of punitive damages. The typical formula is to limit punitive damages to an amount that is three times the total of all compensatory damages. If the defendant were awarded compensatory damages totaling $1,500, for example, then the most that the jury could assess against the defendant in punitive damages would be $4,500. This amount would be added to the award for compensatory damages and would result in a total award of $6,000.

Consider the following example: Micah has brought suit against Reginald, alleging that Reginald willfully endangered him by driving down a sidewalk one evening. Micah managed to jump out of the way of the speeding car and thankfully only received a scratch on his face. He has sued Reginald for emotional distress, negligence, lost time from work, and other compensatory damages in the amount of $5,000. He has also requested that the jury assess punitive damages against Reginald. Micah's case is brought in a state that has recently enacted a maximum award on punitive damages. The jury determines that Reginald's actions were particularly dangerous and assesses a $1 million award for punitive damages. The jury also finds that Micah should receive compensatory damages in the amount of $500. Will Reginald be able to reduce the total award when he appeals the case?

Answer: Yes. Because this is a tort reform state, the most that the jury can award—even in an egregious case—is three times the total of the compensatory damages. Micah's compensatory damages were only $500; therefore, the total punitive damages are limited to $1,500.

LEGAL LEGWORK ■ PUNITIVE DAMAGES

Has your state imposed limitations or caps on punitive damages awards? If so, what are those limitations? Copy out the statute, summarize it, and place it in your portfolio.

C. NOMINAL DAMAGES

The final category of monetary damages is nominal damages. A nominal damage is the jury's award of a small amount of money to the plaintiff. In some cases, the plaintiff may have received a legal injury, but the jury does not believe that a large payment is either warranted or justified. In such a case, the jury may award the plaintiff the amount of $1, in order to show that although the plaintiff presented a technically proficient case, the plaintiff's actual injuries are nonexistent as far as the jury is concerned.

PRACTICE POINTER ▶ EXAMINING OPINIONS

When courts review the award of damages in civil cases, they will first summarize the important facts and then the plaintiff's injuries. Many times, you can anticipate the court's final decision in the case by examining the court's word choice early in the opinion. If the court downplays the plaintiff's injuries or emphasizes the failure of the plaintiff to effectively preserve certain issues for appeal, you can often see the writing on the wall for what the ultimate decision will be. This language is important because it signals the outcome and it gives you a checklist of what not to do in your own cases.

III PROVING DAMAGES

We now know that the plaintiff must present proof of her damages at trial, but that spurs an additional question: How much proof is required? Can the plaintiff simply make an allegation that she is entitled to X amount of dollars, or is more required? If more is required, how much more?

The general rule about proof of damages is that the same degree of proof is required to prove losses as was required to prove the other elements of the case. In many jurisdictions, this means that the plaintiff must present proof to a preponderance of the evidence that he is entitled to an award. The practical side of this burden of proof is that the plaintiff must prove not only that the defendant was the cause of his injuries, but also the nature, extent, and full amount of the financial, property, and emotional losses he suffered as a result of the defendant's actions.

Courts also require certainty in calculating damages. A trial judge will not authorize damages when the plaintiff's claim is based on mere conjecture or a vague idea of what her injuries are. Trial judges are also authorized to overturn a jury's award of damages if the judge believes that the jury did not rely on testimony and evidence and instead simply voted with their feelings.[7]

A. DISTINGUISHING BETWEEN GENERAL AND SPECIAL DAMAGES

Why is there a distinction between general and special damages? The first answer to that question goes to the practical difficulties of presenting evidence about both at the trial.

General damages, because they are difficult to quantify, are harder to prove than special damages. After all, special damages involve specific and quantified items, such as medical bills, while general damages involve intangibles such as pain and suffering and loss of emotional support. Proving these damages often involves testimony from the plaintiff's friends and family about the effect that the accident has had on him. This testimony is, by its very nature, purely subjective. On the other hand, special damages involve presentations of bills and other hard evidence. They are not subjective and present the jury with a straightforward proposition. If the jurors believe that the defendant is responsible for the plaintiff's damages, they will usually award special damages with little difficulty. It should come as no surprise, then, that another important difference between general and special damages is that an award of general damages is more easily appealed than an award of special damages.

B. PRESENTING PROOF AT TRIAL

Because of the inherent difficulties in proving general damages, attorneys have been very creative over the years in attempting to show the jury why the plaintiff is entitled to general damages. One excellent presentation tool is the "day in the life" video.

A day in the life video is a professional presentation that tracks the plaintiff's activities during the day, following her from the moment that she wakes up and through bathing, eating, and driving to see doctors. A day in the life video can be a powerful

Tech Topic
DAY IN THE LIFE VIDEO

This chapter mentions using "day in the life" videos as a way to show the jury exactly what a typical day is like for an injured plaintiff. Such videos can have a dramatic effect on the jury. Instead of simply hearing about how difficult it is for someone without the use of her legs to get out of bed, put on clothes, make breakfast, and go to work, the jury can actually see it. They can hear the plaintiff grunt with effort when climbing into a wheelchair, see the plaintiff navigate through a house that was never designed with a handicapped person in mind, and get an idea of the thousand little indignities such a handicap can bring.

If your firm is considering using a day in the life video, it is important to do the preparation work necessary to pull it all together. Long before the cameras come out, spend some time with the plaintiff going through his daily activities and make extensive notes. The videographer will need this information to set up the cameras, lights, and microphones. Shooting a day in the life video isn't as simple as following the plaintiff around with a camera. In order for the jury to see and understand what is happening, it is often necessary for the videographer to shoot a scene from several different angles. That means using more than one camera or having the plaintiff reenact certain actions from different viewpoints. Both you and the plaintiff must be aware of the procedures involved. If you are in doubt, talk with the videographer long before the day of the shooting. It will make for a much smoother process, with less stress on the client.

evidentiary tool, especially when the plaintiff suffers from terrible injuries. The jury can actually see just how difficult common tasks have become for the plaintiff. The video will also show the plaintiff interacting with others, such as home health care nurses. As a visual aid, they are unsurpassed for giving the jury an accurate, and often unforgettable, view of the plaintiff's life. The final award in the case usually justifies the added expense of creating it.

C. PROVING PROPERTY LOSSES

Different types of evidence are required to prove the existence of different types of damages. Property losses, for example, are handled differently than the evidence presented to prove pain and suffering.

When the plaintiff claims damage to or reduction in value of her property, she must present some evidence showing what the value of the property was before the defendant's actions and what the value of the property is after the defendant's negligence. This often involves calculations of the **fair market value** of the property. Fair market value is usually determined by an appraiser — that is, someone who is an expert in the field and can give an accurate estimate of the property's value.

Fair market value
The amount that a willing buyer would pay for an item that a willing seller would accept

Consider the following example: Juan was recently in a car wreck. His car was rear-ended by the defendant while he was waiting for a traffic light to change. The damage to Juan's car was drastic, and an appraiser has set its value at $100. Before the accident, Juan was in negotiations to sell the car to a friend. The final sale price that they had reached was $5,500. The appraiser agrees that the value of the car prior to the accident was probably at least $5,500. How much in property damages can Juan request in his complaint against the defendant?

Answer: Juan's property damages will be $5,500. Because an expert can testify that the sale price Juan and his friend had agreed to was approximately what the fair market value would have been, Juan can request that amount. If he receives it, the jury will deduct $100 from the total amount. Why?

D. THE COLLATERAL SOURCE RULE

There are some important legal doctrines that can affect the total amount that a plaintiff may receive. One such critical doctrine is the **collateral source rule** (Fig. 10-1). When a jurisdiction follows the collateral source rule, it means that the jury cannot be told that the plaintiff has already been compensated for part of her loss through insurance or other benefits. The theory is that the plaintiff should not be penalized for a reduction in the final award simply because she has taken the precaution of obtaining insurance or receiving some other form of compensation for injuries received. Many states follow the collateral source rule, believing that if the jury knows that the plaintiff has already been compensated out of other sources, they may reduce the total amount of the damage award to the plaintiff. The proponents of the collateral source rule also point out that if the jury does award a plaintiff damages for which she has already been compensated, the plaintiff is not permitted to keep them. Instead, any excess will go to the plaintiff's insurers to defray their costs for compensating the plaintiff in the first place.

Collateral source rule
A rule of evidence that prohibits the jury from being informed about the plaintiff's other sources of compensation, such as insurance, worker's compensation, and so on

The purpose of the collateral source rule is to exclude evidence of payments made to the plaintiff by sources other than the defendant when this evidence is offered for the purpose of diminishing the defendant's liability to the injured plaintiff. The policy behind the rule is to prevent a tortfeasor from reducing his own liability for damages by the amount of compensation the injured party receives from an independent source. This rule is punitive in nature and is intended to prevent the tortfeasor from a windfall when a portion of the plaintiff's damages have been paid by a collateral source.[8]

FIGURE 10-1

Collateral Source Rule

In cases where an insurance company has compensated the plaintiff for her injuries, the company is entitled to seek payment of those damages from the defendant through the principle of **subrogation**. When an insurance company brings a subrogation action against the defendant, it is entitled to sue in the plaintiff's place for reimbursement for the funds paid out to the plaintiff under the insurance policy.

Subrogation
The principle that allows one party to bring suit in the name of another, usually in an insurance setting

E. MITIGATION OF DAMAGES

In addition to the collateral source rule, there are other important legal principles that often come into play in assessing damages. For example, the concept of **mitigation of damages** often plays an important role in determining a final award amount.

Mitigation of damages
The doctrine that holds that it is the plaintiff's responsibility to lessen his potential injuries or losses by taking reasonable actions to seek medical treatment or take other precautions when a reasonable person in the same situation would have done so

Under the doctrine of mitigation of damages, a plaintiff is required to lessen his damages whenever reasonably possible. This means that the plaintiff is not permitted to refuse medical treatment for the injuries caused by the defendant's negligence or allow property to be destroyed when the plaintiff could have taken reasonable steps to protect it. The consequences for failing to mitigate damages are that the plaintiff's ultimate monetary award at trial will be reduced.

Consider the following example: When Juan was injured in his car wreck, he refused medical treatment. His back continued to ache, but he ignored all advice to seek medical help. Two weeks later, when Juan was in unbearable pain, an emergency room doctor diagnosed him with an aggravated and herniated disk in his spine. The disk would not have been in such bad shape had Juan gone to the hospital immediately after the accident and been put into a proper restraint. At trial, the defendant alleges that he should not be liable for the additional medical bills related to Juan's failure to seek medical assistance. Will the defendant be successful?

Answer: Yes. Because Juan, like all plaintiffs, is required to mitigate his damages when reasonable, his failure to seek medical aid appears to be a clear case where the doctrine of mitigation will affect his total amount of damages.

Although we have framed the issues surrounding mitigation in terms of medical treatment, the concept also holds true for other civil disputes. In contract litigation, for example, a vendor has the obligation to sell perishable merchandise to other customers, even when the original customer wrongfully refuses to buy. Without such action, the vendor would be barred from seeking damages for the loss of the entire order. Of course, the vendor can always sue the original customer for the difference between what she would have gotten from the original transaction and the lower amount the vendor received when forced to sell to another.[9]

F. PRIOR INJURIES

One of the most effective attacks that the defendant's attorney can mount against the plaintiff is a claim that the plaintiff was actually injured in a prior accident and that this prior accident is what caused his pain, not the incident involving the defendant in the current case. A paralegal should always ask the plaintiff about any prior medical problems, including prior accidents or collisions. Any prior injury that is even vaguely like the current injury should be closely documented. At trial, the plaintiff's attorney will have to address this issue of prior injuries to make sure the jury comprehends the difference in the injuries received in the pending case and those suffered by the plaintiff in other situations.

IV EQUITABLE REMEDIES

In addition to requesting an award of monetary damages, a plaintiff is also allowed to request specific actions by the court. There are times when a plaintiff's demands cannot be satisfied by monetary damages. Instead, the plaintiff might request an injunction to prevent the defendant from taking some action. Courts in the United States have the power both to assess monetary damages and to use their **equity** powers to force individuals to do (or in some cases not do) specific things. *Equity* refers to a court's power to enforce justice through a wide variety of means, including contempt powers, injunctions, and other mechanisms. Although the U.S. court system is closely patterned on the English judicial system, the early colonies made some important changes. In the English system, a party was forced to go to one court to request an equitable action, such as an injunction, and another court to request an award of money damages. Our system combined these powers into one court, thus giving American judges both judicial and equitable powers.

Equity
A trial court's authority to order individuals and corporations to do (or not do) certain activities because they are unjust

Consider the following example: Carl believes that recent development in his area of town has endangered the water supply and violated state and federal environmental laws. He brings suit but is not requesting money. Instead, he wants the court to order a halt to all new sewer hookups until the county complies with statutes to undertake an environmental impact study on the rapid growth in the area. Does the court have the power to order such an action?

Answer: Assuming that Carl brings his suit in the correct court, yes, the trial judge can order an injunction that bars any new sewage hookups in the county (effectively bringing all new building to a halt) until the county complies with the judge's order.

When a plaintiff brings suit requesting an **injunction**, as Carl is doing in the example above, the plaintiff is asking the court for an order specifically directing someone to stop doing a specific action. In this case, the court could order that the county cease issuing new sewage permits until an environmental study has been completed. If it does not, the judge has the power to impose a wide variety of sanctions, including daily fines and possible jail time under the court's contempt powers.

Injunction
A court order that demands a certain action or that prohibits a certain action

Of course, we have oversimplified the issues a bit. A court generally would always hold a hearing before ordering any injunction and would give county officials the opportunity to address the issues raised in Carl's suit.

A court's equity power can be exercised alongside its normal powers. For example, it is common for the parties in a personal injury suit to seek a **declaratory judgment** about a particular issue in the case. An insurance company might file such an action to determine if it is legally bound to provide (and pay for) a legal defense in a situation where their insured is sued.

Declaratory judgment
A court order that specifies the duties and obligations of a party

Another example of an equitable remedy is a **temporary restraining order**. This order specifically directs a person to stop doing a specific action and sets a date for a full-blown court hearing on the plaintiff's request. Temporary restraining orders are usually seen in situations where immediate action is required and there is no time to set a later court date. They are a common feature in domestic violence cases.

Temporary restraining order
A type of injunction issued by the court without benefit of a hearing; it specifically describes actions that a person is barred from carrying out and sets a hearing date so that the parties can address the court.

V EVALUATING POTENTIAL DAMAGES

One of the first questions that a plaintiff usually asks her attorney once the lawsuit is under way is, "How much money am I going to get from this case?" The defendant might ask, "How much am I likely to lose?" Unfortunately, there is no perfect predictor to this question. An attorney can often give a ballpark estimate, but she certainly cannot promise an outcome. The final award in any case is the result of a variety of almost innumerable factors and is what makes litigation such an exciting field. No one can predict what a jury will do, and the best that the legal team can do is to prepare for every possible contingency and keep the client as informed as possible.

However, it is not impossible to evaluate a case for a likely outcome. Whether you are the paralegal for the plaintiff or the defense, it makes sense to understand some of the factors that go into evaluating a case.

Case evaluations are not an exact science. They rely on both objective facts and an intuitive understanding of judges and juries. The most important starting point for any case evaluation involves an objective and hard-nosed review of the facts.

A. REVIEWING THE FACTS OF A CASE

Even before you review the plaintiff's injuries, careful attention must first be paid to the defendant's liability. Without a clear showing that the defendant is responsible for the plaintiff's injuries, it is unlikely that the plaintiff will recover anything, no matter how severe his injuries. The defendant must be the person against whom the jury imposes an award, and if the jury does not find the defendant liable, there is no possibility of a judgment in the plaintiff's favor.

Most case evaluations begin at the end of the case: the likelihood of actually recovering anything from the defendant. There are times when the case against the defendant is easy to prove, but the defendant has no assets. Pursuing such a claim would only be an exercise in futility. No matter how good the case against the defendant, if she has no financial resources, then it is ultimately going to be a waste of time to bring a lawsuit against her. These are inescapable facts of modern legal finances. The practice of law is a business, and no attorney can afford to take on cases where a win is not balanced by a large payday.

B. ASSET SEARCHES

Most case evaluations begin with an asset search. The plaintiff's legal team will dig into the public records and other sources to get a rough picture of the defendant's financial resources. This is actually much easier than you might imagine. The local courthouse offers tremendous data on a person, including recent lawsuits, UCC filings, and other information that can provide an indication of the defendant's wealth, including real estate holdings, the value of his home, and other resources. If the defendant is covered by an insurance policy, then knowing the policy limits is an important consideration (if they can be learned prior to filing the complaint). In the practical world that legal professionals must inhabit, a seemingly great case could easily become one that an attorney passes up for the simple reason that the defendant has no financial resources and is unable to pay any judgment (commonly referred to as *judgment proof*). Such a defendant has no assets, no insurance coverage, and no other way of paying any damages assessed against him by the jury. In such a case, an asset search prior to filing would be an excellent precaution.

C. THE JURY'S ROLE

In a jury trial, the jury has two purposes: It must first determine liability and then determine damages. If the jury determines that the defendant is not liable, then they are not empowered to assess damages against the defendant. When the jury's verdict finds the defendant liable for the plaintiff's injuries, however, the next stage in the deliberations is to consider how large an award to make to the plaintiff. Judges give jurors legal instructions about how they should conduct their deliberations and how they should make awards.

Not all cases are heard before juries. In some cases, the parties may request a bench trial. In that situation, the judge acts as both the final determiner of the legal issues in the case as well as the fact finder. The judge will consider whether the defendant is liable and to what extent.

1. JURY INSTRUCTIONS

Before the jurors retire to consider the verdict, the judge will inform them about the law in the case. In a jury charge, the judge reads the applicable law to the jurors to help guide them in their deliberations. For instance, suppose the plaintiff has requested punitive damages. The jury instruction in that case might read something like the charge provided in Figure 10-2.

FIGURE 10-2

Jury Instruction Sample

"Ladies and Gentlemen of the jury, I hereby instruct you that you are authorized to award punitive damages, but only if you find by a preponderance of the evidence that the conduct of the defendant was intentional, malicious, or in reckless disregard of the safety of others."

2. JNOV

In most civil cases, the judge has the power to overturn the jury's verdict and award of damages. (Figure 10-3 shows a sample jury verdict.) A judge can issue a JNOV, or a *judgment non obstante verdicto* (a "judgment notwithstanding the verdict"). The judge can make such a ruling after a motion by the losing party in the case or can initiate the decision on her own authority.

FIGURE 10-3

Jury's Verdict in a Civil Case

Doe v. Charles
Jury Verdict Form

(Circle the party indicated) We the jury in this action find for the plaintiff Jane Doe/ defendant Nicholas Charles.

QUESTION 1: Do you find in favor of the plaintiff and against the defendant as to the claim of Count One, negligence?

Answer "yes" or "no."
Answer ____________

Proceed to the next question.

QUESTION 2: Do you find in favor of the plaintiff and against the defendant as to the claim of Count Two, willful failure to obey the rules of the road?

Answer "yes" or "no."
Answer ____________

If you answered any of the above questions "yes," proceed to VERDICT FORM.

VERDICT FORM

We, the jury in this action, having found for the plaintiff, Jane Doe, and against the defendant, assess the total amount of Jane Doe's damages at $42,234, broken down as follows:

Past damages: $8,213
Future damages: $34,021

This the 18th day of November, 2015.

/s/ Leslie McKesson
FOREPERSON

Tech Topic
CALCULATING DAMAGES

The traditional method for evaluating damages in a case is to use a spreadsheet such as Excel or even to prepare the individual points in Word and then use a 10-button calculator to tally up the various amounts. But there are software packages that can do that work and a great deal more besides. This software can be configured to calculate damages in a wide variety of cases, including personal injury, medical malpractice, workers' compensation, and Social Security disability. Instead of simply listing a category, such as "medical bills," this software allows users to enter a spreadsheet with every possible category already present. Besides entering the amount, the software can track when and where the medical treatment was given, whether it is a repeating treatment such as physical therapy, and can even calculate future medical payments to help in creating a workable settlement offer. But software has advanced even further in the calculation of damages. In addition to helping calculate items such as medical bills, the software can also track medical records, insurance payments, and personal damages, including lost time from work and loss of future earnings.

It may soon become mandatory to use some type of software package to track damages just to avoid potential legal malpractice actions. After all, if one attorney can show that she was able to recover a specific sum using a software package, such a practice may become recommended or even required in future cases. In that case, attorneys who simply rely on the old-fashioned way of calculating damages may find themselves not only at a disadvantage, but also engaging in questionable practices in representing their clients.

Case Excerpt

When does the plaintiff's lifestyle become an issue when assessing damages in a medical malpractice case?

ZAK V. RIFFEL
115 P.3d 165 (Kan.App.,2005).

Before MALONE, P.J., GREEN and BUSER, JJ.

MALONE, P.J.

Kathleen S. Zak filed a medical negligence case seeking damages for the wrongful death of her husband, Michael Zak, a 48-year-old business executive, from dilated cardiomyopathy. The case proceeded to trial against only Dr. Lawrence D. Riffel. The jury returned a verdict finding Dr. Riffel to be 51% at fault and Michael to be 49% at fault. The jury awarded $100,000 in total damages. The primary issue we will address on appeal is whether the trial court erred by giving an instruction which allowed the jury to allocate fault to Michael because of his "obesity and lifestyle." We will also address whether the trial court violated the collateral source rule by admitting evidence of a $262,500 payment made to Kathleen by Michael's employer after Michael's death.

Factual and procedural background

In 1988, Michael became a patient of Dr. Fred Farris at the Kenyon Clinic. In 1992, Michael was diagnosed with aortic stenosis, a congenital defect in one of the valves of his heart. Michael underwent surgery for an aortic valve replacement on April 2, 1992. As a result of the damage due to the defective valve, however, Michael was left with a chronic condition known as left ventricular dysfunction in which the left ventricle of the heart was unable to pump the normal amount of blood from that chamber. Michael was obese and significant weight loss and lifestyle adjustments were suggested as a way to manage the left ventricular dysfunction.

In May 1996, Dr. Farris referred Michael to his partner, Dr. Riffel, for evaluation and consultation regarding weight loss. On May 30, 1996, at the time of the initial consultation with Dr. Riffel, Michael weighed 309 pounds and had borderline elevated blood pressure. Michael's cholesterol, triglycerides, and LDL cholesterol were all high. In a letter memorializing the consultation, Dr. Riffel advised that Michael's chest x-ray appeared normal and his electrocardiogram (EKG) was unchanged from previous EKG's in 1992 and 1994. The letter concluded that Michael was in good health and an excellent candidate for the weight loss program.

Dr. Riffel put Michael on a weight loss program of diet, exercise, and medication, which included a prescription for phentermine. Michael's goal was to lose about 80 pounds. The weight loss program was initially successful. Michael lost 89 pounds to a weight of 220 pounds. Blood pressure and cholesterol readings were down, and the weight loss program was stopped in May 1997.

By the time of his annual physical on November 25, 1997, Michael had regained 18 pounds. Dr. Riffel concluded that Michael was in excellent health, but he stressed the importance of continuing to exercise and watching his diet. In February 1998, Michael saw Dr. Riffel because he was concerned and upset that he was gaining weight despite exercising regularly. Dr. Riffel gave Michael another prescription for phentermine, but he did not continue taking the prescription beyond 30 days.

On December 21, 1998, Michael had his annual physical. Dr. Riffel noted that Michael's weight had gradually increased to 265 pounds. Michael reported that his appetite had been difficult to control. Michael's blood pressure, cholesterol, and LDL cholesterol were elevated. Dr. Riffel concluded that Michael's chest x-ray was clear and his EKG had not changed significantly. He did not refer Michael to a cardiologist because he felt comfortable managing the left ventricular dysfunction.

On February 12, 1999, Michael went to the St. Joseph Health Center Emergency Room after he woke up experiencing chest pain and shortness of breath. Dr. Michael Reilly performed an examination and ordered a chest x-ray and EKG. Dr. Reilly reported the results of the tests as normal and diagnosed Michael with gastritis. He was given a gastrointestinal cocktail and discharged with a 10-day supply of Prevacid. The next day, Michael and Kathleen left for a scheduled vacation to Hawaii after reporting the emergency room visit to Dr. Riffel.

On February 22, 1999, after returning from vacation, Michael saw Dr. Riffel. Michael informed Dr. Riffel of the details of the emergency room visit on February 12, 1999. Michael also related to Dr. Riffel that he had several episodes of mild chest discomfort in the middle of the night while on vacation. Michael told Dr. Riffel that he had never had symptoms like this before. Dr. Riffel examined Michael and concluded he had gastroesophageal reflux disease (GERD). He continued the Prevacid medication.

On March 17, 1999, Michael left work early because he was not feeling well. On March 18, 1999, Michael again came home from work early and told Kathleen he was not feeling well. About 9:45 p.m., Michael began to have problems breathing, and Kathleen called 911. The paramedics arrived and found Michael in respiratory arrest. Efforts to resuscitate began, and Michael was transported to the hospital. After resuscitation efforts failed at the hospital, Michael was pronounced dead at 10:37 p.m., by Dr. Kevin Koch. Dr. Koch concluded that Michael had a cardiopulmonary arrest with pulmonary edema and called the coroner's office to schedule an autopsy.

Dr. Michael Handler conducted the autopsy and concluded that Michael died of an arrhythmia due to an enlarged heart, or dilated cardiomyopathy culminating in a cardiac arrest. Dr. Handler testified that Michael's heart weighed 880 grams at the time of the autopsy where a normal heart would weigh 350–420 grams. Any heart weighing over 600 grams is considered electrically unstable. Based on the scar tissue found on the heart, Dr. Handler believed that Michael had two previous heart attacks, but he could not date the attacks. At the time of his death, Michael weighed 272 pounds.

Kathleen filed her petition for medical negligence and wrongful death on March 15, 2001. Kathleen originally brought her lawsuit against Dr. Riffel and several other providers. Prior to trial, settlement agreements were reached and all the other providers were dismissed with prejudice, leaving Dr. Riffel as the sole defendant. Kathleen alleged that Dr. Riffel failed to properly diagnose and manage Michael's heart condition, failed to refer Michael to a cardiologist for treatment, and failed to advise Michael of the abnormal tests performed at the Kenyon Clinic.

On June 16, 2003, the case was tried to a jury. Dr. John Daniels, Kathleen's internal medicine expert, testified that Michael's EKG was "very abnormal," and his chest x-ray taken by Dr. Riffel in 1996 showed an enlarged heart at that time. Dr. Daniels testified that the standard of care required that Dr. Riffel place Michael on an ACE Inhibitor rather than prescribing phentermine as part of a weight loss plan. An ACE Inhibitor operates to decrease the workload on the heart, and Dr. Daniels testified it was standard therapy to use ACE Inhibitors on patients with left ventricular dysfunction by the mid-1990's. Dr. Daniels noted that phentermine was contraindicated for individuals with cardiac disease.

Based upon his review of the test results from Michael's December 21, 1998, annual physical, Dr. Daniels concluded that Michael had substantial left ventricular dysfunction that presented a life-threatening problem requiring treatment. Dr. Daniels testified the results from the December 1998 echocardiogram indicated that the heart was getting larger and the disease process was getting worse. Dr. Daniels opined that the standard of care required Dr. Riffel to have referred Michael to a cardiologist at that time.

Based upon his review of the records from Michael's emergency room visit on February 12, 1999, Dr. Daniels concluded that Michael was clearly in congestive heart failure. Dr. Daniels stated that Michael's further complaints of pain while on vacation should have alerted Dr. Riffel to be suspicious of the GERD diagnosis. According to

Dr. Daniels, Michael required an urgent cardiac evaluation at that time, and Dr. Riffel's failure to provide proper management of Michael's condition contributed to his death. He believed that Dr. Riffel's failure to manage Michael's heart condition reduced his life expectancy by 5 to 10 years. Dr. Bresnahan opined Michael's life expectancy could have been 7 to 10 years with proper care.

At trial, Dr. Riffel admitted that Michael's chest x-ray and EKG results were abnormal. He testified that his entries in the medical records to the contrary meant that the results were "normal for Michael's condition." Dr. Riffel did not believe that Michael's heart condition was getting worse because he had not developed any symptoms of heart failure.

Dr. Riffel's experts testified that the use of ACE Inhibitors was not the standard of care for asymptomatic left ventricular dysfunction. They testified that weight loss and lifestyle changes were effective treatment for the condition. They also testified there was no indication in Michael's medical history which should have alerted Dr. Riffel to refer Michael to a cardiologist.

Dr. John Ward, economist, testified regarding a calculation of lost wages. Michael was an executive with BHA Group at the time of his death. Dr. Ward testified that BHA Group was a rapidly growing company from 1996 to 1998. Michael earned $592,000 in 1996, $363,000 in 1997, and $693,000 in 1998. According to Dr. Ward, total wage loss for a 5-year life expectancy was $1,077,737; total loss for a 10-year life expectancy was $2,132,797.

Prior to trial, Kathleen filed a motion in limine to exclude evidence of the $262,500 payment on the grounds that it constituted a collateral source payment. Dr. Riffel argued that he should be allowed to cross-examine Dr. Ward regarding this information because Dr. Ward had not counted the payment in his calculations and conclusions regarding economic loss. According to Dr. Riffel, this omission showed a bias by Dr. Ward which affected his credibility as a witness. The trial court ruled that it would allow the evidence of the $262,500 payment to be presented to the jury for the limited purpose of laying a foundation for the defense to cross-examine Dr. Ward about his report.

At the conclusion of the trial, the district court instructed the jury to compare fault between Michael and Dr. Riffel. The jury returned a verdict, finding Dr. Riffel to be 51% at fault and Michael to be 49% at fault. The jury awarded $100,000 in total damages, which included $25,000 for medical expenses and $75,000 for past economic loss. The jury did not award any damages for past or future noneconomic loss, past or future loss or impairment of services, or future economic loss. Kathleen filed a motion for a new trial which was denied. She timely appeals.

Kathleen raises five issues on appeal: (1) the trial court violated the collateral source rule by admitting evidence of the $262,500 payment; (2) the trial court erred by giving Instruction No. 14 because it allowed the jury to allocate fault to Michael because of his obesity and lifestyle; (3) Kathleen was denied a fair trial due to juror misconduct; (4) the damage award was inadequate and contrary to undisputed evidence; and (5) the trial court erred in limiting the cross-examination of an expert witness regarding Dr. Riffel's prescription for phentermine as part of Michael's weight loss program. We will begin with the claimed error involving Instruction No. 14.

Instruction No. 14

Kathleen claims the trial court erred by giving jury Instruction No. 14 because it allowed the jury to allocate fault to Michael because of his obesity and lifestyle. Kathleen had objected to the instruction at trial on the basis that it was not supported by the evidence.

"The trial court is required to properly instruct the jury on a party's theory of the case. Errors regarding jury instructions will not demand reversal unless they result in prejudice to the appealing party. Instructions in any particular action are to be considered together and read as a whole, and where they fairly instruct the jury on the law governing the case, error in an isolated instruction may be disregarded as harmless. If the instructions are substantially correct and the jury could not reasonably have been misled by them, the instructions will be approved on appeal." *Wood v. Groh*, 269 Kan. 420, 423-24, 7 P.3d 1163 (2000).

The trial court gave Instruction No. 14 to the jury which identified the party's "claims and defenses" as follows:

> "Issues-Plaintiff's Claim
>
> "The plaintiff, Kathy Zak, claims that she sustained damages as a result of the death of her husband and due to the fault of the defendant.
>
> "The plaintiff claims that she sustained damage due to the fault of the defendant, Dr. Lawrence Riffel, in:
>
> 1. Failing to properly manage Michael Zak's heart condition;
> 2. Failing to refer Michael Zak to a cardiologist; and,
> 3. Failing to advise Michael Zak of the abnormal diagnostic test results performed at the Kenyon Clinic.
>
> "Burden of Proof-Plaintiff's Claim
>
> "The plaintiff has the burden to prove that it is more probably true than not true that she sustained damages caused by any one or more of the claimed negligent acts or omissions of the defendant. When more than one specified negligent act or omission is alleged against a defendant, agreement as to which specific act or omission is not required.
>
> "Issues-Defendant's Admissions and Denials
>
> "The defendant denies any and all claims of negligence asserted against him by plaintiff, and specifically, denies that he departed from acceptable standards of medical care with respect to the care and treatment provided to Michael Zak by him under the circumstances of this case. This defendant asserts that the care and treatment provided by this defendant was within acceptable standards of care for similarly situated physicians given the circumstances of this case.
>
> "This defendant asserts that the death of Michael Zak was not the result of, or caused by, any act or omission on the part of this defendant. Instead, the death of Michael Zak was the result of a pre-existing cardiomyopathy that was aggravated by Michael Zak's obesity and lifestyle.
>
> "This defendant denies the nature and extent of the damages alleged by to have been sustained by the plaintiff."

Instruction No. 14 provided the basis for the trial court to further instruct the jury on the comparative fault of Michael and Dr. Riffel. Kathleen failed to object to any of the comparative fault instructions except for Instruction No. 14. However, the standard of review requires us to view the instructions as a whole in order to establish whether they are substantially correct.

Michael was obese and had a heart condition. However, a patient's prior condition which required him to be under a physician's care cannot be a basis for comparative fault in a negligence claim against the physician:

> "Conduct prior to an injury or death is not legally significant in an action for damages, unless it is a legal or proximate cause of the injury or death. It is inconsistent with the reasonable and normal expectations for the court to excuse or reduce the medical provider's liability simply because it was the patient's own fault that he or she required care in the first place." *Huffman v. Thomas*, 26 Kan.App.2d 685, Syl. ¶2, 994 P.2d 1072, rev. denied 268 Kan. 846 (1999).

On appeal, Dr. Riffel asserts the basis for the jury to assess fault against Michael was his failure to follow Dr. Riffel's reasonable treatment advice. Kansas law recognizes a patient's duty to follow reasonable directions and advice given to the patient by a health care provider. See *Cox v. Lesko*, 263 Kan. 805, 819-20, 953 P.2d 1033 (1998) (patient failed to complete her physician-ordered physical therapy); *Wisker v. Hart*, 244 Kan. 36, 39-41, 766 P.2d 168 (1988) (patient disregarded his physician's warnings to refrain from strenuous work and returned to his physically demanding job soon after he suffered internal injuries in a motorcycle accident).

However, the evidence at trial supporting Dr. Riffel's assertion that Michael failed to follow reasonable treatment advice was tenuous. The only specific evidence cited by Dr. Riffel to support this claim was Michael's failure to keep his weight down and his failure to renew the phentermine prescription in 1998. The evidence was undisputed that Michael was overweight. However, the mere fact that Michael regained much of the weight that he had initially lost does not prove that Michael failed to follow Dr. Riffel's treatment advice. To the contrary, the testimony supported the fact that Michael continued to watch his diet and exercised regularly. In fact, Dr. Riffel testified that Michael was an "excellent patient," and Dr. Riffel was shocked when he learned of Michael's death. Furthermore, Michael's failure to renew his prescription for phentermine could hardly be considered as fault in light of the evidence that phentermine was contraindicated for individuals with cardiac disease.

During the closing argument, Dr. Riffel's counsel never even asserted Michael was at fault for his injuries and death. To the contrary, defense counsel described Michael's conduct as follows:

> "What else is going on at that time with Michael Zak? He is starting to eat better, and I think we have heard it from just about every witness who knew him in this trial, including Dr. Riffel, he was exercising much, much more, which is also in and of itself good for the heart and good for a heart with left ventricular dysfunction."
>
> In summing up the case for the jury, defense counsel stated:
>
> "I think we can conclude that nobody is at fault here. This was a death that was very unfortunate, tragic. Mr. Zak was taken way before his time, everybody agrees, but is it anybody's fault? . . .

> "And my suggestion to you would be that when you go back to the jury room, that you answer question number one, no. No fault; nobody caused Michael Zak's death. That's the most appropriate and the fairest answer based on the evidence."

Clearly Dr. Riffel's trial strategy was to convince the jury that no one was at fault for Michael's death. In any event, whether there was sufficient evidence at trial to support a comparison of fault between Michael and Dr. Riffel is not the issue in this appeal. The real question we must decide is whether Instruction No. 14 adequately apprised the jury of each party's claims and affirmative defenses concerning fault. Regarding Dr. Riffel's contentions, we conclude Instruction No. 14 was fatally defective in two respects. First, Instruction No. 14 failed to specify any allegations of fault on Michael's part. Second, the instruction failed to set forth Dr. Riffel's burden of proof on this issue.

Kathleen's claims against Dr. Riffel were clearly identified in Instruction No. 14. She made three specific allegations of fault against Dr. Riffel. The instruction further informed the jury that Kathleen had the burden to prove that her allegations of fault were more probably true than not true. The instruction did not contain the same information regarding Dr. Riffel's claims, if any, against Michael.

The instruction stated that "defendant asserts that the death of Michael Zak was not the result of, or caused by, any act or omission on the part of this defendant. Instead, the death of Michael Zak was the result of a pre-existing cardiomyopathy that was aggravated by Michael Zak's obesity and lifestyle." At best, this language constituted a claim that Michael's death was caused by his obesity and lifestyle. However, causation is only one component of fault. The instruction did not include any specific allegations of fault against Michael which could be compared with the specific allegations of fault that had been made against Dr. Riffel. Although the jury was informed in another instruction that a patient has a duty to follow his or her physician's reasonable treatment advice, the jury was not given any guidance in the instructions as to what advice Michael failed to follow. This problem was exacerbated by the fact that defense counsel never pointed to any specific allegations of fault against Michael during the closing argument.

More importantly, Instruction No. 14 was fatally defective because it failed to inform the jury that Dr. Riffel shouldered the burden of proof to establish Michael's comparative fault. The trial court instructed the jury that Kathleen had the burden to prove her claims of fault against Dr. Riffel, but Instruction No. 14 never informed the jury that Dr. Riffel had a similar burden to prove any claim of fault against Michael. In another instruction, the jury was informed that "a party who has the burden of proof must persuade you that his claim is more probably true than not true." However, this instruction would be meaningless to the jury unless at some point the jury was informed Dr. Riffel had the burden to prove his claims. This important information was not contained anywhere in the entire set of instructions given by the trial court, and this omission resulted in the instructions as a whole being clearly erroneous.

PIK Civ.3d 106.01 provides that in outlining affirmative defenses, the defendant should "set forth concisely the defendant's specific grounds of negligence that are supported by the evidence." Also, PIK Civ.3d 106.01 includes a statement that "the defendant has the burden to prove that any of (his)(her) claims of fault on the part of the plaintiff are more probably true than not true." The use of PIK instructions by trial courts is strongly recommended. *State v. Kleypas*, 272 Kan. 894, 1035, 40 P.3d 139

(2001), cert. denied 537 U.S. 834, 123 S.Ct. 144, 154 L.Ed.2d 53 (2002), overruled on other grounds *State v. Marsh*, 278 Kan. 520, 102 P.3d 445 (2004).

Here, Instruction No. 14 did not include specific allegations of Michael's fault, nor did it set forth Dr. Riffel's burden of proof. The instructions as a whole were not substantially correct, and the jury could have reasonably been misled by them. We conclude the trial court committed reversible error in instructing the jury and, as a result, the case must be remanded for a new trial. Upon retrial, we make no determination whether Michael's alleged fault can be compared with Dr. Riffel's. That will depend on the evidence presented at trial. However, an assertion of fault based only upon Michael's "obesity and lifestyle" would be legally deficient because that is what required Michael to seek medical care in the first place. Furthermore, if fault is to be compared, the trial court must correctly instruct the jury on the specific claims of fault by each party and the respective burdens of proof pursuant to PIK Civ.3d 106.01.

Collateral source benefit

Kathleen also claims the trial court erred by admitting evidence of a $262,500 payment by BHA Group after Michael's death because the admission of the evidence violated the collateral source rule. The trial court admitted the evidence for the limited purpose of laying a foundation for the defense to cross-examine Dr. Ward about his report. We will address this issue because it is likely to be raised upon a retrial of the case.

Generally, the admission of evidence lies within the sound discretion of the trial court. An appellate court's standard of review regarding a trial court's admission of evidence is abuse of discretion. *Wendt v. University of Kansas Med. Center*, 274 Kan. 966, 975, 59 P.3d 325 (2002). An abuse of discretion must be shown by the party attacking the evidentiary ruling and exists only when no reasonable person would take the view adopted by the trial court. *Jenkins v. T.S.I. Holdings, Inc.*, 268 Kan. 623, 633-34, 1 P.3d 891 (2000). However, an abuse of discretion has occurred where the trial court clearly erred or ventured beyond the limits of permissible choice under the circumstances. *Unwitting Victim v. C.S.*, 273 Kan. 937, 944, 47 P.3d 392 (2002).

"The collateral source rule provides that benefits received by the plaintiff from a source wholly independent of and collateral to the wrongdoer will not diminish the damages otherwise recoverable from the wrongdoer." *Farley v. Engelken*, 241 Kan. 663, 666, 740 P.2d 1058 (1987) (quoting *Allman v. Holleman*, 233 Kan. 781, Syl. ¶8, 667 P.2d 296 1983). The purpose of the collateral source rule is to prevent the tortfeasor from escaping full liability resulting from his or her actions by requiring the tortfeasor to compensate the injured party for all of the harm, not just the net loss. *Rose v. Via Christi Health System, Inc.*, 276 Kan. 539, 544, 78 P.3d 798 (2003), modified on rehearing 279 Kan. ____________, 113 P.3d 241 (2005).

"A benefit secured by the injured party either through insurance contracts, advantageous employment arrangements, or gratuity from family or friends should not benefit the tortfeasor by reducing his or her liability for damages. If there is to be a windfall, it should benefit the injured party rather than the tortfeasor." (Emphasis added.) 276 Kan. at 544, 78 P.3d 798.

Dr. Riffel disputes the fact that the $262,500 payment from BHA Group to Kathleen constituted a collateral source payment and claims this was a factual issue for the jury to decide. He argues BHA Group's promise that Michael's salary would be continued for 1 year from the date of his death indicated that the payment was compensation to Michael rather than a death benefit. He also points to the fact that the payment was recorded in the company books as a payment from a "bonus account," to which payments of cash bonuses to employees were ascribed.

However, it was the trial court's function to determine whether the payment received by Kathleen constituted collateral source evidence. The testimony established that both BHA Group and Kathleen considered the payment to be a death benefit. It was irrelevant whether the payment was based upon BHA Group's promise to continue Michael's salary for 1 year from the date of his death. Even if this evidence is taken at face value, it was apparent that the payment was not compensation earned by Michael during his lifetime. Rather, it was a benefit paid upon his death. Furthermore, it was irrelevant whether the payment was voluntary or an obligation. The collateral source rule applies to payments received gratuitously as well as those received as a result of an obligation. *Johnson v. Baker*, 11 Kan.App.2d 274, 278, 719 P.2d 752 (1986). The evidence was undisputed that the $262,500 payment was a death benefit received by Kathleen as a result of an advantageous employment arrangement between BHA Group and Michael. This constituted inadmissible collateral source evidence as a matter of law. See Rose, 276 Kan. at 544, 78 P.3d 798.

Dr. Riffel also asserts that the evidence of the $262,500 payment was admissible to impeach the credibility of Dr. Ward because he had failed to account for the payment in his damages calculations. According to Dr. Riffel, this omission provided evidence that Dr. Ward's calculations were biased and not credible.

Dr. Riffel is correct in asserting that although evidence of a collateral source payment is generally inadmissible as a matter of law, such evidence may be admissible if it "carries probative value on an issue not inherently related to measurement of damages." *Wentling v. Medical Anesthesia Services*, 237 Kan. 503, 515, 701 P.2d 939 (1985). Apparently the trial court adopted this reasoning when it ruled that evidence of the $262,500 payment would be admissible for the limited purpose of laying a foundation for the defense to impeach Dr. Ward.

Prior to allowing the jury to hear evidence of the $262,500 payment, the trial court gave the following limiting instruction to the jury:

> "Members of the jury, we are about to receive some evidence which is going to be received for a limited purpose only. This is evidence concerning some compensation that was paid by Mr. Zak's employer to Ms. Zak as his surviving spouse, and this evidence is being introduced, and I'm permitting it to be introduced solely for the purpose of being used in examination of an expert witness that's going to testify tomorrow, and it will become apparent which expert witness and what . . . it's being considered for when it happens.
>
> "This evidence is not being admitted for the purpose of permitting you to understand or in any way diminish or reduce the economic losses suffered by Ms. Zak, if any, as a result of Mr. Zak's death due to the negligence of the defendant.
>
> "In other words, later in this case you are going to have to determine the amount of damages that the plaintiff has suffered because of the negligence of the defendant and to the extent that you determine those amounts, this evidence is not being offered. It's being offered but not being received for the purpose of using that to reduce or to diminish the amount of damages that you may find Ms. Zak may be recovering.

> "It's only being used and received for the purpose of laying a foundation for some questions and calculations made by an expert witness who is going to testify presumably tomorrow, and so you are to consider it, and remember that it's being received only for that purpose."

After evidence regarding the payment was presented to the jury, the trial court again admonished the jury:

> "Members of the jury, these two exhibits that we have just been talking about, Exhibits 139 and 140, were received in evidence by me earlier this afternoon for the limited purposes that I have talked about before. They are merely being introduced for the purpose of laying a foundation to determine some calculations that have been made by an expert witness who will testify tomorrow. They are not received for the purpose of presenting evidence to diminish the amount of economic loss, if any, that the plaintiff has suffered as a result of the defendant's negligence."

The problem in this case is that the limited purpose for which the trial court admitted the collateral source evidence never became clear to the jury. After successfully convincing the trial court that the evidence of the payment should be admitted for the limited purpose of impeaching Dr. Ward, defense counsel failed to use the evidence for this purpose. Dr. Ward was never cross-examined about the $262,500 payment. After evidence of the payment was initially presented to the jury, the subject was not addressed throughout the remainder of the trial. Although the trial court had admonished the jury that it was hearing the evidence for a limited purpose that would "become apparent" in later testimony, no evidence was ever presented for the jury to make a connection. The jury could only have been confused by the limiting instruction given by the court.

Furthermore, the evidence of the $262,500 payment had no probative value on any issue other than the measurement of damages. As previously discussed, the question of whether the payment was compensation or a death benefit was not a factual issue for the jury to decide. The payment was collateral source evidence as a matter of law. Dr. Ward was correct in not including the payment in his calculations, and his failure to do so could not have properly been used to show bias by Dr. Ward. Thus, although collateral source evidence may be admissible in certain instances if relevant to an issue other than the measurement of damages, this case does not present such an instance.

Finally, Dr. Riffel argues that Kathleen should have filed a motion to strike the testimony regarding the $262,500 payment once Dr. Ward was not cross-examined on the issue. However, the burden was not on Kathleen to file such a motion, and it may have only caused further prejudice by reemphasizing the collateral source evidence. Furthermore, Instruction No. 5A, which instructed the jury that evidence admitted for one purpose should not be considered for any other purpose, did not cure the error because the limited purpose that the evidence was admitted in this case never became clear to the jury.

We conclude the $262,500 payment from BHA Group to Kathleen constituted inadmissible collateral source evidence as a matter of law. The trial court abused its discretion in admitting this evidence. Upon retrial, the evidence should not be admitted even for the limited purpose of impeaching Dr. Ward.

We recognize that Kathleen has raised other significant issues on appeal. Because we are already remanding this case for a new trial, we will not address the remaining issues. Reversed and remanded.

QUESTIONS ABOUT THE CASE:

1 How did Michael's physical condition and lifestyle affect his medical condition?
2 How did the doctors treat Michael's reports of chest pain?
3 According to expert testimony, how did the doctor's negligence affect Michael's life expectancy?
4 What were the calculations concerning Michael's income and his future damages?
5 Did the jury award damages for future loss?
6 Explain the court's decision based on the collateral source rule.

Chapter Summary

When the plaintiff files a complaint, he includes a demand for an award of damages. Damages are the payments by the defendant to the plaintiff to compensate the plaintiff for physical, financial, or emotional losses. Damages come in several different forms, including general damages for unspecified or difficult-to-quantify losses suffered by the plaintiff. Examples of general damages include pain and suffering and emotional distress. Special damages, on the other hand, refer to specific losses, such as medical bills, lost time from work, and other specific and identifiable economic losses. In order to prevail at trial, a plaintiff must prove that the defendant is liable and that the defendant is responsible for paying the plaintiff's damages. There are provisions that allow the plaintiff to seek additional damages against the defendant. Punitive damages are a prime example. When the plaintiff seeks punitive damages against the defendant, he requests the court to make an example of the defendant and punish him by assessing additional monetary fines because of the defendant's conduct. Not all cases involve claims for punitive damages. The plaintiff may prove a case for liability against the defendant but then fail to show any significant loss. In such an event, the plaintiff might receive nominal damages or a token award from the jury.

In addition to requesting monetary reimbursement, a plaintiff may also request that the court exercise its equity powers. Equitable remedies include declaratory judgments, injunctions, and other mechanisms through which the court can order a defendant to cease certain activity or to dismiss specific claims in the case. Both the plaintiff's attorney and the defendant's attorney will evaluate a civil case prior to trial and make an assessment about possible damages that could be awarded. The plaintiff's attorney will make this assessment in order to ensure that there are sufficient damages to justify the plaintiff's contingency fee. The defense attorney will evaluate the case for damages in order to adequately represent her client and to advise the client about possible losses. In most cases, the jury assesses final damage awards, but the trial judge also has a supervisory role in the process and may overturn an excessive award.

SKILLS YOU NEED IN THE REAL WORLD

Classify the following as particular types of damages (medical malpractice case):

- Plaintiff's medical bills
- Doctor's notes
- Nurse's notes
- Admitting documents to hospital for plaintiff's stay while attended by defendant doctor
- Photos of the plaintiff's neck injuries that he alleges were the result of the defendant doctor's negligence
- Day in the life video showing how the defendant's actions have affected the plaintiff's quality of life
- Calculation of future lost time from work
- Insurance payments to the plaintiff during the time that the case has been pending
- Video transcript of the defendant's doctor
- Wife's testimony regarding the impact of the plaintiff's injuries on their intimate relationship

THE LIFE OF A PARALEGAL

Technology

Dana Martin is a paralegal for the national law firm of Greenbaum, Doll & McDonald. She likes to emphasize the importance of technology in the everyday practice of law. For instance, she uses her iPhone to keep herself organized. "We have Microsoft Outlook and it gives wireless access to Outlook, my address book, everything." With new technology, a phone has become a valuable evidence-gathering tool. She can take photos with it, text her boss and coworkers, and review PDFs and other files while she's waiting for clients. These days, the office is pretty much where you happen to be with your phone, your laptop, or your tablet.

Dana Martin works for a large firm."We're extremely hi-tech and cutting edge. All of our offices are connected. Our professional staff has access to our network.

"We have a very complex piece of software that keeps track of client information, accounting, and billing software. Our whole office is really tied together. We have offices in Louisville, Lexington, Frankfurt, Cincinnati, Atlanta, and Washington, D.C. We are a regional firm. Everybody can get to the same documents. They can work from their home computer and access our system from a secure network.

"Federal courts are requiring briefs to be filed in Adobe Acrobat. The day-to-day life of a paralegal is filled with technology and if you're going to get a good job, you need to know all about it."

ETHICAL ISSUES FOR THE PARALEGAL

When the Client Exaggerates Injuries

There are times when the legal team representing the plaintiff has reason to believe that the plaintiff may be exaggerating the extent of his injuries. The plaintiff may feel that by exaggerating the injuries in a case, he will receive a much larger award. However, gross exaggeration is equivalent to deceiving the court, and no legal professionals should work in conjunction with the client in order to carry out fraud. The same rule applies if the client is attempting to deny the fact that he has previous injuries. In either case, it is a violation of ethical rules to deceive the court. There are methods to double-check the veracity of the client's claims. For instance, if the client's reported symptoms are out of proportion with the injuries and medical professionals in the case suggest that the client is exaggerating, it may be time for a frank discussion with the plaintiff. It is better to resolve these issues prior to trial and in the safety and security of the attorney's office than on the witness stand. If the jury becomes aware that the client is exaggerating the extent of his injuries, they may refuse to award any damages to the plaintiff, even if the initial complaint was valid.

Websites

- **Federal District Court Civil Trials**
  www.uscourts.gov/about-federal-courts/types-cases/civil-cases
- **'Lectric Law Library — Damages, Compensatory**
  www.lectlaw.com/def/d004.htm
- **American Tort Reform Association, Punitive Damages Reform**
  www.atra.org/issues/punitive-damages-reform
- **U.S. Chamber of Commerce — Punitive Damages**
  www.uschamber.com/press-release/chamber-hails-high-court-ruling-punitive-damages

Key Terms

Collateral source rule
Compensatory damages
Damages
Declaratory judgment
Equity
Fair market value
General damages
Injunction
Loss of consortium
Mitigation of damages
Per diem
Punitive damages
Special damages
Subrogation
Temporary restraining order

Review Questions

1. What is the function of compensatory damages?
2. Define general damages.
3. Explain "pain and suffering" damages.
4. Explain how an attorney would raise a per diem argument to jury for an assessment on damages.
5. What are special damages?
6. How would you classify lost wages and medical bills? Are they general damages or special damages?
7. Can a plaintiff recover for future losses? Explain your answer.
8. What is the function of a "day in the life" video?
9. What is the collateral source rule?
10. Explain mitigation of damages.
11. Under what circumstances can a plaintiff recover for emotional distress?
12. What is loss of consortium?
13. What are "bad faith" damages?
14. Explain punitive damages.
15. What are nominal damages?
16. What are equitable remedies?
17. What is a court's power of equity?
18. Explain circumstances that would justify a declaratory judgment.
19. Explain how legal professionals evaluate cases for possible damage awards.
20. What is the purpose of an asset search?
21. What is the role of the jury in assessing damages?
22. How does the attorney present damages to the jury?
23. What are arguments for and against punitive damages?
24. Many states have passed tort reform statutes that limit punitive damages or prohibit them in certain types of cases. Have these statutes gone too far or not far enough? Justify your answer.

Applying What You Have Learned

1. Based on a case you find online, prepare an exhibit summarizing all of the plaintiff's damages and categorizing them as general or special.

2. Go through any civil case you can find online, and prepare a summary of all medical bills incurred by the client. Create a list showing the name of the provider and the amount. What is the total for the medical bills?

3. Review your state's statutes on general, special, and punitive damages, and prepare jury instructions for the plaintiff in the case you created in Chapters 4 and 5. What issues does this case suggest that would be a factor in an award of general or special damages? Is this case appropriate for a request of punitive damages?

4 Prepare a three-page, double-spaced paper discussing the differences and similarities between compensatory damages and punitive damages. Include references to special and general damages, future damages, punitive damage caps, and how these damages are proved at trial.

5 Review the pleadings you created in Chapters 4 and 5, and then prepare an evaluation of the case based on the material in this chapter. Is there a strong possibility of proving damages in this case? Is it likely that the jury will find the defendant liable for these damages? Can the defendant pay a large judgment? You should consider these and additional factors in preparing your Baker case evaluation.

6 Last year, Mary was admitted to the hospital with chest pain. The doctor diagnosed her problem as acid reflux and sent her home with some antacids. Because Mary is a self-employed graphic artist, she only gets paid when she completes projects. Her continuing chest pain prevented her from completing an assignment, and the client fired her and went with another company. That cost her a $5,000 fee. Two weeks after first reporting to the hospital with chest pain, Mary lost consciousness and was taken to the emergency room in cardiac arrest. She is now completely unable to work. Before the first incident, Mary earned about $3,000 per month. She is now on disability. Beyond that, her marriage has suffered, and that has contributed to a bout of depression. Categorize all of Mary's potential damages claims and put as many dollar amounts to them as possible.

Endnotes

[1] *Origin and History of Hebrew Law*, John M.P. Smith, Hyperion Press, 1990.
[2] Restatement of Torts, 2d §902.
[3] Restatement of Torts, 2d §621 (1977).
[4] *Tancredi v. Dive Makai Charters*, 823 F Supp 778 (DC Hawaii1993).
[5] *Davis v. Green*, 188 F Supp 808 (W.D.Ark.,1960).
[6] *Edwards-Warren Tire Co. v. Coble*, 102 Ga App 106, 115 SE2d 852 (1960).
[7] *Walston v. Greene*, 246 NC 617, 99 S.E.2d 805 (1957).
[8] *Wilson v. Burch Farms, Inc.* 627 S.E.2d 249 (N.C.App., 2006).
[9] *International Correspondence School, Inc. v. Crabtree*, 162 Tenn 70, 34 SW2d 447 (1931).

11

Arbitration, Mediation, and Settlement

Chapter Objectives

- Explain the importance of alternative dispute resolution
- Describe the difference between arbitration and mediation
- Explain how an arbitration hearing is held
- Discuss the differences between common law arbitration and statutory arbitration
- Describe the duties of the arbitrator
- Explain how a mediator's role is different than that of an arbitrator
- Describe the significance of an offer of judgment
- Explain the purpose of a settlement brochure
- Describe how a settlement brochure is created and what it contains
- Define "dismissal with prejudice"

I INTRODUCTION

In this chapter, we will address the topic of resolving a case prior to trial. Most civil cases are resolved ahead of time. Resolution may come in the form of alternative dispute resolution, primarily through the means of arbitration or mediation, or it may come in the form of settlement. In each of these instances, the case never reaches trial because of the actions of the parties to resolve all outstanding claims and to end the case before a jury has the opportunity to hear it. We will begin our discussion with the topic of alternative dispute resolution, concentrating particularly on arbitration and mediation, and then move on to the separate issue of settlement.

ARBITRATION

Arbitration
The process of bringing both sides in a civil suit together to negotiate a resolution

Arbitration is a contractual proceeding, whereby the parties to any controversy or dispute, in order to obtain an inexpensive and speedy final disposition of the matter involved, select judges of their own choice and by consent submit their controversy to such judges for determination, in the place of the tribunals provided by the ordinary processes of law.[1] The purpose of arbitration is clear: It avoids the lengthy process of taking a case to trial. It also saves the court money and personnel and helps alleviate the court's backlog of pending cases. In addition to that, arbitration may also save the client a great deal of expense by avoiding additional attorneys' fees, expert fees, and the multitude of other charges that build up as a case readies for presentation to a jury.

Arbitration is a separate proceeding from other types of alternative dispute resolution, such as mediation. It is not a judicial proceeding and therefore is not required to follow the judicial procedures normally found in a courtroom. Arbitration rules were specifically designed to be less formal and complicated than the procedures followed in a courtroom. It truly is an alternative to a judicial proceeding, both in the procedures used and in the eventual outcome of the case.

A. THE HISTORY OF ARBITRATION

Not surprisingly, there is a long history of parties with disputes submitting them to a third party for resolution. Arbitration has a long common law history and has always been seen as a way of resolving issues between contesting parties instead of taking the case to trial. Arbitration is a voluntary process and cannot be compelled; the parties must have agreed to enter into arbitration. This agreement can be in the form of a contract clause in the original agreement between the parties. In fact, in many ways, arbitration itself resembles a contractual agreement between the parties. The parties agree to submit their claims to a third party for a complete resolution of all issues and also agree to be bound by the arbitrator's final decision.

Arbitration has gained a strong foothold in the legal community in the last few decades. Taking a case through arbitration is seen as an advancement of public policy to lessen the burden on the court system and to encourage parties to reach agreements among themselves.[2] In order to further the public policy favoring arbitration agreements, courts will generally uphold them unless the parties can show some irregularity in their creation. If the parties voluntarily agreed to arbitration when they created their original agreement, chances are that they will get it.[3] Arbitration is a now a universally accepted medium for resolving a wide variety of cases.

Consider the following example: Irving applied for a credit card last year. When he signed the credit card agreement, he did not read the provisions very closely. One of the clauses provided for mandatory arbitration of any dispute between Irving and the credit card company. Last week, Irving received a credit card statement that contained errors. He has tried to work out this disagreement with the credit card company, but they have been unwilling to compromise. Irving wishes to bring a civil suit against them, but the company has recently pointed out the arbitration clause and is now saying that Irving must submit to binding arbitration and cannot proceed with a civil suit. Are they correct?

Answer: Yes. Because Irving signed a credit card agreement and entered into a contractual relationship with the credit card company, and because one of the provisions of that agreement was Irving's consent to submit challenges and controversies to arbitration, he cannot attempt to bypass that provision. This is true even though Irving did not read the agreement very closely.

B. THE FEDERAL ARBITRATION ACT

The Federal Arbitration Act was first enacted in 1925 but has been revised several times since then. It provides the general framework for, procedures for, and obligations of parties seeking arbitration. The Act also clearly establishes the right of the parties to seek arbitration and places it on the same level as mediation as a legitimate way to avoid lengthy court battles and reach a fair and just resolution in civil cases.[4]

The Federal Arbitration Act has been held to preempt state law, where the agreement in question falls under the Commerce Clause of the U.S. Constitution. Because there is such a diversity of transactions that potentially fall under the heading of interstate commerce, the Federal Arbitration Act can apply to a vast array of agreements.[5]

The federal approach found in the Federal Arbitration Act is also reflected in the law of the states.[6] States have followed the federal example and enacted their own alternative dispute resolution laws that specifically authorize arbitration and mediation in certain types of cases. Most states that have created their own alternative dispute resolution schemes have based their legislation in whole or in part on the Federal Arbitration Act.

C. COMPARING ARBITRATION TO APPRAISAL

Arbitration is only one type of alternative dispute resolution. Other types include mediation and appraisal. We will discuss mediation in the next section, but we should also briefly discuss appraisal.

An **appraisal** is an informal investigation carried out by experts to evaluate the value of a particular item. It is not a form of arbitration; it merely sets value. Arbitration, on the other hand, determines rights, liabilities, and the final outcome in a case.

Appraisal
The evaluation by an expert of the cash value of a contested item

D. TYPES OF ARBITRATION

There are two types of arbitration: common law (voluntary) and statutory (mandatory). Under the common law of old, it was considered a violation of the court's power to require that all contentions and claims between parties be resolved by arbitration. But these limits were slowly eroded by acts of state legislatures, which gradually expanded the statutory right of arbitration in a wide variety of cases.

Common law arbitration can be triggered by the express agreement of the parties or by their failure to meet the minimum requirements set out in state law.[7] Statutory arbitrations, however, can change the basic formula between the parties. For instance, a statute might require arbitration for specific types of disputes even when the agreement between the parties does not provide for it.[8] Statutes that provide for compulsory or mandatory arbitration often provide mechanisms for appellate review of the arbitrator's decision and may even provide that a party disputing the final arbitration award may take the case to court.[9] When the state requires arbitration, it must also provide a mechanism for appealing the final award.[10] Whether a particular action falls under the provisions of voluntary arbitration or mandatory arbitration depends on the applicable statutes.

Binding arbitration is a clause found in many contracts that requires the parties to submit their dispute to arbitration instead of bringing a civil suit. In such a situation, as long as the provisions do not violate state or federal law, one party can compel the other to submit any disputes to an arbitrator and bar that party from bringing a civil suit. See Figure 11-1 for a sample state statute governing binding arbitration.

FIGURE 11-1

New York Arbitration Statute

Section 28.2 Mandatory submission of actions to arbitration.

(a) The Chief Administrator may establish in any trial court in any county the arbitration program authorized by this Part.

(b) In each county where an arbitration program is established by order of the Chief Administrator, all civil actions for a sum of money only, except those commenced in small claims parts and not subsequently transferred to a regular part of court, that are noticed for trial or commenced in the Supreme Court, County Court, the Civil Court of the City of New York, a District Court or a City Court, on or after the effective date of the order where recovery sought for each cause of action is $6,000 or less, or $10,000 or less in the Civil Court of the City of New York, or such other sum as may be authorized by law, exclusive of costs and interest, shall be heard and decided by a panel of arbitrators. The Chief Administrator may also, at any time, upon the establishment of the program in any particular court or county or thereafter, provide for the submission to arbitration of actions, seeking recovery of such sums, that are pending for trial in those courts on the effective date of the order.[11]

E. ISSUES THAT CAN BE SUBMITTED TO ARBITRATION

When there is no specified limitation, nearly any dispute can be submitted to arbitration, including medical malpractice cases, divorces, and even crimes.[12] Arbitration actions can be directed solely to the interpretation of statutes or a determination about facts and the law that applies to them.

Examples of cases that may be required to be submitted to arbitration include:

- malpractice cases (medical and legal malpractice);
- disputes between contractors and third parties in highway construction;
- negligence claims against the state highway system;
- wills;
- torts;
- the construction of a statute;
- spousal support payments; and
- the effect of bankruptcy on other actions.

F. LIMITATIONS ON ARBITRATION CASES

Although the general approach is to enforce arbitration agreements, there are some exceptions. For instance, the courts will usually not compel a party to go through arbitration when that party did not originally agree to the process.[13] Similarly, if the parties clearly intended that arbitration would not be an option for disputes between them, the courts will generally not force them to go through it.[14]

Courts have been very liberal in allowing parties to negotiate arbitration provisions among themselves, but there are some limitations. Certain issues have been determined to be inappropriate for arbitration:

- The right of a person to enter into a profession, such as law or medicine
- Custody and visitation rights for minor children
- An interpretation of the state or federal constitution
- An action based on a criminal enterprise or invalid contract

G. ARBITRATORS

The parties generally select the arbitrator, either by express terms of the agreement or by the consent of the parties prior to the arbitration hearing.

The authority of the arbitrator flows from the contractual terms between the parties where the original provision authorizing arbitration is found. Because of this, an arbitrator may have limited powers and authority that varies considerably from case to case. However, this is not true when the arbitration process is mandatory under state statutes. In those situations, all arbitrators have the same authority: to decide the issues pending between the parties and to make a final determination that resolves the case.

There are provisions for selecting an **umpire** to decide a dispute. Not all states use this terminology, but for the ones that do, an umpire is a person who acts alone in deciding an issue, often after the original arbitrator has been unable to reach a decision.

Umpire
A person with greater authority than an arbitrator; this person has the authority to make a final and binding decision when an arbitrator has been unable to do so

H. THE ARBITRATION AGREEMENT

Submission
The agreement to arbitrate a specific matter or issue raised between the parties

The agreement to arbitrate is often referred to as a **submission** or an *agreement for submission*. This agreement is central to the determination that the parties voluntarily entered into an arbitration agreement. At its most basic, submission is the agreement where the parties specifically agree to submit their dispute to a third party who will make a determination about the case and also make a final award.[15]

The submission, like the original agreement between the parties, is a contract and is enforced and evaluated under contract law principles. This means that the submission must meet the same criteria for any contract, including mutual assent, consideration, capacity, and legality (discussed further later in this chapter).

MEDIATION

Mediation
The process of submitting a claim to a neutral third party who then makes a determination about the ultimate liability and award in a civil case

In the 1980s and 1990s, many states began adopting statewide **mediation** programs in order to help with the backlog of cases pending in civil courts. In states that adopted mandatory mediation, statistics show that nearly 50 percent of all cases referred to mediation were resolved successfully. Mediation saves precious court time and resources by encouraging parties to settle before the case comes to trial. (See Figure 11-2 for a defintion of mediation.)

FIGURE 11-2

Mediation Defined (Maryland)

(d) Mediation. "Mediation" means a process in which the parties work with one or more impartial mediators who, without providing legal advice, assist the parties in reaching their own voluntary agreement for the resolution of the dispute or issues in the dispute. A mediator may identify issues and options, assist the parties or their attorneys in exploring the needs underlying their respective positions, and, upon request, record points of agreement reached by the parties. While acting as a mediator, the mediator does not engage in arbitration, neutral case evaluation, neutral fact-finding, or other alternative dispute resolution processes and does not recommend the terms of an agreement.[16]

Mediation differs from arbitration in several important ways. The first is that arbitration is a process selected by the parties long before there is ever a dispute between them. The contract will usually set out the requirement to submit disputes to an arbitrator and even create the procedure for doing so. On the other hand, it is the court who often suggests mediation after litigation has begun. It is a mutual attempt to resolve difficulties and to conclude a case. If we were to compare arbitration, mediation, and the judicial process, we would have to say that arbitration most closely resembles the hearing it is designed to avoid. An arbitrator has the right to evaluate the evidence, listen to witnesses, and reach a binding result. A mediator, on the other hand, works with the parties to help them reach a voluntary agreement among themselves. If the parties are unwilling or unable to work out an agreement, then they go back to the litigation process.

A. STATE MEDIATION PROGRAMS

All states have enacted some form of mediation program. The most typical provisions provide that judges can send specific types of cases to nonbinding mediation, where there is a good chance that the case will be resolved and removed from the court's dockets. If the parties are unable to work out an agreement, they are in no worse a position than they were before and can still proceed to litigation.

SEARCH SUGGESTION • STATE STATUTES

You should always keep in mind that different states have different rules regarding arbitration and mediation. Some states, for instance, require mandatory, binding mediation for certain types of cases. Always review your state's statutes to find out if a particular case is obligated to go through mediation.

B. CERTIFIED MEDIATORS

In states that have mediation programs, there are certified mediators. These are individuals who have qualified as mediators with the state. They are often attorneys, counselors, psychologists, or others who have received state training. Certified mediators understand the limited role they can play in this process. They cannot, for example, give legal advice to either side, reach binding decisions, or enforce a particular approach. What they can do is work with the parties to help them reach an agreement themselves. This is perhaps the biggest and most important difference between mediation and arbitration. An arbitrator can reach conclusions and enforce them against the parties, even when the parties don't like the result. This is not true in mediation. A successful mediation session results in a mutual agreement between the parties to resolve the case.

LEGAL LEGWORK ■ MEDIATOR CERTIFICATION

What is the law in your state regarding mediators? Is there a board that certifies mediators? Are they required to go through specific education before they can qualify as mediators for the court? Is there a certification process? How are mediators paid?

Before mediation begins, the parties are allowed to select a mediator. They can choose from a wide variety of individuals, including former judges, currently practicing attorneys, and other professionals who have been certified by the state board, including paralegals. Most states also have provisions that allow the parties to choose someone who is not board certified. If the parties find it impossible to select a mediator on their own, the court may select one for them. Mediators are paid a fee for their services, which is typically $100 per hour.

C. THE MEDIATION CONFERENCE

Sidebar

Mediators are protected by judicial immunity in the same way as a trial court judge.

The mediation settlement conference can be scheduled at the courthouse or any other public building. Responsibility for actually reserving the place and making arrangements for the conference falls on the mediator. The mediator is also responsible for setting the time and date of the hearing and notifying all parties to make sure that they can attend.

D. PERSONS REQUIRED TO BE PRESENT AT MEDIATION

Before the mediation can begin, there are several persons who are required to be present:

- The parties
- The insurance company representative(s)
- The attorneys

The plaintiff and defendant must be present in order to proceed with mediation for the simple reason that they will be actively involved in reaching an agreement. They will have input during the process and final approval over any deal reached during mediation. Simply put, if the parties do not agree to the proposed solution, there is none.

Insurance company representatives are often required to be present at mediations because they provide the pool of funds that will cover some of or the entire settlement amount. For example, in a typical automobile collision case, the defendant's insurance company will pay the final settlement to the plaintiff. Because of this, a representative from the insurance company is required to be present and actively involved in the mediation process. Obviously, the insurance representative will attempt to reserve as much of his company's money as possible. The most that the insurance company will be required to pay out is the policy limits on the defendant's insurance policy.

The parties will also have their attorneys present in order to provide them with legal advice and other counseling. The mediator is specifically barred from giving legal advice and therefore cannot advise any party about the legal consequences of the agreement. But the party's attorney can provide that information. In situations where one of the parties is not represented, then she bears the burden of the legal consequences because there is no one present at the mediation who can provide legal advice to that person.

PRACTICE POINTER ▶ CLIENT COMMUNICATION

Long before the arbitration or mediation hearing is ever held, make sure to communicate with the client the significance of alternative dispute resolution hearings and how they differ from actual trials. You should explain to the client that arbitration and mediation hearings are much less formal than the actual trial and what effect the decision in the hearing will have on the case. Your client should know that there will be no jury present to hear the issues and that the presentation is much less formal than a trial. By explaining these details to the client before the hearing, you can save the client a great deal of confusion and frustration.

E. THE MEDIATOR'S AUTHORITY

The mediator is the person responsible for controlling the conference and setting the procedures to be followed during the hearing. Mediators are authorized to meet privately with any of the parties or attorneys prior to or during the conference. They can work behind the scenes to encourage a settlement and can shuttle back and forth between the parties with various proposals to move the settlement process along. The duties of the mediator include:

- setting the procedures at the hearing;
- explaining the differences between mediation and other forms of alternative dispute resolution, such as arbitration;
- explaining that the mediation conference is not a trial, that the mediator is not a judge and does not have judicial power, and that the parties retain their right to trial if they do not reach a settlement in the mediation hearing; and
- explaining that the agreement reached will be by mutual consent of the parties.

F. IMPASSE

The mediator has the final responsibility for declaring an **impasse** in a hearing. An impasse occurs when the parties are unable to reach an agreement and the mediator determines that there is no possibility of a mutual agreement by extending the hearing. Once an impasse has been declared, the case is sent back to the trial docket, where it will be rescheduled for trial. None of the conversations that occurred during the mediation can be repeated in the trial, and the mediator cannot be compelled to testify about the settlement discussions. As far as the trial is concerned, the mediation never happened.

Impasse
A declaration by the mediator that the parties are unable to reach an agreement

This protection allows the parties to engage in frank discussion without the fear that anything they say at the mediation hearing might be used against them during the trial. This policy also explains why mediators cannot be called to testify about discussions held at the mediation. Without such protection, there would be very little the parties would be willing to communicate during the mediation.

PRACTICE POINTER ▶ MEDIATION DRESS REHEARSAL

Before going to a mediation or arbitration hearing, it is always wise to try a dress rehearsal. Bring in the client and any others who will participate in the actual hearing and do a run-through. Have someone play the role of the mediator. Do you have all of the exhibits and material that the legal team plans on presenting at the hearing? If not, where is this material? Present your case to the mediator and see what problems arise. Better to have a misstep in practice than at the actual hearing.

IV. SETTLEMENT

Settlement
A negotiated termination of a case prior to a trial or jury verdict

When a case is settled, it means that the parties have reached an agreement about terminating the case. A case can be settled at any point in the litigation process, although most are settled shortly before the trial begins. There is something about the looming prospect of a jury trial that tends to make parties begin to see reason. **Settlement** often involves payment by the defendant to the plaintiff in exchange for the plaintiff dismissing his claim. When the case is dismissed through settlement, it cannot be brought against the defendant at a future date.

The concept underlying a settlement is similar to other legal concepts, including accord and satisfaction, novation, and release. *Accord and satisfaction* is a term that is usually reserved for the negotiations between debtors and creditors. *Novation* is a term used by contracting parties to substitute one contract provision for a new one. *Release* is a term even more closely associated with settlement. In a release, a party surrenders a specific right, often in exchange for something of value.

A good working definition of *settlement* is the dismissal of the plaintiff's suit against the defendant in exchange for a monetary payment by the defendant. There is a strong public policy argument in favor of allowing the parties to settle their differences prior to trial. In fact, courts are encouraged to allow the parties to work out any agreement that they find satisfactory and to enforce that agreement, as long as it does not violate the basic legal requirements of contract law or public policy.[17]

Consider the following example: Carla was in a car wreck last year. A large delivery truck, owned and operated by Fuzzy Cola and driven by Randy, ran a red light and smashed into her car. She was severely injured and brought suit earlier this year, seeking several million dollars in damages. Fuzzy Cola representatives have recently approached Carla with a settlement proposal: They will pay her $1.2 million in exchange for her dismissing her suit and also agreeing not to testify against Randy in the upcoming criminal action. It seems that Randy was cited for failure to stop at the red light, and the company is concerned about bad press as a result. Is this settlement agreement in violation of public policy?

Answer: Yes. The parties can certainly agree to settle the case for money and a dismissal of the suit, but the company cannot insist that Carla refuse to testify in a criminal action. Paying a person to refuse to testify could be considered witness tampering; at the very least, it is a violation of public policy to encourage witnesses not to testify, if not an outright criminal action. When it comes to enforcing the settlement, a judge will undoubtedly refuse to implement that provision.

A. REASONS TO SETTLE

Settlement discussions can occur at any time during the litigation. The parties might discuss settlement before the plaintiff ever files suit, or they could discuss settlement as the jurors file into the courtroom at the beginning of the trial. There are several compelling reasons that would make both parties interested in bringing about a settlement of the case before it goes to trial.

For the plaintiff, there are several important reasons to settle a case. First, even if the plaintiff believes that she has a strong case, there are no guarantees with jury trials. A strong case for the plaintiff could easily result in a verdict for the defendant, and a weak case might just as easily go the other way. It is virtually impossible to predict what a jury will do in any given case; therefore, the plaintiff's attorney often advises the client to take a certain sum of money instead of gambling on receiving more at trial.

Besides the inherent risks of taking a case to trial, there are other reasons to settle. Up to this point, the plaintiff and the attorney have invested a great deal of time in the case. There have been depositions to attend, interrogatory questions to answer, and a host of pretrial issues to address. But the trial will take up even more time, and after months of dealing with the case, the plaintiff may just be tired of the whole thing. A large check and a resolution might be very attractive at that point, especially when the plaintiff considers even more lost time to attend the trial and put his life on hold for an additional period of time.

On the defendant's side, the pressures to settle the case are similar. The defendant is also facing the possibility of a jury decision that could go either way. Of course, for the defendant, a loss could equate to a huge jury award. Rather than face that possibility, a defendant might be willing to pay an amount up front. The defendant may also be facing litigation fatigue and might want a resolution to the case just as much as the plaintiff.

You will notice that in our discussions of the reasons to settle a case, we did not include the preferences of the individual attorneys. Both the plaintiff and the defense attorney might want a resolution of the case before trial, but their needs are always secondary to those of the client. The client has the final say in whether to settle the case or not, and even if the attorney believes that taking the case to trial is a bad idea, if that is the client's decision, then that is what the attorney will do.

B. SETTLEMENTS ARE CONTRACTS

When both sides to a suit seek to settle a case, they are actually engaging in a form of contract. The plaintiff agrees to dismiss her complaint against the defendant in exchange for the defendant's agreement to pay the plaintiff a sum of money. Because they are contracts, settlements must meet all of the minimum requirements of any contract, including:

- mutual assent;
- capacity;
- consideration; and
- legality.

1. MUTUAL ASSENT

Mutual assent is the contract requirement that the parties to the contract have a "meeting of the minds" about the details provided in the agreement. They must know and understand what they are agreeing to and must have an understanding about the basic arrangements involved in the contract.

2. CAPACITY

Capacity is the requirement that a party to a contract knows and understands the consequences of creating a legally binding agreement. A party who lacks capacity cannot enter into any contract, including one to settle a case. Examples of individuals who lack capacity include persons under the age of 18, persons who have been declared mentally incompetent, persons acting under the influence of drugs, or persons suffering from a physical impairment that prevents them from understanding what they are doing.

3. CONSIDERATION

Consideration is the contract requirement that both parties to the agreement surrender something of value in exchange for receiving something else of value. The idea behind consideration is simple: It ensures that both parties have a vested interest in the contract. A contract that obligates only one party is not a contract at all. In the typical settlement agreement, the plaintiff surrenders his right to continue with a suit in exchange for a monetary payment. The defendant, on the other hand, surrenders money in exchange for the benefit of having the suit dismissed.

4. LEGALITY

The fourth and most obvious element of any contract is that the agreement must be legal or in accord with public policy. Courts will not enforce contracts for illegal subjects, such as to carry out a crime. Contracts that are considered to be in violation of public policy will also not be enforceable through the court system. An example of such an agreement would be one party's insistence that the other party surrender all possible rights before the contract is carried out. Such a sweeping provision is a violation of public policy, and any settlement agreement that imposed such a requirement would be deemed void for public policy reasons and considered unenforceable.

C. PROCEDURES IN BRINGING ABOUT A SETTLEMENT

The procedures for bringing about settlement vary depending on the particular nature of the case. In some cases, settlement will be achieved through a demand letter. Other times, a more formal offer of judgment serves as the settlement mechanism. In most cases, the process begins with a settlement brochure.

1. SETTLEMENT BROCHURE

At some point in the litigation process, the plaintiff's attorney may prepare a settlement proposal or settlement brochure and forward it to the defendant. No matter what name is used to describe this document, its basic purpose remains the same: The plaintiff makes out her case against the defendant and suggests a figure that, if paid, will result in a dismissal of the suit.

Typical settlement brochures will contain several sections, including:

- the factual basis of the plaintiff's claim;
- a summary of the plaintiff's physical, financial, and emotional injuries;
- an overview of the law as it applies to the issues in the case;
- a summary of recent jury awards; and
- an offer to settle the case for a specific sum.

a. Factual Basis of Plaintiff's Claim

The settlement brochure will present an overview of the plaintiff's claim against the defendant. A settlement brochure is a one-sided affair; it does not seek to present the defendant's version of the case. Instead, it puts the best possible spin on the plaintiff's claims. The defendant might well dispute some of the assertions, but the factual statements contained in the settlement brochure are at least one possible interpretation that the jury could bring to the case.

b. Summary of Plaintiff's Damages

In addition to presenting the factual basis of the plaintiff's claim, the settlement brochure will also set out the plaintiff's physical injuries, financial losses, and any claims for mental distress. Again, these are points seen in the best possible light and may not necessarily be how the case will be presented to the jury or even how the jury might view the claims. The plaintiff presents a strong case for damages in the settlement brochure to put psychological pressure on the defendant to settle the case. After reviewing the damages, the defendant might decide that it would be cheaper to settle the case early in the litigation process than to spend money throughout the discovery and pretrial phases and still risk a large verdict in the plaintiff's favor at trial.

c. Overview of the Law

Although not all settlement brochures contain an overview of applicable law, there are times when it is appropriate. If a recent appellate decision clearly favors the plaintiff's case, the plaintiff's attorney would be well advised to include it in the materials. This inclusion is more for the defendant than for the defendant's attorney. The attorney is probably already aware of that case and any others that have a direct bearing on the issues in the case, but the defendant might review this recent decision and begin to think the case law is against his position. The plaintiff's attorney hopes that after reviewing an overview of the law on the issues in the case, the defendant will begin to feel that the appellate courts will favor the plaintiff, and that is all the more reason to settle.

d. Summary of Recent Jury Awards

A good settlement brochure will also include a section on recent jury awards from similar cases. This information can have a devastating impact on the defendant, especially if the plaintiff can point to recent jury awards in millions of dollars. A defendant might easily conclude that it would be far cheaper to settle the case before trial than risk a similar jury award in the present case.

The question often arises, Where does the plaintiff obtain information about recent jury awards? In the past, researching these details was often difficult. A paralegal might be required to read dozens of appellate decisions and even go to courthouses around the state to discover exactly what a jury's award was in particular cases. However, these days there are companies that do such research for legal professionals for a fee. Companies such as Jury Verdict Research have researchers scattered across the country who review this information and provide it to the company's database. Some companies provide this service as a regular publication, while others will provide data on a case-by-case basis.

e. Offer to Settle

After setting out all of this information, the settlement brochure concludes with an offer to settle the case for a specific sum. This offer often contains a deadline. If the defendant fails to respond or make a serious counteroffer by the deadline, the plaintiff will proceed to trial.

2. DEMAND LETTER

In some cases, a full-blown settlement brochure would be considered overkill. Cases involving smaller amounts of money might involve something as simple as a demand letter (Fig. 11-3). In this letter, the plaintiff's attorney follows some of the same conventions as in a settlement brochure but simplifies and shortens them. A demand letter serves the same function as a settlement brochure: It offers to settle the case for a specific sum of money.

FIGURE 11-3

Demand Letter

Bevans & Bevans, P.A.
1001 Burkemont Avenue
Bohemia, PL 28655
828-555-1212 (phone)
828-555-1213 (fax)

April 24, 2015

Allnation Insurance Company
300 Money Street
Capitol City, PL 28888

Re: Claimant: Sherlock Holmes
Insured: James Moriarty
Date of Loss: August 23, 2014
Claim No.: 665421-1457

Dear Sir or Madam:

I have been retained by Mr. Sherlock Holmes with respect to recovery of damages due to personal injuries suffered by Mr. Holmes in a train collision, which occurred on August 23, 2014, and which involved your insured, James Moriarty.

I have been directed to do everything that is necessary to present, settle, and collect this claim for damages.

I have evaluated this claim for settlement purposes. This letter and the enclosures are presented to you for the purpose of attempting to settle this claim.

I. Liability

James Moriarty is owner and operator of Moriarty Trucking Company. On the 23rd day of August 2014, Mr. Moriarty disregarded a red traffic light in his lane of traffic and negligently crashed his truck into the 2012 Honda Civic owned by my client and driven by his wife, Irene Adler Holmes. The force of the impact caused severe physical and psychological damages to my client and ended the life of his beloved wife.

Numerous witnesses can testify that your client failed to stop for a red light in his lane of traffic and that he acted in disregard of the rules of the road. Traffic reconstruction testimony also shows that Mr. Moriarty failed to apply his brakes before striking the vehicle occupied by the plaintiff and his wife.

II. General Damages

As a result of the incident, Mr. Holmes has suffered a number of injuries, endured medical examinations, and suffered short-term and long-term health consequences. Injuries resulting from the collision include a closed-head injury, fractured left tibia, internal hemorrhaging, hemopneumothorax, and severe abdominal trauma. In addition, he had five broken ribs and a left hip fracture. Seven days after the collision, Mr. Holmes had a tracheostomy placed. Infection set in thereafter, causing acute and chronic bronchitis.

For several weeks after the collision, Mr. Holmes remained in a coma, with his breathing controlled by mechanical ventilation. It took several weeks after coming out of the coma for Mr. Holmes to reorient himself to his surroundings. Doctors noted that Mr. Holmes suffered from short-term memory loss.

In November 2014, Mr. Holmes began suffering severe and debilitating migraine headaches from which he has been unable to receive any relief. Mr. Holmes did not suffer from migraines prior to the accident, and medical diagnosis has determined that the head trauma he received has caused these painful migraine headaches. As a result, Mr. Holmes has been unable to return to his former profession, that of professional consulting private detective.

III. Loss of Consortium

As a result of the collision, Irene Adler Holmes, Mr. Holmes's wife of many years, was killed. Because of her death, Mr. Holmes is without her companionship and assistance in his own recovery. He has lost her companionship and affection forever.

IV. Enclosures

Enclosed are the following records and reports for your review:

1 Emergency Room Record, London County Hospital
2 Operative Report, London County Hospital
3 Medical Report from Dr. Thorne MD, London County Hospital
4 Medical Report from Dr. Kaitland Burnett, King's Road Rehabilitative Hospital

V. Settlement

If this case can be resolved within 30 days and without the expense of litigation, I would recommend settlement in the amount of $3,000,000.00.

Very truly yours,

____
Neal Bevans

Attorney for Plaintiff Sherlock Holmes

Tech Topic
DIGITIZING FILES

With the widespread availability of computers, scanners, and huge storage capacities, it is natural to assume that the law office is swiftly moving away from the use of paper. However, practitioners are not seeing a move toward "paperless pleadings." Simply because it is possible to make digital copies of nearly every aspect of a case does not mean that digital files will replace paper. In fact, some legal professionals have begun seeing more paper produced, rather than less. According to paralegal Dana Martin, "I love technology, but I've seen more paper since technology has been the thing. I've seen more copies of things since we became high-tech than I did before. Now it's on the computer, and everybody wants their own copy. So instead of seeing two copies of a thing, now I'm seeing eight copies. Because everybody has to touch it."

Although it is always a good idea to back up all computer files, do not make the mistake of thinking that the days of paper are ending. Digital files and hard copies will probably coexist in the legal field for years to come.

3. OFFERS OF JUDGMENT

In some states, there is a more formalized approach to settling cases. These states use a document referred to as an *offer of judgment*. Like the settlement brochure and the demand letter, an offer of judgment seeks to settle the case without taking it to trial. However, unlike those two devices, the offer of judgment comes from the defendant. Offers of judgment are governed by the Rules of Civil Procedure (Fig. 11-4). In the federal courts (and many state courts), Rule 68 of the Rules of Civil Procedure expressly authorizes a party defending a suit to serve on the opposing side an offer to settle the case via a judgment. The rule provides that a party defending a claim may serve an offer of judgment 10 days or more prior to trial.

FIGURE 11-4

Federal Rules of Civil Procedure, Rule 68 Offer of Judgment

At any time more than 10 days before the trial begins, a party defending against a claim may serve upon the adverse party an offer to allow judgment to be taken against the defending party for the money or property or to the effect specified in the offer, with costs then accrued. If within 10 days after the service of the offer the adverse party serves written notice that the offer is accepted, either party may then file the offer and notice of acceptance together with proof of service thereof and thereupon the clerk shall enter judgment. An offer not accepted shall be deemed withdrawn and evidence thereof is not admissible except in a proceeding to determine costs. If the judgment finally obtained by the offeree is not more favorable than the offer, the offeree must pay the costs incurred after the making of the offer. The fact that an offer is made but not accepted does not preclude a subsequent offer. When the liability of one party to another has been determined by verdict or order or judgment, but the amount or extent of the liability remains to be determined by further proceedings, the party adjudged liable may make an offer of judgment, which shall have the same effect as an offer made before trial if it is served within a reasonable time not less than 10 days prior to the commencement of hearings to determine the amount or extent of liability.

Offers of judgment have two aspects. First, if the offer is accepted, the clerk may then enter the offer of judgment as the final resolution in the case and mark it closed. Second, if an offer is not accepted within 10 days, it is considered withdrawn. When the case is ultimately resolved, if the final verdict is less than what the party would have received had she accepted the offer of judgment, then the party who refused must pay the opposition's attorney's fees and other costs.

Rule 68 encourages parties to be reasonable and to try settling their lawsuits before the case actually goes to trial, and it puts some teeth into the process by creating monetary penalties when parties fail to do so. In addition to assessing costs against the party who could have accepted an offer that was greater than what he ended up receiving after a long and expensive trial, this rule also encourages parties to settle their cases by an assessment of interest charges. There are statutory provisions that allow increases or decreases in prejudgment interest rates depending on whether an offer of judgment was tendered or accepted (Fig. 11-5).

FIGURE 11-5

Prejudgment and Judgment Interest

(a) Except as provided in subsection (b) of this section, recovery of prejudgment or pre-award interest and the rate of interest to be applied in the action or distribution proceeding shall be determined by the substantive law governing the right to recovery under the conflict of laws rules of this State.

(b) The court or arbitrator shall increase or decrease the amount of prejudgment or pre-award interest otherwise payable in a judgment or award in foreign money to the extent required by the law of this State governing a failure to make or accept an offer of settlement or offer of judgment, or conduct by a party or its attorney causing undue delay or expense.[18]

Tech Topic
MEDIATION ARBITRATION SOFTWARE

In these days of high-tech touching every part of our lives, it should come as no surprise to learn that there is now software available to help the legal team prepare for an upcoming mediation or arbitration hearing. Alternative Dispute Resolution (ADR) software is becoming more and more available and is bringing down the price so that even small law offices can afford to purchase it. A good ADR package allows legal professionals to prepare for an upcoming arbitration or mediation hearing and even provides reminders about specific items that should be incorporated into the presentation. These software packages also offer enhanced features that allow users to access features online or through cloud backup:

- E-mail notifications of pending cases, hearings, or appointments
- Comments section that allows users to insert notes, comments, or strategy details concerning a specific hearing or the use of particular testimony, evidence, or case law in the hearing itself
- Case law that reports on recent decisions in similar cases
- Scanning, review, and revision of documents digitally uploaded into the file
- Reminders about the next steps required in specific cases
- Contact information about the mediator, witnesses, attorneys, paralegals, and anyone central to the case
- Assistance in creating a mediation or settlement brochure
- Individualized reports on specific cases, including expenses and awards
- Access files remotely from various devices, including laptops, cell phones, and tablets
- Searchable database on other cases, including cross-referencing by name, issue, mediator, or jurisdiction

In some states, there is another option for defendants that is closely associated with offers of judgment: confessions of judgment. In a confession of judgment, a defendant who does not wish to contest a lawsuit is not required to do so. Instead, she can file with the clerk of the superior court a confession of judgment. This is a statement in writing, signed and verified, authorizing the entry of judgment for the amount stated in the complaint. Confessions of judgment are often seen in foreclosure proceedings where the homeowner chooses not to contest the action and simply allows the house to be turned over to the mortgage lender.

D. RELEASES

Once a case is settled, the parties release one another from the claims in the lawsuit. A **release** is an official relinquishment of the plaintiff's claim against the defendant in exchange for the money payment through the settlement. When a party signs a release, he is foregoing all possible actions against the other party. The end result of the settlement is a complete dismissal of the complaint, often in the form of a *dismissal with prejudice* (although it may be called by another name in some jurisdictions). A dismissal with prejudice means that, once the settlement is filed, the plaintiff is relinquishing any right to renew the action. A *dismissal without prejudice* gives the plaintiff the right to revive the action at a future date. Obviously, a defendant who negotiates the settlement of a case would require a dismissal with prejudice.

Release
To surrender a legal right to sue another, often in exchange for monetary payment

Case Excerpt

Can a court lose jurisdiction because of a mandatory arbitration clause in a contract?

JOYNER'S MECH., INC. V. MILLER
85 Va. Cir. 80, (Va. Cir. Ct. 2012)

OPINION
Judge John W. Brown

On Wednesday December 14, 2011, counsel for all parties appeared before this Court and presented arguments on Defendants' previously filed Demurrer and Motion to Dismiss. The Court received the transcript of that hearing on January 10, 2012. On January 23, 2012, counsel for the Plaintiff submitted a Brief in Opposition to Demurrer and Motion to Dismiss ("Brief 1"). Counsel for the Defendant submitted a Reply Brief in Support of Demurrer and Motion to Dismiss on February 6, 2012 ("Brief 2"). Plaintiff's counsel submitted a Response to Defendants' Reply Brief in Support of Demurrer and Motion to Dismiss on February 14, 2012 ("Brief 3"). The Court has considered the evidence, arguments, and briefs of counsel and makes the following decision.

Facts

Plaintiff, Joyner's Mechanical, Inc. ("Joyner's"), provides heating, ventilation, and air conditioning ("HVAC") services to a variety of structures in Virginia and the surrounding states. Joyner's was formed on February 28, 2006, when its predecessor company, Joyner's Holdings Corporation, entered into an Agreement for Purchase and Sale of Assets ("Purchase Agreement") with Atlantic Mechanical, Inc., then wholly owned by AMC, Inc., which in turn was wholly owned by Defendant William G. Miller. Under the Purchase Agreement, Joyner's acquired substantially all of Atlantic Mechanical's assets, including intangible assets such as goodwill, customer lists, "information base," and trademarks. Article 6.4 of the Purchase Agreements states that, "at the closing, Holdings and each of: (i) Seller and (ii) each of the Stockholders will enter into a Noncompetition Agreement. . . ."

On that same day, February 26, 2008, Joyner's Holdings Corporation and Defendant William G. Miller entered into a Noncompetition, Noninterference, and Nonsolicitation Agreement ("Noncompetition Agreement") by which Miller agreed to certain restrictive covenants, including an agreement to refrain from disclosing Joyner's trade secrets and other confidential information for a certain period of time, an agreement to refrain from competing with Joyner's, and an agreement to refrain from soliciting Joyner's customers or employees. Paragraph 8 of the Noncompetition Agreement states that:

> The Seller shall agree that any such dispute relating to or in respect of this Agreement, its negotiation, execution, performance, subject matter, or any course of conduct or dealing or actions or conduct under or in respect of this Agreement, shall be submitted to, and resolved exclusively pursuant to arbitration . . . in Chesapeake, Virginia . . . subject to the substantive laws of the Commonwealth of Virginia . . . and binding on the parties.

Subsequent to these agreements, Miller was allegedly employed by Joyner's until January 2008. Miller allegedly had a relationship with SMJ Enterprises, a company that obtained a license to provide HVAC services in Virginia in February 2008. Plaintiff alleges that Miller improperly disclosed confidential information to SMJ, solicited seven employees away from Joyner's from March 6 to May 1, 2010, continued to solicit other employees to leave Joyner's for SMJ, and solicited customers and accounts away from Joyner's.

On May 27, 2011, Plaintiff filed suit in the Court against William G. Miller for (1) and (2) Breach of Contract and the Covenant of Good Faith and Fair Dealing, (3) and (5) Breach of Contract, and (4) Breach of Contract Regarding Non-Solicitation of Employees. Plaintiff sued all Defendants for (6) and (7) Intentional Interference with Existing and Prospective Contracts, (8) Statutory Conspiracy, (9) Commercial Defamation a.k.a. Trade Libel, and (10) Violation of the Uniform Trade Secrets Act.

Defendants demurred and moved to dismiss these claims by motion on July 6, 2011. In the motion to dismiss, Defendants assert that this Court is without jurisdiction over the claims against Defendant Miller because of the mandatory arbitration clause in the Noncompetition Agreement. During oral arguments on December 14, 2011, and in Brief 2, defense counsel modified the motion and admitted that there is no way to fit the defamation claim against Miller into the mandatory arbitration clause. Therefore, the Court has considered the applicability of paragraph 8 of the Noncompetition Agreement to all counts against Miller except (9), Commercial Defamation, a/k/a Trade Libel.

Law

TA's written agreement to submit any existing controversy to arbitration or a provision in a written contract to submit to arbitration any controversy thereafter arising between the parties is valid, enforceable, and irrevocable, except upon such grounds as exist at law or in equity for the revocation of any contract. This article also applies to arbitration agreements between employers and employees or between their respective representatives unless otherwise provided in the agreement.

Decision

Plaintiff has made various arguments in opposition to the applicability of the mandatory arbitration clause, none of which the Court finds persuasive. First, Plaintiff argues that the Noncompetition Agreement is "expressly incorporated by reference in the asset purchase agreement" and, therefore, the law of New York governs. See Transcript, p. 10. As stated above, the relevant language is that, "at the closing, Holdings and each of: (i) Seller and (ii) each of the Stockholders will enter into a Noncompetition Agreement. . . ." There is certainly a reference to the Noncompetition Agreement, but the Purchase Agreement is devoid of any express language of incorporation by reference. The Purchase Agreement and Noncompetition Agreement are two separate and distinct contracts, and the Court thus does not find it necessary to decide between potentially conflicting arbitration agreements and choice of laws provisions.

Next, in Brief 1, Plaintiff argues that nonsignatories to a contract, in this case, SMJ and Miller Mechanical, cannot benefit from the arbitration clause. The Defendants, however, have not attempted to compel arbitration of the claims against SMJ and Miller Mechanical and have conceded that those claims will remain in this Court.

Furthermore, in Brief 1, Plaintiff argues that judicial economy and the specter of inconsistent judgments weigh in favor of trying all of the claims together in this Court. The Court finds that the public policy that favors clear and unambiguous arbitration clauses outweighs these other concerns.

Finally, in Brief 2, Plaintiff cites *Ulloa v. QSP, Inc.*, 271 Va. 72, 624 S.E.2d 43 (2006), for the proposition that Joyner's claim under the Uniform Trade Secrets Act is not arbitrable. In that case, the parties submitted the issue of an award of attorneys' fees in their dispute under the Uniform Trade Secrets Act to the jury to be determined pursuant to the fee-shifting language of their contract. Id. at 78. The Court reversed, holding that "the Uniform Trade Secrets Act provides a statutory remedy for the misappropriation of trade secrets, including the award of attorneys' fees, when it is shown that the misappropriation is 'willful and malicious.' A successful claim under the Act, including an award of attorneys' fees, is therefore not dependent upon provisions contained in a contract between the parties." Id. at 81. Due to the fact that the contract provision for attorney's fees excluded an independent action for attorneys' fees under the Act, the award of attorneys' fees for the trade secret claim under the contract was reversible error. Id. at 82. The Court stated the Plaintiff's misappropriation of the trade secrets claim did not qualify as "any action relating to" the parties' conduct as contemplated by the contract's fee shifting agreement. Id.

Plaintiff argues that the holding in Ulloa is broad; a contract cannot exclude any independent action under the Uniform Trade Secrets Act. This Court declines to adopt such an expansive reading. The contract at issue in Ulloa violated the Uniform Trade Secrets Act because §59.1-338.1 of that Act deals specifically with attorneys' fees. There is no such specific provision in the Act that deals with arbitration. To the contrary, a later section of the Act states that "This chapter does not affect . . . contractual remedies whether or not based on misappropriation of a trade secret. . . ." See Virginia Code §59.1-341. The Court finds that parties to a contract can agree to submit a trade secret dispute to arbitration without violating the Uniform Trade Secrets Act.

The Court holds that all claims against Defendant William G. Miller except the Commercial Defamation claim are subject to the mandatory arbitration clause in paragraph 8 of the Noncompetition Agreement. Paragraph 8 is clear and broad; any dispute relating to or in respect of the Noncompetition Agreement shall be submitted to arbitration. Claims (1), (2), (3), (4), (5), (6), (7), (8), and (10) all fall within the ambit of this arbitration provision. Further, the Court finds that the Plaintiff cannot avoid arbitration by filing suits against third parties or adding counts upon which relief is sought which are not related to the subject contract.

Pursuant to Virginia Code §8.01-581.02(D), the Court stays the entire action, including the demurrers to the claims for Intentional Interference with Existing and Prospective Contracts, Statutory Conspiracy, and Violation of the Uniform Trade Secrets Act against Defendants SMJ Enterprises, L.L.C., and Miller Mechanical, Inc., and the demurrer to the Commercial Defamation, a/k/a Trade Libel, claim against all Defendants.

QUESTIONS ABOUT THE CASE:

1 What were the basic provisions of Miller's noncompete clause?
2 Why does Miller claim that the arbitration clause in this case is not mandatory?
3 How does the court rule on this claim?
4 Can the court order mandatory arbitration when one of the issues in the case is the application of the Uniform Trade Secrets Act?

Chapter Summary

Alternative dispute resolution has become very prominent in the last few decades. It is now a common practice to have disputes between parties referred to arbitration instead of proceeding through the court system. Many contracts, including many consumer agreements, have arbitration provisions in them as a matter of course. When a case is referred to arbitration, an arbitrator is authorized to make a final and binding decision on the issues pending between the parties. Another form of alternative dispute resolution is mediation. Mediation is a consensual process wherein a mediator works with the parties to help them reach a resolution of the issues between them. Mediators cannot impose rulings; they help the parties resolve the issues on their own. Many states now require mediation for many different types of lawsuits. If the parties are unable to work out a case through mediation, then it simply returns to the docket with other cases pending trial.

Settlement is the resolution of the case between the plaintiff and the defendant. The most common method of settlement is for the defendant to pay a monetary amount to the plaintiff in exchange for the plaintiff's dismissal of his case. Plaintiffs often send settlement offers to defendants that set out the basis of the plaintiff's claim against the defendant and request a specific amount that the plaintiff will accept to dismiss the case. Settlement offers can come in the form of settlement brochures, demand letters, or offers of judgment. A plaintiff will usually sign a release and file a dismissal with prejudice of all claims pending against the defendant in exchange for the defendant's payment.

SKILLS YOU NEED IN THE REAL WORLD

Research your state's laws and prepare excerpts that list all applicable rules of civil procedure governing settlements, including offers of judgment, pre- and post-trial interest rates on judgments, and the various methods used to enforce judgments.

THE LIFE OF A PARALEGAL

The Details

Jean Jurasin started in the legal field when she was 15 years old. "I took a secretarial program in high school, and part of the curriculum called for an internship at the local courthouse. I worked for the local prosecutor a couple of hours a day, 10 hours a week. It was a great job.

I learned that when you work for a team, everybody has to pull their weight. I typed up pleadings, did filing, answered the phone, and even took out the trash."

These days, technology has made huge inroads in the practice of law. "We're living in a cell phone world. Everything is done so quickly. E-mail, faxes, scanners make for a more stressful world, because everybody waits until the last minute. You're always rushing to get it done. One of our biggest concerns is e-mail. You have to be real careful about e-mail. Our firm includes a provision in the fee agreement that the client has no objection to being contacted by e-mail. If the client objects, we don't use it. For a lot of clients, it's easier. We worry all the time about someone intercepting communications from our clients. You can't be too careful.

"Some of what we do can be very boring," says Jean. "You have to be detail oriented with your cases. Keeping track of all the evidence and exhibits in a case is so important because they get so jumbled up all the time. The attorney is constantly pulling things out of the client file to review it, and it doesn't always get back where it belongs. That's where you come in. You have to know where everything is. On top of that, you are also dealing with a dozen other things going on at the same time. It's my job to do anything to make my lawyer's life easier. I don't think that [the attorney] should have to worry about anything other than what she's been trained to do."

ETHICAL ISSUES FOR THE PARALEGAL

Frivolous Lawsuits

One ethical challenge that constantly taxes legal professionals is the specter of frivolous lawsuits. There is a small percentage of plaintiffs who bring cases just on the off chance of receiving a large award from a defendant, either because of a sympathetic jury or, more likely, because the defendant is willing to settle the case prior to trial to avoid additional expenses. The problem with such suits is that bringing them is a violation of ethical rules. A claim that has no basis in law or fact is one that should never be brought in the first place. In situations where the legal team only realizes after the pleadings have been filed that the case lacks merit, this fact should be pointed out to the attorney handling the case as soon as possible. Maintaining a frivolous lawsuit can result in legal penalties, including bad faith damages and the award of attorney's fees for the opposition. More importantly, a firm that makes a habit of bringing groundless lawsuits will soon lose the respect of others in the legal field. Beyond simply losing prestige, this lack of respect will reflect in more concrete ways, including a sudden unwillingness of other law firms to accommodate the firm for scheduling depositions, requesting extensions on the deadlines for pleadings, and so on. Although this may not sound like such a bad thing, in the real world, this can have a cumulative effect and can eventually drive a law firm out of business. No matter how big the city, the legal community is always small and close-knit. Word of unscrupulous or unethical behavior by one firm spreads quickly in this community.

Websites

- **Hieros Gamos — Arbitration and Mediation**
  www.hg.org/adr.html
- **American Arbitration Association**
  www.adr.org/
- **Global Arbitration Mediation Association**
  www.beyondintractability.org/internal-biblio/20959
- **Connecticut Board of Mediation and Arbitration**
  www.ctdol.state.ct.us/medarb/regs.htm

Key Terms

Appraisal
Arbitration
Impasse
Mediation
Release
Settlement
Submission
Umpire

Review Questions

1. What is alternative dispute resolution?
2. Why has alternative dispute resolution become popular in recent years?
3. What is arbitration?
4. Describe the history of arbitration.
5. What is the Federal Arbitration Act?
6. Compare and contrast appraisal and arbitration.
7. What are the two types of arbitration?
8. What are some examples of issues that commonly result in arbitration?
9. Explain limitations on the issues that can be submitted to arbitration.
10. What is the scope of the arbitrator's authority?
11. What is submission of an arbitration agreement?
12. What is mediation?
13. Compare and contrast mediation and arbitration.
14. Why have many states adopted mandatory mediation programs?
15. What is a certified mediator?
16. Who is normally required to be present at a mediation hearing?
17. What are the normal duties of a mediator?
18. What is an impasse in regards to mediation?
19. What is settlement?
20. Explain the contractual elements of a settlement agreement.

21 What are some of the reasons that a plaintiff and defendant would wish to settle a case?
22 What is a settlement brochure?
23 What is a demand letter?
24 What is an offer of judgment?
25 What is a confession of judgment?
26 Does the modern settlement process encourage frivolous lawsuits? Explain your answer.

Applying What You Have Learned

1 Research your state's laws and prepare excerpts to include in your trial notebook, listing all applicable Rules of Civil Procedure governing settlements, including offers of judgment, pre- and post-trial interest rates on judgments, and the various methods used to enforce judgments.

2 Discuss alternative dispute resolution, with a particular emphasis on the similarities and differences between arbitration and mediation.

3 Based on the case you created in Chapters 4 and 5, prepare a settlement brochure based on the example provided in this chapter and the details discussed. What is the final amount that the plaintiff will offer to settle the case? That amount should figure prominently in your settlement brochure. Remember to summarize the important facts and the plaintiff's damages and to include any relevant case law from your state that would help sway the defendant toward settling the case prior to trial.

4 Create an offer of settlement in the case you created in Chapters 4 and 5. What would the plaintiff propose if he genuinely wishes to settle the case prior to trial? What justifies the amount of your proposed offer?

5 Contact your state's board or organization that regulates mediators. What standards are mediators required to follow during their hearings? Can anyone be a mediator? When and where can a mediation hearing be presented? What rules govern a mediation hearing? Locate these rules, and place a copy of them in your portfolio.

6 Mary and Jorge have entered into a partnership to run a small craft store. Part of their agreement provides that any issue arising out of the partnership will be resolved through arbitration, much like the provisions found in this chapter's case excerpt. However, after working closely for several months, Mary and Jorge fall in love and get married. Six months later, the marriage ends and Mary files for divorce. The biggest asset of the marriage is the business. Do Mary and Jorge have to go through arbitration, or can they apportion the assets through a divorce proceeding?

Endnotes

[1]*Gates v. Arizona Brewing Co.*, 54 Ariz. 266 (Ariz.1939).
[2]*Weeks v. Harden Mfg. Corp.*, 291 F.3d 1307 (11th Cir. 2002).
[3]*Hart v. McChristian*, 344 Ark. 656, 42 S.W.3d 552 (2001).
[4]Title 9, US Code, Section 1-14.
[5]*Ex parte Ephraim*, 806 So. 2d 352 (Ala. 2001).
[6]*Allstate Ins. Co. v. Stinebaugh*, 374 Md. 631, 824 A.2d 87 (2003).
[7]*Beattie v. Autostyle Plastics, Inc.*, 217 Mich. App. 572, 552 N.W.2d 181 (1996).
[8]*Malted Mousse, Inc. v. Steinmetz*, 150 Wash. 2d 518, 79 P.3d 1154 (2003).
[9]*Dearborn Fire Fighters Union Local No. 412, IAFF v. City of Dearborn*, 42 Mich. App. 51, 201 N.W.2d 650 (1972).
[10]*Mount St. Mary's Hospital of Niagara Falls v. Catherwood*, 26 N.Y.2d 493, 311 N.Y.S.2d 863, 260 N.E.2d 508 (1970).
[11]22 NY ADC 28.2.
[12]*American Safety Equipment Corp. v. J. P. Maguire & Co.*, 391 F.2d 821, 3 A.L.R. Fed. 901 (2d Cir. 1968).
[13]*Commonwealth Equity Services, Inc. v. Messick*, 152 Md. App. 381, 831 A.2d 1144 (2003), cert. denied, 378 Md. 614, 837 A.2d 926 (2003).
[14]*Board of Water & Sewer Com'rs of City of Mobile v. Bill Harbert Const. Co.*, 870 So. 2d 699 (Ala. 2003).
[15]*Schoolnick v. Finman*, 108 Conn. 478, 144 A. 41 (1928).
[16]MD R ADR Rule 17-101.
[17]*Gates Corp. v. Bando Chemical Industries, Ltd.*, 4 Fed. Appx. 676 (10th Cir. 2001).
[18]N.C.G.S.A. §1C-1828.

12 Appeals

Chapter Objectives

- Explain the function of a motion for new trial
- Describe the basis of appellate jurisdiction
- Explain the purpose of the record
- Define *certiorari*
- List and describe the contents of an appellate brief
- Explain a notice of appeal
- Describe why a state supreme court would grant certiorari in a particular case
- Explain the actions than an appellate court can take with a case on appeal

I INTRODUCTION

At the end of a civil trial, there is always a winner and a loser. The party who loses has the right to appeal the verdict to a higher court. In this chapter, we will examine the issues that arise on appeal, explain how appellate courts are organized, and examine the actions that these courts are authorized to take.

STARTING AN APPEAL

Before a party can appeal to a higher court, there must be some final determination in the trial court. Parties are barred from appealing issues until the trial phase is over. A final determination in a case can come from the jury's verdict, but it can also come from a judge's decision granting a summary judgment or any other ruling that effectively ends the case. For purposes of simplicity, we will phrase our discussion about appeals on the facts found in the following example:

Kara was a smoker for over 30 years and 2 years ago was diagnosed with lung cancer. She brought suit against the manufacturer of the brand of cigarettes that she smoked for those three decades: Smokey Smokes. At trial, Kara produced testimony that the officers of the company knew that their product probably caused lung cancer but continued to market their "low-tar" cigarettes as safer than the other brands. Kara's theory at trial was that Smokey Smokes violated her state's consumer protection statute by failing to disclose the dangers of cigarette smoking and by marketing low-tar cigarettes with an implied message that they were somehow safer and thus less likely to cause lung cancer. At trial, the jury awards Kara a total of $1.14 million. Smokey Smokes intends to appeal.

In Chapter 9, we examined the trial of a civil case. There, we saw that when a jury returns a verdict, the judge enters that finding as the official judgment of the court. What we did not point out is that the official entry of judgment is the trigger point for the next round of litigation in the case: the appeal.

When a judge enters the judgment in the case, the losing party has the right to file a motion for new trial. This request is actually the first step in beginning the appellate process. If the motion is denied, the party then has the right to invoke the jurisdiction of the appellate court and to begin the long process of appealing a case. On the other hand, if the party's request for a new trial is granted, there is no need for an appeal. Instead, the parties will return to a pretrial footing and everyone must behave as though the first trial never occurred. It will be retried with the same witnesses and evidence introduced. Only a small percentage of motions for new trial are actually granted. In the vast majority of cases, the trial judge denies the motion and the parties then move to an appellate footing.

In the example above, Smokey Smokes filed a request for a new trial, citing several instances in the original trial that it believed were unfair. For one, Smokey Smokes alleges that Kara's reliance on the state's consumer fraud statute was inappropriate because the company complied with all the provisions of that law, at least as they existed at the time that Kara was smoking. The trial judge disagrees and denies the motion for new trial. At this point, the jurisdiction in the case shifts to the appellate courts and the appeal has begun.

CHANGING COURTS

Jurisdiction is an important term for any court proceeding. In the example involving Kara and Smokey Smokes, we have seen that the trial judge's ruling denying the motion for new trial triggers appellate jurisdiction. This has more than record-keeping consequences. At the point that appellate courts obtain jurisdiction, the trial judge is no longer empowered to make any additional rulings in the case. All issues are now pending in the appellate court, and the parties must go to that court to seek any relief or further rulings in the case.

With the trial judge's denial of the motion for new trial, the losing party can file a notice of appeal with the appellate court.

A. NOTICE OF APPEAL

The court systems in the United States are often discussed as a pyramid, with the base composed of the numerous trial courts. In the center of the pyramid are the intermediate appellate courts, and at the top is the Supreme Court. This metaphor is instructive whether we discuss the state appellate court system or the federal. What this pyramid structure means is that each court occupying the lower tier of the pyramid must respect the authority and the rulings of the next highest court. Trial courts are bound by the decisions of the court of appeals, and that court is bound by the decision of the State Supreme Court.

This model is instructive when we discuss the appeal mentioned in the example. Smokey Smokes filed a motion for new trial, and that motion was denied. Now they must file a **notice of appeal** in order to begin the appellate process. That notice must be filed in the state court of appeals.

Notice of appeal
A request to an appellate court that it assume jurisdiction in the case and docket the case for an appeal

A typical notice of appeal contains the names of the parties, a brief statement establishing appellate jurisdiction, and a request that the jurisdiction be transferred to the state court of appeals. Filing the notice has important consequences for deadlines. For instance, the party filing the notice of appeal now has a specific period of time to file its briefs in support of its contention that the trial court's ruling be overturned. The notice of appeal will also be filed on the opposing party, and that party will have a specific time period to reply to the briefs filed by the opposition.

One of the most important elements in a notice of appeal is the allegation establishing appellate jurisdiction. The party on appeal must explain to the appellate court why it has jurisdiction in the case. If the party fails to do so, the appellate court might refuse to hear the case. See Figure 12-1 for an example of the phrasing that a party might use in alleging appellate jurisdiction, and see Figure 12-2 for a sample notice of appeal.

FIGURE 12-1

Allegation of Appellate Jurisdiction in Notice of Appeal by Smokey Smokes

Appellant, Smokey Smokes, now alleges that jurisdiction is proper in this Court because of a final judgment entered on the jury's verdict for the Appellee, dated December 1, 2014. With this verdict, all issues pending between the parties were resolved, leaving no further issues pending in the trial court and jurisdiction is proper in this court according to Rule 10, Appellate Rules of Procedure.

FIGURE 12-2

Notice of Appeal

STATE OF PLACID
DISTRICT COURT
LONDON COUNTY

Sherlock Holmes
(Plaintiff)
v. File No.: ____________
Professor James Moriarty, individually
and as owner, operator of Moriarty
Transport Trucking Co.
(Defendant)

NOTICE OF APPEAL

Notice is hereby given to Plaintiff Sherlock Holmes that the Defendant in the above-styled action, James Moriarty in his individual capacity and as owner and operator of Moriarty Transport Trucking Company, hereby appeals to the Placid State Court of Appeals from the final judgment and verdict entered against the defendant on December 1, 2014.

____
Deborah Bolstridge

Attorney for Defendant James Moriarty

B. TERMINOLOGY ON APPEAL

When a case goes to an appellate court, there are some important changes in terminology. At the trial level, the party bringing the claim is usually referred to as the *plaintiff* and the person against whom the suit is brought is referred to as the *defendant*. However, on appeal, these terms change. The party bringing the appeal is referred to as the **appellant**, and the party against whom the appeal is brought is referred to as the **appellee**.

Appellant
The person bringing the current appeal from an adverse ruling in the court below

Appellee
The person who won in the lower court

Consider the following example: In the case involving Kara and Smokey Smokes, which party is the appellant and which the appellee?

Answer: Because Smokey Smokes lost on the trial level and has filed a notice of appeal, the company is the appellant and Kara is the appellee.

C. THE RECORD

Record
The entire body of evidence, witness transcripts, pleadings, motions, discovery materials, and any other material admitted during the original trial

The notice of appeal informs the appellate court that an appeal will be forthcoming, and it requests that the trial court forward the **record** to the appellate court. The record consists of all the evidence and pleadings that have been admitted at trial. This record, along with the transcript of the witness testimony, will be sent to the appellate court and docketed there during the time that the appeal is pending.

D. APPELLATE DOCKET NUMBER

When a case is filed with the state court of appeals, it is immediately assigned a docket number that must be used on all subsequent pleadings or filings by the parties. This docket number is similar to and serves the same purpose as the case file number originally assigned to the case in the trial court. It identifies the case and ensures that anything filed in the case will be stored in the appropriate location for later review.

IV BRIEFS

Once a notice of appeal has been filed and the case has been assigned a docket number, the next event in the appeal is the filing of briefs by both sides. The appellant usually has 30 to 60 days from the date that the case was docketed to file a brief with the court. After that, the appellee typically has 30 days to file a responding brief.

SEARCH SUGGESTION • SAMPLE BRIEFS

Online pay sites, such as Westlaw, offer briefs that accompany the final appellate opinions presented. Often, it is very instructive to review the briefs along with the court's final decision.

A. APPELLANT'S BRIEF

The purpose of the appellant's brief is to explain and advocate for that party's position — that is, that the ruling against the party in the lower court was wrong and should be overturned. The appellant's brief will have a very stylized and formal presentation, containing an analysis of the factual elements of the plaintiff's case, a summary of the court's rulings, and a position statement by the appellant declaring why these actions were clearly in contravention of prevailing legal authority. It is important to note that while paralegals can — and often do — draft appellate briefs, they cannot sign them. That right is reserved for the attorney. Appellate court briefs have a specified format, often set out in the state's Rules of Appellate Procedure (Fig. 12-3).

All briefs and responses shall be typed or printed on letter size (8 1/2" x 11") paper with covers on the front and back, STAPLED on the left-hand side in booklet form. Covers shall be of recyclable paper, heavier than regular stationery, and shall bear the style of the case, the case number, and the name or names of the persons preparing the brief, along with their bar numbers, if attorneys.[1]

FIGURE 12-3

Appellate Court Rules: Format and Appearance of Appellate Briefs

LEGAL LEGWORK ■ BRIEF RULES

Before you begin to draft a brief for an appellate court, make sure that you have the most up-to-date rules from that court. The rules govern a wide variety of activities associated with bringing an appeal, including the formatting of the actual documents, when and where they should be filed, how many copies should be filed, and even the font size that should be used in printing the briefs.

1. CONTENTS OF AN APPELLATE BRIEF

An appellate brief has specific subsections, including:

- title page;
- statement of facts;
- enumerations of error;
- argument; and
- conclusion.

a. Title Page

A brief must have a title or cover page, listing the names of the parties, the appellate docket number, and the name of the court. See Figure 12-4 for a sample title page.

FIGURE 12-4

Appellate Brief Title Page

IN THE COURT OF APPEALS

FOR THE STATE OF ANYWHERE

Smokey Smokes, Inc.,
Appellant,
vs. Docket No: 2015-1232
Kara Smoker,
Appellee

BRIEF OF APPELLANT

b. Statement of Facts

After the title page, the next part of an appellant brief is the statement of facts. This section describes the underlying claim and any relevant facts that figured prominently in the lawsuit and that have implications on appeal. The purpose of the statement of facts is to apprise the court of appeals about the relevant events in the case, but most attorneys draft their statements of facts so that they also emphasize the client's points on appeal. See Figure 12-5 for a sample statement of facts.

FIGURE 12-5

Statement of Facts by Smokey Smokes

STATEMENT OF FACTS

Appellant Smokey Smokes, hereafter referred to as Appellant, was in the business of manufacturing and marketing cigarettes. (Answer, p. 4.) All phases of the production cycle were under the close scrutiny of government inspectors, and Appellant complied with all state and federal laws in producing its product. (Trial transcript, p. 208.) Appellant complied with all requirements under this State's Consumer Safety Statute, including a filing specifying the dangers of smoking and its tendency to result in addiction to nicotine, including "low-tar" varieties. (Trial transcript, p. 45.)

As you can see, the appellant's statement of facts sets out specific incidents and cross-references these details to the transcript of the trial. This makes it easier for the appellate justices to double-check facts and locate specific testimony. While presenting accurate information, the statement of facts also plays up critical features of the appellant's case.

c. Enumerations of Error

Once the appellant has drafted the statement of facts, the next part of the brief is the enumerations of error. These are usually single paragraphs, set off in boldface and indented in order to make them easy to find and even easier to read. The enumerations of error specify the appellant's points about the errors that occurred at trial and why these errors should result in the appellate court overturning the trial court's decision.

An appeal can have dozens of enumerations of error, but for purposes of simplicity, we will limit our discussion to the single enumeration set out in Figure 12-6. As you can see, an enumeration is something more than a bare allegation that something at the trial was incorrect. In its own way, the enumeration also urges a particular point of view. The appellant could simply have stated, "Trial court committed error in its ruling on the Consumer Safety Statute." Although that would have been technically correct, a brief is not simply a recitation of facts. At every point in the brief, the legal team will seek to argue a position. That accounts for the additional language in the enumeration that the appellant "followed all procedures set out by statute." This is both an enumeration of error and an argument.

FIGURE 12-6

Enumerations of Error by Smokey Smokes

ENUMERATIONS OF ERROR

I. The trial court committed reversible error when it ruled that the state Consumer Safety Statute did not create an exemption for the Appellant, even after the Appellant followed all procedures set out by the statute.

d. Argument

Following the enumerations of error, the appellant will then argue his position. The argument portion of a brief brings together the facts, the law, and the position urged by the appellant. The argument must be based on a solid foundation of legal research and an equally firm grasp of the facts in the case. Essentially, the argument is based on a simple principle referred to as **stare decisis**. This principle is one of the most important and pervasive in the American judicial system.

Stare decisis
Latin for "stand by the decision"; the principle that appellate courts will follow clearly established precedents in their decisions

Stare decisis is a Latin term for "stand by the decision." Its importance is that all courts are bound by the principle that similar cases with similar facts should result in similar rulings. For instance, if the State Supreme Court has recently decided a case that has similar issues and similar facts as a case currently pending before the state court of appeals, that court should rule in exactly the same way as the State Supreme Court did. Of course, if things were that simple, there would be very little for appellate courts to do. After several centuries of running a legal system, most of the issues that a party could bring on appeal should already have been decided at some point or other. However, language is open to interpretation, and attorneys and judges are constantly inventing new ways of approaching a legal concept. This results in an ever-growing slew of cases pending before the various appellate courts.

For instance, in Figure 12-6, we saw the enumeration of error raised by Smokey Smokes. How would Kara's brief handle the same issue? It might read something like, "The trial court did not commit reversible error when it ruled that the state Consumer Safety Statute did not create an exemption for the Appellant because courts in this state have been consistent that the statute does not apply to tobacco companies."

As you can see, the parties will have very different approaches to these issues, and it is up to the appellate court to evaluate the merits of both arguments, review the applicable law, and reach its decision, justifying it based on the facts in the case and the requirements of stare decisis.

e. Conclusion

The conclusion is usually a short statement at the end of the brief that reiterates the party's position and requests specific relief. It will emphasize what the party wants the appellate court to do (Fig. 12-7).

FIGURE 12-7
Conclusion

For all of the foregoing reasons, appellant urges the Court to reverse the decision of the trial court and order a new trial.

2. FILING DEADLINES

Both parties on appeal have strict time limits for preparing and submitting their briefs. Failure to meet those deadlines will often result in the appeal being dismissed or some other sanction.

Tech Topic
ELECTRONIC FILING

Because most federal (and many state) courts have gone to electronic filing, it is absolutely essential for all legal professionals to know and understand how to use programs such as Adobe Acrobat. Electronic filing allows an attorney to file a pleading over the Internet instead of the old-fashioned method of driving over to the courthouse and presenting a hard copy of the pleading or brief to a clerk. Electronic filing has obvious advantages: It saves time and money and, in some cases, allows a party to file as late as 11:59 p.m. instead of 5:00 p.m. An attorney can file a pleading while she is sitting on the beach in Hawaii just as easily as if she were sitting behind a desk at the firm. But there are complications to electronic filing. Many appellate courts still do not allow the practice, and many require that the firm establish an account, with username and password, before the first filing. The firm's bank account is then debited for the cost of the filing. If a deadline is approaching quickly, that is not the time to try to learn the complexities of electronic filing. However, it is obvious that more and more courts will move to this format.

3. SERVING COPY ON APPELLEE

Once the appellant's brief has been written, copies are served on the appellee and filed in the clerk of appellate court's office. The appellee then has a specific time limit in which to respond to the appellant's brief. This time period varies, but it is usually 30 days.

B. APPELLEE'S BRIEF

The appellee's brief will be very similar in appearance to the appellant's brief. It will contain the same elements but will have a very different approach to the law and the facts. For instance, the appellee's statement of facts will tend to emphasize his argument and will reiterate that the trial court was correct in its rulings. The appellee's argument will obviously argue that the trial court's decision against the appellant was correct under the principle of stare decisis.

PRACTICE POINTER ▶ BRIEF BANK

It is always wise to maintain a brief bank. A brief bank consists of previously written briefs in a wide variety of cases. Storing all of these briefs in the same location has obvious advantages. If you have a new case that raises issues similar to those of a previous case, you have a ready source of information, case law, and reasoning to draw on. A brief bank also gives you a practical example of what a brief should look like and has already taken into account the formatting and other issues required by the appellate court.

C. ORAL ARGUMENT

Most appeals before the state court of appeals are conducted in writing. Although appellate rules do allow for oral argument, most parties do not request it. Oral argument is usually reserved for unusual cases, where the parties feel that a face-to-face meeting with the justices will somehow be beneficial to them. There are also times when the justices require oral argument to consider an unusual appeal.

If oral argument is scheduled for a case on appeal, the attorneys representing the parties will travel to the courthouse, usually located in the state capitol. There, they will present their arguments to the justices in a very stylized and formal way. Witnesses do not testify at appellate court hearings, and attorneys are not allowed to present any evidence that is not already part of the record. The attorneys argue their positions from podiums in the large appellate chambers. Justices can interrupt the attorneys' presentations at any time to ask questions to clarify specific points or request additional information. When the presentations are concluded, the justices retire to consider their decision and may not actually announce it for months. Given the restrictions and pressure of oral argument, most attorneys opt out of oral argument and rely on their written briefs to make their points.

V. THE POWERS OF THE APPELLATE COURTS

Although we have said that the court system is structured as a pyramid, with the trial courts at the bottom and the appellate courts at the top, this oversimplifies the organization and powers of these courts. Appellate courts are higher courts, but they have greater restrictions than one might assume. These courts have very limited options in what they can do with a case on appeal. The decisions for appellate courts are limited to the following rulings on an appellate case:

- Affirming the lower court's decision
- Reversing the lower court's decision
- Modifying the lower court's decision
- Remanding a case for further proceedings

A. AFFIRMING

Returning to our hypothetical case of *Kara Smoker v. Smokey Smokes*, the cigarette company has now appealed its case to the state court of appeals. If that court agrees with the decision in the lower court, it will issue an order affirming the decision. When a higher court **affirms** a lower court's decision, it leaves it intact and does not change it. An order affirming the lower court's ruling would be a loss for the cigarette company.

Affirm
The appellate court's final decision supports the decision made by the lower court

B. REVERSING

When a higher court **reverses** a lower court's ruling, it issues an order overturning that court's decision, making the appellant the winner in the case. If the court of appeals were to do that in the case involving Kara and Smokey Smokes, it would be a clear win for the cigarette company.

Reverse
The appellate court's final decision sets aside the decision made by the lower court

C. MODIFYING

Appellate courts are also authorized to create a hybrid decision that partly affirms and partly reverses a lower court's decision. This is common when there are numerous issues in the appeal. Although we have only addressed a single enumeration of error in the case of *Kara Smoker v. Smokey Smokes*, it is clear that there would likely be numerous issues, and the most likely result would be a series of decisions by the court of appeals, some of which affirm and some of which reverse.

D. REMANDING

If an appellate court requires additional information, such as witness testimony or evidence, the only option for the court is to return the case to the trial court for additional hearings. Appellate courts are not equipped to hear new testimony. They are not trial courts, and no one ever testifies before them. When an appellate court **remands** a case, it returns it to the trial court with directions that the court hold a hearing on specific issues.

Remand
The appellate court requires additional information or an evidentiary hearing because it cannot conduct such a hearing itself; the case is temporarily transferred to the trial court for a hearing and then resent to the appellate court.

PRACTICE POINTER ▶ PENDING ISSUES LIST

As you stay abreast of recent appellate decisions, keep a list of pending issues from current client files. As you come across cases that have particular relevance to a client's case, send the client a letter describing the cases and attach a copy of them to the letter. This helps a client know that you are actively involved in pursuing her legal matters and gives her a better feel for the legal complexities involved in bringing the case. One of the biggest complaints that clients have about attorneys and other legal professionals is that they fail to communicate with them on a regular basis. Letting the client know about recent appellate decisions is one way of staying in constant contact with the client.

VI THE STATE SUPREME COURT

We have discussed the function and limitations of the court of appeals; now we will focus on the role played by the State Supreme Court. If Smokey Smokes loses its case in the state court of appeals, it can attempt to bring the case before the State Supreme

Court. However, there is at least one hurdle that the company must clear before the State Supreme Court will accept the case: certiorari.

State Supreme Courts have the right to decide which cases they will hear, a right known as certiorari or cert. State supreme courts, like the U.S. Supreme Court, refuse to hear the vast majority of cases that apply to them for appeals. Supreme courts have different standards than courts of appeal. Before a supreme court will consider an appeal, the parties must show that the case has statewide significance or involves an interpretation of the state constitution. Simply showing that the case is important to the individual parties is not enough. A party must meet the hurdle of certiorari by explaining the significance of the case in its petition for cert.

A. PETITION FOR CERT

The appeal to the state court of appeals in the case of *Kara Smoker v. Smokey Smokes* was a relatively simple and straightforward proposition. The cigarette company simply moved for a new trial, and when that request was denied, it filed a notice of appeal in the appellate court. But before the State Supreme Court will even consider the merits of the appeal, it must be satisfied that the case warrants a grant of certiorari. The company must show that the issues involved in its case have broader implications for the entire state. One way that it might raise such an argument is set out in Figure 12-8.

FIGURE 12-8

Excerpt from the Petition for Certiorari by Smokey Smokes

. . . Appellant Smokey Smokes, Inc., shows that the issues involved in this case involve an interpretation of the state Consumer Protection Statute and that the trial court's ruling in this case will result in the filing of hundreds of cases by smokers against any cigarette company that has ever conducted business, shipped product, or marketed cigarettes in this state.

The appellee also has the right to file a motion opposing the granting of certiorari in this case. Here, the appellee will argue that the decision in the case has no broader implications than the rights of the parties involved in the case. The ultimate decision to grant cert and allow the case to be appealed to the State Supreme Court is in the hands of the justices.

B. GRANTING CERT

If the State Supreme Court grants cert, it means that the court has agreed to hear the case. The appeal will now proceed in an almost identical fashion to the procedure followed in the state court of appeals. The parties will submit written briefs that include all of the features that we saw in our previous discussion of appellate briefs. Simply because a party has been granted cert does not mean that she will ultimately win the appeal. Granting cert simply authorizes the continuation of the appeal. The court is free to rule any way that it sees fit.

C. DENYING CERT

If the State Supreme Court denies cert, it means that the court has refused to hear the appeal (Fig. 12-9). At this point, the appellate process is essentially over. The party can file a motion for rehearing that asks the court to reconsider its ruling, but the court rarely overturns its own decision. At this point, the only option left to a litigant is to file a petition for cert with the U.S. Supreme Court.

"The petition for certiorari filed by appellant Smokey Smokes, Inc., is denied."

FIGURE 12-9

The State Supreme Court's Ruling in *Kara Smoker v. Smokey Smokes, Inc.*

VII THE U.S. SUPREME COURT

Our discussion about appeals has so far centered on the state appellate system. The federal appellate system is organized in almost exactly the same way. However, instead of covering a single state, the federal system covers the entire nation. Because of the size of the United States, the country has been divided up into different circuits, with one

Tech Topic
APPEALS

This chapter mentions several specific parts of an appellate brief, but there are also numerous sites on the Internet that provide a valuable resource for anyone considering writing even the first draft of an appeal. There are brief banks online that provide templates for cases involving similar issues as the law firm's pending appeal, and there are even YouTube videos that explain how briefs are created for specific states and the federal level. In fact, there is so much detail provided online about appellate briefs that the truly difficult part about using online sources is deciding which sites provide the best advice and which do not. One way of evaluating the bona fides of any website devoted to appellate practice is to ensure that the material provided is current, that it cross-references to rules of appellate procedure for the court where the brief will be filed, and that it is not posted as a means of simply drumming up business for another law firm.

Besides simply locating samples of appellate briefs, there are several sites that explain how a brief can be formatted to meet the specific requirements of the court. The sites explain how to format a brief in Word or Adobe Acrobat PDF software.

The Internet also provides services that would have been unthinkable even a few years ago. Just as some attorneys specialize in certain areas of law, some attorneys specialize in appellate work. Surprisingly, some of that appellate work can be outsourced. Some of the firms or individuals who write some or all of the briefs are located overseas or in areas that we traditionally associate with outsourcing, but not necessarily legal work, such as India. Although this author would strongly urge caution when outsourcing any legal work, especially briefs.

circuit often encompassing several states. Appeals from federal trial courts (called *federal district courts*) are brought to the federal circuit court of appeals that has jurisdiction over those states. These courts are situated in a major city in one of the states inside the federal circuit. All of these courts are governed by a uniform set of appeal rules. The Federal Rules of Appellate Procedure govern everything from when a party is permitted to appeal to the typeset and format that a brief must follow when it is presented to an appellate court for filing.

Like a State Supreme Court, the U.S. Supreme Court is the final authority on the interpretation of the U.S. Constitution. In the United States, there is no court higher than the U.S. Supreme Court. Because litigants in the state court system always have the option of appealing to the U.S. Supreme Court, that court has become the de facto court of final appeals.

Case Excerpt

What effect does the filing of bankruptcy have on a pending appeal?

CITY OF RIVERSIDE V. HORSPOOL
223 Cal. App. 4th 670, 167 Cal. Rptr. 3d 440 (Cal. App. 4th Dist. 2014)

Opinion by: Ramirez, P. J.

Opinion

RAMIREZ, P. J. — The City of Riverside (City) filed a nuisance abatement action as to property owned by William F. and Kelly Horspool, and sought the appointment of a receiver pursuant to Health and Safety Code section 17980 et seq. Defendant William F. Horspool (William)1 appealed from the order appointing the receiver in case No. E051500,2 but failed to obtain an undertaking on appeal. Kevin Randolph, in his capacity of receiver, obtained an order permitting the sale of the property to a party who rehabilitated the property after defendants frustrated his efforts to do so. A notice of appeal on behalf of both Horspools was filed in case No. E053605, from the order permitting the sale of the property and an order awarding the receiver extraordinary costs and fees. J.P. Morgan Chase Bank, the holder of the mortgage on the property, did not appeal.

On appeal, William raises 12 issues challenging the adequacy of the prelitigation notice of the proposed receivership, the appointment of the receiver, the propriety of the order for posting bond to challenge the appointment of the receiver, the entry of the defaults of both Horspools, the orders precluding them from opposing the receiver's ex parte application to sell and the order permitting the sale of the property, and asserting error in allowing the receiver to sell the property for less than its fair market value, in precluding them from opposing the loan stripping effect of the sale of the property, in awarding the receiver $114,000 in fees and costs, and in allowing the receiver to conduct a private sale of the property. We affirm.

BACKGROUND

On December 10, 2008, the City received a complaint regarding a vacant house on Mt. Vernon Avenue. A code enforcement officer conducted an aerial inspection of the property and observed a dilapidated roof. The following day, the officer inspected the property from a public right of way and observed the landscaping and house were in a condition of dilapidation and disrepair ranging from landscape maintenance issues, including structural maintenance issues, and fire hazards caused by overgrown and dried weeds, as well as accumulated dead leaves. The officer posted a notice of violation instructing defendants William and Kelly to remediate specified issues before December 30, 2008.

On December 30, 2008, the code enforcement officer reinspected the property and observed no changes or improvements. On January 8, 2009, an administrative civil penalties notice and order (ACPNO) was issued for violations of sections 6.14.020, subdivision B, 6.14.030, 6.15.020, subdivisions B, C, and 6.11.040 of the Riverside Municipal Code. Notice of the ACPNO was sent by mail to the property owners and interested parties on January 8, 2009. William was personally served with the ACPNO on January 10, 2009. On February 18, 2009, the officer reinspected the property and observed the violations had not been corrected.

On March 5, 2009, a notice of the administrative civil penalties hearing was sent to the property owners and interested parties, seeking an order assessing administrative costs incurred. The notice was served by certified mail to William and Kelly, as well as the banks having a security interest in the property. An attorney for defendants William and Kelly appeared at the hearing for defendants. After the hearing, an administrative order was issued assessing daily civil penalties against defendants.

On June 11, 2009, the Horspools filed for chapter 13 bankruptcy (it was converted to a chapter 7 bankruptcy on June 29, 2009, case No. 6:09-bk-22815-PC) and obtained a stay, preventing the City from moving forward with the receivership. Between April 1 and September 29, 2009, the code enforcement officer reinspected the property once per month, but no changes or improvements were observed.

On October 2, 2009, another notice of hearing was served by certified mail on defendants regarding a new ACPNO. On November 6, 2009, an administrative hearing order was issued assessing daily civil penalties in the amount of $500 a day. Additionally, the property was determined to be a public nuisance.

On April 20, 2010, the City obtained relief from the automatic stay in bankruptcy. On June 9, 2010, the City filed a complaint for nuisance abatement and an injunction, and a petition for appointment of a receiver, pursuant to Health and Safety Code section 17980.7. Proofs of service show the complaint was personally served on William. After three successive attempts to serve Kelly on different dates, substitute service was effected by leaving the summons and complaint with William, followed by mailing a copy of the summons and complaint to Kelly at her address.

On July 30, 2010, a hearing on the City's motion to appoint a receiver was held. William personally appeared at the hearing (in propria persona) to request additional time to respond to the complaint. He represented to the court that he was in the process of refurbishing the property, although the City provided photographs taken the day before the hearing, which showed no improvements had been undertaken. The court agreed to postpone the hearing until August 2, 2010, on the condition William provide pictures showing significant improvement.

On August 2, 2010, the court held a hearing on the City's motion for appointment of a receiver. William appeared with counsel and made a general appearance. William's counsel informed the court William could not do anything to the property due to the fact he had filed for bankruptcy. The City demonstrated it had obtained an order exempting these proceedings from the automatic stay by the bankruptcy court. The court granted the City's motion and appointed Kevin Randolph as receiver.

On August 3, 2010, a notice of appeal was filed by William. On August 6, 2010, William filed an ex parte motion for an order fixing the amount of the appeal bond or dispensing with the bond pending appeal. On August 13, 2010, the court ordered an appeal bond in the amount of $80,000 to be posted within 10 days. No bond or undertaking on appeal was posted.

On the same day William filed his first appeal, he also filed a notice of related case, *Horspool v. City of Riverside*. Another action, apparently seeking an injunction against the City to prevent it from proceeding with the receivership, was also filed in superior court under case No. INC080588. The trial court in the injunction action recognized that the action was in response to the appointment of the receiver in the instant action by another judge and refused to grant a temporary restraining order on August 24, 2010, informing William that the pending appeal was the appropriate remedy.

On August 20, 2010, the receiver submitted his initial inventory of property and initial report. The report indicated that William had refused to allow access to the property, under the belief that the appeal automatically stayed the receivership. Although William had represented he lived on the property, there was no evidence of human occupancy: the kitchen was gutted, asbestos debris was piled on the floor, there was mold on the walls of the den/patio, exposed wiring, no functioning bathroom due to lack of toilets, sinks and bathtubs, and there were no beds in the bedrooms.

On August 23, 2010, the clerk entered the defaults of both William and Kelly. On August 28, 2010, the Horspools filed a second chapter 13 bankruptcy petition (case No. 6:10-bk-37614-MJ), obtaining a stay of all proceedings. On September 17, 2010, the bankruptcy court granted relief to the City, and issued an order declaring the automatic stay is not in effect as to the City's nuisance actions "pursuant to 11 U.S.C. §362(b)(4)." Because the motion for relief did not specifically address the receiver's authority to proceed with the receivership, the City sought a more specific order (its third application for relief) from the bankruptcy court, which granted the relief on October 8, 2010, and made the relief binding on any future bankruptcy.

On October 18, 2010, a motion to set aside default was filed as to both Horspools along with a motion to quash the complaint as to Kelly. The motion was not immediately heard because on November 19, 2010, defendants filed an ex parte application in the bankruptcy court to reopen their chapter 7 bankruptcy in case No. 6:09-bk-22815-PC, requiring the City to file a fourth motion for relief from the automatic stay on December 16, 2010. On December 22, 2010, the bankruptcy court issued an order confirming that the City's action to enforce code violations was exempt from the automatic stay.

On January 7, 2011, the receiver filed an ex parte application for an order approving the receiver's proposed rehabilitation plan, outlining the steps to be taken to bring the property up to code. On January 14, 2011, the Horspools filed a notice of removal of the receivership action to the bankruptcy court, but the bankruptcy court remanded the matter to the superior court on March 3, 2011, because the matter was not a removable claim.

On April 6, 2011, the receiver filed an ex parte application for an order approving the sale of the property. The application was made on the ground that the Horspools' actions had made it impossible for the receiver to obtain financing to pay for the rehabilitation of the property. Further, the multiple bankruptcy filings prevented the receiver from filing the motion earlier and required the City to seek four separate applications for relief from the bankruptcy stays.

The delays resulted in further deterioration and vandalism of the property, increasing the expense of rehabilitation. The estimated cost of rehabilitation ranged from $123,550 to $131,650, but the property was appraised, "as is," at a value of only $117,000. Thus, an as-is sale to an investor-buyer with the personal resources and willingness to complete repairs was the best option. The receiver had identified a buyer who was willing to purchase the Mt. Vernon property, "as is," for $75,000, and to fund the cost of repairs, under the oversight of the receiver.

William opposed the proposed sale of the property on the ground his due process rights had been violated due to failure to serve the ex parte application on him. On April 28, 2011, the court granted his motion to set aside the default. However, because William's counsel had substituted in as attorney for William only, he was deemed to lack standing to make the motion on Kelly's behalf. The court made no ruling as to Kelly.

The following day, the court granted the receiver's motion for an order approving the sale of the Mt. Vernon property "as is," free and clear of all liens and encumbrances. On May 9, 2011, William filed a motion for reconsideration of the order approving the sale of the property. Before that motion could be heard, William filed a notice of appeal in case No. E053605, from the order approving the sale, purportedly on behalf of both defendants William and Kelly. The motion to reconsider could not be heard because the filing of the appeal deprived the trial court of jurisdiction.

On June 21, 2011, the receiver filed a motion for approval of fees, as well as attorney fees and costs. Escrow closed on the sale of the Mt. Vernon property on June 30, 2011.

DISCUSSION

All Notice and Due Process Issues Relating to the Manner of Service of Process on William Were Forfeited by William's General Appearance

Without any citation of authority, in arguments 1, 2, 3, and 4, William challenges the court's in personam jurisdiction over himself (and his wife) due to defective service of (a) the code violations, (b) the prelitigation notice, and (c) the complaint for the appointment of the receiver. He complains, in part, that he was personally served by a nonregistered process server and, in part, that his wife was served by substitute service. None of his complaints have merit.

William made a general appearance in the proceedings in the trial court. Where a person makes a general appearance, such appearance operates as a consent to jurisdiction of his person. A general appearance occurs when a defendant takes part in the action or in some manner recognizes the authority of the court to proceed. A request for a continuance constitutes a general appearance because the relief could only be requested on a theory that a defendant was submitting to general jurisdiction of the court.

William appeared (in propria persona) at the initial hearing on the City's motion for appointment of a receiver, where he requested a continuance to answer the complaint. He made a general appearance and cannot now complain.

William argues at length about the manner of service by an unregistered process server, although he never made a motion to quash service in the trial court, and Kelly's motion is not before us because it was heard after the second notice of appeal was filed. There is no requirement that the person serving notices or a summons must be a registered process server and William cites no authority so holding. A summons may be served by any person who is at least 18 years of age and not a party to the action. (Code Civ. Proc., §414.10.) A notice or other paper may be served by mail, express mail, facsimile transmission, or electronically. (Code Civ. Proc., §1013.) A notice of code violations pursuant to Health and Safety Code section 17980.6 may be provided by both posting a copy of the order or notice to repair or abate in a conspicuous place on the property and by first class mail.

Although William denies being served with or receiving notice, a review of the entire record shows otherwise. William relies upon Evidence Code section 647 providing that service by a registered process server raises a presumption that service was proper. This does not mean that other forms of service or notice are invalid. The City served the notice of the pending proceedings in person and by mail as provided by statute. (Code Civ. Proc., §§414.10, 1013.) William and Kelly were both properly served with all notices.

Additionally, none of the issues relating to notice or due process were preserved for review by a timely motion to quash service prior to making a general appearance. Failure to make a motion to quash constitutes a waiver of the issues of lack of personal jurisdiction, inadequacy of process, inadequacy of service of process, inconvenient forum, and delay in prosecution. None of the issues relating to defective notices or service of process (issues 1–4) are cognizable on appeal.

Finally, William's failure to make a proper challenge to jurisdiction in the trial court (as by a motion to quash service prior to any general appearance) forfeits any such challenge on appeal.

3. Kelly Cannot Appeal

Kelly was duly served by leaving a copy of the summons and complaint with her husband, William, at the address they used in all their correspondence and litigation, and was subsequently served by mail on July 6, 2010. On August 23, 2010, her default was entered. On October 18, 2010, counsel for William filed a motion to vacate the judgment (which William had appealed) and to quash the complaint as to Kelly. However, because counsel had substituted in as attorney for William only, the relief from default was granted only as to William.

On May 26, 2011, Kelly filed a supplemental motion to set aside her default, but on June 6, 2011, the court denied the motion without prejudice. Kelly subsequently sought reconsideration of the denial, but that request was denied as well. No default judgment was entered prior to the institution of these appeals.

On appeal, defendants (issue 5, which purports to be on behalf of both) claim that the court erred by entering their defaults. Defendants cite no legal authority in support of the argument that the orders were void, which renders the issues forfeited. Because

William's default was set aside, the issue is moot as to him because he is no longer aggrieved by the entry of the default.

As to Kelly, the entry of the default terminates her rights to take any further affirmative steps in the litigation until either the default is set aside or a default judgment is entered. No judgment by default has been entered to date, so Kelly is barred from appealing the denial of her motion to set aside the default. The denial of such a motion is not appealable.

Propriety of the Order for Costs and Fees of the Receiver

In argument 11, William argues that the trial court erred in awarding the receiver $114,000 in fees and costs. He cites a single, incomplete authority, but the proposition for which the authority was provided is that the appointment of a receiver is often a "legal luxury," frequently representing an extravagant cost to losing litigants, and requiring courts to weigh the appointment of a receiver carefully. His authority does not address the propriety of receiver's fees and costs, and William has failed to cite any authority for the proposition that the trial court abused its discretion in awarding the receiver $114,000. The issue is therefore forfeited.

Nevertheless, on the merits, the amount of fees awarded to a receiver is in the sound discretion of the trial court and in the absence of a clear showing of an abuse of discretion, a reviewing court is not justified in setting aside an order fixing fees.

Here, the trial court's findings are supported by the record and must therefore be accorded a deferential standard of review. (*Melikian v. Aquila*, supra, 63 Cal.App.4th at p. 1368.) William relentlessly abused the processes of both the state and bankruptcy courts in his efforts to thwart the City's attempts to correct structural defects on his property that were dangerous to health and safety. In fact, he has been deemed to be a vexatious litigant in the case of *Horspool v. Updike*, Riverside Superior Court case No. RIC10021157. In the bankruptcy court, his fourth and final effort at removal of the action was finally met with an order that the City's exception from the bankruptcy stay would apply to any future bankruptcy filing, and specifically directed that no subsequent filing would stay the actions of the City respecting the property.

Given the extraordinary actions the receiver was required to take, the award of fees to the receiver was reasonable.

DISPOSITION

The judgment is affirmed. Respondents are entitled to costs on appeal.

QUESTIONS ABOUT THE CASE:

1 What was wrong with the property that forms the basis of this appeal?

2 The appellants were given until February 2009 to make improvements on the property. Did they?

3 What action did William take that postponed any immediate action on the property by the city?

4 William represented to the court that he lived on the premises. What, if any, evidence was there to contradict this?
5 William contested the trial court's jurisdiction over him and his wife. How does the appellate court deal with this contention?

Chapter Summary

When a party loses at trial, she has the right to appeal the decision to an appellate court. The appeals process begins when the losing party files a motion for new trial. When that motion is denied, the party then has the right to file a notice of appeal and have the case transferred to the jurisdiction of the appellate court. In most states, and on the federal level, the first level of appellate court is the court of appeals. The appellant files a brief in this court requesting that the court of appeals reverse the trial court's decision. The appellee also files a brief requesting that the court leave the trial court's finding intact. Appellate briefs have a standard format, with specific sections for the statement of facts, the enumerations of error, the argument, and the conclusion. Most cases that are heard on appeal do so through written briefs, but there are provisions that allow parties to request oral argument before the appellate court.

Appellate courts have limited jurisdiction and can only take four different actions in a case on appeal. When the appellate court affirms the lower court's decision, it agrees with that decision and allows it to stand. However, when a court reverses the lower court's decision, it disagrees with the trial court and overturns that court's decision. Appellate courts can also modify lower court decisions or send the case back to the trial court for additional hearings on a remand.

Appellate courts are organized in a hierarchy, with the most powerful court at the top and the trial courts at the bottom. On the state level, the most powerful court is usually called the State Supreme Court, and it has the final say about interpretations of state law. The U.S. Supreme Court is the highest court in the country. It is the court of last resort for all types of appeals.

SKILLS YOU NEED IN THE REAL WORLD

One of the most important skills you can develop is to recognize a good appellate brief when you see one. Your firm and your colleagues may have all developed a solid brief bank that they store on their computer or in some other digital format. Before you begin to draft any appellate brief, you should always check with attorneys and paralegals in your firm or in other friendly venues to see if they already have a brief that is at least close to the issues that you are dealing with in your case. This other brief will give you some idea of what your finished brief should look like, and it will provide you with some solid cases to rely upon as you begin your draft. However, you should never take anything you see in someone's brief as an accurate expression of the law. It always pays to research, even if you are checking on the cases provided to you in a brief that is very closely "on point." Form books, checklists, and other aids are always helpful, but nothing replaces contemporaneous research and well-thought-out writing.

THE LIFE OF A PARALEGAL

Using Technology

For Janice Johnson, who spends a lot of her time working on personal injury and Social Security cases, computer programs are her lifeblood. "We use Abacus as a database and tracking system here in our office. I don't know how we survived as well as we did before we went to this system. Today, not to have some type of product program for client information and management along with a deadline system is living in the dark ages and asking for a malpractice situation to occur. I don't know how many work hours we've saved over the years since we began using Abacus, merely in looking at the computer file rather than hunting down the physical file when a client or contact called me, but I daresay over the past five-plus years since we got Abacus, we've probably saved a number of days if not a few weeks in man-hours spent looking for files alone. Unless something was logged onto the system incorrectly, nothing is ever filed incorrectly on Abacus. I wish I could say that for our physical files.

"I encourage all my clients who have e-mail addresses to please contact me in that manner. I get the contacts in an extremely timely manner without having an interruption while a client is in my office. I can also respond back without getting caught on a call that ends up going entirely too long because a client can't stop him- or herself from going on and on and on with questions that I've already answered or which really aren't that pertinent to the handling of the case anyway. Also, I have a word-for-word record of what information was given to the client through the e-mail contacts."

At the office where Janice works, they emphasize the team approach to working on their cases. "When certain events occur in cases, we may have two or more persons working on different aspects of one case simultaneously. This is much more effectively done when each person can access the file via technology at his or her desk rather than trying to split up the physical file between us.

"We still use the old 'client list' file on our word-processing system along with other forms files that we've developed over the years. I highly suggest that an office go with Microsoft, as we have had some problems when we needed to transfer data electronically and we find almost everyone in the world uses Microsoft but us.

"I use the Internet on a nearly daily basis. Due to my narrow area of practice, I don't generally use traditional legal research but tend to look for medical dictionaries online and drug listings. I track down obscure medical providers out of my normal area of operations, and used it last summer after the death of a client to track down in minutes where and what was required to obtain the death certificate and autopsy reports in a 'crossroads' metropolitan area which had three different offices which could have been my correct source depending on the exact location of the death within the city. I research medical conditions online extensively."

ETHICAL ISSUES FOR THE PARALEGAL

Unfavorable Case Law

You might have a natural tendency to downplay or even ignore adverse case law as you research issues on appeal. The situation can arise in several contexts, but the most common is that as you research a particular issue, you find cases that both support your client's position and that clearly go against your client's position. The tendency is to focus on the cases that are helpful to the appeal and to put aside those cases that are not. But that is a mistake. Most courts have rules that require the parties to submit both the cases that support a position and the ones that do not. Beyond that, ignoring cases that go against your own position can only end up hurting the client. The opposition will certainly find those cases and play them up in their own brief. Better that you discuss them in yours and show how they don't apply or that they should be overruled than to simply ignore them and hope they go away.

As you research cases in preparing any document, especially a brief, you should always be careful to point out any cases that run counter to your argument. Make sure that the attorney knows about these cases and has fashioned an argument to deal with them. In the long run, it is not only the ethical thing to do, but also the most practical. If there are numerous cases going against your client's position, perhaps it is time to reconsider the appeal, or even to settle the case before it goes to appeal.

Websites

- **California Courts of Appeal**
  www.courts.ca.gov/courtsofappeal.htm
- **Supreme Court of Texas**
  www.supreme.courts.state.tx.us/historical/recent.asp
- **Supreme Court of Ohio**
  www.supremecourt.ohio.gov/
- **Florida Court System**
  www.flcourts.org/florida-courts/
- **Court of Appeals of Georgia**
  www.gaappeals.us/

Key Terms

Affirm
Appellant
Appellee
Notice of appeal
Record
Remand
Reverse
Stare decisis

Review Questions

1 What is a motion for new trial?
2 Explain the basis of appellate jurisdiction.
3 What is a notice of appeal?
4 What is the appellate "record"?
5 What is an appeal?
6 What is a brief?
7 List the basic components that an appellate brief contains.
8 What is the purpose of a statement of facts in an appellate brief?
9 What is an enumeration of error?
10 What is oral argument?
11 The chapter suggests that appellate courts have limited powers. Explain.
12 Explain the possible rulings that an appellate court can make in a case.
13 What is the difference between affirming and reversing an appeal?
14 What is the purpose of a remand?
15 Explain the organization of state courts.
16 What is certiorari?
17 What is the basis for granting or denying certiorari?
18 What types of cases do not have certiorari requirements?
19 What is the name of the highest court in the United States?
20 What is the purpose of federal circuit courts?
21 What is a brief bank?
22 If you were going to organize a system for appealing cases, which aspects of the current system would you keep and which aspects would you eliminate? Explain your answer.
23 What are some arguments for and against certiorari?
24 Are there some types of cases where appeals should not be allowed? Why or why not?

Applying What You Have Learned

1 Locate your state's rules of appellate procedure, and copy out the provisions related to the appearance of appellate briefs. What do the courts require in terms of formatting, paper selection, and font size? How many copies of the brief must be served on the court? Does the court allow for electronic filing of briefs?

2 Use an Internet search engine to locate appellant and appellee briefs from various sites. What do these briefs have in common? What conclusions can you draw about the presentations, formatting, and argument you should use in creating your own briefs?

3 Based on the jury verdict form provided in the Baker case, prepare a motion for new trial on the defendant's behalf.

4 Danny recently lost his case against his ex-wife. He alleged that she had, on several occasions, slandered him by reporting him to the police. Apparently, Danny had been stalking his ex-wife for several months and had been arrested on more than one occasion. Danny's ex-wife moved for summary judgment on his action for slander, and the motion was granted. Danny filed a proper motion for new trial, which was denied. To protest, Danny wrote his appellate brief to the state court of appeals on tissue paper. Will the court consider the merits of Danny's appeal?

5 If your firm does not already have a brief bank, perhaps you should create one. A brief bank is an archive of the appellate briefs filed in previous cases that can be quickly and easily retrieved. There are many issues in appeals that recur over and over again. Why reinvent the wheel each time when you can rely on previous research and writing when creating a new brief? In the old days, paralegals would make hard copies of appellate briefs and then file them according to subject, or put appellate subjects on index cards to help retrieve the briefs later. These days, most paralegals keep brief banks on a computer. Why not use this same system to create a brief bank?

Each argument section of old briefs could be pulled out and indexed separately. The subjects could be saved like this:

- Appeal: Waiver of issue by failure to object at trial
- Appeal: Failure to conform to appellate rules
- Cert: Petition for cert to State Supreme Court
- Cert: Petition for cert to U.S. Supreme Court
- Evidence: Hearsay exceptions
- Evidence: Demonstrative
- Witnesses: Unavailable for trial
- Witnesses: Expert witness in auto reconstruction
- Witnesses: Expert witness in medical standard of care

Prepare the basic formulation of a brief bank by reviewing recent decisions from your state's highest appellate court. Choose topics related to civil litigation, including evidence law, expert witnesses, pleadings, and motions, to name a few.

Endnotes

[1]Ga. Sup.Ct.Rules, Rule 18.

Glossary

12(b)(6) motion A motion under the provisions of Rule 12 of the Rules of Civil Procedure that challenges the basis of the complaint for failure to state a claim upon which relief can be granted.

Admissibility A ruling on whether the jury will be allowed to view proffered evidence.

Admit To agree or stipulate to the allegations presented in a complaint.

Affidavit A written document containing the statement of a person who then swears that the contents are true and correct to the best of his or her knowledge.

Affirm The appellate court's final decision supports the decision made by the lower court.

Affirmative defense A defense that goes beyond a simple denial; affirmative defenses state that the defendant is entitled to judgment in his or her favor for specific reasons.

Answer The document filed by the defendant in a civil action that responds to each of the allegations raised in the plaintiff's complaint, denies or admits to the factual allegations, and denies or admits to responsibility for the plaintiff's injuries.

Appellant The person bringing the current appeal from an adverse ruling in the court below.

Appellee The person who won in the lower court.

Appraisal The evaluation by an expert of the cash value of a contested item.

Arbitration The process of bringing both sides in a civil lawsuit together to negotiate a resolution.

Associate attorney An attorney who is an employee of an attorney partnership.

Attorney-client privilege The evidentiary privilege that bars a court or other authority from compelling an attorney or a client to divulge the conversations that either had with one another.

Authentication Proof that evidence is what it claims to be.

Bad faith A claim that a party to litigation is interposing legal claims or making other allegations not based on fact, but out of a desire to harass, intimidate, or otherwise waste the court's time.

Bar examination A test administered to graduates from approved law schools that determines the applicant's knowledge of the law and suitability to practice in the state.

Beyond a reasonable doubt Proof of the elements of a crime against the defendant to a point where a juror has no substantive uncertainty about the defendant's guilt.

Burden of proof The amount of proof that the plaintiff must present in order to substantiate his or her claims as made in the complaint.

Calendar call A mandatory court hearing where the judge inquires about the readiness of the parties to go to trial; also known as a docket call.

Caption (Style) The heading or title used in all legal pleadings.

Case evaluation The process of investigating the facts, issues, and legal implications of a proposed lawsuit before it is ever filed.

Case law The decisions written by appellate courts explaining the outcome of a case on appeal.

Cause of action A personal, financial, or other injury for which the law gives a person the right to receive compensation.

Certificate of service A party's verification that a copy of a pleading or necessary document was served on the opposing party, either through the U.S. postal system or by personal hand-delivery.

Certification The recognition of the attainment of a degree of academic and practical knowledge by a professional.

Certiorari (Cert) Latin for "to make sure"; an appellate court's authority to decide which cases it will hear on appeal.

Challenge for cause When a panel member is removed because he or she cannot sit on the jury.

Circumstantial evidence Evidence that suggests a conclusion.

Class action A lawsuit involving a large group of plaintiffs who have been certified by a court as having mutual interest, common claims, and a representative plaintiff who will pursue the action on the basis of the entire group.

Clear and convincing evidence Having a high probability of truthfulness; a higher standard than preponderance of the evidence.

Clerk A government official responsible for maintaining public records.

Collateral source rule A rule of evidence that prohibits the jury from being informed about the plaintiff's other sources of compensation, such as insurance, worker's compensation, and so on.

Commingling Combining funds from different sources into one, such as using a client's money as personal funds.

Common law The large body of decisions and principles created by judges as they decide individual cases.

Compensatory damages An award by the jury (or judge) designed to compensate the plaintiff for physical or financial losses.

Complaint Also known as a petition, it is the pleading filed by the plaintiff and served on the defendant that sets out the plaintiff's factual allegations that show the defendant is responsible for the plaintiff's injuries.

Compulsory counterclaim A claim by the defendant against the plaintiff that must be raised in the case or it will be barred.

Concurrent jurisdiction When two or more courts have contemporaneous jurisdiction over a civil action.

Conflict letter A letter sent by an attorney to the judge explaining that the attorney has several different appearances scheduled for the same date and detailing which courts the attorney will go to first.

Contingency fee The attorney's fee calculated as a percentage of the final award in a civil case.

Counterclaim A claim by the defendant against the plaintiff where the defendant seeks damages.

Court reporter A person who is empowered to administer oaths and records oral testimony, usually by stenography.

Cross-claim A claim by one party against another party on the same side of the action; for example, a plaintiff against another plaintiff or a defendant against a co-defendant.

Cross-examination The questioning of a witness to show bias, prejudice, or lack of knowledge.

Damages Monetary payments assessed against a party who has been deemed liable to another party in a civil case.

Declaratory judgment A court order that specifies the duties and obligations of a party.

Default judgment A judgment entered against a defendant who has failed to file an answer to the plaintiff's complaint.

Defendant The party who is named in the complaint and against whom the plaintiff has a cause of action; the individual, company, or institution against whom a lawsuit is brought.

Demonstrative evidence Any object, visual aid, model, scale drawing, or other exhibit designed to help clarify points in the trial.

Deny To disagree with or contest the allegations presented in a complaint.

Deponent The person questioned during a deposition.

Deposition Oral questions asked of a witness, under oath, by an attorney and later preserved in a transcript.

Deposition digest Also known as a deposition summary; a document that summarizes the important points of a deposition transcript by cross-referencing topics with page numbers.

Direct evidence Evidence that establishes a particular fact without resorting to other testimony or evidence.

Direct examination The questioning of a witness by the side that called the witness to the stand.

Disbarment Temporary suspension or permanent revocation of an individual's license to practice law.

Discovery The exchange of information between the sides involved in a lawsuit.

Dispositive motion A motion that resolves some or all issues in pending litigation.

Domicile A party's permanent residence, where the party has lived and where the party intends to return.

Equity A trial court's authority to order individuals and corporations to do (or not do) certain activities because they are unjust.

Evidence Any fact, testimony, or physical object that tends to prove or disprove allegations raised in a case.

Exclusive jurisdiction The authorization of a specific court to hear particular actions.

Exhibit A document attached to a pleading that is incorporated by reference into the body of the pleading.

Fair market value The amount that a willing buyer would pay for an item that a willing seller would accept.

Forum The location of the court; a court that possesses both personal and subject matter jurisdiction over the case.

General damages A monetary award by a jury (or judge) that is closely tied to the defendant's actions but has no preset or easily quantifiable amount.

General jurisdiction The power of a court to hear a broad range of case types, including civil and criminal issues.

Guilty A verdict only available in criminal cases where the jury determines that the defendant is responsible for committing a crime.

Impasse A declaration by the mediator that the parties are unable to reach an agreement.

Impleader The involuntary addition of a new party to the litigation; a party without whom all issues raised in the case could not be resolved.

Injunction A court order that demands a certain action or that prohibits a certain action.

In rem jurisdiction The power of a court to exercise jurisdiction based on the location of real property within the forum.

Interpleader The deposit of contested funds with the court, followed by the removal of the filing party from other action in the lawsuit.

Interrogatories Written questions posed by one side of a civil action to the other side.

Intervention The voluntary insertion of a third party into a pending civil action, often to resolve issues directly related to the third party's interests.

JNOV Also known as a judgment notwithstanding the verdict; a motion filed by a party at the conclusion of a trial asking the judge to overturn the jury's decision and rule in favor of the unsuccessful party.

Judge A person either appointed or elected to serve as the final arbiter for legal questions in a court of law.

Judgment A court's conclusion about a specific issue in controversy.

Judgment on the pleadings A motion that alleges that if all of the allegations raised in the pleadings are true and correct, the movant would still be entitled to a ruling in his favor and a dismissal of the opposition's pleadings.

Judicial notice The authority of a judge to agree that certain facts are true without the necessity of proof.

Jurisdiction A court's power to enter rulings and make findings that bind the individual parties.

Jurors Those people who have been selected to sit on a jury; they will consider the evidence and reach a verdict in the case.

Jury charge Oral instructions given by the judge to the jury about how they should deliberate and what law they should follow.

Jury strike The removal of a jury panel member, also known as a jury challenge.

Lay the foundation The presentation of sufficient background material to establish the relevance and competence of a particular piece of evidence.

Legal document assistant A specialized type of paralegal, legally able to provide assistance to clients in preparing forms.

Liability A jury's determination that one party is responsible for injuries to another party; the basis for an award of damages.

Licensure The requirement of governmental approval before a person can practice a specific profession.

Limited jurisdiction The expressly confined powers of a court to hear specific types of cases only.

Loss of consortium A claim filed by the plaintiff's spouse for the loss of companionship in the marriage, caused by the injuries.

Marital privilege The evidentiary privilege that prevents spouses from being compelled to testify against one another.

Material fact A contested fact in litigation; a fact that, if different, might alter the entire outcome of the case.

Mediation The process of submitting a claim to a neutral third party who then makes a determination about the ultimate liability and award in a civil case.

Medical authorization A form, signed by the client, that allows the legal team to review and obtain copies of the client's medical records.

Mitigation of damages The doctrine that holds that it is the plaintiff's responsibility to lessen his potential injuries or losses by taking reasonable actions to seek medical treatment or take other precautions when a reasonable person in the same situation would have done so.

Motion A request made by a party to a judge requesting a specific action.

Motion for directed verdict A motion which, if granted, takes the case away from any consideration by the jury and enters a judgment in favor of one party over the other.

Motion for more definite statement A motion that cites specific deficiencies in a pleading and requests a court order that the judge force the opposition to provide additional detail to support the claim.

Motion for new trial A motion made by the party who lost at the trial court level; this motion requests a new trial on specific grounds; if denied, it triggers the appellate process.

Motion for summary judgment A written motion filed by a party requesting a ruling in its favor and dismissal of the opposition's claims.

Motion in limine A motion at the conclusion of a trial, often made orally, that may request a wide variety of forms of relief, including a ruling on evidentiary matters.

Notice of appeal A request to an appellate court that it assume jurisdiction in the case and docket the case for an appeal.

Ordinance A law passed by a local government, such as a town council or city government.

Overrule A judge's ruling in disagreement with the party who raised the objection.

Panel A group of people who have been called for jury duty; the final jury will be selected from this group; also known as venire.

Paralegal A legal professional who handles many aspects of legal practice but is not authorized to give legal advice; also known as a legal assistant.

Partner A person or corporation who is a co-owner of a business and shares in profits and losses.

Partnership A business model wherein two or more individuals pool assets, run a business for profit, and share in the profits and losses of the business.

Per diem Latin for "by the day"; daily.

Peremptory jury strike The removal of a jury panel member for any legally permissible reason.

Permissive counterclaim A claim by the defendant against the plaintiff that may be raised in the case; it may also be brought as a separate action.

Personal jurisdiction A court's power over the individuals involved in the case; when a court has personal jurisdiction, it can compel attendance at court hearings and enter judgments against the parties.

Petition A request made to a government entity; often used synonymously with "complaint," although "petition" is a more general term.

Plaintiff The party who has a cause of action; the person who initiates a lawsuit against another.

Preponderance of the evidence The level of proof required in a civil case; "more likely than not to be true."

Pre-trial conference A conference between the judge, plaintiff, and defendant before the trial commences; the parties discuss witness issues and evidence, and finalize their agreements in a pre-trial order.

Pre-trial order An order, prepared by the trial judge with the input of the parties, that summarizes key issues in the case, including witness order, evidence, and other critical concerns.

Prima facie Latin for "at first sight"; the presentation of a minimum of evidence to establish the party's case.

Private reprimand A private letter to an attorney advising of possible ethics violations.

Probate court The court empowered to settle estates for those individuals who have died with or without a will.

Province of the jury An issue that must be determined by a jury, not a judge.

Public reprimand A published notice concerning an attorney's ethical violation.

Punitive damages Monetary assessments by the jury against a party that are designed to punish or make an example of the party for others.

Record The entire body of evidence, witness transcripts, pleadings, motions, discovery materials, and any other material admitted during the original trial.

Release To surrender a legal right to sue another, often in exchange for monetary payment.

Relevance The characteristic of evidence that makes it tend to prove or disprove some fact or allegation in a case.

Remand The appellate court requires additional information or an evidentiary hearing because it cannot conduct such a hearing itself; the case is temporarily transferred to the trial court for a hearing and then resent to the appellate court.

Removal The transfer of a case from a state court to a federal court.

Reply The responsive pleading, provided in Rule 7, to a counterclaim.

Request for production of documents A request by one party to another in a civil case for copies of all documents relevant to that case.

Res judicata Latin for "the thing has been adjudicated"; the principle that a court's decision on a particular matter is binding on future litigation between the parties; sometimes referred to as "res adjudicata."

Reverse The appellate court's final decision sets aside the decision made by the lower court.

Rule 11 One of the major rules under the Rules of Civil Procedure; it requires an attorney to investigate an action before bringing it.

Self-authenticating document A document, usually from the public record, that receives the benefit of special legislation that specifically avoids the necessity of requiring a witness to testify about the document's accuracy or competence.

Settlement A negotiated termination of a case prior to a trial or jury verdict.

Skip tracing agency A company or individual who charges a fee for locating a witness or potential civil litigant.

Special appearance A temporary appearance authorized by the Rules of Civil Procedure that allows a defendant to contest a court's personal jurisdiction without submitting to it through the challenge.

Special damages Damages, such as lost wages or medical bills, that can be calculated with specificity.

Standing The requirement that a party to a lawsuit has a legally recognized interest in the proceedings, or a party's rights will be infringed upon by the rulings in the litigation.

Stare decisis Latin for "stand by the decision"; the principle that appellate courts will follow clearly established precedents in their decisions.

State bar The organization that licenses and oversees the practice of law and the conduct of attorneys in the state. An attorney must be a member of the state bar before she will be allowed to practice in that state.

Statute A law that is voted on by the legislative branch and enacted by the executive branch.

Statute of limitation A statute that imposes a time limit on the initiation of a civil action.

Stipulation An agreement between parties as to facts or an agreement between attorneys about procedural matters.

Subject matter jurisdiction The power of a court to entertain specific legal actions and to make rulings on those issues.

Submission The agreement to arbitrate a specific matter or issue raised between the parties.

Subpoena duces tecum A court order commanding a witness to produce documents or physical evidence for presentation to a judge.

Subrogation The principle that allows one party to bring a lawsuit in the name of another, usually in an insurance setting.

Sustain A judge's ruling in agreement with the party who raised the objection.

Temporary restraining order A type of injunction issued by the court without benefit of a hearing; it specifically describes actions that a person is barred from carrying out and sets a hearing date so that the parties can address the court.

Temporary suspension A sanction that prevents an attorney from practicing law for a specified period, usually because of a serious ethics violation.

Tendering The process of seeking admissibility of a particular item of evidence.

Testimonial evidence Oral statements made by a witness under oath.

Umpire A person with greater authority than an arbitrator; this person has the authority to make a final and binding decision when an arbitrator has been unable to do so.

Unauthorized practice of law (UPL) When a person who is not an attorney gives legal advice or counsel to a client.

Verification A sworn statement by a party attesting to the truth and accuracy of the statements made in a complaint.

Voir dire French for "to look" or "to speak"; the process of questioning jurors about their potential biases in the case.

Witness locator service A company that provides information about a witness's former addresses, telephone numbers, employment, and current location.

Work product An attorney's notes, impressions, charts, diagrams, and other material used by him or her to prepare strategy and tactics for trial.

Index

12(b)(6) motion, 266

A

Accident reconstructionist report, 74-75
Accident, documenting the scene, 84-86
Administrative rules and regulations, 9
Admissibility, 178-179
Admit, 139
Affidavit, 122, 256
Affirm, 396
Affirmative defenses, 146-147
Amount in controversy, 106-107
Ancillary jurisdiction, 107-108
Answer, 4
  bad faith, 143
  denying claims, 140-142
  drafting, 139-140
  failure to respond, 145
  function, 138
  minimum requirements of, 138-139
  other responses, 142-143
  serving on plaintiff, 144-145
Appeal, affirm, 396
  appellant, 390
  appellee, 390
  briefs, 391-395
  cert, 398 399
  courts, 388-389
  docket number, 391
  modifying, 397
  notice of, 389-390
  oral argument, 396
  petition for cert, 398
  powers of appellate court, 396-397
  record, 390
  remand, 397
  reversing, 397
  starting, 388
  state supreme court, 397-399
  terminology, 390
Appellant, 390
Appellate courts, 17
Appellee, 390
Appraisal, 361
Arbitration, 360
  agreement, 364
  appraisal, 361
  Federal Arbitration Act, 361
  history of, 360-361
  limits on, 363
  submission, 364
  types of, 362-363
  umpire, 363
Arbitrators, 363
Asset search, 342
Assistants, legal document, 49
Associate attorneys, 41
Attorney–client privilege, 198
Attorneys, 35-38
  associate, 41
  bar examination, 36
  defendants', 38
  disbarment, 35
  law school, 36
  partnership, 41
  plaintiffs', 37
  specialization, 37
  state bar, 37
Authentication, 194
Authorization, medical, 72

B

Bad faith, 143
Bad faith damages, 334
Bar examination, 36
Best evidence rule, 190
Beyond a reasonable doubt, 5
Birth, marriage, and death records, 88-89
Brief
  appellant's, 391-395
  appellee's, 395
  argument, 394
  conclusion, 394
  enumeration of errors, 393
  filing deadlines, 394
  serving, 395
  stare decisis, 394
  statement of facts, 392-393
  title page, 392
Burden of proof, 5-6
Business records, 193

C

Calendar call, 306
Capacity, 109-110
Caption, 3
Case evaluation, 64-67
Case law, 10
Case or controversy requirement, 113
Cause of action, 68
Cert
  denying, 399
  granting, 398
  petition for, 398
Certificate of service, 256
Certifying, paralegals, 46-48
Certiorari, 16
Circumstantial evidence, 186-187
Civil case, evaluating, 64-70
Civil law
  how different from other areas, 3-7
  outcome, 7
  parties, 3-4
  what is, 2
Claim, investigating, 80
Class action, 161-162
Clear and convincing evidence, 6
Clerk, 50
Clerk of court, 50
Clerk of courts office, 87
Clients, 49
Closing argument, trial, 314
Codes, ethical, 42
Collateral source rule, 338-339
Commingling funds, ethical violation, 43-44
Common law, 11
Competence, 178
Complaint, 4
  demand for judgment, 120-121
  elements of, 114-121
  factual contentions, 118-119
  identification of court, 114-115
  jurisdiction, 117-118
  style or caption, 115-117
  title of action, 117

Compulsory counterclaim, 148
Concurrent jurisdiction, 109
Conflict letter, 306
Consent, jurisdiction, 14
Constitution, 8
Contingency fees, 38-40
Counterclaim(s), 148-149
  compulsory, 148
  permissive, 148
  replies, 150
  res judicata, 149
Court reporter, 224
Court
  clerk of, 50
  probate, 51
Courts
  appellate, 17
  general jurisdiction, 105-106
  trial, 16-17
Criminal prosecution, 43
Cross-claims, 153-155
  answers, 155
  time limits, 155
Cross-examination, 310

D

Damages, 7, 329-330
  bad faith, 334
  calculating, 331
  collateral source rule, 338-339
  compensatory, 330-332
  emotional distress, 334
  evaluating, 341-343
  fair market value, 338
  future losses, 333
  general, 331
  loss of consortium, 334
  lost wages, 332-333
  medical bills, 333
  mitigation, 339
  nominal, 336
  pain and suffering, 332
  per diem, 332
  prior injuries, 340
  proving, 336-339
  punitive, 335
  special, 332-334
Declaratory judgment, 341
Deed room, 87-88
Deeds, registrar, 50
Defendant, 3, 102
Defenses, 146-150
  affirmative, 264-266
Demand letter, 372-374
Demonstrative evidence, 188-189
Deny, 139
Depositions, 224-234
  after, 232-235
  conducting, 228-230
  cross-examination, 230
  digests, 234
  duration, 232
  exhibits, 230
  notice of, 226
  permissible questions, 229-230
  persons present, 231-232
  preparing for, 225
  reserving objections, 229
  setting, 226-228
Direct examination, 309
Directed verdict motion, 271
Disbarment, 35, 43
Discovery, 209
  avoiding surprise at trial, 211
  clarification of facts, 210
  compelling, 240-241
  constitutional rights, 237-238
  e-discovery, 215-217
  expert witnesses, 215
  failure to respond, 240
  interrogatories, 218-222
  introduction, 209-210
  methods, 217-236
  narrowing the issues, 211
  objections to, 236-239
  preservation for late use, 211
  protective orders, 238-239
  purpose of, 210-211
  rules of civil procedure, 213
  sequence, 213-214
  short history of, 211-212
  software, 241-242
  stipulation, 211
  supplementing responses, 214
  trade secrets, 238
  unduly burdensome, 237
  work product, 237
Diversity of citizenship, 106
Documentary evidence, 187
Domicile, 13

E

E-discovery, 215-217
Electronic discovery, 215-217
Emotional distress damages, 334
Enumeration of errors, 393
Equitable remedies, 340-341
Equity, 340
Ethical violation(s), 43-44
  commingling funds, 43-44
  lack of diligence, 44
Ethics
  attorney, 42-44
  criminal prosecution, 43
  disbarment, 43
  paralegal, 48-49
  temporary suspension, 43
Evidence
  admissibility, 178-179
  authentication, 194
  best evidence rule, 190
  circumstantial, 186-187
  competence, 178
  demonstrative, 188-189
  direct, 185
  documentary, 187
  eye witness testimony, 185-186
  gathering, 86-87
  hearsay, 190-194
  improper conclusion, 183
  judge, 35
  judicial notice, 195-196
  laying the foundation, 180-181
  objecting to, 183-184
  prejudice, 184
  privileges, 197-198
  relevance, 177
  relevance, objection, 184
  scientific, 190
  self-authenticating document, 196
  specific rules, 190-194
  tendering, 182-183
  testimonial, 188
  types of, 184-190
  what is, 176
Excited utterance, 192-193
Exclusive jurisdiction, 108
Exhibits, 121-122

F

Fair market value, 338
Federal Arbitration Act, 361
Federal question, 106
Federal versus state law, 17-18
Fees, contingency, 38-40
Forum, 13
Foundation, laying the, 180-181

G

General jurisdiction, 12
General jurisdiction courts, 105
Guilty, 7

H

Hearsay, 190-194
  business records, 193
  documents, 191-192
  exceptions, 192-194
  excited utterance, 192-193
  statements for medical diagnosis, 193-194
HIPAA, 72

I

Impasse, mediation, 367
Impleader, 156
Initial client meeting, 70
Injunction, 340
In rem jurisdiction, 13-14, 109
Interpleader, 158
Interrogatories, 218
  answering, 222
  drafting, 220-222
  limitations, 219
  time limits, 222
  verification, 218
Intervention, 158
Investigative reports, 74
Investigators
  attorneys and paralegals, 80
  paralegal, 81-84

J

JNOV motion, 271
Judges, 31-35
  appointment, 33
  becoming, 33-34
  election, 33
  fact finders, 35
  role, 34-35
Judgment, 316
  enforcing, 316
Judgment on the pleadings, 264
Judicial appointment, 33
Judicial notice, 195-196
Judicial selection committee, 33-34
Jurisdiction, 11-14
  amount in controversy, 106-107
  ancillary, 107-108
  complaint, 117-118
  concurrent, 109
  consent, 14
  diversity of citizenship, 106
  domicile, 13, 103
  exclusive, 108
  federal question, 106
  forum, 13-14
  general, 12
  in rem, 13, 109
  limited, 12
  minimum contacts, 14, 104
  pendent, 107-108
  personal, 13-14
  removal, 108
  special appearance, 104
  subject matter, 12 105-108
Jury
  challenge for cause, 307-308
  panel, 307
  peremptory strike, 307
  strike, 307
  voir dire, 307
Jury charge, 314
Jury deliberation, 315
Jury instructions, 314
Jury selection, 307-308

L

Lack of diligence, ethical violation, 44
Law office, organization, 40-41
Law school, 36
Law
  case, 10
  common, 11
Legal document assistants, 49
Liability, 7, 67
Licensing, paralegals, 46-48
Limited jurisdiction, 12
Loss of consortium, 334

M

Marital privilege, 198
Material fact, 269
Mediation, 364-367
  certified mediators, 365
  conference, 366
  impasse, 367
  mediator's authority, 367
  persons required to be present, 366
  state programs, 365
Medical authorization, 72
Medical bill damages, 333
Minimum contacts, jurisdiction, 14, 104
Mitigation of damages, 339
Mootness doctrine, 113-114
Motion, 34
  bringing, 254
  for default judgment, 268
  for directed verdict, 271, 311
  for more definite statement, 266-268
  for new trial, 271-272
  for partial summary judgment, 264
  for summary judgment, 262-263
  in limine, 261
  to strike, 153
Motions
  affidavit, 256
  arguing, 259-261
  certificate of service, 256
  clarifying issues, 270
  construing the language in, 254
  directed verdict, 271
  dispositive, 262
  drafting, 254-255
  filing, 258
  for new trial, 271-272
  JNOV, 271
  judge's role, 268-270
  material fact, 269
  oral, 261
  pre-trial, trial, and post-trial, 270-272
  purview of the jury, 269
  ruling, 261
  serving , 255-256
  written, 261

N

Nominal damages, 336
Notice of appeal, 389-390

O

Offers of judgment, 375-377
Oral argument, brief, 396
Ordinance, 10
Overrule, 179

P

Pain and suffering, 332
Panel, jury, 307
Paralegal, 44
  ethics, 48-49
  investigators, 81-84
Paralegals, 44-49
  daily activities, 45-46
  development of the profession, 44-45
  licensing and certifying, 46-48
  unauthorized practice of law, 48
Parties to a civil case, 3-4
Partners, attorneys, 41
Partnership, 41
Pendent jurisdiction, 107-108
Per diem damages, 332

Peremptory strike, jury, 307
Permissive counterclaim, 148
Personal jurisdiction, 13-14, 102
Petition, 4
Petition for cert, 398
Plaintiff, 3, 102
Police report, 74
Prejudice, 184
Preponderance of the evidence, 5
Pre-trial conference, 303-304
Pre-trial order, 303
Private reprimand, 42
Privileges, 197-198
- attorney-client, 198
- marital, 198

Probate court, 51
Process, summons and service, 124-125
Proof
- beyond a reasonable doubt, 5
- burden of, 5-6
- clear and convincing evidence, 6
- preponderance of the evidence, 5

Public records, researching, 87-89
Public reprimand, 42
Punitive damages, 335
Purview of the jury, 269

R

Record, 390
Registrar of deeds, 50
Releases, 377
Relevance, 177-178
Remand, 397
Removal, 108
Reply, 150
Reprimand
- private, 42
- public, 42

Request for physical and/or mental examination, 235
Request for production of documents, 223-224
Request to admit, 236
Res judicata, 149
Reverse, 397
Ripeness doctrine, 113
Rule 11, 66
Rule 12(b)(6) motions, 151-153
Rules of civil procedure, discovery, 213
Rulings, judicial, 34-35

S

Self-authenticating document, 196
Service
- by other means, 126
- corporation, 126
- personal delivery, 126

Settlement, 368-377
- as a contract, 369-370
- brochure, 370-372
- demand letter, 372-374
- offers of judgment, 375-377
- procedures, 370-375
- reasons to, 368-369
- releases, 377

Skip tracing agency, 81
Special appearance, jurisdiction, 104
Special damages, 332-334
Specialization, 37
Standing, 111
- elements of, 111-112

Stare decisis, 394
State bar, 37
State court, levels of, 16-17
State supreme courts, 17
Statements for medical diagnosis, 193-194
Statute of limitations, 74
Statutes, 8
Stipulation, 211
Strike, motion to, 153
Striking the jury, 307
Style, 3
Subject matter jurisdiction, 12, 105
Subpoena duces tecum, 224
Summons and service of process, 124-125
Supreme Court, U.S., 399-400
Supreme courts, state, 17
Sustain, 179

T

Tax office, 51, 89
Temporary restraining order, 341
Temporary suspension, 43
Tendering evidence, 182-183
Testimonial evidence, 188
Third-party claims, 155
- impleader, 156
- interpleader, 158
- intervention, 158

Trial courts, 16-17
Trial
- attorney's role, 287
- calendar call, 306
- charge conference, 312-314
- chronology of events, 288
- closing argument, 314
- cross-examination, 310
- direct examination, 309
- issue table, 291
- judgment, 316
- jury deliberation, 315
- jury instructions, 314
- jury selection, 307-308
- master index, 290-291
- mock, 303
- motion for directed verdict, 311
- opening statements, 308
- paralegal's role, 287-289
- phases, 303-316
- plaintiff's presentation, 308-310
- preparing witnesses, 297-300
- presenting the defense, 312
- pre-trial conference, 303-304
- pre-trial order, 303
- resting the case, 311
- reviewing deposition, 297
- role of the paralegal, 300-302
- trial notebook, 294-295
- verdict , 315
- witness cross-reference, 291-292
- witnesses, 308
- witness summary, 293

U

UCC filings, 88
Unauthorized practice of law, 48
U.S. Circuit Courts of Appeals, 15
U.S. Federal District Court, 15
U.S. Supreme Court, 15-16, 399-400

V

Verdict, 315
Verifications, 121
Voir dire, 307

W

Witness locator services, 81
Witnesses, what to tell about testifying, 298